◎毛晓霞 主编

中国文化导读

Guide to Chinese Culture

中国农业科学技术出版社

图书在版编目（CIP）数据

中国文化导读 = Guide to Chinese Culture：英文/毛晓霞主编．
—北京：中国农业科学技术出版社，2008.6
 ISBN 978 - 7 - 80233 - 547 - 9

Ⅰ. 中… Ⅱ. 毛… Ⅲ. 文化-中国-英文 Ⅳ. G12

中国版本图书馆 CIP 数据核字（2008）第 048193 号

责任编辑	孟磊
责任校对	贾晓红
出 版 者	中国农业科学技术出版社
	北京市中关村南大街 12 号　邮编：100081
电　　话	（010）62150979（编辑室）（010）68919704（发行部）
	（010）82109703（读者服务部）
传　　真	（010）62189012
网　　址	http://www.castp.cn
经 销 者	新华书店北京发行所
印 刷 者	北京富泰印刷有限责任公司
开　　本	889 mm×1 194 mm　1/16
印　　张	18.5
字　　数	560 千字
版　　次	2008 年 6 月第 1 版　2008 年 6 月第 1 次印刷
定　　价	98.00

Guide to Chinese Culture

Chief Editor: Xiaoxia Mao

Writer: Xiaoxia Mao

Xue fei Yang

Catherine Gu

Helen Yang

Li Min

Frits Buijs

Miao Zhang

Jonathan Hoddinott

Adam A. Marx

Proofreader: Joe Wagner

Frits Buijs

Dermot Stewart

Ron Lowe

Potographer: Feibao Du

Chenjie Yang

随着改革开放的不断深入，沉寂多年的东方巨龙逐渐苏醒了。一个伸开双臂拥抱世界的中国，再次吸引了全球的目光。人们热切地关注中国，希望了解发生在这古老大地上的一切事情，不仅是它的现在，也包括它的过去。人们在惊诧于中国经济高速发展的同时，也对延续几千年的传统文化充满好奇。这就提供了一个契机，全面地了解中国既然是世界的客观需要，那么真实地弘扬中华文化就是我们的历史责任。

笔者多年从事外语教学工作，并有机会参与多批外国来华研修班学生的中国历史与文化课程培训。其间感受了他们对中国历史与文化的浓厚兴趣，但也了解了他们对中国事物认知的局限及对中华文明的陌生！这种日常交往频繁而客观认知遥远的巨大反差不能不令人遗憾。究其原因，一方面是由于近代中国闭关锁国的状况而导致国力的衰败，使整个民族被世界所忽视；另一方面，则是因为国家之间意识形态的差异而造成的相互隔膜，使彼此丧失了更多交流与沟通的机会。中国历史的持续性、统一性、交融性，与其特定的人文、地理相结合，构成了其特殊的文化内涵。油然而生的责任感与使命感使笔者产生了急切想向他们介绍中国历史与文化的冲动。

考虑到来华研修学生时间短暂和边学习、边考察、边体验的实际情况，同时兼顾了不同层次学员群体的特殊需求，我们推出了不同的专题讲座，内容主要有：朝代历史纪元，民族及少数民族政策，宗教，儒家思想对中国的影响，科举与教育体制，节日与民俗，图腾，饮食文化，文学与戏剧，书法及绘画，园林与建筑，音乐，工艺品，中医药，旅游景点与世界文化遗产等等。接受培训的外国学生在亲眼看到和亲身感受到中国文化所具有的不同特点和独特魅力之时，也实际感受到世界文化的多元性，自觉增进跨文化交流的意识，从而帮助他们真切地了解中国人的观念、学习、工作和生活，进而对中国产生真实的认知。

中外学生的渴望和认可给予了我们巨大的鼓舞，它启示和激励笔者与几位中外朋友将这些专题讲座的内容整理成文，以便有机会提供给更多的有兴趣了解中国的朋友们。本书力求深入浅出，通俗易懂，为初步接触中国历史与文化的外国朋友提供一个生动有趣的读物；同时也希望成为在进一步探索中国历史与文化道路上游兴正浓的中外朋友们的一个尽职向导。

此外，由于国人在对外交流中普遍存在语言障碍，对于广泛而深入的文化交流更是如此。如果本书能为国人在对外交往中用英文表述中国文化与历史提供点滴有益的借鉴与参考，笔者将会感到莫大欣慰。

借此，还要感谢为本书的出版作出贡献的各位人士：

周维先生和张馨禾女士对本书的内容提供了宝贵的指导。韩惠鹏先生、刘荣乐先生、王秀玲女士、王春霞女士、赵庆惠先生、闫庆健先生等为本书的出版发行提供了许多建设性意见及大力支持，没有他们的帮助本书将不会呈现在大家的面前。

编者
2008 年 6 月于北京

The genesis of this book comes from the authors teaching materials. It represents an extended and thoroughly revised version of a collection of lecture notes on Chinese history and culture as presented to English speaking undergraduate college students. The focus as well as content is academic but accessible to anyone who cares to read it. It is intended to appeal to readers and students for whom the study of Chinese history and culture is a relatively new experience.

The authors' pride in their heritage and love of their country and its traditions are evident throughout. They have utilized these materials to bring aspects of China's history and culture alive for westerners with the hope that this cultural exchange of knowledge and understanding might in some way contribute to world peace. This book was not meant to provide a comprehensive treatise on the centuries of Chinese history and culture, but to bring highlights, appreciation and understanding of China's history, music, arts and crafts, social customs, religions, strengths and weaknesses and pride to students who will return home as ambassadors from their country.

The authors illuminate many of the basic aspects and activities of the Chinese way of life. They stress China as a symbol of man's capability and place in nature. They speak to the new world economy, new world politics and the modernization (not necessarily westernization) of China. Advances in travel and communication, plus increased trade and investments have opened China to the world.

Most of the writers are residents of Beijing, their descriptions capture the uniqueness, continuity, progress, richness, creativeness and diversity of Beijing. They allow the readers to visualize the Great Wall of China, Tian'anmen Square, the Forbidden City and the Summer Palace. Additionally, one can get a glimpse of the hutongs, the traditional gardens and the temples.

Readers can gain an insight into China's minorities, folk music and customs, festivals, traditional medicines, religions, philosophies, literature, poetry, martial arts, cooking, science and art. As someone who has visited China, reading these chapters brings back to me the smells of their spicy foods, the beauty of their traditional gardens, the sounds of traditional Chinese music and opera, their fine craftsmanship, their intricate calligraphy and their myriad of people.

I, along with the authors, believe if we can help others see beyond their own way of life, understand something outside their own experiences and to value diversity, world understanding and peace become real possibilities.

Joseph Wagner

Contents

Part 3   Philosophy and Religion

Chapter 5   Great Thinkers in the Warring States Period

Chapter 6   Lao Zi, Zhuang Zi and Taoism

Chapter 7   Buddhism

Part 4   Civilization and Culture

Chapter 8   Chinese Characters

Chapter 9   Chinese Calligraphy

Chapter 10   Chinese Painting and It's Component Parts

Chapter 11   Traditional Chinese Medicine

Part 5   Science and Technology

Part 6   Literature and Art

Part 7   **Tradition and Customs**

Part 8   China—a Big Family of 56 Nationalities

Chapter 28　Traditional Chinese Minority Festivals

Part 1

Basic National Conditions and History

Chapter 1

Geography of China

Xiaoxia Mao

Section 1 Area and Position

China's land area covers approximately 9. 6 million square kilometers. It is nearly one-fifteenth of the world's land.

China is situated in eastern Asia on the west coast of the Pacific Ocean. The territory of China extends 5,500 kilometers from north to south, and it measures 5,200 kilometers from west to east. The centre line of the main navigation channel of the Heilong River, north of the town of Mohe in Heilongjiang Province, is the northern boundary of China. The territory extends to the Zengmu Reef of the Nansha Islands in the South China Sea. It stretches from the Pamirs, west of Wuqia County in the Xinjiang Uygur Autonomous Region, to the east where the main navigation channels of the Heilong and the Wushli rivers meet in Fuyuan County, Heilongjiang Province.

China is bordered by about 20 countries with a land boundary exceeding 20,000 kilometers.

The coast line of China, running 18,000 kilometers, is the longest one in the world. The eastern part is flanked by the four seas from north to south: the Bohai, the Huanghai (the Yellow Sea), the East and the South China Seas. The Bohai Sea is the maritime gateway to the nation's capital, Beijing. The Huanghai Sea is a half-closed shallow sea. It is adjacent to Liaoning, Shandong and Jiangsu provinces in the west and to the Korean Peninsula in the northeast. The Huanghe River and the Huaihe River flow into the Huanghai Sea. The Huanghai Sea gets its name because its coastal water is yellow, caused by the enormous amount of silt and mud carried by the Huanghe River (the Yellow River). The East China Sea is situated at the east of the mainland and leads the country's sea areas in resources. It is contiguous to Japan's Ryukyu Island in the east and the Taiwan Straits in the south. The Changjiang, Qiantang and the Qujiang are among the 40 rivers flowing into the East China Sea. Being a deep-sea basin, it is separated from the East China Sea at the southern tip of the Taiwan Straits. It is an approach to many of the world's key ports and is a vital seaway between China and other countries. Zhujiang, Hanjiang as well as the Honghai rivers are the principal rivers flowing into the South China Sea.

The three straits from north to south off China's shores are: the Bohai, the Taiwan and the Qiongzhou straits. The Taiwan Strait controls the seaway between China's north and south. The Taiwan Strait teems with fish because it is situated at the site where the cold and warm currents meet.

China's nearshore continental self is very wide. It occupies a large area off China's coast. Both the Bohai and Huanghai Seas' floors are entirely on the continental shelf, At least 70% of the East China Sea and more than 50% of the South China Sea are on the continental shelf. The nearshore continental shelf is richly endowed with oil and natural gas.

The eastern coast of Taiwan Island is bounded directly by the Pacific Ocean. Most of the coast north of the Hangzhou Bay is flat, while mountainous coasts line Taiwan's eastern shore and Hainan's southern shore. The coasts are favored with approximately 5,000 islands and large, deep natural harbors. About 60 percent of the islands are in the East China Sea. More than 90 percent of them are less than one square kilometer. More than 90% of the Chinese islands are rock islands, including Taiwan Island and Hainan. Most of the alluvial islands are at the mouths of the Changjiang, Zhujiang and other rivers—formed out of the mud and silt from these rivers. The coral islands, built from the deposits of tropical marine organisms, are the Dongsha, Xisha, Zhongsha and Nansha island groups. The South China Sea islands have been a part of China since ancient times. The area is rich in tropical resources, fish and other valuable marine products.

Section 2　Physical Features

Being a mountainous country, two-thirds of China is covered with hills and mountains. The main three groups of mountains run west-east and northeast-southwest. China has varied topography and diverse physical features such as plains, hills, plateaus and basins. The land surface of China slopes down from west to east in a three-step staircase. Plateaus cover about one-fourth of China's total area and are mainly located in the western and central parts of China. The four major plateaus are the Qinghai-Tibet, the Loess, the Yunnan-Guizhou and the Inner Mongolia plateaus. The stupendous snow mountains on the Qinghai-Tibet Plateau supply headstreams to the major rivers in East, Southeast and South Asia. The melting water from the stupendous snow mountains flows into the following rivers: the Changjiang (the Yangzi River), the Huanghe (the Yellow River), the Lancang, the Nujiang, the Indus, the Yarlungzangbu and the Trim. The plateau is studded with lakes and is rich in hydro-power. Being the second largest plateau in China, the Inner Mongolia Plateau consists of three parts. The eastern part is mostly grasslands due to a semi-arid climate. Hetao Plain is the major farming area. The eastern part has a comparatively humid climate. The grasslands in the Hulunboir and Xilingol leagues rank among China's major grasslands and stockbreeding areas. The western part is desert, covered with drifting sands and poor soil. The Loess Plateau is the biggest loess plateau in the World. The greater part of the plateau once was covered with forest, lush grasslands and fertile soil. That area, the cradle of the Chinese nation, was the birthplace of ancient Chinese culture. However, the loss of soil, the sparse vegetation and the frequent rainstorms in summer have caused serious soil erosion. The yellowish-soil land is carved into gullies and the fertility of the earth is reduced. More than a billion tons of mud and silt are carried down into the Huanghe River every year. The Qinghai-Tibet Plateau is "the roof of the world," composed of high and super-high mountains and massive highlands. The highlands' altitudes average 4,000 meters or more above sea level. Most mountains in China run west-east and northeast-southwest and consist of mainly three groups: the northern group includes the Tianshan range and the Yinshan range, the middle group includes the Kunlun range and the Qinling range, and the southern group consists of the Nanling Mountains. Nine of the world's 14 mountains exceeding 8,000 meters are in China. They are geographically important to provide headwaters for major rivers and to form climatic or river basin divides. Over 100 mountains in China exceed 7,000 meters and 1,000 mountains exceed 6,000 meters. The Himalayas are the most majestic, highest and longest mountain range in the world. The main chain has an average elevation of more than 6,000 meters. Mount Qomolangma, which lies on the border of China's Tibet and Nepal, with its northern slope in China, towers 8,848.13 meters. It is the highest mountain in the world.

The five deep and large basins are found in the west, while the medium and small ones are mainly found in the east. More than 10 percent of the country's total area consists of plain. The main large basins are the Tarim Basin (Xinjiang), the Junggar Basin (Xinjiang), the Turpan Depression (Xinjiang), the Qaidam Basin (Qinghai) and the Sichuan Basin (Sichuan Province). The Tarim Basin in Xinjiang is the country's largest inland basin which has an arid climate with little rainfall. Its surface structure consists of a series of concentric belts of the outer mountains, the foothills of stones area, a ring of oases and desertland with salt lakes in the center. Deep in the luxuriant forests of the Tianshan Mountains, the outermost belt dotted with snow-capped peaks, are many natural grazing grounds. The Sichuan Basin, drained by many rivers, is divided into three parts. The eastern part consists of mountains and valleys. Access to the mountainbound Sichuan basin used to be as difficult to get to as travel to heaven in ancient times. The central part is a major farming area with numerous flat-topped hills. Chengdu Plain at its western border has fertile soil and numerous rivers. It is the most affluent area in the basin. The Sichuan Basin, green with trees and crops in all four seasons, has become a major industrial base in southwest China.

The three important plains are the Northeast, the North China and the Middle-Lower Changjiang Plains. They provide a base for China's major agricultural production and industry. The Northeast Plain, consisting of the Songnen Plain, the Liaohe Plain and the Sanjiang Plain, is the largest plain in China. Its temperature is low in winter with a long freezing period, and high in summer. The famous fertile black soil is ideal for crop growth. Prior to 1949, the plain was considered to be the "Great Northern Wilderness." It is an important commodity grain growing area and provides a well-developed heavy industry base for China. The North China Plain, the second largest plain in China, has a long history of agricultural development. The vast, flat shallows on the shores of the Bohai and Huanghai are ideal salt-fields. The easily accessible plain has a well-developed mining business and other industries. Many of its major cities, Beijing, Tianjin, Jinan, Xuzhou and Zhengzhou, are well-known. The Middle-Lower Changjiang Plain, created by mud and silt from the Changjiang River, is woven with streams, rivers and lakes. The "water country" is known for its intensive farming cultivation. It is called "a land of fish and rice" and is one of the country's major grain-producing regions. The plain has a well-developed economy, convenient communications and a dense population. Its many major cities include such well known cities such as Shanghai, Nanjing and Hangzhou.

Hilly regions are located in many regions such as plateaus, basins and coastal plains in China. Many hills are located in east China. For example, the vast areas of red hills are in the Middle-Lower Changjiang Plain. The major hilly regions in the eastern part of the country are the Liaodong and Liaoxi hills, the Shandong Hills, the Jiangnan Hills, the Zhejiang-Fujian Hills and the Guangdong-Guangxi Hills.

Deserts cover 11.4 percent of China's total land area. Most of them are found in northwestern and northern China, including Xinjiang, Qinghai, Gansu, Inner Mongolia and Shaanxi, which are situated deep in the inland. The climate there is a typical continental climate. The Taklimakan Desert (Xinjiang) is the largest desert in China. Its name means "no emergence upon entry" in Uygur. Other big deserts are the Gurbantunggut Desert, the Badinjaran Desert, the Tenger Desert and the Muus Desert.

Section 3 Climatic Characteristics

China's climate is featured by monsoonal winds and a variety of climatic types. China is world-famous for its monsoonal climate because of the difference in heat reserves between the world's largest continent and the biggest ocean. Most regions have a distinct continental climate. North winds bring dry-cold air masses from Siberia and Mongolia under high pressure across most part of China, except the Qinghai-Tibet Plateau, on their way south. Most of China is colder and drier than other parts of the world on the same latitude because of the continental climate of China in winter. The winter monsoons last from October to March each

year.

The southeast monsoons from the Pacific and Indian Oceans influence the most of China. The warm and moist summer monsoons bring abundant rainfall to the mainland so that the annual rainfall is concentrated in the period from May to September. The summer monsoons withdraw from the mainland in October when the winter monsoons increase in momentum. The summer monsoons create higher summer temperatures than in other regions of the world on the same latitude. Summer and winter in China are longer than spring and autumn.

The temperature in the eastern half of the southern part is high and gradually decreases from south to north. On the other hand, the temperature in the western half of the southern part is lower than in the north. For instance, when the Qinghai-Tibet Plateau is below zero, the temperature in the Tarim and Turpan basins is more than 12℃. China can be divided into five temperature zones; the greater part of China belongs to the temperate and sub-tropical zones. The Qinling range has great influence on the climate of China, for it forms a natural geographic and climatic divide between southern and northern China. It blocks the northern cold air masses from moving south in winter and the moisture-bearing south winds from moving north in summer like a shelterbelt.

It rains more in the southeast than in the northwest in China. The farther away from the coast, the more the rainfall decrease. It rains mainly in summer and the amount of rainfall varies from area to area and from year to year due to monsoon activity. The irregular variation in annual precipitation harms agricultural production because it causes constant drought and floods.

The cold waves, "plum rains" and the typhoons all affect industrial and agricultural production as well as people's lives. Cold waves usually start from the Arctic Ocean, and move across northern Siberia and the Mongolian area before they reach China. They sweep southward along three routes and cause the temperature to drop by about 10 degrees within 48 hours. The abrupt drop in temperature often causes frost between late autumn and early spring, which is harmful to farm crops. "Plum Rains" (Intermittent Drizzles, "mould rains") is weather peculiar to the eastern region comprising the middle-lower Changjiang River valley. These rains come every year beginning in mid-June and ending in mid-July. The warm and moist air of the southeast monsoons and the cold air currents from the north meet in the Changjiang and Huaihe River valleys, neither being strong enough to drive the other out. Therefore, it causes a rain belt for about a month. The rainfall is favorable to the growth of rice, though an excess may result in water-logging. Typhoons strike China at the rate of 7 annually, which is more frequent than in other countries. They mainly affect Guangdong and Taiwan between July and September. The typhoons' rainstorms and tidal waves can cause tremendous damage. On the other hand, the rainfall sometimes contributes to the relief of the heat and drought.

The character of China's climate is one of large daily and annual ranges of temperature. The vast eastern areas are cold and dry with frequent northerly winds in winter. The summers are warm and humid with the rainy season coinciding with the hot season. Temperatures vary greatly in northern and southern China in winter while they are high throughout the country in summer.

Section 4　General Introduction of Rivers

There are more than 50,000 rivers in China, with a total length of 226,800 kilometers. China leads the world in hydroelectric power potential.

The Changjiang River is the largest river in China and the third largest river in the world. A total 40 percent of the country's total population live near its trunk and branch rivers. It plays an important role in China partly because it is the major water transport artery between the west and the east. Flooding has been a major problem. For instance, the big flood in 1997 caused huge damage to the local economy and the agricultural industry. Therefore, the Three Gorges Dam was built a few years ago. This dam is the biggest one in the world.

The Huanghe River is the second longest river in China. Ancient Chinese civilization and the cradle of the Chinese nation began in the Huanghe River valley. It has over one-fifth of the countries' total cultivated land in northern China. The river provides precious water resources for the northern areas that lack enough water. The headstream is crystal-clear. However, it changes to a yellow color because large quantities of yellow soil are washed away by torrential rains. Grass and trees are planted annually to help prevent soil erosion. Annually, 400 million tons of silt from the middle reaches is deposited on its widening riverbed along the lower section. The riverbed has risen from about 3 cm to 10 cm above the two banks, making it virtually an "above-ground river. " Water conservancy projects have been built along its upper, middle and the lower reaches during the recent decades.

The Zhujiang River is the largest river in southern China, formed by the Xijiang, Beijiang and Dongjiang rivers. The three rivers meet at the Zhujiang River Delta, formed of silt deposits at the river mouth. The Zhujiang valley is the region with the largest rainfall. It ranks fourth among China's rivers. However, its flow is eight times that of the Huanghe River and is second only to the Changjiang River. It is also second to the Changjiang River in the volume of water transport.

The land of China has many freshwater and saltwater lakes. Over 2,800 lakes exceed one square kilometer, and more than 130 lakes exceed 100 square kilometers. Most of them are concentrated in the Middle-Lower Changjiang Plain and the Qinghai-Tibet Plateau. The rest are scattered in the Yunnan-Guizhou Plateau, the Inner Mongolia Plateau, Xinjiang and in the northeast. There are freshwater lakes connected with exterior rivers in southeast China. The five largest freshwater lakes are Poyang in northern Jiangxi, Dongting in northern Hunan, Hongze in western Jiangsu, Taihu in southern Jiangsu, and Chaohu in central Anhui. Qinghai Lake is the largest inland saltwater lake in China. Lop Nur in Xinjiang and Nam Co in Tibet are also famous saltwater lakes.

There are more than 100 major waterfalls throughout China. These waterfalls are a source of hydroelectric power. The Huangguoshu Waterfall, situated over the Baishui River southwest of Guizhou. The Baishui River's bed is like a staircase descending step by step, forming nine falls at each step. The Huangguoshu Waterfall, 30 to 40 meters wide in summer, is the largest one in China. The Hukou Waterfall on the Yellow River, and the Diaoshuilou Waterfall on the Mudan River are among the famous waterfalls in China.

Chapter 2

Chinese Culture's Formation and Development

Xiaoxia Mao

China is renowned for her ancient civilization, which has greatly contributed to the civilized world. China has undergone eight phases in the formation and development of its traditional culture.

Section 1　Prehistoric Culture

The prehistoric culture indicates the culture of the primitive society. The earliest known ancients in China were Yuanmou ape-men, who existed 1,700,000 years ago. Chinese culture departed from the Paleolithic era and entered the Neolithic Age about 10,000 years ago. The ruined sites of Hongshan Culture, Dawenkou-Longshan Culture, Yangshao Culture and Majiayao-Qijia Culture along the Yellow River in northern China and the Hemudu-Majiabang Culture in southern China, found in the lower reaches of the Yangtze River, are evidences of the Neolithic culture. The earliest primitive religion emerged during this time. The totem, as a form of religious manifestation, mixed the worship of ancestors and nature. The Chinese dragon and phoenix were the totems of ancient China's clans.

Of the various tribes, three of them, named Western Xia, Eastern Yi and Miaoman Man, gradually created their own regional culture and characteristics. The Western Xia and the Eastern Yi gradually became integrated through a long process. Being the predecessor of ancient China, they laid the foundation for the formation of China's ancient civilization. They eventually conquered the Miao tribe. The embryonic form of the Chinese nation was formed. They held a memorial ceremony for the establishment of their ancestors, Yandi and Huangdi. The Chinese nation claims to be the descendants of Yandi and Huangdi.

The emergence of primitive agriculture was a major achievement in this prehistoric culture. Foxtail millet (in northern China) and rice (in southern China) were the chief products.

Primitive characters were invented and carved on pots. Pottery was another great invention, including painted pottery and black pottery.

Section 2　Xia, Shang and Western Zhou Dynasties

The Xia (founded around the 21st century B. C.) was the earliest slave society.

The Shang Dynasty (16th Century B. C. —1066 B. C.) replaced the Xia in the 16th century B. C. The custom of succession for choosing the next emperor followed the principle of "the young brother succeeding after the elder dies" in the Shang Dynasty. The Zhou Dynasty (770 B. C. —221B. C.) rose and exterminated the Shang Dynasty.

The system culture, material culture and spiritual culture were highly developed around the period of the Western Zhou Dynasty. During this period, China advanced into the Bronze Age and achieved great progress in comparison with the Stone Age. Succession started with "the wife's eldest son" and the other official positions were held by nobles who had a blood relationship to the emperor in the Western Zhou Dynasty. The system of rites and music was codified for the nobles. It has become traditional in the Chinese culture.

The Nine-square's system became the agricultural pattern. The arable land in a field was divided into nine squares. Eight squares were designated for the peasants as private land to make a living. The middle square was a public plot that was planted by the eight peasants' families for their hereditary master, feudal lord.

People had superstitious beliefs in the deity, fate and charities. "Heaven" and "Emperor" were the common dominators of the human world during the periods of the Xia, Shang and Western Zhou dynasties.

Both material and spiritual cultures continued to develop. The brilliant Bronze culture came into being. The Shang period was the biggest bronze vessel in the world.

The development of Chinese characters matured and ancient writing gradually expanded during the Shang and the Zhou periods. About 4,000 various characters are found inscribed on bones and tortoise shells (the Shang Dynasty). The character inscriptions found on ancient bronze objects were mainly characters from the Western Zhou Dynasty. Early documents, which recorded ceremonies, political or military activities and rituals, proliferated with the maturity of writing.

Section 3　Spring and Autumn Period, Warring States Period

The slave society collapsed during the Spring and Autumn Period of Chinese history, between 770B. C. and 476 B. C. The use of ironware and the technique of using a till pulled by a cow helped to develop economic production as China entered the Iron Age.

During the Warring States Period, a feudal system was established. The existence of six states, Qi, Jin, Qin, Chu, Wu and Yue, caused endless wars, as well as providing close political contacts. These close contacts among the states prepared the way for the final political unity.

Numerous schools of thought emerged during the Warring States Period. The well-known schools were the Confucian School, the Taoist School, the Moist School, the Military Strategists, the School of Logicians and the School of Naturalists. These schools contended with each other and exerted influence on each other in academic study. The various schools taught an extensive number of subjects, including ethics, logic, political theory, natural laws and modes of social development. The resulting free academic debate pushed forward the academic culture. The cultural progress provided a theoretical basis for the social reform. The emergence of the Confucian school promoted the Chinese traditional culture. Although the Confucian political inclination was conservative, it has remained remarkable throughout the ages.

Section 4　Qin and Han Dynasties

The Qin-Han periods witnessed significant achievements in various fields. The feudal society reached maturity during the Qin (221 B. C.) and the Han (206 B. C. —220A. D.) dynasties. Although the Qin Dynasty lasted for only 15 years, it greatly influenced the Chinese feudal society.

The Qin established the first centralized feudal autocratic dynasty after the State of Qin united China. The Qin system was the centralized autocratic political system intended to meet the needs of a feudal au-

tocracy. The emperor had supreme power. The prime minister assisted the emperor in governing the country, while the marshal took charge of military affairs and the censor supervised officials of all ranks. The country was divided into prefectures, with each prefecture comprised of several counties. The emperor appointed or dismissed all officials, those in the imperial court and those in local areas. This centralized autocratic political system had a lasting influence on the government throughout the 2,000 years of the feudal society.

The First Emperor called Ying Zheng of the Qin Dynasty ordered that the land system, the weights, the measures, the roads and the writing forms should be standardized. These standards proved helpful for cultural exchange and the merging of nationalities. He introduced series of reforms to strengthen the united country and develop the economy. Standardizing of weights and measures was one of the reforms. It was not only used for the easy collection of tax and rent and the distribution of salaries to officials, but assisted the exchange of goods in the market and promoted business activities impartially as well.

Ying Zheng adopted cruel methods against the Confucian scholars who criticized the court and the reform carried by him. He ordered to burn all the books owned by the Confucian scholars and buried the scholars alive. The tragedy damaged the development of the Chinese culture and set a very bad example for pressuring culture in the Chinese history.

Emperor Wu Di of the Han Dynasty adopted Confucianism as the official philosophy. Scholars from other schools were denied to civil service positions.

Cai Lun invented papermaking technology during the East Han Dynasty. Mathematical works such as *Zhoubi Suanjing and Nine Chapters on Mathematical Art* were important achievements in mathematics. An armillary sphere, which was the world's first seismograph, was invented by Zhang Heng. *Classic of Internal Medicine and Febrile and Other Diseases* was one of the medical classics. After Zhang Qian was sent as an envoy to the western regions, the Silk Road became the main passage for cultural exchange between China and western Asia and even Europe. The Han court sent missions to countries like Iran, Iraq, India and the Roman Empire. During this time, China developed their foreign relations and spread their advanced culture.

Section 5 the Wei and the Jin, the Northern and the Southern Dynasties

The five major minority nationalities included the Huns, Jie, Di, Qiang and Xianbei. There ensued an upsurge of ethnic mergence in northern China. These minorities conquered the Han nationality with force, but then were gradually assimilated into the advanced Han culture.

Large numbers of the Hans fled from the Yellow River area and poured into the Yangtze River area due to the oppression and discrimination of the northern minority nationalities. They provided advanced production and labor techniques to land development in the Yangtze River area. A solid foundation was formed for economic development in the south.

Buddhism was introduced into China during the Qin and Han period. It began to spread and flourish during the Wei-Jin period. Some grottoes for their engravings were dug during this period. For instance, the Dunhuang Mogao Grottoes, Longmen Grottoes and Datong Yungang Grottoes are among the world-famous grottoes known for their engravings.

Jia Sixie compiled an agricultural work, *Important Arts for the People's Welfare*. Zu Chongzhi worked out the ratio of the circumference of a circle to its diameter. *Treatise on the Pulse* was written by the noted physician, Wang Shuhe.

This period witnessed the rise of the Dark Learning, a new sect in the realm of philosophy, and brought a new atmosphere to the academic and ideological circles. The principal exponents were Guo Xiang and Wang Bi. The natural, genuine and profound aesthetics at that time exerted much influence on traditional music and painting.

Section 6   The Sui and Tang Dynasties

The division and turmoil, lasting more than 300 years, was put to an end by the founder of the Sui Dynasty (581—618). The Sui abolished the official selection system which selected officials according to family status. The Sui emperors developed an imperial civil examination system. Examinees were selected to be officials because of their ability and originality. It opened a new channel for more people to have official careers.

There was a comparative freedom of thought. Scholars did research on Confucianism, Buddhism and Taoism. The Sui Dynasty also witnessed closer relations between China and foreign countries.

The Tang Dynasty (618—907) is one of the most glorious eras in Chinese history. The tax reform provided for tax payments in proportion to the land property, which lightened the burden of peasants.

Buddhism and Taoism were equally prevailing religions in the Tang period. The cultural and academic policy helped the assimilation of Confucianism, Buddhism and Taoism.

Supported by the economy and national strength, this culture saw its achievements surpassing that of previous dynasties. Tang poetry attained its peak in Chinese history. Hundreds of noted poets left behind tens of thousands of poems, contributing an incomparable heritage. Some noted calligraphers and painters were also recognized during this era.

The golden age of the Sui-Tang period witnessed closer relations between China and foreign countries. Foreign emissaries, merchants and ecclesiastics came to China bringing with them various products and cultures. The growing international contacts enriched the cultural life of the Chinese. Meanwhile, Chinese culture and advanced technology were also passed on to the world and made tremendous contribution to the world culture.

Section 7   The Song, Liao, Xia, Jin and Yuan Dynasties

The Northern Song Dynasty (960—1127) restored a unified central authority and brought an end to the prolonged partition created by the Five Dynasties (907—979). The Song rulers weakened the powerful and independent to ensure their rule and to avoid a similar downfall, as occurred in the Tang Dynasty. As a result, the strengthened feudal autocracy and the political corruption weakened the defensive power when the Northern Song confronted the military threat from the Liao (907—1125) and Xi Xia (1032—1227) regimes on the north-western border. A passive and appeasement policy in exchange was taken in the Northern Song Dynasty. After gaining strength and conquering the Liao regime, the Jin occupied the Yellow River basin. The Northern Song emperor fled south and established the capital at Lin'an (Hangzhou, Zhejiang Province) known to historians as the Southern Song Dynasty (1127—1279).

Economic production continued to increase despite the internal problems and the trouble on the northern border. The south quickly became the economic center of the country.

The invention of gunpowder, the compass and printing techniques were three great Chinese inventions which contributed greatly to the civilized world. An indication of the splendid achievements in natural science was written by the great Northern Song scientist, Shen Kuo, in *Sketchbook of Dream Brook*. The encyclopedia covered a wide range of scientific fields such as mathematics, physics, chemistry, biology, astronomy, geography, meteorology, medicine and engineering.

The art of Chinese painting was further developed. Poetry of the Song Dynasty created a new form called "Song Ci."

Li Xue (Neo-Confucianism or the Cheng-Zhu Li Xue school of Confucianism) was developed by combining Confucianism, Taoism and Buddhism by Cheng Hao, Cheng Yi and Zhu Xi. They put forward the ethical slogan: "eradicate human desires to maintain the heavenly principle." As the consummate ideological system in Chinese feudal society, it advocated supreme morality, internalized as cultivation, and externalized as the governance of virtue. This principle encouraged the cultivation of scholars' morality and loyalty to the sovereign and to the country. However, it exaggerated heavenly principles and suppressed human nature causing major tragedies, such as massacres, in later generations.

The Song Dynasty was an important period for the merging of nationalities in Chinese history. The economic and cultural exchanges between the Han nationality and other nationalities, such as Dangxiang, Nüzhen, Qidan and Jin, never ended.

The Mongols rose and became powerful. After vanquishing the Western Zia, Jin, and Southern Song, Hublai Khan founded the Yuan Dynasty (1279—1368) and reunited China.

The communications between the Han nationality with other nationalities developed to a new level because of the vast domain and easy communications. Hui nationality was formed as a fruit of the ethnic merging.

Yuan opera represented the zenith of literature during the Yuan period. Guan Han Qin, a noted Yuan opera writer, created many famous works.

Section 8　The Ming and the Qing Dynasties

China's feudal society declined during the Ming (1368—1644) and the Qing (1644—1911) dynasties. Espionage and literary inquisition were employed after the autocratic system developed. The emperor selected his officials according to their stereotyped writing in exams. As a result, intellectual and creative thought was suppressed. Farmers personal attachment to the agriculture career was released due to the reform of taxes and corvee. However trade was still restricted and maritime trade with foreign countries was banned. These policies not only curbed China's economy, but also stymied China's social and global development, and left them behind the western world. Western countries experienced the Industrial Revolution and became capitalistic, while China was blinded to these big changes in the outside world. China retained their feudal society system through the Ming and the Qing dynasties. The sprouting of capitalism and the merging and developing of the urban areas was not encouraged.

Chinese ancestors contributed to a mature traditional culture that has survived for five thousand years. The rulers of the Ming and the Qing dynasties employed plenty of manpower and abundant financial resources to collect and systemize a tremendous number of ancient books. The encyclopedias and concordances included books such as *Great Encyclopaedia of Yongle*, *A Collection of Books Ancient and Present and Complete Library in the Four Branches of Literature*. General anthologies of prose and verse are, *Complete Collection of Prose in the Tang Dynasty* and *A Complete Collection of Poems in the Song Dynasty*. *Exegesis of Classical Works and The Kangxi Dictionary* are large reference books. The study of textual criticism began while these ancient books were collected. Therefore, the forming of the Qian Jia School made an important contribution toward preserving the traditional Chinese culture for later generations.

A large number of novels were created in this period. The following four ancient classical works were among the most successful from this period: *The Romance of the Three Kingdoms*, *Water Margin*, *Pilgrimage to the West and A Dream of Red Mansions*.

There came into being some great academic works of summa in science and technology. The medical work, *Compendium of Material Medicine* (by Li Shizhen), the agricultural work, *A Complete Treatise on Agriculture* (by Xu Guangqi), and the geographic work, *Travel Notes* (by Xu Xiake) are among the works having a big influence on Chinese history.

Part 2

Ancient Capital Cities—Epitome of the History

Chapter 3

Beijing—an Ancient and Modern Capital City

Xiaoxia Mao, Xuefei Yang, and Frits Buijs

Beijing, literally meaning "Northern capital", is located in the northwest part of the North China plains and covers an area of 16,800 square Kilometers. As the capital of the People's Republic of China (PRC), Beijing with a population of approximately 16 million inhabitants is not only known as China's cultural, economical, political and transportation center, but also as a famous historical city (Oriental Travel, 2007, para. 1). This chapter covers Beijing's ancient history and its modernization, particularly during the new century, as well as its world famous historical sites and other places of interests such as ancient architectures, parks, museums and temples.

Section 1 Beijing as an Ancient Capital

Five hundred thousand years ago, the ancestors of human beings called "Peking Man" kindled the fire of ancient civilization in Zhou Kou Dian. By the first millennium B. C., there were already cities in the vicinity of Beijing, and the founding of Beijing as a city dated to the vanquishing of the Shang and setting up of the fiefdoms of Yan and Ji in 1045 B. C. In other words. Beijing had become a capital of the Yan kingdom during the Warring States period. The city was successively called Zhoujun, Youzhou, Nanjing, Yanjing and Beijing. In the early 10th century, Khitan, a nomadic tribe in northeast China, established the Liao Dynasty, and during the Liao dynasty, Beijing was referred to as Yanjing.

In 1125, the Jurchen Chin Dynasty annexed Liao, and in 1153 moved its capital to Liao's Nanjing, calling it Zhongdu (the central capital), which is slightly to the southwest of central Beijing. It is interesting to mention that the pattern of the city here was similar to that of the Song Dynasty's capital Bianjing. The palaces which were enclosed by the imperial city formed a three-layer city wall system, which means that the layout of Zhongdu followed a well defined central point, the Central Tower, and a north-south axis (Gu, 2006, p. 256). The first circle of the wall was constructed around the palaces, a second around the imperial city, and the third around the outer city. During the Yuan, Ming and Qing dynasties, this pattern was maintained.

In 1215, Mongol forces burned Zhongdu and the Chin (金) rulers were forced to move their capital to Bianjing (Kaifeng), which is a city in Henan province. In order to conquer all of China, Kublai Khan's, the Yuan emperor founded its capital Dadu (the grand capital) in the north of modern central Beijing. After the accession to the throne, Kublai Khan decided to locate the capital of Yuan in Yanjing. Thus, Kublai Khan issued an order to build a new city to the northwest of Zhongdu as his capital in 1267. After thorough reconnaissance and well-conceived planning, a majestic capital city was built at the northeast of

Yanjing's Old City, which was entitled Dadu (presently Beijing). It centered on what is now the northern stretch of the 2nd Ring Road, and stretched northwards between the 3rd and 4th Ring Roads. There are remnants of the Mongol-era wall still standing (Wikipedia, 2007, para. 10). Beijing became the national capital of the Yuan Dynasty (1277—1368). With regard to scale, magnificence and prosperity, Dadu City outperformed two renowned European metropolises, Paris and Rome, during the same period.

In 1368, the mercenary Zhu Yuanzhang led an uprising, taking over the city and claiming the start of the Ming Dynasty. The city was renamed Beiping and for the next 35 years Zhu Yuan Zhang moved the city to the south and took Nanjing as his capital (Harper, 2002, p. 156). After his death, Zhu Di rebelled and took power from his nephew, the young emperor. Zhu Di moved the capital from Nangjing to Beiping (1421) and renamed it Beijing. The capital was also known as Jingshi, simply meaning capital (Wikipedia, 2007, para. 11).

Many of Beijing's historical structures, such as the Forbidden City and the Temple of Heaven, were built in the Ming Dynasty. The capital City of the Ming period was rebuilt, expanded, and modeled after the capital of the Yuan. After the Manchus overthrew the Ming Dynasty and establishing the Qing Dynasty in 1644, Beijing remained China's capital throughout the Qing period. In the Ming and the Qing dynasties, the security system for imperial palaces was comprehensive and strict. The Qing emperors spent large sums of money and a lot of manpower to rebuild new pleasure grounds in and around Beijing during the Qing Dynasty (1644—1911).

The city was divided into three sections: the Forbidden City (the Palace City), the Imperial City and the Great City (Inner City). Many large-scale buildings such as palaces, temples and even walls were constructed. The capital city continued to develop and became much larger than Dadu. While building the imperial palaces in Beijing, the Ming emperor ordered the construction of high city walls for the Palace City and the imperial city to form two important lines of defense. Parallel to the alignment were two thoroughfares from north to south on both sides, which linked a number of lanes to form a network of streets stretching from east to west. This layout of the city formed the square-patterned style of the Inner City.

The outside walls were built to the south of the capital to strengthen the defense of the Outer City, which was composed of business centers and the handicraft industry. There was an axial alignment from north to south measuring about 7.5 kilometers long, along which the city of Beijing was located. The gates of the city wall were used for different functions, such as defenses, for example, most of the carts passing through Chongwenmen were carrying liquor in the past.

When the New Republic of China was set up in 1949, Beijing became the capital of the new republic. After 1949, the walls around the Imperial City were successively demolished with the improvement of city infrastructure in the 1950's and 1960's. Most of the ancient city wall, which was about 47 kilometers long, was mostly destroyed in 1950. Only a few hundred meters have been rebuilt. The Yongding Gate was rebuilt in 2003. More than forty outer and inner city gates gradually disappeared from 1952 to 1967. Only four inner city gates have remained. People can only read the names of the gates from the names of the subway stations around Beijing, for the subway was built just beneath the site of the ancient city wall. Front Gate (Zhengyangmen, South-Facing Gate), a 38-meter-high brick fortress-like structure, is one of the few remaining gates of the Beijing city wall located at Qianmen area. It was built for the city's defense in 1439. This gate was a pass that was only used by the emperor, the imperial sedans and carriages to go to the Temple of Heaven for worshipping ceremonies. The 94 windows were watchtower windows from which archers could shoot arrows. Before it was reconstructed in 1914, the tower burned down several times. The gate was renovated in 1977. The tower was opened to the public in 1990 and exhibitions are held in the three-story tower.

The whole eastern part of the outer city was commonly considered as Xuannan. Archaeological findings and a number of historical relics provide evidence to support the conclusion that Xuannan was where Beijing city originated. In 2003, the building of Memorial Que was established in Binhe Garden, which is a relic site as a symbol of great significance, showing the special status of Xuannan area in the historical development of Beijing.

All in all, Beijing is an ancient city with a long cultural history. Thirty-four emperors made Beijing their capital and the four feudal dynasties—Chin, Yuan, Ming, and Qing all set up their capital here, which is the reason why it has the biggest concentration of the country's scenic spots and historical sites. Beijing's splendid architectural sites, picturesque landscapes, abundance of cultural heritage, together with its well known historical sites, numerous palaces, imperial gardens, temples, ancient stone carvings, pagodas, etc. all make Beijing an intriguing and mysterious ancient city. Nevertheless, viewing Beijing as only a historical city is far from enough. Nowadays, Beijing should, or can be viewed to develop into a modern international metropolis (Oriental Travel, 2007, para. 8). Recognized as one of the cities that has the most potential for the fast development and modernization, Beijing will become a new world tourism center in the near future.

Section 2　Beijing as a Modern City

In the recent decades, Beijing city has undergone an ongoing modernization. People at home see Beijing as an ancient city, as well as an attractive new city with growing prosperity. For people in the rest of the world, Beijing is seen as a fast developing metropolitan city with a blend of old and new things. To know Beijing better one should not only know its past, but also know its present and future development.

Since the foundation of the new China in 1949, the new leaders soon embarked on a building program that started Beijing urban construction on an unprecedented scale. First of all, the 1950's saw the construction of apartment blocks, factories and Beijing 's first subway line (CCTS, 2007, para. 13). Secondly, in 1964 the old city walls were torn down to make way for the roadway that would become today's Second Ring Road. Tian'anmen Square was dramatically expanded and this transformation of the ancient palace square to Tian'anmen Square created a new face for Beijing. It had a significant influence on the development of the city's reconstruction. For Chinese people, the Forbidden City is the very heart of Beijing, and Tian'anmen Square is regarded as the second most important element in the planning and reconstruction projects in Beijing. Thirdly, the economic reforms initiated by Deng Xiaoping in 1978 set the stage for Beijing's ongoing development boom (CCTS, 2007, para. 14). Since China's opening up to the world in the 1980's, rapid economic growth combined with preparations for events like the 1990 Asian Games and the 50th anniversary of the People's Republic of China in 1999 fuelled countless construction and infrastructure projects all of which represented the city's continuing drive to become an international city and a world destination. Especially after the success of Beijing's bid to host the 2008 Olympic Games, Beijing has changed beyond recognition. Major construction projects give the old city a new appearance and it seems that apartment blocks and office buildings have sprung up like mushrooms overnight. Moreover, commercial streets such as Wangfujing Commercial Street, International Financial Street and Xidan Commercial Street have been transformed into well-lit pedestrian commercial areas. For example, there are five big commercial districts that have been formed, they are Wangfujing, Xidan, Dazhalan (Dashilan), Longfusi and Chaoyangmenwai. From the urban areas to the suburban areas, tall buildings rise one after another, and modernized symbolic structures with different characteristics can be seen everywhere.

To fulfill the requirements of modern construction, Beijing drew up Beijing Overall City Plan (2004—

2020) in 2004, setting new goals and extending new space for the long-term development (Liu, 2007, p. 10). For instance, the Beijing Municipal Government defined "two axes-two belts-multi-centers" new city development pattern and aims to develop Beijing into an international metropolis (BilinChina, 2004, para. 2). To be specific, the "two axes" represent the cross axes formed by Beijing traditional middle axis and Chang an Avenue. The "two belts" refer to the southern development zone which starts from the north along Huairou and Miyun with Shunyi, Tongzhou and Yizhuang as key areas, and the so-called "western ecological zone", which includes Yanqing, Changping, Liangxiang and Huangcun. "Multi-centers" means the construction of several comprehensive service districts in downtown areas including the CBD, Olympic Park and Zhongguancun, and of several new towns in the areas covered both by the city and the Two Belts (BTM Beijing, 2004, para. 5-7). Thus, the "two axes-two belts-multi-centers" in the city spatial structure foundation form the "city center-new city-towns" i. e. a "city and town" structure (People's Daily Online, 2005, para. 6).

Furthermore, during the Capital Alliance Meeting, the Vice Director of Beijing Municipal Commission of Reform and Development, Zhi Liu, pointed out three stages for Beijing to reach its development goals. First, from 2004 to 2008, Beijing "shall primarily realize and construct the basic framework of a modern international metropolis". Second, from 2009 until 2020, Beijing shall completely realize modernization with its own characteristics and be recognized world wide. During the final stage, which is by 2050 Beijing will develop into a sustainable city in the economic, social and ecological aspects, hence become a well-known world metropolis (Liu, 2007, p. 11).

In sum, efforts are being made to update the infrastructure, improve the environment and increase the construction of satellite townships. Modern technology, natural landscaping and ancient sites form a brilliant picture of Beijing today.

However, the rapid modernization of Beijing is not without problems and drawbacks. It is undeniable that the modernization and economic development also brings serious environmental challenges and other related problems. Such as the air pollution, water pollution, energy usage, supply issues and overcrowded traffic. Especially during the past few years, air pollution has become serious due to the increase in number of vehicles and natural occurrences such as sandstorms. To prevent further deterioration and to protect the environment, the Beijing government has introduced 69 urgent measures to reduce coal and fuel emissions which are the main cause of air pollution in the capital. One of the future aims of Beijing is to improve appreciably the air quality and once again bring back the blue sky. And in the near future, namely, by 2008 the greenery coverage in Beijing will reach 40% providing an average of 10 m^2 of green space per resident.

Secondly, although it is widely known that Beijing still has a long way to go in realizing the construction of the city together with the development of environmental protection, Beijing government is determined to improve its waterway system. For example, in 2000, 30 rivers and 26 lakes in and around the city were dredged and cleaned.

Furthermore, with regard to the use of natural resources, Beijing government claims that by 2020 the demand and supply of water will be balanced and clean energy will occupy more than 90% of the total final energy consumption of Beijing (Liu, 2007, p. 18).

Moreover, although there are many of Beijing's ancient constructions which are in need of protection, Beijing people's awareness for protecting the ancient heritage of the city is gradually becoming stronger. Consider the newly reconstructed Yongdingmen Gate Tower (Eternal Stability Gate Tower) at the south area of Beijing (2002—2005). The entire Tower was rebuilt according to the original design and style of building, which is unique in the world. To support the reconstruction, more than 2,000 enterprises, companies and residential homes, which were built at the site after the former Yongdingmen moved away, were re-settled.

To put it simply, by 2020, Beijing will be built into "an ecologically sustainable city with beautiful mountains, fresh air, friendly environment, excellent ecology, and a harmonious relationship between human and nature". The "forest coverage rate of Beijing will reach up to 55%; the greenery coverage rate shall reach up to 44% ~ 48%" and "the public green area per capita shall be 40 ~ 45 m^2" (Liu, 2007, p. 17).

Finally, as far as Beijing's overcrowded traffic problem is concerned, measures are being taken to cope with the problem. As pointed out by Liu, by 2020, public transportation will become the main mode of passenger transport, and there will be more travel choices with higher efficiency. Therefore, traffic congestion will be better dealt with.

Famous Lanes and Streets: Dongjiaominxiang Lane

Dongjiaominxiang starts at the Chongwenmen Gate in the east, and ends at the eastern side of Tian'anmen Square in the west; it stretches to eastern Changan street in the north, and reaches Qianmen Gate Street in the east.

The street was originally called East River's Rice Lane. The name, Glutinous Rice Lane, came into being during the Yuan Dynasty because it was the place where glutinous rice was stored. In 1421, after the Emperor Yongle of the Ming Dynasty moved the Capital to Beijing, he constructed important government offices at both sides of the line that links Qianmen Gate with the Main Gate of Imperial Palace. He designed these buildings after the Palaces in the city of Nanjing. The Qing Dynasty continued to locate the six Ministries of the central government at the east and the west sides of Chessboard Street, copying systems and regulations from the Ming Dynasty. Dongjiaominxiang is situated at the east side of Chessboard Street and became the gathering place of government offices of the Qing Dynasty. Many imperial palaces were built in Dongjiaominxiang during the Qing Dynasty, including the palaces of Prince Suwang, Prince Chunwang, Prince Yixianginwang, etc. The palace of Prince Suwang, which is located at the eastern side of the Imperial River, is a fairly typical example of these palaces.

During the Qing Dynasty there were frequent contacts among different ethnic groups, and an increasing exchange of foreign diplomatic envoys. Students and visiting businessmen from other countries all preferred to live at Nantong Assembly Hall which was located in this lane. Dongjiaominxiang, consequently, turned out to be the lane where residents of different nationalities intermingled.

After the Qing Dynasty was defeated during the Second Opium War, China reached the Tianjin Agreement and the Beijing Agreement with England and France respectively. According to these agreements, these foreign countries were entitled to build embassies and to send permanent envoys to Beijing. That same year, the government of the Qing Dynasty rented the imperial palace of Prince Qingong to France as its embassy. Later, embassies of various countries such as Germany, Portugal, Belgium, Netherlands, Spain, Italy, Japan and Austria mushroomed in Dongjiaominxiang. At that time, Dongjiaominxiang experienced the convergence of government offices, imperial palaces, local residences and foreign embassies.

Most of the buildings in the area have been repaired and ameliorated since 1949.

The most valuable thing about the area lies in the fact that it preserves the exotic beauty of foreign architectures in this historical and cultural street. It possesses a unique value for the preservation of the traditional architectural cultures of old cities. Additionally, it is the special conveyer of China's modern history. The exotic beauty of the foreign architectures in the area has existed for over 100 years. It not only serves as the special carrier of history at special historical moments, but is a witness to the tremendous historical transformation of China.

Guozijian Street (Chengxian Street)

Guozijian Street (Chengxian Street) is situated inside Andingmen, Xicheng District, which is near Andingmendongdajie. Guozijian Street, where the Confucius Temple and Yonghe Lamasery are located, was constructed in the same period as Dadu, the capital city of the Yuan Dynasty, and it was the area where temples and official buildings were concentrated in Beijing's old city. While the Confucius Temple and Guozijian are important architectures in term of cultural value, Yonghe Lamasery and Bailin temple distinguish themselves as the main historical architectures in this area.

Guozijian not only served as the highest organ for educational administration for the whole nation during the Yuan, Ming and Qing Dynasties, but also was the location of China's highest learning institution, Taixue (Supreme Learning). In particular, Biyong, where the ancient emperors gave lectures, was an elegant edifice of great cultural and historical significance in Guozijian. As one of "Beijing's 6 greatest palaces" credited by the famous architect, Mr. Liang Sicheng, Biyong hall serves as a reminder of Emperor Qianlong who emphasized both academic and military might during the Qing Dynasty (1784). In the 49th year of Qianlong's reign, this hall was designed and supervised by Liu Yong. Biyong was completed successfully. It was unique in style and high in standard, which symbolized the great importance that the emperor Qianlong attached to education. Serving as the highest administrative body for China's educational system through several dynasties, Guozijian is preserved in relatively good condition. As witness to China's imperial examinations, Biyong Hall is of great significance to the study of China's history.

Four magnificent and exquisitely decorated cross street archways constituted an integral element of China's ancient architectural history. They render Guozijian Street the focus of the world. It is noteworthy that there is hardly any well-preserved cross-street Pailou other than these four.

Guozijian Street was among the first group of Beijing's protected historical and cultural streets opened in November, 1990. It is one of the 15 protected areas in Beijing.

Fuchengmen Street and Xisi Street

Fuchengmen, which was located along the nine Gates of Beijing's inner city during the Ming and Qing Dynasties, was situated in the southern part of West Beijing. Fuchengmen Street has been the most important thoroughfare in West Beijing since the Ming Dynasty. Inner Fuchengmen Street's position was attributable to the renovation of the City Wall during the Ming Dynasty, to the increase in freight transportation, and to the rising business markets. Notably, Inner Fuchengmen Street was the main thoroughfare for coal transportation, coal-mine workers, camels, and for coal carriages to go through.

The Inner Fuchengmen Street has been a key religious and business area in Beijing since the Ming Dynasty. The area from Inner Fuchengmen Street to Xisi Pailou has been the largest business center in West Beijing too. In fact, the emergence of this business area could be dated back to the Yuan Dynasty.

Execution grounds were once located in Xisi Street during the Ming Dynasty. People gathered around Guangji Temple, Baita Temple and the Shrine of Emperors of Past Dynasties, which were located along the Street. As an old saying goes, the flourishing of the temples makes people gather and the gathering of people makes the markets appear. Taking advantage of the convenient traffic patterns and the prosperity of businesses, the densely-populated and stores-concentrated area between Fuchengmen and Xisi has been the largest business center in West Beijing for more than 700 years.

Located in West Beijing, the advantageous geographic location, the frequency and convenience of freight transportation, as well as the prosperity and convergence of businesses and markets, contributed to this street's position as a main thoroughfare. Through the years, this area became the important business, religious and cultural center of Beijing.

Liulichang Street

Visitors, who walk through Xinhua Street, go out the Heping Gate, and turn to the south, see that Changqiao Haiwangcun (village of the sea king) park is not far from them. Haiwangcun is located in the famous Liulichang Culture Street running north to west. While the street running south to north, Xinhua Street, divides it into two parts, the west and the east. Traditional culture and businesses were the main focus of Liulichang Culture Street.

Liulichang gets its name from the kiln factory that made colored glazed tiles for the imperial houses during the Yuan and Ming Dynasties. "Liulichang" means a glazed-ware factory. The Liulichang area has a 900 years history. It was one of the four big kilns built in the city during the Yuan Dynasty (1279—1368). These big kilns made glazed tiles for the imperial palaces. Therefore, the street took its name from the glazed ware factory. It became one of the most popular quarters in Beijing during the Qing Dynasty (1644—1911). It is noted for antiques, ceramics, paintings, rubbings and jewelry.

The bookstores, south paper stores, curio stores, mount painting stores, stamp stores and ink box stores are all located on this street. These stores formed Liulichang's unique character and provided a window from which to view a sample of China's two-hundred-year cultural history. The buildings in the Liulichang Street maintain a unified traditional form. Others are China-style shop fronts made of brick and wood. Most of the bookstores there sell the old books. In the past, the business of the bookstores in the Liulichang Street included the arranging and rebinding of ancient books, and the seeking of rare books.

The South Paper Stores sell Four Treasures for study, including pens, ink, paper, and ink stones. It is called "South Paper Store" because the goods came from the south. It manufactured stone stamps and carved characters on seals. The South Paper stores, bookstores and curio stores are three significant industries of the Liulichang Culture Street.

The culture and businesses of the Liulichang region were the most prosperous during the Qing Dynasty, during which many famous scholars lived. However, book stores and curio industries were going downhill and many old stores were on the brink of bankruptcy during the period from the Japanese invasion and occupation of Peking (Beijing) in 1937 to the eve of 1949. It is estimated that there used to be 122 curio stores, but only five curio stores remained in the Liulichang Culture Street at the end of the 1940's Republic of China. During the period, the restoration of Liulichang Street took place from 1978 to 1985. Beijing's government has been rehabilitating this area since the 1980s. A lot of well-known old stores in the Liulichang Culture Street attract a great number of customers coming from throughout China and from other countries. The history, culture, and unique character of Liulichang Street is very appealing. Liulichang Culture Street has become a governmental protected culture street area of historical importance.

Wangfujing Street

Wangfujing Street lies on the north side of Changan Boulevard next to the Forbidden City. The 700-year-old street is one of Beijing's oldest and most famous commercial areas. The street came into being in the Yuan Dynasty (1279—1368). One Qing emperor wanted all of his ten brothers to build their mansions in Beijing so that it would be easy for him to keep an eye on them, for he was suspicious that they might pose a direct threat to him. These ten brothers lived on Shiwangfu Street (Wangfujing Street). This street became a prosperous commercial area during the Qing Dynasty.

The local government spent about one billion Yuan on renovating the entire street between 1992 and 2000. It was a quality renovation and quite comprehensive. The area is now fashionable, and hosts many so-

phisticated cultural activities. It presents a shining, modern, new look. The Beijing Municipal government and other government offices in this area make the area a strategic location. This wide street accommodates over 200 shops along its 810-meter length and is free of vehicles. This renovated street has retained some of its traditional cultural atmosphere in spite of being modern. Twelve famous old shops from the area have been set on the southern wall. A group of sculptures depicting the lives of Beijing's local residents from the old times has been established. The ancient well, also related to the street's name was symbolically restored.

Section 3　Beijing's World Cultural Heritage

the Great Wall

" The Great Wall, a massive project constructed in a long span of time, is not only an ancient defensive project, but also one of the greatest ancient construction projects worldwide. Several hundred years ago, it had been named as one of the seven wonders in the world. The Great Wall is known in the world for its complicated and laborious construction, decisive strategic position and grand and firm structure. The Great Wall is of historical, cultural and scientific value. In the past 2,000 years, although repair and renovation never stopped, it still has maintained its profound historical, cultural and scientific value to this day. " ("Statement of significance" from the World Heritage Convention in 2003.)

"You are not a real man until you have climbed the Great Wall"! The Great Wall of China, as it is called, is undoubtedly one of the most wonderful monuments ever made by mankind. This miracle of the world is well known and deeply admired and praised by people of all nations. Spanning more than 2,000 years and stretching approximately 6,700 kilometers from east to the west of China, it snakes up and down across the undulating terrain land, like a gigantic dragon.

No one can tell precisely when the construction of the Great Wall started but it is popularly believed that the construction began in the 15th century BC when China was divided into a number of rival kingdoms. Then it served as a military fortification against intrusion by tribes on the borders during the earlier Zhou Dynasty (China Travel Guide, 2007, para. 1) . According to historical records, the king of the Zhou Dynasty ordered the wall to be built around the cities to ward off the frequent harassing activities of the cavalries of the northern nomadic tribes. Dukes or Princes of various states, such as Qi, Wei, Qin, Zhao, Zhongshan and Yan, all had their own walls built to carry on wars in the competition for hegemony during that period. In order to strengthen its defense capability, the ducal states extended and built "great" structures to prevent the attacks from other states in the Spring-Autumn Periods (770—476 B. C.) . However, before the Qin Dynasty in 221 B. C. , the great wall consisted only of separate walls. The emperor, Qin Shihuang, the first emperor in Chinese history, who unified the country in 214 BC, ordered the construction of the wall (China Travel Guide, 2007, para. 1) . Since then, separate walls, constructed by different kingdoms to keep out marauding nomads, were linked up. The effort required hundreds of thousands of workers, most of which were General Meng Tian's 300,000 troops, laborers, prisoners and other captives. It took ten years to finish the wall which stretched from Lintao (a part of today's Gansu Province) in the west to Liaodong (a part of today's Jilin Province) in the east (China Travel Guide, 2007, para. 1).

There are some legends and tales about the construction of the Great wall. The most popular legend is about *Lady Meng Jiangnu*. Meng Jiangnu's husband was press-ganged to build the Great Wall on the night of their wedding. Lady Meng broke her white jade hairpin into two halves and gave her husband one half as a token of her love. Subsequently, Lady Meng had a bad dream. She dreamed her husband was yelling, "Cold! Cold!" She recalled that her husband was wearing thin clothes when he left home. She quickly made some padded clothes and left home to look for him. When she was told her husband was already dead and buried beneath the wall, she felt overcome with grief and burst into tears. Heaven heard her sad voice and moved a part of the Great Wall. She found her husband with her white jade hairpin among many other dead bodies under the collapsed Great Wall. She wrapped her husband's body in her arms and committed suicide by jumping into the sea. People built a temple at Shanhaiguan Pass near the sea in memory of this lady.

The Great Wall was continuously renovated and newly constructed in almost every dynasty after the Qin Dynasty. For example, during the Han Dynasty, Emperor Wu (Han Wu Di), sent three expeditions to fight against the Xiongnu, an ancient tribe that lived in North China, in 127 BC, 121 BC and 119 BC. To maintain the safety of the Hexi Corridor (today's Gansu Province), the emperor ordered the extension of the Great Wall westward into the Hexi Corridor and Xinjiang region (China Travel Guide, 2007, para. 2).

The vast project which was carried out during the Ming Dynasty brought about the climax of the development of the Great Wall. It is in this period (1368—1644) that the last major repairs were carried out. The Ming authorities divided the Great Wall into nine zones and placed each under the control of a Zhen (garrison headquarters) to strengthen the military control of the northern frontiers. Most of the wall was about 25 feet high and 19 feet wide at the top, with about 25,000 towers about two arrow-shots apart so that the guards could cover its entire length, from the Yellow Sea to the Gobi Desert (Tales of Old China, para. 6). The idea of the wall was to keep out the northern barbarians and, although it is still debatable whether the wall succeeded in preventing other tribes from invading China or not, the Great Wall indeed established a border within which China's civilization could develop (Tales of Old China, para. 6).

Today, the Wall has become a must-see for every visitor to China, and the north section, called Badaling is the most frequently visited section. Why is the Badaling section (built in 1505) of the Great Wall in northern Beijing among the most representative segments? First of all, the geographic position of the Badaling section is crucial throughout history. After the Yuan Dynasty was overthrown and driven into the northern wilderness, Shundi of the Yuan Dynasty launched frequent southward raids. The Tarta and Wa-la Tribes were powerful invaders later in time. Since the capital of the Ming Dynasty was based in Beijing, the regime attached great importance to the construction of the Great Wall in the Beijing area. This section in Beijing is the most magnificent, most solid and most alarmingly dangerous with the forts and watch towers densely and solidly built with brick-and-stone-covered surfaces. Therefore, the section does not only provides the best views of the ancient construction, but was also important for the security of Beijing city, and it can be also perceived from the name of this section-with Bada literally meaning stretching in all directions. Furthermore, the history of the Badaling section is rather meaningful in the eyes of the Chinese people. Credit should be given to the designer Qi Jiguang, who was a famous general transferred from the south. He also resisted the invasions of Japanese pirates who were operating in Chinese coastal waters. Moreover, the structure of this section is also considered to be significant. Being a general, as well as an eminent architectural engineer, he developed the Great Wall by covering most parts of the construction with bricks and stones. He also built spanning watch towers which were like the watch houses in common residential quarters. There were also rooms for the soldiers, their arms and grains. In these rooms, small shooting windows were open on walls facing the four different directions and protected by crenels. These rooms were forts for defense, storage and also provided observation posts. In fact, the construction project of the Great Wall continued without interruption over the 200 year rule of the Ming Dynasty. Built over time by different dynasties, it is generally believed that the wall enhanced the development of trade by creating safe, secure and unthreatened areas for people to live in. These areas became the backbone of trade between China and the western world.

Last but not the least, the beautiful scenery of this section should not be missed, since the landscape

of Badaling Great Wall changes every season, with numerous sceneries to catch one's attention. As the Badaling section is vividly described as "A sunlit and enchanting scene of spring, with the valley covered in greens. When the rain from mountain comes, the vista will look vast and hazy. The sky in autumn is high with unsoiled stratosphere, while the maple forest is dyed in golden color. White snow covers the whole scene in winter" (Oriental Travel, 2007, para. 5). It would be a pity if one were to visit the Great Wall without climbing the Badaling section!

Nevertheless, the impressive scenery of the Badaling section is only a small part of the whole Great Wall. The broad walls, with an inconceivable pose, wind upward along the mountains like two giant Chinese dragons. It is a spectacle by virtue of its imposing manner and huge construction. The Ox Horn, the Single Side, and the Arrow Trigger of the Mu Tianyu section in northern Beijing, are examples of the Great Wall's magnificence and solidity. The Huang Huacheng section, located to the northwest of Beijing, is not only a sheltered strategic pass, but also a magnificent and well-preserved section of the wall. The four famous sections of the Great Wall in Beijing are Badaling (Eight Prominent Peaks), Juyongguan, The Mutianyu Great Wall and the Simatai Great Wall. Badaling, in Yanqing County, was the first section to be developed and is the most famous section in the world. It is also the best-preserved. The Juyongguan section of the Great Wall in Changping District includes a pass as well as the wall located outside it. It looks like a complete military castle with a supreme headquarters or command post. The Mutianyu Great Wall in the Huairou District includes watchtowers designed by Qi Jiguang (1528—1587) who was an important Ming general. The architectural style of the brick watchtowers is from southern China. The Simatai Great Wall in Miyun County features many aspects, such as a strategic pass carpeted by a dense growth of foliage and strange mirages. It also has superb craftsmanship, an excellent nature and panoramic views. Most parts of the Great Wall are inaccessible to tourists because of the extreme terrain. So it is easy to imagine the incredible difficulties experienced by the ancient builders. These renovated sections are outstanding representatives of the Great Wall and the quintessence of the Ming Dynasty Great Wall. The Juyong section is one of the eight scenes of Beijing. In spring, the mountains look verdant, and peach and plum flowers flourish. The place is also an ideal summer resort in Nankou, for the temperature is 5 ~ 6 ℃ lower than that in Beijing city. Red leaves, ancient purple forts and yellow clouds can be seen from the towering structures in autumn. When the snow falls, the long wall on the mountain ridges looks like a soaring white dragon in the vast icy expanse. People view the Great Wall as a picture scroll and a long song, for it is both beautiful and rhythmic. Battered by the elements for centuries, the walls and forts in its many parts have toppled and fallen. The remains arouse peoples' recollections. Both the Fort and the Great Wall at Badaling were pronounced key cultural relics in 1961 by the State Council of China. The great Wall was listed as one of the cultural legacies of the world in 1987 by UNESCO. The program, "Love China and Renovate the Great Wall," has acquired support from the Chinese as well as from people of other countries. The renovation to repair the Badaling section began in 1984. A 2369 meter length of the Great Wall and nine watch towers have been renovated during the restoration work. Some parts are restored and some are not, making it an interesting outing for casual travelers or for those who are hoping for a more intense experience. Visitors, as well as modern explorers from around the world, climb and walk on it. Sometimes people scramble over sections of broken wall, slip on crumbing stairs, and brave precarious rocky paths on the sides of the cliffs.

The Great Wall is both a construction and a spirit! It is the symbol of the "indestructible" spirit of the Chinese people. It is one of the several world wonders in the history of mankind, for it incorporates victory, humiliation and the prosperity and the decline of the Chinese nation. The imposing but graceful bearing, the aesthetic value, and the defensive functions show the military strategies which are rarely seen in the cultural legacies of this world.

the Summer Palace

The Summer Palace is " An outstanding expression of the creative art of Chinese landscape garden design, incorporating the works of humankind and nature in a harmonious whole. "

(UNESCO, December 1998)

The largest and best-preserved imperial garden in China, the Summer Palace lies in the northwest suburban area of Beijing and covers a total area of two hundred ninety hectares. The garden includes the Longevity Hill (59 meters high) and the Kunming Lake (290 hectares), which take up three quarters of the area, and is widely known as a country palace during the Qing Dynasty.

The history of the Summer Palace dates before the Qing Dynasty, which means that being a famous classical imperial garden already for several dynasties, it has a history spanning 800 years. The Summer Palace was first constructed in the Jin Dynasty (1115—1234), and during the succeeding reign of feudal emperors, it was expanded continuously (Travel China Guide, 2007, para. 2). For instance, the Mongol Emperor Kublai Khan (Yuan Dynasty, 1279—1368), who wanted to improve Beijing's water supply, ordered the construction of canals to transport water from the Western Hills to the Summer Palace. He also enlarged the lake (now called KunMing Lake) to act as a reservoir (China Summer Palace, para. 8). By the time of the Qing Dynasty (1644—1911), it had become a luxurious royal garden providing royal families with rest and entertainment. In 1750, to celebrate his mother's birthday, Qianlong emperor ordered to rebuild the garden and named it Qingyi Yuan (Garden of Limpid Ripples) and changed the name of the hill to Longevity Hill. To make the garden more graceful, Qianlong's appointed designers reproduced the styles of various palaces and gardens from around China. KunMing Lake was extended to imitate the West Lake in HangZhou (China Summer Palace, para. 8). In 1860, the Anglo-French Allied Forces burned down the palace when they invaded Beijing and during the Boxer Rebellion (1900), the Summer Palace was attacked by the eight allied powers. Subsequently, the big temples and halls at the back of Longevity Hill were all seriously sacked. But the garden survived and was rebuilt in 1886 and 1902 respectively (Wikipedia, 2007, para. 2). In 1903, the Empress Dowager spent a considerable amount of money which originally was assigned to the Chinese navy to have the palace reconstructed and enlarged for the second time. Since 1949, the Chinese government has been funding the renovations of the most ramshackle buildings and scenic spots restoring them to their original designs (Harper, 2002, p. 166). The Summer Palace was then opened to the public as a park.

As the largest, the most well-preserved imperial royal garden in the history of China, the Summer Palace not only displays the particular styles of the Chinese royal gardens through successive dynasties, it also combines different classical building characters, skills and techniques through the successive dynasties. Moreover, inside the garden, natural scenery is ingeniously combined with man-made scenes to form a breathtaking scenario. For example, three-quarters of the area of the Summer Palace is a lake divided into three parts by long and short dykes. The slope of Longevity Hill is covered by several groups of giant buildings. The halls, pavilions, bridges and temples, Kunming Lake and Longevity Hill all blend together harmoniously in spite of their individual styles. Artfully conceived and masterly designed, the Summer Palace, featuring the garden styles of both northern and southern China, is justifiably known as the "garden of gardens" (China Summer Palace, para. 19). One will constantly find each scenic area different and uncrowded when strolling in the garden.

Although the Summer Palace is an artificial garden, the magical masterpiece looks like a natural scene with a group of buildings. There are many buildings of different types, comprising about 3,000 compartments. As far as the structure of the imperial garden is concerned, strictly speaking, the whole Summer Pal-

ace is divided into three parts: the administrative area, the imperial residential area and the scenic area (Beijing International, 2007, para. 5). With regard to the administrative area, it is right inside the East Palace Gate and northeast of Kunming Lake. For instance, the Hall of Benevolence and Longevity-the main building in the administrative area-is the place where Empress Dowager Cixi and Emperor Guangxu met officials and handled state affairs.

Further west, past the Administration Area is a complex of courtyard buildings that served as the residences of the Empress Dowager Cixi and Emperor Guangxu (Beijing International, 2007, para. 7). The residential area is made up of the Hall of Jade Billows, which is the main building in this area, the Garden of Virtue and Harmony, and the Hall of Joyful Longevity. In the Garden of Virtuous Harmony (Deheyuan), Emperors and empresses of the Qing Dynasty were entertained with Beijing Opera performances. The Garden of Virtuous Harmony is the best preserved and largest ancient theater in existence in China today. The Hall of Joyful Longevity used to be Empress Dowager Cixi's residence chamber when she stayed in the Summer Palace. The central suite used to be the sitting room, the western suite the sleeping chamber and the eastern suite the change room. Opposite the Hall of Joyful Longevity, there stands a huge rock, which is called the Blue Iris Hill. There is an interesting story about this strange-shaped rock. According to history an official, during the Ming Dynasty, found this large stone in Fangshan district near Beijing. During his effort to bring it home, he went bankrupt and had to discard it. Hence, the nickname of the stone is "home-breaking stone". Later, Emperor Qianlong had it moved to his place and named it "Blue Iris Hill". This is the largest stone decoration in ancient Chinese gardens.

As to the scenic area, it is the essence of the Summer Palace. After entering the East Palace Gate and the Hall of Benevolence and Longevity, walking along the road at the left side, within a minute's time, one will see the vastness of the Kunming Lake with an area of 220 hectares. In China, rulers think that still waters are a sign of longevity and stability of the nation (Beijing International, 2007, para. 8). The lake, which is separated by dams and causeways and connected by different bridges, is divided into three parts: the main Kunming Lake, the West Lake and the Back Lake (Beijing International, 2007, para. 8). In the southeastern part of the lake is an Island, containing the Dragon King Temple, which is connected to the eastern bank by the Seventeen Arch Bridge. The Dragon King Temple is the site for the members of the imperial family to pray for rain. The 17-arch bridge spans 150 meters from the South Lake Island, to the nearby mainland where a beautiful bronze ox is placed. There are 17 arches in the bridge because the middle arch is always 9 arches away from each side. The ancient Chinese regarded odd numbers as masculine and even numbers as feminine. The number 9 in Chinese culture is given the greatest value as the most important and is associated with the dragon and the emperor (Beijing Guide, n. d. para. 10). In addition, the number 9 is also believed to symbolize the "ultimate masculinity and is emblematic of Heaven."

Located on the northern bank of Kunming Lake is Longevity Hill dotted with many examples of garden architecture. This area is the highlight part of the Summer Palace. Magnificent buildings such as Gate of Dispelling Clouds, Hall of Dispelling Clouds, Hall of Moral Brilliance, Tower of Buddhist Incense (also called "Pavilion of Buddhist Fragrance") and Sea of Wisdom form a north-south axis in this part (Beijing International, 2007, para. 9). "Cloud-Dispelling Hall" and "Pavilion of Buddhist Fragrance" are the main constructions on the south side of Longevity Hill. Being built on a base constructed with carved marble, and surrounded by a terrace with marble railings, these graceful and magnificent buildings were the site where emperors and empresses received congratulations during their birthday ceremonies (China Summer Palace, 2007, para. 1). The octagonal, 3-storied and quadruple-eaved wood-constructed Pavilion of Buddhist Fragrance (Fo Xiang Ge) is the highest and largest grand architecture in the Summer Palace (China Summer Palace, 2007, para. 2). It is also considered to be a masterpiece of ancient Chinese architecture. The tower stands out strikingly in the midst of green trees, and it forms the very center of the garden. Within the complex you will enjoy many beautiful places and views while from the top one can look back down at the buildings, courtyards and the KunMing lake beyond.

Returning to the lake and taking the Long Corridor to the west until the end, one can find the Marble Boat, which is off the northern shore of the lake. The marble base of the boat was originally a platform for a Ming dynasty Buddhist monastery where fish and birds intended for the marketplace were released by the devout in order to gain karmic merit. The ship itself is a reproduction of a steam paddleboat (China Summer Palace, 2007, para. 2). It was built entirely of huge stone slabs, and it enables a good view of the sights around the lake and symbolizes the rock-firm nature of the Qing Dynasty.

Along the north shore of the lake is the Long Corridor, and the 273-section corridor runs for a total distance of 728 meters from The Gate for Inviting Moon through The Cloud-dispelling Gate. Of all the corridors in Chinese classical gardens, the Long Corridor is the largest. On the beams are more than 8000 colorful paintings depicting stories from Chinese classic novels, folk tales, landscapes as well as the flora and fauna. In 1990, the Guinness Book of World Records determined it to be the largest painted corridor in the world.

Situated in the northeast corner of the Summer Palace, the Garden of Harmonious Interests (Xiequyuan) is fashioned according to the design and layout of The Garden for Ease of Mind in Wuxi of Jiangsu province. It forms a quiet environment reflecting the atmosphere of the southern Chinese garden. The Garden of Harmonious Interests is also seen as the garden within the garden. It is remarkable because of its eight settings, each with a particular theme. They are, Interest of Seasons, Interest of Water, Interest of Bridge, Interest of Calligraphy, Interest of Pavilion, Interest of Painting, Interest of Corridors, and Interest of Imitation (China Summer Palace, 2007, para. 6).

The Summer Palace has two main entrances, one is the East Palace Gate and the other is the North Palace Gate. One can proceed straight ahead to Suzhou Market Street from the north gate. Suzhou Street, known as the Buy and Sell Street, was a 300-meter-long shopping street, with over 60 stores extending along the street, running along the banks of the "Back Lake". It was built according to a typical street scene in the lower Yangtze valley, where the empresses and imperial concubines took their strolls in times of leisure, and to them, walking along the street was like enjoying a day in the outside world.

Last but not least, there are also some beautiful bridges of various designs in the Summer Palace which all deserve to be visited, such as the Glazed-Tiles Pagoda, Wenchang Gallery, Pavilion for Perceiving the Spring and the Six Bridges along the West Lake.

the Temple of Heaven

Situated in the southern end of Beijing, the Temple of Heaven was first established during the 18th year reign of emperor Yongle the Ming Dynasty (1420) and reconstructed in 1503. The Temple of Heaven encompasses 273 hectares. It is the largest group of temple buildings of its kind in China.

Sacrifices to heaven have a history of about 5,000 years. The King of Zhou, claiming to be the Son of Heaven, made the first offering to Heaven 3,000 years ago. The Temple of Heaven was the place where the emperors of the Ming and Qing dynasties worshipped heaven, prayed for good harvests, and offered sacrifices to heaven. In ancient China, emperors of almost all dynasties called themselves "the Son of God." They were so respectful to God that every emperor in history believed sacrificing to heaven and earth was a very important political and spiritual activity. An emperor regarded sacrifice to heaven as his duty and tried to consolidate his rule through sacrifices to heaven. Twenty two Ming and Qing emperors held about 600 ceremonies in all to worship heaven in this temple. It is the largest architectural complex in the world for rituals

to pay homage to heaven. The brilliant and grand buildings one sees today were reconstructed by Emperor Qianlong of the Qing dynasty. In 1911, the Republic of China abolished the activities of sacrificing to heaven. Yuan Shikai (1859—1916), a warlord, made the last sacrifice to Heaven in 1914 after he became the "emperor" of China. The temple was opened to the public in 1919.

The architecture of the Temple of Heaven has two themes. One is "in the heaven." The entire building complex was designed in a way to make one feel close to heaven. In making the heaven-like structures, the designers made good use of color, geometric figures, sound and changes in height. The design embodied the philosophy of the "replacing more with less" principle by creating the flat Altar of Heaven, the delicate Imperial Vault of Heaven with single cornices and a spiral top, and the Hall of Prayer for Good Harvest with three-tiered eaves and a spiral piercing top amidst the vast span of woods along the alignment. The alignment is a wide, high causeway running through the cypress woods. There are more than 100,000 trees of varieties, of which 60,000 are evergreen pines. More than 2500 trees are ancient cypresses. One hundred trees have reached the age of 1,000 years. The Temple of Heaven has the most ancient trees in Beijing. While walking along the alignment, one can feel the solemn and quiet atmosphere. The combination of buildings and gardens seem to appear mysterious and magical. While ascending the bridge, one can look over the roaring cypress woods and feel as if enveloped by a rolling sea. The sky seems more open, deeper and wider above the woods. It creates an atmosphere in which the mysterious Heaven is close, and other living beings and creatures are far away. The idea of unity of nature and man was expressed by using natural materials in constructions for ritual ceremonies. The Temple of Heaven was built against the backdrop of a cypress forest. The Danbiqiao constitutes a single axis connecting the northern and southern groups of main buildings in the Temple of Heaven. The 360-metre road ascends gradually. One might have the feeling of coming toward Heaven while walking along this road.

Many cypress and pine trees were planted in the garden during the Ming and Qing Dynasties, creating an atmosphere of grandeur and quietness.

Another theme of the Temple of Heaven is "on the earth." The square-shaped palace for fasting, in the western part of the temple, appears like a miniature "Forbidden City."

The Temple of Heaven, built in a later stage of the feudal society, is the most representative work among the numerous buildings. It forms an architectural system with its own axial line. The design and symbolic layout embodied the thought of "complete harmony of man and nature." It is a masterpiece that seamlessly combines architecture with scenery, as well as representing a distinct and simple demonstration of the cosmic outlook in Chinese traditional culture. The limited group of constructions achieves a great artistic appeal, contrasting with the shape of the cypresses and their grave hue. The ancient Chinese believed that Heaven is round and the Earth is square. This belief was symbolized by building a circular northern part and a square southern part of the Temple. Located in the northern part of the temple is The Alter of Prayer for Grain. In The Hall of Prayer for Good Harvests, emperors sacrificed animals and burned incense sticks to pray for good harvests in springs. In the southern part houses, emperors held ceremonies for worshipping Heaven.

The Hall of Prayer for Good Harvests, the main building, is a lofty cone-shaped structure with triple eaves, and the top is crowned by a gilded-ball. The Hall of Prayer for Good Harvests was first built in 1420 on a round 5.2-meter-high white marble base comprising three tiers. Each tier is surrounded by white marble railings and balustrades. The hall which is 32 meters in height, looks as if it were a colossus that might prop up the sky from the ground. This building is not only splendid in outer appearance, but also unique in its inner frame. Without the use of steel, nails or cement, without even the use of large beams and crossbeams, this 38 meters high and 30 meters in diameter vault is solely supported by 28 massive wooden pillars plus a number of bars, lathes, joints and rafters. The 28 pillars are painted with designs of composite flowers representing the four seasons. The 12 gilded pillars in the middle ring represent the 12 months; the outer 12 pillars represent the 12 hours of a day. The 12 gilded pillars and 12 outer pillars together represent the 24 solar terms of one year; all 28 pillars represent the 28 constellations in the universe. The 8 small pillars setting above the four central pillars represent the 36 stars in space. All the beams and lintels of the building are painted with patterns of 5,000 dragons and phoenixes and colorful imperial paintings. They look splendid and elegant. On each wing of the main hall, there are subsidiary halls, where the Gods of the Sun, the Moon and the Stars as well as the Gods of Rain, Wind, Thunder and Lightning were worshipped. It was rebuilt according to its original design in 1889, after the Hall of Prayer for Good Harvests was struck by lightning and burned down. The Hall of Prayer for Good Harvests is arranged in a straight line with the Imperial Vault of Heaven and the Circular Mound Altar. The wall to the south is square while the wall to the north is semi-circular. This pattern again represents the ancient belief that heaven was round and the earth was square.

The Heaven-worshipping Terrace (Circular Mound Altar), the principal structure of the Circular Mound Altar, is known as Jitiantai where the emperors offered sacrifices to Heaven each year on the day of the Winter Solstice. As a representative of ancient stone-made structures, the number of the stones in the first ring was 9, in the second ring was double 9, on up to 81 in the ninth ring. The number nine, being the largest positive number, was regarded as the symbol of the supremacy of Heaven by the ancient Chinese. Builders applied their knowledge of mathematics by utilizing symbolic numbers in their structures. This integration reflects the thought of "a complete harmony of man and nature." When one stands in the center of the upper terrace and speaks in a low voice, one's echo will sound much louder to himself than to others, because the sound waves are sent back by the marble balustrades to focus at the center.

The round Echo Wall encircles the building. A whisper at any point close to the wall will send the sound traveling along it so the echo of that whisper can be heard clearly at the other end. This phenomenon is due to the fact that the wall is round and the eaves and all the bricks are hermetically laid. If one stands on the first stone and calls out, the sound will be echoed once; on the second stone, the sound will be heard twice; and the sound will be repeated three times if standing on the third stone. This is made possible because the sound waves have to travel from the stone to the Echo Wall from different distances. The sound waves returning at different intervals create various echoes.

The temple is both a masterwork of Chinese architecture and a precious heritage of existing ancient architecture. It was inscribed on the World Heritage List by UNESCO in 1998.

Section 4   Beijing's Hutong and Siheyuan

Hutong in Beijing-step back in time and lose yourself in Beijing's ancient alleyways...

Hutong is a small street or a lane between rows of neighbouring Siheyan (traditional-style, single-story houses with rows of rooms around the four sides of a courtyard). These alleys were built between the quadrangles for access purposes. When more and more families began sharing the quadrangles, new sets of access alleys were built. It is said that if linked end to end, Beijing Hutong would be longer than the Great Wall. As a unique form of community that exists only in China, Hutong has a history of more than 800 years. There are thousands of hutongs in Beijing City and most of them were built in the Yuan, Ming and Qing Dynasties (1271—1911).

The history of the *Hutong* can be traced back to the Yuan Dynasty (1271—1368).

"Hutong" is a Mongolian word, meaning "water well". During that time, the water well was the center around which people settled (Travel China Guide, 2007, para. 2). When the Emperor of the Yuan Dynasty constructed Dadu (Yuan's capital city) in 1267, the 9 north-south streets and 9 east-west streets intersected each other and divided the city into rectangular blocks with single-story houses grouped around courtyards. Some alleys today are very twisted and confusing, for example, among the numerous Hutongs in Beijing, Beixinqiao Hutong has the most turns. There are more than 20 in which you can easily get lost.

The single-story houses along the alleys grouped around the courtyards were situated facing south, north, west and east. They were low and grey at first sight, but there are a great number of legends, anecdotes, and much hearsay associated with them. They are an important part of the culture and the way of life for Beijing residents, as well as a symbol of Beijing. One feels as if he entered a museum when walking along the Hutongs. It is a way to experience the local culture too. If a person is really willing to learn something meaningful about the lives of the local residents, a jaunt down the intricate maze of Beijing's Hutongs is essential. Perhaps the best way for visitors to see it is taking a pedicab-tour offered by the Beijing Hutong Tourist Agency. The Hutong tour may bring you right into people's lives. It provides opportunities to interact with locals and to participate in their daily activities. Quadrangles located around these small lanes are the witnesses of the lives of the ordinary Beijing people. The life of ordinary people in these lanes contributes greatly to the charm of the ancient capital. It is in these alleys that families play, buy goods, gossip and connect with one another.

This particular example of Beijing's local culture can be seen at the gates of these compound houses. One should especially note the exquisitely carved bricks, the stone blocks supporting the pivot of a door, the various shapes of the wood; the ancient trees, and the stone carvings and the screen walls. With their unique style of building, the Hutongs tell stories of old Beijing and the lives of ordinary people. These Hutongs remain from the ancient capital of the Yuan, Ming and Qing dynasties.

Hutongs contain the rich flavour of Beijing's culture. The Hutongs are a symbol as well as the pride of Beijing. They are unique in the world.

Visitors can learn about Beijing while sight-seeing in the Shichahai Lake area which consists of numerous quadrangles, such as the former residence of Imperial Prince Gong, the former residence of Soong QingLing, and the former residence of Guo Moruo.

No one knows the exact number of lanes in Beijing. The disappearance of lanes and quadrangles every year wakes the Chinese people's awareness of the need to protect this precious culture heritage. About 37% of old Beijing is protected. For instance, alleys near the Gulou area and the Shichahai area have been well preserved.

Siheyuan (Quadrangles)

Siheyuan literally means houses with four-sided enclosed courtyards. The main buildings in the Hutong were almost all quadrangles—a building complex formed by four houses around a quadrangular courtyard (Sino Hotel Guide, n. d., para. 3).

Throughout the Chinese history, the Siheyuan composition was the basic pattern used for residences, temples, palaces, monasteries and families. Records show that even during the Shang Dynasty (1046-17th century) homes were built around courtyards, even though houses may look very different depending on the different designs and climate in various areas. According to some historical records, such residences were first built during the Han Dynasty (206 B. C. -220 A. D.), and have a long history of about 2,000 years in Beijing. They were improved during the Yuan, Ming, and Qing Dynasties, and became one of the representative types of residences in China. Most of the existing courtyards are relics of the Ming (1368—1644) and Qing (1644—1911) Dynasties. They are the reflection of old China (Travel China Guide, 2007, para. 7).

Basically, the Siheyuan consists of four houses facing four directions enclosed by walls, forming the shape of a square. As mentioned earlier, because the Hutongs are connected with each other, the Siheyuans are also connected with each other, forming a block with other blocks which have the same structure, in this way they form the whole city (About. com, 2007, para. 4). The inside structure of a Siheyuan follows certain principles based on the traditional Chinese culture. First of all, the position of a *Siheyuan* is very important. Normally, the entrance of a Siheyuan is built at a lane (*hutong*) running from east to west, and faces south, satisfying Fengshui requirements. Fengshui is the ancient Chinese practice of placement and arrangement of space to achieve harmony with the environment. According to Fengshui, the south-facing aspect guarantees plenty of sunshine, and the whole house is protected from negative forces from the north. Second, the four houses that form the Siheyuan each have their own importance and function. Of the four houses, the principal one is in the north, and is enclosed by high walls. The main gate is situated in the southeast corner, and the northern house usually has three main chambers and two flanking ones; the eastern and western houses each have three chambers; and the southern house, four chambers. Finally, generally speaking, quadrangles were roofed with grey tiles and built with grey bricks. The pillars were painted vermilion and the steps were made of marble. Bricks of the walls were finely laid. The buildings on four sides were usually one story high.

The quadrangles varied in size and design according to the social status of the residents. There are small, medium and large quadrangles. As an old Chinese way of living, Siheyuan was also constructed according to the Confucian code. It was a type of traditional Chinese courtyard house according to its clear hierarchical structure, therefore, it is not difficult to tell if a quadrangle belonged to a private individual and how wealthy or powerful its owner was. Taking big quadrangles for example, a large *Siheyuan* is customarily known as "big mansion" (*dazhaimen*). Stepping over the high wooden base of the front gate, one sees a brick screen located a few feet inside. The screen wall ensures inside privacy when the large main door to the courtyard is opened to admit visitors. A red-painted gate leads through the north wall of the outer court into the inner yard. Both the southern and the northern houses may have five or seven chambers. The principal house may have as many as nine or eleven chambers and it is usually made up of several quadrangles connected lengthways (BTA, 2007, para. 7). The main chambers were for the older generations and the other rooms were for the younger generations. The main chambers have the best position and are the warmest in the winter when the sun is low, and the coolest in summer when the sun is high and the room is shaded by the overhanging leaves. The rooms facing east or west are for the juniors and the women live in the inner courtyard. The few houses in the front courtyard were for the guests. The courtyard, which is the center of the Siheyuan, is spacious, containing trees, flowers, and gold fish jars. It serves for passage and providing good light, ventilation and cool shades. It may also contain beautiful rocks or stones and a water supply. People would like to take a rest or do the housework here (BTA, 2007, para. 3). In the past, wealthy families were not satisfied with a simple courtyard and would add one or more courtyards along the north-south axis, forming courtyard complexes. When the family grew, courtyards would also be added on both sides of the main axis.

Residents of the Siheyuan could tell the time by looking at which side of the courtyard was casting shadows on the cobblestones under their feet. They could wake in the morning and come out the door of the master house, knowing that the sun would shine on their face. They stored their food in the eastern part of the west house knowing that that location was the coolest. They also knew where to put their flower pots and where the birds would nest. Their courtyard was built according to the principles of maximizing sun exposure

to provide protection from cold north winds. It was designed according to the ancient Chinese rules for house construction. The courtyard was an outside space protected from the noise and dust of the streets. It also provided total privacy. To the residents, the atmosphere of Siheyuan was harmonious, calming and sensitive. However, a large number of Siheyuan disappear annually and are replaced with high-rise buildings. This situation is becoming critical and the Chinese people are realizing that they must protect this important architectural heritage.

The local customs and traditional culture are displayed through the decorations, fittings and paintings in Siheyuan. The decorations and the paintings also reflected the owners' wishes for happiness, well-being and good luck. People also liked to grow trees and flowers in the courtyards to make their homes pleasant and lovely.

Shichahai, a Typical Place for Hutong and Siheyuan

With a total area of 34.5 hectares, Shichahai is composed by three interlinked seas: Front Sea, Back Sea and West Sea. Shichahai was also named "Three Back Seas" as the extension of Zhongnanhai and Beihai to the north. It is the only cultural heritage preservation unit and tourism resort that combines water scenery, temples, official residences, Hutongs and folklores together in Beijing.

This area was a belt-shaped natural lake along the ancient Kaoliang river course before the Chin Dynasty (1115—1234). During the Chin Dynasty, its rulers built a magnificent palace named Taining Palace. At that time, Shichahai was just like a most beautiful landscape painting in the eyes of the royal families and aristocrats. Shichahai was first recorded as "Jishuitan" or "Haizi". It was a relatively wide riverbed along the ancient Kaoliang River, and was once part of the passing course of the Yongding River during the prehistoric period. The earliest history of Shichahai could be traced back to the Tang Dynasty. In 1153, during the Jin Dynasty, the capital was moved to Beijing. Due to the building of the Taining Palace, that section of the Kaoliang riverbed was once again greatly developed. The northern part was later recorded as Jishuitan. Due to the building of Deshengmen, the running of Deshengmennei Street and the silted mud on the south-west corner of Jishuitan, the original wide surface of the water was greatly narrowed. Jishuitan was transformed from the vast expanse of water in Yuan Dynasty into three connected pools of waters separated by the Desheng and Silver Ingot Bridges. The northern part is still called "Jishuitan," the other two parts (the middle and southern parts) are generally called "Shichahai." These three parts together are named the "Three Back Seas", while the silted land became a fertile field for planting rice. It became the ruling center of the capital city, and the Shichahai came to be an important water transport wharf— "Haizi," which was the terminal of the north-south Grand channel during the Yuan Dynasty. At that time, the northern and western banks of the North Sea were the royal families' forbidden areas. From the map of Dadu City in the Yuan Dynasty, Jishuitan and Taiye Pool are situated in the most important part of the city. This vast expanse of water was located in a very strategic position. This area demonstrated the power and grandeur of the water as well as the unusual ingenuity of the designers of the capital city during the Yuan Dynasty! Another important reason that the capital city was moved here in the Yuan Dynasty was to take advantage of this water. Appointed by Kublai Khan, the first emperor of the Yuan Dynasty, the water conservancy specialist, "Guo Shoujing built a famous water introduction project" called the Tonghui River Project. During this period, the amount of water and the width of the Jishuitan were unprecedented. In the Yuan Dynasty, Haizi was not only an important source of water in the capital city, but it also contributed to the economic life by transporting food and cloth from other regions to Beijing. The Shichahai is the "mother river" to Beijingers. Huitong Ancestral Temple is located in the Jishui Tan area, the Shichahai is like a "Water Suppressing Kwan-yin" that brings blessings to Beijing city. Throughout history, there were quite a few temples around the Shichahai; 165 of them have their own records. Hugou Temple (Dalongshan Hugou Temple) is situated at No. 85, Hugousi Street. It was first built in the Yuan Dynasty, and then repaired many times during the Ming and Qing Dynasties. The main construction inside the temple is Jingangdian which is still preserved, and is one of the cultural relic preservation objects in Beijing. Since there are a lot of temples a-round Shichahai, many streets and lanes were named after these temples in this district. Some of these temples have ceased to exist, and some of them have been turned into residential compounds, but the name-sake streets and lanes continue to suggest the religious history and the charming and quiet environment of the Shichahai Area. Generally, the people of the Yuan Dynasty called it the "Haizi." All around the "Haizi" were warehouses and shops. Business men from many places gathered here. Between 1403 and 1420, Bei-jing was rebuilt on a larger scale. The channel waters, from Jishuitan to the "front Three Seas," were reo-pened, becoming one water system once again.

After the Ming and Qing Dynasties, the blocking water channel was blocked and the east terminal of the Grand channel was moved. Then the Shichahai's economic significance gradually gave way to its cultural importance. Since the Ming Dynasty, many private villas have been built for the local magnates. Surrounded by water, these villa gardens were just like heaven on earth for scholar-officials to enjoy during their leisure time. The villa scenery area of the Shichahai gradually moved to the Front Sea and the Back Sea during the Qing Dynasty. This was a unique street in Beijing that existed for hundreds of years with several court officials' residences. In the Qing Dynasty, there were some residences of princes scattered around the Three Seas of Shichahai. The primary ones were the Residence of Prince Chun, the Residence of Tao Beile and the Residence of Prince Qing. Dingfu Street is situated between the Front Sea of Shichahai and the Hugou Temple, with a length of about 200—300 meters, and a history of 600—700 years. Its appearance was con-nected with Minister Xu Da who helped to found the Ming Dynasty.

Among the many palatial residences, the Residence of Prince Chun occupied an eminent position in Beijing at the end of the Qing Dynasty. Its owner was the younger brother of Emperor Guangxu—Zaifeng, and the son of Zaifeng was the last emperor Puyi, who was born there.

The Residence of Prince Gong was the former residence of Scholar He Shen, and was first built in the late Qianlong period. During the Xianfeng ruling period, it was given to the younger brother of Emperor Xianfeng-Prince Gong from whom it derived its name. It is said that the Residence of Prince Gong was the Daguanyuan under the pen of Cao Xueqin. At the beginning of the 1960's, the idea that the Residence of Prince Gong was just a Daguanyuan in the classical fiction Dreams of the Red Mention caused great concern among people from all circles of society. This idea created enough interest to bring many famous visitors, such as Zhou Enlai, and Guo Moruo.

Prince Chun's Mansion was a well-preserved Qing imperial garden located near the north bank. Prince Chun was the father of the last Emperor Pu Yi of the Qing Dynasty. The mansion had many famous inhabit-ants during the Qing Dynasty, such as Na Lan Ming Zhu (a famous scholar from the Emperor Kang Xi pe-riod), He Shen (the prime minister from the Emperor Qian Long period) and Prince Cheng during the Jia Qing Period. It became the Prince Chun Mansion in the 14th year of Emperor Guang Xu's reign. In 1963, Premier Zhou En Lai supervised the renovation of this imperial residence into a tranquil and elegant resi-dence for Soong Ching Ling (Madam Sun Yat-Sen). She is the late Honorary President of the People's Re-public of China. The mansion became a key site for state protected cultural relics after Soong Ching Ling passed away in 1981. After extensive renovation, it was opened to the public in 1982. The famous residence of Soong Ching Ling not only retains the style of the original garden, but also blended the features of a western villa. Therefore, it is a combined Chinese and Western style garden. Aspects of modern, contempo-rary Chinese history can be viewed through this exhibition of Soong Ching Ling's life and work.

The former residence of Guo Moruo is situated at No. 18, West St., Front Sea, which was originally a garden during Qing Dynasty. The construction was courtyard-style quadrangles with a fine and quiet environment.

Mei Lanfang's former residence is situated at No. 9, Huguosi Street, North Ping'anli. Mei Lanfang was a famous Beijing opera artist, a leader of the National Beijing Opera Theater, and the president of the Institute of Chinese Opera in 1950's. He was the symbol of China's performing arts and the pride of the Chinese people. In the courtyard, there are two persimmon trees, one apple tree, and one Chinese flowering crabapple tree, implying "safety on everything."

Wan Rong's former residence, "Keyuan" is situated at Mao'er Hutong, east side of bridge, back gate, Shichahai. Both Guo Buluo-Wan Rong and Wen Xuy were married to the last Qing emperor, Pu Yi, at the same time at the age of seventeen.

"Viewing mountains from silver Ingot Bridge" —one of the Eight Small Scenes in Beijing is an important Shichahai scene. The lake, the hill, the garden, the temple and the palace enhance each other's beauty. The site combines the natural scenery and a place of cultural interest. Additionally, some business atmospheres were left by the past prosperous market, and myths and legends and anecdotes on many historic figures and historic relics still survive. All this contributed to giving the Shichahai area a lot of cultural interest, and made it one of the representative regions with the strongest cultural atmosphere and charm in Beijing. Successively, there appeared dozens of temples. The name, Shichahai, evolved from a famous temple situated by the lakeside in the Ming Dynasty. After the founding of new China, Shichahai was again dredged. Now, this well-equipped river and lake system again ripples with blue water.

The Bell Tower was first built as a time-keeping center in 1272 A.D. (Yuan Dynasty). It was rebuilt in 1420 after it was ruined by fire. It was rebuilt again in 1745 in the Qian Long period. It was listed as an important cultural relic by the Beijing People's Conference in 1957. The government allocated special funds to repair and renovate the tower in 1996. The bronze Yongle Bell inside the Bell Tower is 7.02 meters high, with an inner diameter of 3.1 meters and the thickness of the bottom edge is 24.5 cm. The bell weighs 63 tons.

The Drum Tower, located 100 meters south of the Bell Tower, was also used as a time-giving tower during three dynasties: the Yuan, Ming and Qing dynasties. It has now become an important symbol of the history, culture of Beijing, and of the splendid sights at the center of the city. Once there were 25 drums in the Drum Tower: one master drum and 24 more drums arranged according to the annual 24 solar terms. The drums represented different periods and natural conditions as precisely derived by the ancient Chinese according to their agricultural experiences and the lunar calendar. The Drum Tower installed a Bronze Clepsydra for announcing the time. The clepsydra was handed down through the dynasties due to its fine and ingenious workmanship. It became a cultural relic from the earlier Song Dynasty. The structure contained four bronze clepsydras. The God of Cymbals was fixed in this timing device with a mechanical structure. On the quarter hour, the God of Cymbals would beat the cymbals in his hands eight times. However, the original Bronze Clepsydra was lost. Experts from the Beijing Bell and Drum Tower Maintaining Agency and the Suzhou Institute for Ancient Chronometers succeeded in imitating the Bronze Clepsydra according to relevant historical documents. The imitation one is currently kept in the Drum Tower. The Tablet Shaped Clock, another kind of ancient chronometer, was once kept in the Drum Tower. The original one is nowhere to be found now. Experts from the Beijing Bell and Drum Tower Maintaining Agency succeeded in reproducing the Tablet Shaped Clock. It is 2.2 meters high and 1.4 meters wide. All 3,600 metal balls roll, one by one, along the copper tube in the Tablet Shaped Clock until they beat on the cymbal at the bottom. Each ball rolls for 24 seconds. All 36 balls take 14.4 minutes to roll through the tube. The whole time for the 3,600 balls equaled 24 hours. The Ancient Chinese utilized this method to ensure an accurate measure of time in China.

In 1924, China ceased using the Drum Tower and Bell Tower to measure time and the drums and bells no longer sounded. On the eve of 2001, the drum in the Drum Tower sounded once again, expressing people's hopes for a prosperous new century.

All the old Beijing residents know the Water Lili Market. The sentence "Take a stroll along the river bank" embodies people's great interest in it. The market is a "precious and popular city area" and is the Daguanyuan of Beijing civilians. In the past, the tea house of the market was like today's tea ceremony house, and could be regarded as a kind of refined establishment. The Water Lily Market combines the features of Zhongshan Park, North Sea, Tianqiao and multiple temple fairs; its special wild flavor of the southern Yangtze River area offers people a unique spiritual enjoyment. With the passing of time, many changes have taken place in the Shichahai area, but many important features that embody its historical styles and cultural values still exist, and the traditional city customs basically remain. Many of the important cultural relics and historical ruins are well preserved here. Colorful sights exist in the main streets of the Shichahai area, and gray is still the prevalent color in most street lanes, Hutong' construction surfaces and roofs today.

Section 5　Museums

Beijing boosts 118 public and private museums in the downtown and the suburban areas. More than 50 museums of them scattered in the downtown area. They cover a wide range of fields related to art, architecture, history, tradition, mines, animals, science, agriculture, politics and industry. Beijing will increase the number of its museums to around 150 by 2008.

Palace Museum (the Forbidden City)

Located in downtown Beijing, the Forbidden City could be divided into the southern part and the northern part in Ming and Qing dynasties. The southern part is centered on the three grand halls straddling the Central Axis. It was here the emperor met with high-ranking officials to handle national affairs and grand ceremonies were also held. The northern part, centering on two palaces, was the area where the emperor lived. The Forbidden City includes the Taihe Hall, Zhonghe Hall, Baohe Hall, Qianqing Palace, Imperial Garden, Yanxin Hall and Chuxiu Palace. This museum reflects China's splendid ancient civilization.

Since Beijing City, built by Zhu Di, imitated Nanjing City, the Imperial Ancestral Temple was built on the east side of the Forbidden City. Both the emperor and his sole empress were enshrined in the Imperial Ancestral Temple of the Ming Dynasty. Once, the emperors of the Qing Dynasty would personally come to this temple to offer sacrifices to their ancestors. These emperors followed the etiquette of "three-genuflection and nine-bow" traditions. The imperial Ancestral Temple became the Cultural Palace for Working People after the founding of the People's Republic of China.

Ming emperor ordered that a Shejitan (Temple for Sheji) had to be installed in administrative offices at every level to show the great importance attached to agriculture. Thus, Shejitans spread over China in large number during the Ming Dynasty. Emperors of the Qing Dynasty would hold sacrificial events at the Shejitan on the west side of the Forbidden City whenever important incidences occurred. Today, the Shejitan has become Zhongshan Park.

The largest cluster of wooden buildings in the Forbidden City Museum today used to be the symbolic heart of the capital of China. Twenty four emperors of the Ming and Qing Dynasty lived there during the past 500 years. Construction of the Forbidden City took place from 1406 to 1420 during the Ming Dynasty. It covers an area of 72 hectares, with the 9000 buildings covering some 150,000 square meters. The palaces are

fully surrounded on four sides by a 10-meter high brick wall. The Forbidden City is renowned as the largest and most integrated existing ancient palace complex in China and in the world.

Although being repaired and rebuilt many times during the past 500 years, its basic form and layout remain true to its original pattern. It is divided into the Outer court and the Inner Court, and all the structures are arranged symmetrically in a hierarchical order along the central axis of the palace. The arrangement shows both imperial style and breathtaking magnificence. The emperor held grand ceremonies, exercised his supreme power and summoned his ministers in the Outer Court. The Three Grand Halls: Hall of Supreme Harmony (Taihedian), Hall of Complete Harmony (Zhonghedian) and Hall of Preserved Harmony (Baohedian), were very important. The core structures of the Inner Court are the Palace of Celestial Purity (Qianqinggong), the Hall of Celestial and Terrestrial Union (Jiaotaidian) and the Palace of Terrestrial Tranquility (Kunninggong) . The Inner Court where the emperor and his family lived is again aligned along the central axis of the palace. The six Eastern and Western Palaces, Hall of Mental Cultivation (Yangxindian), and the Imperial Garden are the other principal structures of the Inner Court.

The Meridian Gate (Wumen), the southern entrance to the Forbidden City, is surmounted by five towers. The 9-bayed main gate-tower, with a double-eave hip roof and two massive wings, forms a huge square. Such grand ceremonies as dispatching the generals into the fields of war, celebrating victories and announcing the new calendar for the following year were held here.

The Hall of Supreme Harmony (Taihedian), standing on a three-storied marble terrace, is the largest timbered structure existing in China. It was used to hold grand coronation ceremonies when a new emperor ascended the throne. Ceremonies for an emperor's birthday or wedding, an empress's conferment, celebrating the Chinese New Year, and other important occasions such as dispatching generals into fields of war were also held there.

Standing behind the Hall of Supreme Harmony, the Hall of Complete Harmony (Zhonghedian) served as a place of rest for the emperor on his way to the Hall of Supreme Harmony (Taihedian) . The emperors consulted with their religious ministers in this hall. It was here that the emperor would read prayers prior to his departure for sacrificial rites at the temple of Heaven, Altar of the Earth and Ancestral Temple. During the Qing Dynasty, a special ceremony was conducted every ten years after the revision of imperial genealogy was completed.

The Hall of Preserved Harmony (Baohedian) stands at the northern end of the terrace. Ming emperors usually changed into their ritual garments here prior to the ceremonial installation of an empress or a crown prince. Qing emperors used to hold imperial banquets to entertain princess's bridegrooms, their fathers and other relatives who served the imperial government. Banquets would be held to fete provincial governors, Mongolian princes, civil and military officials here on the eve of the New Year. The final stage of the Palace Examination during the Qing Dynasty was also held here.

Being the core structure of the Inner Court, the Palace of Celestial Purity (Qianqinggong) used to be the place where the Ming and some Qing emperors lived and handled their daily affairs. During the reign of Emperor Yongzheng of the Qing Dynasty, the building was used as an audience chamber where he held ceremonies and received envoys presenting tributes from vassal states. Also, Foreign ambassadors were received and imperial banquets were held here at Chinese festival time. After the death of each Qing emperor, his coffin would be placed here for a few days for memorial ceremonies. After the death of Emperor Yongzheng of the Qing Dynasty, the name of an emperor's successor was placed in a box behind the plaque of "Be Open and Above-Board. " The box was opened only after the emperor passed away. If the name in the box was the same as was retained by the emperor, the named person would be the designated prince and take the crown upon the death of the emperor.

The Palace of Terrestrial Tranquility (Kunninggong), the last major palace in the Inner Court, was the residential palace of the empress during the Ming and early Qing dynasties. From Emperor Shunzhi of the Qing dynasty, it was used to pay homage to the gods of Shamanism. Three grand ceremonies would be held in the first lunar month, spring and autumn, as well as daily and monthly sacrificial rites.

The Hall of Mental Cultivation (Yangxindian) stands south of the Six Western Palaces in the Inner Court. From the time of Emperor Yongzheng of the Qing Dynasty, this was where emperors resided. The rear chamber was where the emperors lived. In the Eastern Warmth Chamber, Cixi (mother of Tongzhi) and Ci'an attended state affairs sitting behind a curtain when Emperor Tongzhi and Emperor Guangxu were young. Cixi was the real monarch ruling China for 48 years in the Qing dynasty.

The Palace of Longevity and Prosperity (Chuxiugong) was home to the imperial concubines during the Ming and the Qing Dynasties. The most noted hostess who lived there was Cixi.

Standing at the northernmost tip of the central axis is the Imperial Garden measuring 130 meters long and 90 meters wide. Arranged symmetrically in hierarchical order, 20-odd architectural structures of different appearances are interspersed with rare trees and flowers, ponds and layered rocks. The architect sought to use diverse forms of buildings and supplements to play up the imposing royal manner of the neat layout. The garden also displays a dense variety of different characteristics. Though similar in layout, the two groups of the buildings vary in shape, decoration and color portraying a totally different look.

At the corners of the Forbidden City are the four corner towers consisting of nine roof beams, 18 pillars and 72 ridges. These towers were used for defensive purposes.

The Gate of Divine Might (Shenwumen) is the north gate of the Forbidden City. It has three openings and an imposing tower. Housed in its tower are drums and bells used in the mornings and evenings to mark time. This gate was used by empresses, imperial concubines and members of the royal family members. The candidates of beauties for selection as the wives of the emperors would also enter the palace through this gate.

After the Foundation of the People's Republic of China, the new government soon opened the Forbidden City to the public as a museum. It was listed among the first group of key cultural sites to be placed under state protection by the Chinese government in 1961. In 1987, it was added to the list of UNESCO World Heritages. The Palace Museum was established in the imperial palace along with other relevant collections from the Qing and Ming Dynasties. Being a comprehensive national museum, it mainly exhibits the history of the Ming and Qing Dynasties, the palaces and ancient art works. Millions of cultural relics are housed in there, and most of them are art treasures from the past dynasties of China. The Forbidden City takes pride in its precious collections of more than 900,000 cultural and art objects, and many of them are state relics. The displays in the museum are composed of Palace Historical Sites Displays and Art Works Displays, which are only a very small part of the precious collections.

A large collection of more than one million precious objects are held in the underground storeroom of the Palace Museum. They include formal and informal robes, accessories and jewelry, arms and armor, scepters and seals, and portraits and paintings. Through these sumptuous visual materials, one enters into the world of ceremony and ritual, banquets and processions, birth and deaths, all part of the lives of the emperors. There are many other precious things belonging to the Forbidden City that were taken to Taiwan by the Kumintang government before 1949. Their leaders asked to build another Forbidden City Museum in Taipei, the capital city of Taiwan. There are more than 250,000 rare culture relics in 5,000 suitcases, and 140,000 ancient books and paintings in the museum. Some other precious culture relics belonging to the Forbidden City of Beijing are held in museums in America, Japan and some European countries such as England, France and Russia. Most of them were taken from China after the Opium War (1860) till the end of

World War II (before 1949).

China Art Gallery (中国美术馆)

The China Art Gallery is a national-class art museum focusing on the display, collection and research of Chinese modern and contemporary art works. With a total coverage of 30,000-square-feet, the museum devoted 6,000-square-feet to an exhibition hall. The construction of the museum was initiated in 1958 and completed in 1962. In recent years, it has been developed and rebuilt again. Since the 1950's, the museum is not only one of China's top ten architectures, but also the largest domestic art gallery. Sometimes foreign and contemporary art works are also exhibited here. The main body of the museum is a modern building in the style of an ancient pavilion with distinct ethnic characteristics. It is decorated with yellow glazed tiles and surrounded by corridors. In the main construction of the museum, there are three floors with 13 exhibition halls with large art works hanging on the walls. The side halls on the first floor have huge glass arks for exhibitions.

Capital Museum (新首都博物馆)

The Capital Museum is located in the Fuxingmen of Changan Street in the Xicheng District of Beijing. Opened to the public in 2005, it is the largest cultural building with moderate equipment constructed in Beijing since 1949, as well as a landmark construction of the capital in the 21st century. The museum is expected to become one of the leading museums in China, with state-of-the-art technology and equipment. Its historical mission presents Beijing Culture to the public. It explains Beijing's uniqueness, continuity progress, richness, creativeness and diversity. The basic exhibition has the theme of the Ancient Capital, stories of the Capital City, Old Beijing Folk-customs Exhibition and a host of other special displays enrich and deepen the foundation and soul of the capital. Other temporary exhibitions held in the museum expand and extend the theme of the ancient capital. Breaking with the tradition of highlighting general history, the Ancient Capital exhibition takes full advantage of the three-dimensional space to present Beijing's history and culture through various perspectives and on different levels. The exhibition attempts to illustrate from political, economic, cultural and social perspectives the historical process of how Beijing has evolved.

The Stories of the Capital City-Old Beijing Folk-customs Exhibition begins with Hutong life. It highlights the etiquette and customs of the ordinary residents of Beijing. Comparing the history of the Qing Dynasty with present life makes the exhibition more analytical.

The seven exhibitions in the museum are divided into precious paintings, calligraphies, bronzes, porcelains, jades, Buddha statues and study utensils. Paintings from the Beijing area were well developed as early as the Tang period. Beijing gathered talent from various fields and became a large stage for developing the art of painting. During the Yuan, Ming and Qing dynasties, this development evidenced a remarkable cultural accumulation and ability to incorporate different ideas. The bronze culture began more than 3,000 years ago in the Beijing area. Beijing was in the northern borderland under the empire of the Central Plains. This facilitated the integration of the farming civilization and the Eurasian steppe civilization. The bronze culture in the Beijing area exhibited a strong identity with the Central Plains culture as well as the distinctive aspect of a multi-national cultural amalgamation. The jade culture of the Beijing area germinated in the Neolithic Age. Prior to the Tang period, the unearthed jades have roughly outlined the evolutionary course of the jade culture. Jades of the Liao, Kin and Yuan dynasties from the Beijing area show the distinct character of the grassland national culture. The Beijing jade culture reached new heights in its development during the Ming and Qing periods. From the Buddhist exhibition, it can be noticed that the art of the Buddhist statue was an important component of the Buddhist culture. After 2000 years of amalgamation and reform of the nationalities' cultures, Buddhist statue art gradually lost its Indian influence and took the artistic form characteristics of the Chinese culture. It has become an important part of the Chinese nation's traditional culture. Stationery and other study utensils on exhibition are both practical and artistic. They have rich cultural contents and reflect pronounced characteristics of the past. They also embody unique local styles. The Beijing study culture exhibition incorporates the cream of Chinese art and culture, and adds a charm to the culture of the ancient capital.

The seven gem exhibitions crystallize Beijing's richness and creativeness. Some of the items are the only ones in existence. They constitute a symphony of Beijing.

China National Arts and Crafts Museum (中国工艺美术馆)

The China National Arts and Crafts Museum, located near the overpass of Fuxingmen on Chang'an Street in Beijing, is the first national arts and crafts museum in China.

The museum is comprised of sections such as the halls of preface, display and treasure. A complete collection of contemporary art works is displayed. The many crafts displayed include jade articles, ivory sculptures, wood and stone sculptures, potteries, porcelains, lacquer works, knitted articles, fancyworks, cloisonné, golden and silver wares, inlaid wares, tin wares, etc. There are many national treasures which have gained national and international awards. There are also four rare Chinese national treasures of emerald: Wonder of Shanzidaiyue, Table Screen symbolizing happiness, Sightseeing with Flower Baskets and Flowers that infer auspiciousness.

Temple of Ancient Monarchs (帝王庙)

Located in Fucheng Men Street, Xicheng District, the Temple of Ancient Monarchs occupies 21,500 square meters and the construction part occupies 6,000 square meters. Its overall arrangement is solemn and vast, which is an elaborate work of classical Chinese architecture. It is one of extremely high-ranking design and imperially grand in style.

The Jing De Chong Sheng Palace of the temple was built in the Ming Dynasty (1530). It has a thick and heavy-eaved roof, golden Nanmu wood pillars and a golden-paved floor. It is regarded as the supreme imperial construction of China. This royal temple received the worship of many successful emperors like Sanhuang (the Three Emperors), Wudi (the Five Emperors) and other successful emperors from the past dynasties as well as some successful and eminent ministers or generals. The Three Emperors and the Five Emperors, the center of the sacrificial system, reflected the great status of the ancestors. Chinese consider their common ancestors are the Sanhuang and Wudi. This belief promoted a strong feeling of unification and intimacy. More and more emperors had been added in the temple later. There were 188 historical emperors, including those who had founded new dynasties, who had safeguarded the heritage in the main hall during the Qianlong period in the Qing Dynasty. It represented the Chinese nation advancing in one continuous line that would never break or separate.

There were 80 eminent historical ministers or generals in the two minor halls on both sides of the main hall (Jing De Chong Palace).

The worshipping ceremony stopped in the temple after 1911. The commemoration for President Sun Zhongshan was held in the Jing De Chong Sheng Palace soon after he died in 1925. The Peking School for Preschool Teachers was established in the temple by Tao Xingzhi and Xiong Xiling in 1931. The Peking School for Preschool Teachers became the No.3 Peking High School for Girls in 1941 and then became the No.159 High School of Beijing in 1972. The cultural relics of the temple were seriously damaged. The government of Beijing Municipality and Xicheng District worked out a plan to protect and utilize the temple. The

State Department declared it to be one of the key cultural relics of China in 1996. The government spent a huge amount of money to execute this plan from 2001. The temple formally opened to the public after three years. The local government of Xicheng District established the Association for Preservation, Utilization and Promotion of Beijing Temple of Ancient Monarchs in 2003. The association accepts donations for renovating the temple buildings, protecting the temple and systematically studying the relics of the temple.

Big Bell Temple (Temple of Awakening)（大钟寺）

Big Bell Temple was built in 1733. Yongle Bell was moved to the Temple of Awakening (Big Bell Temple) in 1743. The bell became an important musical instrument for Buddhist services at the temple. Originally, the emperors of the Qing Dynasty used the temple to pray for rain. This activity usually lasted for several days, or even dozens of days. Monks struck the Yongle Bell on the eve of a new year. Buddhists strictly follow the custom of striking 108 strokes of the bell. It is said that worries are alleviated when the peal of the bell is heard. It is a common practice for people to listen respectfully to the sound of the bell from the Big Bell Temple. The Yongle Bell was so well known that the Temple of Awakening was popularly called the Big Bell Temple. The original name of the temple was rarely known by the public.

The Yongle Bell is a huge bronze bell which weights 46 tons. It has been suspended steadily from wooden beams for hundreds of years. It convincingly attests the consummate skills and scientific design of Chinese craftsmen in ancient times. Three tiers of beams are overlapped so that the weight, carried by the main beam, is shared by ten cross sections to support the heavy bell. The load born by eight pillars should even survive an earthquake. The eight gigantic pillars, decorated with gilded dragon patterns, slant toward the inner side of the bell beams. The design, termed "side angle," plays an important role in resisting any wobble of the beams of the bell and prevents the separation of the mortise and the tenon. A tiny gap appeared between the mortise and the tenon at the northeastern corner of the bell beams because of the earthquake in Tangshan in 1976. Staff members repaired the northeastern corner of the bell beams soon. A stone pit was dug under the bell to spread the sound of the bell. The pit, 0.7 meter in depth and 4 meters in diameter, is in good shape with a bluestone base. The surface of the pit is one meter away from the rim of the bell. The peal could be heard within a circumference of 50 kilometers in the old days, when the bell was struck.

After 1911, the temple fell into disrepair and many cultural relics were lost during the years of the Republic of China. The temple was used as the No. 2 Food Factory from the 1950's to the late 1970's. Fortunately the big bell tower remained. It attracted attention from the Beijing Government in the early 1980's. The food factory was moved. The layout of the original ancient buildings along the central route was restored. The Big Bell Temple Cultural Relics Preservation Office collected several hundred ancient bells and established an ancient bell museum in 1985.

The bells in the museum are of different types and categories dating back to various dynasties in Chinese history. This important Buddhist temple attracts many visitors. People enjoy the game of throwing coins into the bell hole and praying for a life of peace and good luck from year to year.

White Pagoda Temple (Miao Ying Temple)（白塔寺）

Located in the west city of Beijing, Yong An Temple was built in 1096 in the Liao Dynasty (907—1125). It was ruined during the war (1211—1214) when Mongolia overturned the Chin Dynasty (1115—1234).

The first emperor of the Yuan Dynasty decided to rebuild the temple in order to stabilize and improve the relationship with the Tibetan Zang nationality. Tibet became a part of the Yuan Dynasty in 1253. The temple was the first temple for Tibetan Buddhism built in the capital city and it highlighted the high position of Tibetan Buddhism in China. The temple site was chosen because some Sheli (the bones of the famous Buddhist monks) were found there. The emperor ordered four arrows to be shot in four directions at the site of the white pagoda. The area that the arrows reached became the site for building the temple. The area covered about 160,000 square meters, which was a few times bigger than other temples. The temple's name was changed to Da Sheng Shou Wan An Temple after it was rebuilt in 1271. Almost all the emperors in the Yuan Dynasty went to pray in this temple. Famous artists and monks from Nepal and Korea also held activities in the temple. Some Buddhist works were also translated and printed in the temple.

The temple was struck by lightening and burned to ashes at the end of the Yuan Dynasty. Only the white pagoda remained in the ashes. Eighty-nine years later, the temple was rebuilt (1457—1468) in the Ming Dynasty (1368—1644). The new temple was much smaller, utilizing only one eighth of the area used in the Yuan period. Also, the architectural arrangement and style were changed to be like other temples of the Han nationality. Although the temple was renamed Miao Ying Temple, people were more familiar with the name White Pagoda Temple because of the white pagoda in the temple. The delicate and majestic pagoda tower is 50.9 meters in height with an upside-down-alms-bowl-shaped top. The pagoda contains three sections: the base, the body and the head. The nine-meter high base is layered with three stacks, each lying on top of the other. There is a lotus-bloom pedestal with 24 lotus petals encompassing the sides of the base. The pedestal is surrounded with five "King Kong" hoops to make the square base transition into the round pagoda body naturally. The snow white body of the pagoda, which is about 18.4 meters in diameter, is like a huge upside-down alms bowl. The bottom is drawn into a pedestal that shoulders the 13 concentric rings of the vault of heaven. These rings are topped with a plate-shaped canopy at the zenith. There are 36 strings of engraved copper tassels and bells hanging around the edge of the canopy. The gold-covered bronzed crown of the pagoda is 4.2 meters in height, and weighs four tons. The well-known pagoda was designed by a noted Nepalese architect and technologist, Arniger, a government officer of the Yuan Dynasty (1279—1368). The monastery was one of the important projects in the capital city (Dadu) in the Yuan Dynasty. It is the largest Buddhist pagoda of the Yuan Dynasty that has been discovered and preserved in China. It is also the oldest Buddhist pagoda in Beijing city.

The temple had an important influence and position in different dynasties. It was a famous place for spreading the Xian and Mi branches of Buddhism during the Liao Dynasty. People used the temple to pray for good luck and also as an international cultural exchange center during the Yuan Dynasty. It became the temple of the Chan religion during the Ming Dynasty. During the Qing Dynasty, it was an important temple for spreading Tibetan Buddhism.

The Eight Country Union Army took away the precious Buddhist art works in 1900. The temple was repaired by the Qing emperor at the end of the Qing Dynasty (1909—1911). The temple market opened every month from 1922 until 1958. In 1961, the State Council officially designated the White Pagoda Temple as one of the historical relics deserving preservation. Some of the Buddhist statues were damaged during the Cultural Revolution (1966—1969). The white pagoda was seriously damaged after the big earthquake in 1976. The local government decided to repair the pagoda in 1978. Some precious Buddhist relics, preserved in the crown since the 18th year of Qian Long of the Qing Dynasty, were found when the white pagoda was restored in 1978. The bean curd factory at the west side was moved away in 1980. The repair work started again in 1988. The rebuilding program started in 1997 and the pagoda reopened to the public in 1998. About 4,000 square meters were returned to the temple site by the local government in 2001.

Beijing Folk Museum (Dongyue Temple, East-Mount Temple) (东岳庙)

Located in Chao Yang Men (Chao Yang District) in Beijing, this temple was built for the God of the

Tai Mountain (one of the four famous mountains in China) in 1319 in the Yuan Dynasty. There were 376 rooms during its prime and it was the largest temple of the Taoist Zheng Yi School in northern China. It was built for offering sacrifices to gods or ancestors on a national scale. The ancient construction and its appurtenant relics is a precious treasure handed down from the Yuan, Ming and Qing dynasties. The temple is full of historical and cultural value.

Being a valuable cultural and historical heritage site, the temple became one of the National key Cultural Relics Protection areas and is the only national level Beijing Folk Museum. National exhibitions focusing on folk custom are held here. Today, large fairs celebrating the folk customs of Beijing have been held during the festivals, such as the Spring Festival, the Dragon Boat Festival and the Mid-autumn Festival.

Zhandaimen Archway was built in 1322 A. D. It enshrined the Taoist Gods of law enforcement, namely General Dragon (General Heng), General Tiger (General Ha) and the Ten Imperial Guards. Daiyue Hall is the shrine for the God of Mount Taishan, known as God Dongyue, who acted as the divine ruler of China in charge of 76 departments and 18 layers of hell. He is also responsible for all human beings. The Hall of Descendants was built in 1323 A. D. in the Yuan Dynasty. It was the shrine for "Father of the Descendants" and "Mother of the Descendant," who bestowed the fortune of having many healthy children. The Hall of Wealth was built in 1323 for Bi Gan, known as the Civil God of Wealth and Zhao Gongming, the Military God of Wealth. Their jobs were to make profitable commercial transactions through fair competition.

There used to be more than 100 tablets in the east and west parts of the tablet forest in the temple. Most of the tablets recorded the renovation of the temple during different periods and the contributions of various trade societies. The most famous one is the Taoist Tablet, Zhang Gong Bei, written by the celebrated calligrapher, Zhao Mengfu of the Yuan Dynasty. The two Imperial Tablets have the statements written by Emperor Kangxi and Qian Long of the Qing Dynasty. The tablets were carved in the languages of both the Man and Han nationalities. They described the full story of the renovation efforts funded by the state in 1704 and 1761. The Tablet Forest contains important historical records and materials for both the historical research of the temple and the folk beliefs in the Beijing area.

According to Taoist legend, the White Jade Horse symbolized God Wen Chang's riding horse. God Wen Chang was in charge of the world's scholarly honors and official ranks. People believed that by touching the white horse they could enjoy safe travel and business fulfillment. The horse was originally made of white porcelain. Now the White Jade Horse is made of marble. The Bronze Donkey in the temple is also a riding animal for God Wen Chang. The supernatural animal had the head of a horse, the body of a donkey, the tail of a mule and the hoof of a bull. As the legend goes, the magic animal could cure diseases. It used to be a well-known folk custom for Beijing residents to touch it for good fortune.

The Little Golden Bean is a piece of base stone inlaid with natural copper dots as big as beans. The green-and-white base stone lies in the west side of Daiyue Hall; the dots shine in the afternoon sunlight. Therefore, people called it "Little Golden Bean. " It is said that one can obtain good luck by stepping over it.

Five-pagoda Temple (Zhenjue Temple) (五塔寺)

Zhenjue Temple is also called Five-Pagoda Temple because it has five famous pagodas that were built during the Ming Dynasty. The temple was built from 1403 to 1424 and then leveled to the ground by a fire at the end of the Qing Dynasty. Only the pedestal (Vajrasana), which was built in the 9th year of the Chenghua reign of the Ming Dynasty, with the five pagodas survived. Ancient trees, planted 600 hundred years ago, provide a quiet environment. The temple is on the first list of ancient monuments to be protected by the national government.

The temple is used as an ancient stone carvings museum. Laid out in eight subject areas, the museum boasts 500 stone carvings from different dynasties. Another 500 carvings are not yet exhibited for visitors. The most remarkable ones include an inscribed Han Dynasty tomb pillar, Buddhist statues from the Northern dynasties, epitaphs of the Tang Dynasty, important artistic works of the Yuan Dynasty and an exquisite miniature mortuary shrine from the Qing Dynasty. Some unusually shaped tomb stones and inscriptions of famous calligraphic works are also included in the museum. It is, indeed, a history written on stone, for it is a forest of steles from various dynasties. A few stone carving subjects came from the famous imperial garden, *Yuan Ming Yuan* built in the Qing Dynasty. Some are stone carving of the tombs with stone figures of human beings and animals erected on both sides of the tomb passage, marking the dead person's status. The stone altar room and stone altar table were used to offer sacrifices to the dead person. A stone chair was placed in a tomb.

Stone Carvings in History, held in a hall of the museum, traces the stone carvings from the prehistoric era to modern times.

Zhi Hua Temple（Beijing Wen Buo Exchange Museum）（智化寺）

Located in the Xiao Pai Fang Hu Tong of Ya Bao Lu in Dong Cheng District of Beijing, Zhi Hua Temple used to be a Buddhist temple. It was built by Wang Zhen during the Emperor Ying Zong period of the Ming Dynasty. The wood structure from the Ming Dynasty has been well preserved. The roof is paved with black colored glazed tiles, which creates a serious and descent atmosphere. The famous Zhi Hua Temple Jing Music is called the "alive fossil" because it is one of four types of Chinese ancient music with a 500-year history. The music is played in the Zhi Hua Temple everyday.

Zhihua Men was also named the Heavenly King Hall. In the center of the hall, there were statues of the Maitreys Buddha seated on a pedestal with Skanda standing behind. The right and left sides of the hall were partitioned with wooden fences with two of the four heavenly kings on each side.

The only Zhuan Lunzang (a Wheeling Scripture to store Buddhist Works from the Ming Dynasty) in Beijing is kept in the Scriptures Hall. The well-organized structure, perfect carving craftsmanship and profound Buddhist implications are features of the Zhuan Lunzang, which is seldom seen in other Buddhist temples. The workmanship of its caisson ceiling is exquisite.

Zhihua Hall closely corresponded to the Jeweled Hall of the Great Heroes. The statues of Shakyamuni, Amitabha, Bhaisajyaguru and 18 Arhats are enshrined in the hall. Its beautiful caisson ceiling, from the first floor, was removed and exhibited in an America museum in the 1930's. There is a small adjacent building at the back of Zhihua Hall with a mural of the Ming Dynasty named Ksitigarbha Bodhisattva and Ten Kings in the Hell.

Tathagata Hall Myriad-Buddha Pavilion is the largest building in Zhihua Temple. It has statues of Brahmadeva and Vajra-warriors enshrined downstairs and three different incarnations of the Shakyamuni Buddha upstairs. The walls of the hall are decorated with 9,999 small, but elegantly carved Buddha niches. The caisson ceiling was taken away to America in the 1930's.

Chapter 4

Xi'an—an Ancient Capital City, the World's 8th Wonder

Xuefei Yang, Xiaoxia Mao and Frits Buijs

Section 1　Ancient Capital Xian'yang

After Qin people built the Qin state in the territory bestowed by King Ping of Zhou, Duck Qin De moved the capital of the Qin State from a narrow valley at Pingyang to the plain at Rongcheng (the present Fengxiang County, Shaanxi Province) in 677 B. C. Rongcheng served as the Qin state's capital for 294 years. The Qin completed a successful economic reform which caused a rapid change of its economic structure. A centralized political system was formed. This system created a solid foundation for the Qin State to become powerful. Xian'yang's construction projects were supervised by the Prime Minister, Shang Yang. Six Qin kings ruled there during the following 120 years. Xian'yang was responsible for new construction and enlarging projects. A large number of palaces were scattered around this area and it evolved into the largest city in China. Ying Zheng inherited the throne when he was only 13. He assumed power 9 years later and went to war with other states from his base at Xian'yang. When he was conquering other states and unifying China, "he had palaces replicating those of defeated state built in the Xian'yang area. There were many palaces and structures with the characteristics of other states" (by Sima Qian).

Xian'yang became the capital of China after Ying Zheng unified China and became the first emperor in Chinese history. He enlarged the scale of the city. More palaces were built, with Xian'yang Palace as the center. These palaces, pavilions, towers and offices were scattered over 15,000 square kilometers. Each one was linked by straight ways. Chen Zhi in the Tang Dynasty (618—907) described in his San Po Huang Tu, "all the palaces, buildings and towers like stars in the sky were set up along the Wei River which was known as the Milky Way according to the theory of astronomical phenomena. " There had been straight ways from Xian'yang to Inner Mongolia in the north before the unification and many ways to radiate to faraway places. The highways were 50 steps wide with pine trees planted along the edges. The convenient transportation brought about the rapid development of commerce. Xian'yang was the capital of the Qin Dynasty as well as a famous world metropolis in the third century B. C. The first emperor decreed that all weapons from the former six states be melted down and cast into 12 statues. They stood in front of the Epang palace.

Xian'yang, the capital of the Qin State and then of China, lasted 144 years and was occupied by General Xiang Yu in 206 B. C. His army set fire to the palaces and the fire lasted for 3 days. The magnificent City was burned and left in ruins. The first Emperor of the Western Han Dynasty moved his capital to Chang'an City (near present Xi'an) because it was too difficult for him to build a new capital on the ruins of Xian'yang.

The archaeological exploration and excavation of the ancient Xian'yang began in the 1950's. About 230 historical sites in its ruins have been found. Six of them were excavated, covering about 15,000 square meters. One hundred Qin tombs have been found and more than 5,000 relics have been unearthed and collected. It is still difficult to draw an outline of ancient Xian'yang since no remains of the city wall have been discovered. One could speculate that the Wei River, located near the city, moved northwards and flooded the southern wall. The excavated remains of Xian'yang were listed as National Protection Sites of Cultural Relics by the State Council of China in 1988. Located beside the remains of Xian'yang Palace, 10 km. northeast of the present Xian'yang city, the Museum of the Xian'yang Palace, covering an area of 0.7 hectares, was opened to the public in 1995.

Section 2 Ancient Capital Chang'an (present Xi'an)

About 7,000 years ago, China's earliest inhabitants lived in Shaanxi Province and began spreading their culture along the Yellow River. During the New Stone Age, the site of Chang'an was settled at the Wei He area, a branch of the Yellow River. Nearby is also a historical site called Banpo where the Yangshao Culture was discovered (Wikipedia, 2007, para. 2). Except for being an ancient historical site where civilization started, Chang'an is also known as the ancient capital of more than ten dynasties in Chinese history. During 221 and 220 B.C., The Qin Dynasty developed nearby the site where now is the modern city of Xi'an (in the past called Chang'an). During 206 B.C. and 220 A.D., the Han, who conquered the Qin, built their new capital at Chang'an, north of the present-day Xi'an (Naumann, 2007, para. 4). After the Han's wars broke the country apart, the Sui Dynasty (581—618) reunited the country. Under the Sui Emperor, Chang'an started to revive. The Tang Dynasty (618—907), who replaced the Sui Dynasty in 618, moved the capital back to Chang'an and established peace throughout China. In 907 the Tang Dynasty fell, which led to the decline of the status of Chang'an and it became a regional capital (Naumann, 2007, para. 8). During the Ming Dynasty (1368—1644), the city was renamed as Xi'an, meaning Western Peace, which is what it is called today. This section aims to explain in detail about Xi'an's history as a reminder that it represents China's earliest civilization in the Neolithic Age (or the New Stone Age) and as a historical monument of the Chinese ancient, it stood at the very center of China.

Thirteen dynasties such as Zhou, Han and Tang chose Xi'an (Chang'an) as their capital city. Being China's political, economic and cultural center from the 11th century B.C. to the 10th century A.D., and the terminus of the Silk Road, which brought constant exchanges between the East and the West, Xi'an was a cosmopolitan city equaling Rome. Western music, dancing, painting, astronomy, the calendar, plants and Buddhism were introduced into China from this city.

The cultural relics and ruins are plentiful, they are found preserved both above the ground and underground as an important part of the rich history. Xi'an, the "history museum" of Chinese civilization, has contributed abundant information and knowledge to Chinese history. All the unearthed and excavated objects, including bricks, tiles, burial pits, pottery figures and so on are greatly beneficial to the study of Chinese history. For instance, the Yangshao culture of prehistoric times can be studied by visiting the Banpo Village Remains, located in the eastern suburb of Xi'an. Ancient tool and pottery discoveries include 10,000 production tools and a variety of daily utensils, 200 cellars, six kinds of pottery, 174 adult's burial pits, 73 children's burial jars and the remains of 45 houses. From those remains, people can gain an understanding of the Banpo villagers' life in the Neolithic Age, their methods of farming, fishing, hunting and pottery making. Also, of interest is the leading role of women in this community. These villagers produced tools such as axes, chisels, sickles, stones and pottery knives as well as fine and elegant potteries.

Located at Zhanjiawan Village, about 20 kilometers (12 miles) north of Xi'an City, Shaanxi Prov-

ince, the Mausoleum of the Western Han Emperor, Liu Qi is the most well-preserved and integrated Western Imperial Mausoleum (Hanyangling). Built in 153 A. D., and covering an area of 20 square kilometers, the tomb has 40,000 burial objects, such as cavalrymen, infantrymen, utensils, chariots, weapons, painted nude pottery figurines and animals. They not only vividly show the living style and cultures during that era, but also reflect the superb and advanced engraving skills of the labors at that time. Therefore, they are considered to be great Chinese treasures. Other Han tombs such as the Maoling, the tomb of Emperor Wudi (140B. C. —87B. C.) and the tomb of a brave and skillful general under Emperor Wudi, Ho Qubing, are also of great historical significance from the Han Dynasty. It is not extravagant to say that Xi'an is the best place to study the history and culture of the Han Dynasty.

Located about 35 kilometers east of Xi'an city, at the foot of the Lishan Mountains, is Huaqing Hot Springs (Huaqingchi). Water from the hot springs is funneled into public bathhouses, which have 60 pools accommodating 400 people. The Hot Springs Palace was built in the Tang Dynasty by the Emperor Taizong. In the period of Tian Bao (724—756 A. D.), Emperor Xuanong (Li Longji) of the Tang Dynasty had more luxurious palaces built over the hot springs around the mountain. Huaqingchi used to be the Tang Dynasty emperors' favorite springs for it was famous for its beautiful scenery and the romantic love story of Emperor Xuanzong (Tang Dynasty) and his concubine Lady Yang Yuhuan, one of the four most beautiful ladies in China's history (China Travel Agent, 2007, para. 2). The water should have medical power. Even today, many people visit the hot springs for health. Although destroyed by war and time, the present buildings still remain in the Tang style.

The Big Goose Pagoda, situated in the Da Ci'en Temple near the center of Xi'an, is a well-preserved ancient building and a holy place for Buddhists. This fine pagoda was built in honor of the work of Xuan Zang, the great monk scholar, who lived and translated the Buddhist scriptures after his return from India. Originally, the pagoda was 60 meters high with five stories and is now of 64. 5 meters high with seven stories. It is said that after building the additional two stories came the saying, Saving a life exceeds building a seven-storied pagoda (Travel China Guide, 2007, para. 5). As one of the city's most distinctive and outstanding landmarks, the Big Goose Pagoda is rated as a National Key Cultural Relic Preserve and an AAAA Tourist Attraction (Travel China Guide, 2007, para. 1).

As for the reason why it is called the Big Goose Pagoda, there is a legend. There used to be two branches within Buddhism, from which one didn't regard eating meat as a taboo. One day, the monks wanted to eat meat, but they did not have it anymore. Seeing a group of geese flying by, a monk said to himself: I hope the merciful Bodhisattva will give us some meat to eat. A goose broke its wings and fell on the ground at the very moment. All the monks were surprised and they believed that Bodhisattva showed his spirit and encouraged them to be more pious. Since then the monks built the Big Goose Pagoda where the goose fell and stopped eating meat (Travel China Guide, 2007, para. 6).

Da Ci'en Temple (Mercy and Kindness) is the home of the Big Wild Goose Pagoda. It was initially built in the Sui Dynasty (589—618) and the Emperor Gaozong of the Tang Dynasty rebuilt it in 649. The temple was an architectural marvel because it has a sturdy, simple brick-tower structure, which means that it was built with layers of bricks but without any cement in between. Inside the temple, there are two small buildings: on the east side there is a bell, which is an iron cast from the Ming Dynasty, and on the west side there is a drum. Inside the great hall of Buddha, there are three incarnations of sakyamuni. Vivid and exquisite figures of Buddha are carved on the walls and doors, reflecting the profundity in the paintings of the Tang Dynasty. Simple style and high structure, the Big Goose Pagoda is a good example of ancient people's wisdom and talent.

Besides temples and springs, a number of the tombs of the Tang emperors, empresses and their satellites hold extraordinary meanings for Tang history study. The Zhaoling tomb was built for the Emperor Tai-zong (Li Shimin) . The Qianling tomb includes the joint tombs of emperor Tang Gaozong (Li Zhi) and Empress Wu Zetian. Additional examples are the Tomb of Princess Yongtai, the Tomb of Prince Zhang-huai, the Tomb of Prince Yide and so on. In these tombs, a large number of mural paintings, pottery, i-ron, stone, bronze figures, and gold wares are all impressively well preserved. There are over 120 stone statues of men and animals lined along a 500-meter access road. Fine and smooth sketches are carved on the outer stone of the coffins. They offer good examples of the features of the Tang-style carved sketches: smooth, powerful and clear. They are considered to be demonstrations of the superb artistic achievements of the Tang Dynasty. Other famous places in Xi'an, such as the Bell and Drum Towers, the Xi'an City Wall and the Forest of Stone Steles Museum also illustrate the history of the various dynasties.

In the Xi'an Forest of Stone Tablets Museum, the Steles are considered the largest stone library and a calligraphic treasure. Thousand of important steles and tombstones of historical value from the Qin Dynasty (221 B. C. —206 B. C.) to the Qing Dynasty (1644—1911) have been collected. The content of the steles express aspects of Chinese civilization through thousands of years, historical changes and people's hard-ships. Opening the scarlet door of the museum is like opening the gate into Chinese history and entering a hall of Chinese calligraphy. The Xi'an Steles collection is based on preserving the Filial Scripture from the Tang Dynasty (618—907) . Emperor Wenzong of the Tang Dynasty had the Confucionist scripture carved on stones and erected them in the Imperial College. The project was named "Kaicheng Stone Scripture." The stele consists of 114 pieces of stone with carvings on both faces. It took six years to carve 650, 252 characters on the stones. "Mensius", "the Great Learning" and "The Doctrine of the Mean" were carved during the Kangxi period of the Qing Dynasty (1644—1911) . The carving of all the Confucionist scrip-tures was completed. Fei Jiazhu, a Chang'an calligrapher from the Shunzhi Period in the Qing Dynasty, carved *Chunhua Painting and Calligraphy Models* onto 143 pieces of stone, keeping the pictures of all the emperors and important officials and related calligraphic books. Lu Dazhong, a transport minister of the Song Dynasty moved the steles to the present Xi'an Forest of Stone Tablets and built houses, pavilions and corridors to house them.

Xi'an's ancient city wall was originally built during the Tang Dynasty. It was rebuilt based on the wall in the Ming Dynasty 600 hundred years ago. The wall is the best protected and biggest city wall (13. 7 kilo-meters) in China. It was thoroughly repaired in 1985.

Section 3　Qin Mausoleum

There used to be seven states in the Warring State Period (475—221 B. C.) . The Qin State grew from a small and weak state into a large and strong one after several generations. After successively conquering the states of Han, Zhao, Wei, Yan, Chu and Qi, Ying Zheng of the Qin state (221—209) established the first feudal empire in Chinese history. It became one big imperial country—the Qin Dynasty. The simple terms "Zhongguo" and "Zhonghua" have never changed throughout Chinese history. They were adopted in many foreign languages. The foreigners use of "China" for "Zhongguo" mainly came from the sound of "Qin."

As the first emperor of the centralized feudal dynasty, Ying Zheng ordered that a magnificent mausole-um and a palace (Epang Palace) should be built for him immediately after he ascended the throne. There were over 72,000 convicts from all over China working on the two massive construction projects, and it took 38 years to finish the construction designed by Prime Minister Li Si.

Situated at the northern foot of Mount Li in Lintong County of Shaanxi Province, the mausoleum is

one of the earliest and largest imperial mausoleums of ancient China. It is also not extravagant to say that the Qin mausoleum is one of the grandest mausoleums the world had ever seen. It used to be more than 2,000 meters in circumference and was originally more than 100 meters high. However, due to erosion and destruction by humans in the ensuing centuries, it has been reduced to only half of the original height. The remaining area of the outer city is 2,129,500 square meters and the remaining inner city is 7,859,000 square meters.

The pits of Terra-Cotta Warriors and Horses are located to the east of the Mausoleum, while the chariot pits and pits of numerous buried prisoners are located to the west. A large stone material processing ground of the Qin Dynasty was in the northwest corner. Twenty eight vaults of real horses, three vaults of kneeling pottery figures and six vaults of pottery figures and horses together were discovered in 1976 and 1977. Some vaults were scattered to the west of Shangjiao village, east of the tumulus and about 350 meters outside the outer city wall. Others are located between the inner and outer city wall, south-west of the mound. The horses were either buried alive or killed. There are clay lamps, vessels, basins and iron sickles beside the heads of the horses. Why were many horses buried? The Qin State, located in the west, was suited for raising horses. Horses were the main means of transportation and a major force in war. The first emperor, Ying Zheng had stables in the garden of his palace when he was alive. Therefore, the replica stables were built underground with many horses buried after his death. The kneeling pottery figures in the vaults may represent the handlers that tended the animals. Thirty one vaults of rare animals and birds were found between the inner city walls and outer city walls in the southwest part of the Qin Mausoleum.

Farmers in Xiachen Village, southeast of the Qin Mausoleum, found some red soil in 1996. After this unusual soil was reported, archeologists researched this area from 1997 to 1999. They discovered an oblong vault with a length of 130 meters and a width of 100 meters covering an area of 13,689 square meters. It is the largest attendant vault discovered between the inner and outer city walls. The method of the vault's construction is almost identical to the vaults of the Terracotta Warriors and Horses. Eighty seven suits of blue-gray stone armor and 43 stone helmets were unearthed in the corridor. These stone suits of armor can be divided into large, medium and small types. Each suit of armor is comprised of more than 700 stone tiles sewn together with copper thread. The suits were measured at 80 centimeters long and weighed about 20 kilograms. They could not be worn in battle because they were too heavy. The suits were similar to those worn by the terra-cotta warriors. Some bronze arrowheads, terra-cotta figures and pieces of bronze chariots and horses were also unearthed. The vault of armor was built because the First Emperor wanted everything after death to be like it was when he was alive. The vault is a weapons store.

The princes and princesses of the emperor were buried in a group of attendant tombs discovered in Shangjiao village, 350 meters east of the outer city wall of the Qin Mausoleum. Seventeen tombs are in a line running from south to north, and they are two to four meters apart. Eight of the tombs have been excavated and each is in the shape of "甲" with a sloping passage into the burial chamber. Both the decorated outer vaults with their inner coffins were excavated in six of the tombs. The rich burial objects in the tombs are valuable things made of gold, silver, copper, iron, jade, shells and silk pieces.

A man-made dam and ditch was located to the south, protecting the mausoleum from floods. This mausoleum is the earliest example of a grand mausoleum of an emperor in ancient China. The mausoleum is situated at the north foot of Mount Li in Lintong County of Shaanxi Province, 35 kilometers east of Xi'an. Nestling against Mount Li on the south, it commands a view of the River Wei to the north. The tumulus is the converging point of the nine ridges of Mount Li which lie like nine undulating dragons giving protection to it. Looking down at the mausoleum from a plane, one will observe that floods that occurred throughout history, have washed gullies in the loess highland on the north bank of the river forming a pattern like a gigantic lotus flower with the mausoleum sitting at the stamen. The site of the mausoleum was described in history as "nine dragons giving protection to a jade lotus. "

The mausoleum was first robbed by General Xiang Yu's army. According to some historical records, Xiang Yu ordered his soldiers to dig into the tumulus and take what they found. It took 300, 000 people over 30 days to carry away the burial objects and other materials. Then they burned the things which could not be removed. It was recorded that the Chimei insurrectionary army at the end of the Eastern Han Dynasty (25— 220 A. D.), the ruler of the late Zhao kingdom (319—350), the Huang Chao peasant insurrectionary army and the warlords in the early days of the Republic of China (1911—1949), all dug up many tombs and seized a lot of treasure. Additionally, countless nameless grave robbers have robbed the Mausoleum since the Qin Dynasty was overturned.

Archaeological workers have excavated over 40, 000 holes around the Qin tumulus for exploratory research during the past ten years. Fortunately, after nearly 2, 000 years have passed, it appears that the underground palace has never been touched.

It has been found that the more valuable the burial objects are, the closer they were to the underground palace. This has been demonstrated by the unearthed cultural relics already found. The burial objects closest to the tumulus proved to be more valuable than those in the attendant vaults and tombs. It definitely contains something that the world finds thrilling. According to the historical documents of Sima Qian's immortal work—*Historical Records*, the outer coffin in the underground vault or palace was cast in bronze. The bronze ceiling was studded with images of the sun, the moon, and a myriad of stars decorated with pearls and gems. The floor featured mountains and rivers. The rivers, lakes and seas were filled with mercury which flowed incessantly. Other decorations were rare treasures collected from all over the country. The burial chambers were complete with palaces, towers and halls. Though experts are uncertain about the truth of the description, geophysical surveys in 1979 and 1984 determined that there is in fact an area of 12, 000 square meters of unnatural concentrations of mercury in the area under the tumulus. Fine utensils, precious stones and other rarities were everywhere. Automatic crossbows with lethal poisoned arrows were installed in the passageway to forestall any attempt by grave robbers. The mausoleum is encircled by a double wall. The inner wall extends more than 2, 500 meters and the outer one is more than twice that long. The tumulus stands over 50 meters high with a circumference extending about 2, 000 meters. The mausoleum has no precedents in previous history in terms of size or in the quantity and quality of the treasures buried in it.

The Mausoleum Cemetery Garden was poorly protected during the late 1960's and early 1970's. A reporter named Lan Anwen of the News Agency in Beijing, wrote a report about the mausoleum in 1974. He wrote, "The Qin Mausoleum is an important place under the national protection, but is not well protected. Farmers took earth from the tomb area and grew crops there. Pottery Fragments and copper artifacts have been unearthed, but thrown around. " The report attracted the higher ranking leaders' attention. A planned archaeological research and excavation program has been in progress throughout the entire tomb area since 1974. New discoveries around the Qin Mausoleum have been continuing since 1997. The more recent discoveries were vaults of stone armors, vaults of acrobats, vaults of civil officials, pits of bronze water birds and a bronze tripod. The stone armor vault is thought to be the weapons store of the First Emperor after death. As to the eleven life-sized pottery figures with distinctive characteristics scattered within an area of 9 square meters, experts believe they were to serve the First Emperor in his subterranean existence in the afterlife.

Archaeologists found another two vaults in 2000, named No. 6 and No. 7 according to the order of their discovery, southwest of the Qin tumulus. Twelve colored terra-cotta figures, wooden chariots, 20 bones of horses, bronze cranes and other relics have been unearthed in vault No. 6. Bronze birds had never

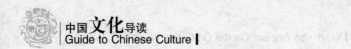

been found before in the Qin Mausoleum Cemetery Garden. The crane was considered to live a long life and to go to heaven after death in ancient China. The unearthed bronze cranes show that the First Emperor wanted to go to heaven after death. Vault No. 6 may be a replica of a pond where birds were raised. The other vault was a replica of a department in charge of prisons of the Qin government. Both the vaults are underground earth-wood tunnel structures.

More discoveries will appear following future archaeological excavations. However, it is very difficult to protect such treasures from natural destruction at present. Experts have pointed out other problems apart from limited preservation techniques. For example, the underground palace, covering an area of 180, 320 square meters, needs a permanent covering to protect the palace. That means a square shaped protective covering should have a span of at least 500 meters. However, such a large structure does not exist. Besides, most of the palace structures are below underground water. The whole palace would be inundated without large pumps to pump out the underground water as excavation occurs. It is also difficult to move the thick earth in and under the tumulus. Mercury concentrations beneath the tumulus are 280 times higher than normal levels. Exposure at these levels is very harmful to humans and difficulty to treat. Thus, major difficulties remain for excavation of the Qin Mausoleum at present.

Section 4   the World's 8ᵗʰ Wonder

The vault's location is 1, 500 meters east of Qin Shihuang's tumulus and used to be covered with brambles. The existence of the Terra-cotta Warriors and Horses was not recorded in any Chinese historical documents. They had been found before but were completely unknown when discovered in 1974. General Xiang Yu, who overthrew the Qin Dynasty, destroyed the terra-cotta figures and set fire to them. Some ancient tombs of the Western Han Dynasty (206 B. C to 24 A. D.) and the Ming Dynasty (1368—1644) were found in Vault 1 and Vault 2. Twelve tombs of modern times were also found in Vault 2. The terra-cotta figures had been disturbed when these tombs were built. A farmer remembered when he was 13 years old (around 1918), his father had found a "strange figure" when digging a well. The well initially had water but became dry afterwards. Farmers thought the "strange figure" had drunk all the water, so they removed it from the well and smashed it to pieces.

They were discovered again in 1974 when local peasants were digging wells in the neighborhood. The vaults containing the terra-cotta warriors and horses were discovered only about five meters below the ground level. Some astonished farmers surmised there must be a pottery statue of a god in the hold. Old men came to the site to burn joss sticks and pray to the god. Fang Shumin, who was responsible for irrigation work came to inspect the well. He was confident they were cultural relics. He told the farmers to stop the digging and reported the discovery to the Lintong County Government. Zhao Kangmin and two others from the Lintong Culture Club, who were responsible for archaeological affairs, were sent to investigate. They were stunned by what they saw and took some fragments back to the Culture Club. They informed the farmers about the National Policy on Archaeology and asked them to hand over their findings. Zhao and his workmates restored the three figures. They did not report the discovery to the relevant department for they were unsure of the historical period of the figures. Lin Anwen, a journalist from the Beijing-based Xinghua News Agency visited his family at that time. He saw the figures and knew they were models for Qin Shihuang's soldiers. He wrote an article entitled *Terra-cotta Warriors of the Qin Dynasty Unearthed in the Tomb Area of the First Emperor*. He sent the article to the People's Daily and it caught Vice Premier Li Xiannian's attention. Li requested immediate action to properly protect the key relic site. The terra-cotta figures then became known to the world.

It further established that the Qin mausoleum is a world-class wonder. The French President, Jaques Chirac, exclaimed in admiration, after visiting the vaults containing the vividly shaped figures arranged in mighty combat formations, "The world used to have seven wonders. The Qin-terra cotta figures must make an eighth...Now I'd say that no one who has not seen these terra-cotta figures can claim to have visited China. " The Qin Dynasty pottery figures created a big stir worldwide soon after they were unearthed in 1974.

These terra-cotta figures constitute the epitome of Qin military prowess under the First Emperor and are an indication of the overall national strength at that time. The excavated vaults in which the terra-cotta figures were found are located some 1,500 meters to the east of the Qin mausoleum. These life-size pottery figures were modeled after the Emperor's guard-of-honor. The pottery figures were situated in battle order in underground vaults supported by wooden frameworks. They are replicas of what the imperial guard should have looked like in those days of horses and vigor. When General Xiang Yu (232—202 B. C.) captured Xian'yang, the capital of Qin, his soldiers set fire to the Qin Mausoleum. This big fire caused the vaults containing the pottery figures to collapse and the figures were buried into oblivion. However, this was a blessing in disguise as the terra-cotta objects were preserved underground during the next 2,000 years, though some were damaged or broken during the fire.

The mausoleum site contains more than 400 tombs and vaults which contain articles buried with Qin Shihuang. The main vaults include the vault of the bronze carriage, the vault of horses, the vault of rare and precious birds and animals, the vault of stables and the vault of warriors and horses (World Heritages, n. d. , para. 2) . There are three vaults 1. 5 kilometers east of the Mausoleum and these vaults contain the terra-cotta warriors and horses. The No. 1 vault is the largest and is 5 meters deep, 230 meters long from east to west, and 62 meters wide from north to south, covering an area of over 14,260 square meters. A hangar-like structure has been built to cover the No. 1 vault. Besides bronze swords, curved swords, spears, crossbows, arrowheads used as weapons in actual battles, altogether 6,000 pieces of pottery warriors and horses were unearthed. The pottery warriors are 1. 8 meters high and the clay horses are 2 meters long and 1. 5 meters high. Both the soldiers and horses are in full battle formation (Travel-in-China, 2007, para. 3) . Based on their weapons, archaeologists classified them as generals, military officers, knights, soldiers, charioteers and cavalry. The vault begins with a row of five ramps, or inclined approaches, at the eastern end leading down to the three rows of terra-cotta warriors in the front. A vanguard of about 210 figures stand together facing east. Three commanders wear armor and the rest wear short battle dresses with puttees and thin-soled, low black slippers. They carry crossbows in their hands. Behind the three rows are eleven tunnel passageways leading to the part where 40 columns of troops are lined up. The outermost of the 40 columns stand on each side facing north and south respectively, while the 38 columns in the middle all look to the east. The last soldier in each column faces west. They are positioned to protect against an attack from the flanks or from behind. Such a formation does not only reflect the perfect organization of the troop in the Qin Dynasty, it is also an embodiment of the military thinking of the First Emperor, faultless military and sharp alertness of the troops.

In addition to the typical specimens of terra-cotta figures, various kinds of weapons, including spears, swords, broad swords, lances, arrowheads, halberds and hooks, which were unearthed from the vaults, are also on display in the No. 1 vault exhibition hall. Those bronze weapons have remained rust-free and sharp even after having been buried underground for 2,000 years. They were not only made from copper and tin, thirteen other kinds of rare metal were used. The surfaces of the weapons were treated with chromium so that they acquired an oxidized coating about ten microns thick. The "overcoat" of the weapon prevents corrosion. It is said it was not until 1937 that German scientists took out a patent for the same kind of chromium-based anti-rust technology. The arrowheads were indeed scary things with a lead content as high as

7. 71% , making them lethal. These arrowheads were the first poisonous ones discovered in human history. The unearthed weapons on display in vault 1 exhibition are a good indication of the melting technology of China at the early date of the Qin period. No wonder that the Qin Mausoleum is regarded as "the Eighth Wonder of the World".

About 20 meters northeast of the No. 1 vault it is the No. 2 vault. Shaped like a carpenter's square, the No. 2 vault covers 6, 000 square meters (approximately half of the vault 1 in size) and houses 1, 000 terra-cotta objects, mainly war chariots and cavalrymen. It looks like a battle formation with a combination of arms (About. com, 2007, para. 4) . Compared with Vault 1, the warriors of the No. 2 vault are of a larger variety and arranged in a more complex battle array. For example, the charioteers in that vault are armored sophisticatedly and carry spears, swords and crossbows, indicating that they could engage in long-range battles, short-range fighting and hand-to-hand combat. All the cavalrymen carry crossbows, which show that shooting on horseback was a common practice in the army at that time.

Northwest of the No. 1 vault is the No. 3 vault covering an area of 520 square meters. It is a modest building more resembling a gallery. It appears to be the command post housing the headquarters that directed the mighty underground army forces of No. 1 and No. 2 vaults. It has 69 pottery warriors with defensive weapons and a wooden chariot pulled by four terra-cotta horses. According to the structure of the gallery and the line-up of the soldiers, it seems that the No. 3 vault is the headquarters of the troops of Vault 1 and 2.

The Qin terra-cotta provides evidence of the high level of artistic ability in China 2, 000 years ago. The Qin artists, who molded the terra-cotta figures, were masters at capturing instantaneous changes of facial expression to express the inner world or even the personality of an individual. Although the terracotta warriors in the museum look much the same at first glance, after paying attention to the details, one can notice that each figure differs in the details of their complexions, expressions, ages, hair styles and beards. The lifelike figures represent individual characters as well as unity. For instance, a terra-cotta figure of a general, with a flowing beard and eyes staring straight ahead, imparts an air of fortitude, self-assurance and resourcefulness. Even the figures of horses, which are based on actual valiant hours, seem to be strong-limbed and well-fed. With heads rearing and ears pricking, they look lifelike and alert. The horses seem ready to charge forward in an instant. In a nutshell, the terra-cotta figures are fully comparable to the sculptures of the ancient Greeks.

In 1980, two rigs of bronze chariots and horses were also found in Vault No. 1 and No. 2. The horses wear gold and silver bridles and the chariots are painted in color on a white background. An oval-shaped umbrella is on top of each chariot. The No. 1 chariot seems to protect the following No. 2 chariot. The No. 2 chariot appears to be for the Emperor's spirit to go on tours of inspection. The No. 1 chariot, with horses, is 2. 25 meters long, and 106 centimeters high. The total weight is 1, 061 kilograms. It can be deduced from the broken pieces that there were four steps in the manufacturing process: molding and sculpting, carving, firing and painting. The body parts are made in molds, or by sculpting. The legs, arms, feet, and hands were made by hand and then joined to the body. The manufacture of the head was the most sophisticated technique. Two molds were used to make the face and other parts of the head, then, the two halves are joined together. The ears, nose and hair were made separately and added later. A plinth was added beneath the feet of the warrior to prevent the figures from toppling over. The roughly made models were exquisitely carved in detail according to various personal characters and military ranks. Before the figures are carried into the kilns, to be fired at temperature of 950 to 1025 ℃ , one to three small holes were made in the bodies to prevent them from deforming or exploding. Painting with colors is the last manufacturing step. The names of eighty seven different artists, who were from both the imperial pottery workshops and local workshops, have been found on the warriors' heads, chests, backs and legs. The names of the makers can be seen on the weapons unearthed from the vaults of the Terra-cotta Warriors and Horses. Those names are inscribed on the sides of the halberds and the necks of spears. Each artist had some apprentices working under him. In general, the making of the bronze chariots and horses involved different techniques such as casting, welding, riveting, mounting, embedding and carving. Knowledge of these techniques demonstrates the advanced design and construction of chariots and the metallurgical techniques of the Qin Dynasty.

Being the most significant archeological excavations of the 20th century, the extraordinary grandeur and transcendental artworks have won the reputation as "the Eighth Wonder of the World." Both, the Mausoleum of the First Qin Emperor and the Museum of Terra-Cotta Warriors and Horses, have been declared to be world cultural heritages by UNESCO (1987). The excavation or the vaults of the Terra-cotta Army with its accompany study has been continuing. These discoveries tell us about the politics, economy, military, art, culture, science and technology of the Qin Dynasty. The Qin Mausoleum, including the Terra-cotta vaults, has become a world famous research and protection base for historical cultural relics.

Section 5 Secret of Famen Temple

Famen Temple was built in the East Han Dynasty (25—220 A. D.) in Fufeng County of Shaanxi Province. It was rebuilt several times. The present construction is divided into three parts: the projection of exhibition hall, the projection of temple and the projection of municipal administration. The buildings in the spindle of the temple were the gate, Mikado Hall, finger-relics hall, scripture hall, bell pagoda and clock tower.

There was a pagoda with a 1700 years history which was built to hold the relics of Sakymuni. It was originally a four-story wooden pagoda, but it was burned in the Longqing period of the Ming Dynasty (1567—1572). It was rebuilt as a thirteen-story brick pagoda. It began to list to the west and cracked because of the earthquake in 1654. The crack became more serious due to the influence of another earthquake in the Songpan area (Sichuan Province) in 1976. The long, heavy rain later caused half of the pagoda body to collapse in the summer of 1981. The department of historical relics has found some rare historical relics, including ten images of Buddha, a bronze pagoda, 19 iron bells, a bronze bowl, some Buddhist scriptures, pears, ambers, and jade.

The Shaanxi Province Government decided to rebuild and reinforce the pagoda. The project of rehabilitation and reinforcement for the pagoda began in 1985. When the Fufeng Government began to remove the remaining half of the pagoda, to rebuild a new one, the underground palace of Famen Temple was unearthed. This was discovered on 29th September, 1986. It was another great discovery following the discovery of Emperor Qin's Warrior and Horse Figure. There are a large number of rare cultural relics of the Tang Dynasty (618—907) kept in the underground palace. They exhibit wide variety and high quality. These discoveries have contributed greatly to China's history, science and the arts, for they successfully express the advanced development of civilization in the Tang Dynasty. They influence the historical study of the Tang Dynasty. The relics are stored in the Famen exhibition hall, an area covering 1817. 1 square meters and situated in the west of the temple. They are in good condition without any damage since the underground palace avoided every impact. For instance, some "Red Guards" broke into the temple one day to dig the underground palace but they failed. No one was able to expose the secret of the underground palace for 1700 years.

It was said a Chinese man, named Wang Ayu of the Zhou Dynasty (1066 B. C.—221 B. C.), asked craftsman to build Buddha figures at the site of Famen Temple to release the suffering of the local people living in poverty. Many people came to burn incense and pray. Later, Wang was killed because the King of the

Zhou believed Wang's behavior encroached on his benefits. Sahyamuni, the founder of Buddhism in India, heard the unfortunate news and was deeply moved by Wang's behavior. He asked the king named Asoka in ancient India to divide his corpse into parts. One part was sent to Famen Temple. After his death, five of his bones were sent to China and buried under five pagodas in different Chinese temples. The pagoda in the temple was built to store the bone of the finger. Four of them have not been kept. Only one of his finger bones was buried in the underground palace. For many years, the monks of the temple and the local people protected this bone. It was discovered in an eight-covered golden box kept in the underground palace for 1113 years in the Temple. Chinese archaeologists accept it as the ninth world-famous wonder in the world.

The emperors offered all of the 121 splendid golden vessels and silver-wares as gifts to the Famen Temple, which was the imperial temple in the Tang Dynasty. Most were offered by Emperor Yizong and his mother. A Buddhist monk's staff, 1.96 meters long with 12 rings, is the longest gold and silver staff in the world. A set of tea-things is very rare and it affirms the tea culture was very popular in the Tang Dynasty. Sixteen pieces of porcelain (called Secret Chinaware or *Mi* Chinaware) were unearthed. The colors were green, dark green, blue and white. The glaze, formula and technology of the chinaware were very secret. The technology disappeared and left an eternal secret. In the past, countless skillful craftsmen have studied the secret technique of making Secret Chinaware in vain. Archaeologists discovered the answer in the underground palace.

The silk kept in the underground palace is the quintessence of the Tang Dynasty. It is also epoch-marking in the research of the Silk Road. Many kinds of silk were unearthed including brocade, yarn, and thin silk. Many of them are golden fabrics, like golden cassock and golden hassock. The most inconceivable thing is that the diameter of the silk of golden hassock is only 0.1 millimeter.

An international Buddhist ceremony related with religious assembly for the finger relices of Sakyamuni was held in Famen Temple on Sakyamunis' birthday on April 8, 1998. Many monks and nuns attended this ceremony to greet the finger of Sakyamuni from Xi'an.

About 500,000 people lined up, waiting for the arrival of Sakyamuni's finger bone. Some people from HongKong, Chinese Taiwan Russia, Japan, Singapore, Thailand, Burma, United States, and Great Britain were also invited to attend.

Part 3

Philosophy and Religion

Chapter 5

Great Thinkers in the Warring States Period

Xuefei Yang, Xiaoxia Mao and Frits Buijs

Section 1 Confucius Confucianism (551—479 B. C.)

Confucianism is a belief system deeply rooted in the Chinese soil. It did not constitute the great Chinese tradition from its very beginning. It developed step by step during the past 2,000 years. Having experienced May 4 Movement in 1919 and the " Cultural Revolution" from 1966 to 1976, Chinese intellectuals began to think critically about Confucianism. New values and thoughts have mushroomed in China with fast economic development since 1980s. Some people believe Confucianism has lost its vigor and it has no ability to adapt to the market economic development. Other intellectuals hold the point that though science and democracy are the two weak points of Confucianism, the humanism of Confucius, which lies in ethics and arts, has its own merit. Confucianism's greatest contribution to China is that it shaped the Chinese character and national soul. The doctrine emphasizes the obligations due to society and how people really behaved since morality and ethics are very important to Confucianism. The following words are well known by Chinese people. "Riches and honor acquired by the unrighteous means are to me as drifting clouds. "

"A gentleman is always calm and at ease while an inferior man is always worried and full of distress. "

"A Man of virtue has nothing to contend with others for. "

"Isn't it a pleasure to learn and then review what you've learned from time to time?"

"Isn't it a joy to meet friends from afar?"

"Isn't he a man of virtue, who doesn't feel annoyed when others do not understand him?

"Learning without thinking is labor lost; thinking without learning is perilous. "

"When traveling in company of two other people, I could find my teachers. I would learn from their good points and guard against their bad ones. "

"A man of virtue is open-minded and always at ease; a man of meanness is full of distress at all times. "

"There is no distinction of classes in education. "

Confucianism has exerted a strong influence on many aspects of the Chinese culture. It has also made great contributions to the world's civilizations. Confucianism is regarded as an ethical-political system in ancient China. It has shaped the civilization of China and exerted a profound influence upon almost one fourth of the human race for more than two thousand years. The study of human relationships in society was of great importance to Confucius. The ethical principle of Confucianism is its discovery of the ultimate in the moral character of human relationships. He upholds the self-valuing role of man in the universe, proposing that benevolence (*Ren*) and righteousness (*Yi*), or virtue and morality are the general law of everything

under heaven. Later on, Chinese Buddhism absorbed some elements in the moral philosophy of Confucianism such as its doctrine of cultivation of the mind to remodel them into Buddhist doctrines. They created a new theoretical system different from the indigenous Indian Buddhism. Their belief that the Buddha-nature is within everyone is similar to the Confucian teaching that everyone can become like the ancient sage-kings Yao and Sun.

Born in 551 B. C. , in the Chinese State of Lu, today's Shandong Province, Confucius' given name was Qiu and his middle name was Zhongni. Early accounts say that his ancestors used to be slave-owners, but during his father's generation, the noble family had fallen financially and became very poor. Confucius' father died when Confucius was three and he was brought up in poverty by his mother (Guoxue, 2000, para. 2) . Later when Confucius was young he became a low-ranking official, belonging to a class whose status lay between that of the old nobility and the common people.

As a traveling teacher of the fifth century B. C. , Confucius, also called Master Kong, and his philosophy had a deep and significant influence on the Chinese culture. The influence of his philosophy even extends until today and does not only include the Chinese people's way of thinking and behaving, but also the concept of governance. As a teacher of 3,000 students (70 of them became well-known in China) and as the first thinker and educator to advance a systematic body of ethical and moral theories in Chinese history, Confucius has laid down the foundation of Chinese education, and thus, he is regarded as the "Great and Revered Teacher" for all generations.

Taking some of his students with him, Confucius traveled from one state to another, talking with his disciples and with any ruler who might be willing to listen. Although Confucius himself never attained the position of power for which he yearned, he made all the efforts teaching his students to help them acquire the necessary skills to get into politics (Moise, 1994, p. 12).

In his fifties, he became an official in charge of criminal punishment and the maintenance of social order in the State of Lu. He held the post for only three months to participate in state administration in the State of Lu. He devoted his time collating and editing literary works. The following are some of his works:

(1) *Books of Odes*

(2) *Book of Changes*

(3) *Spring and Autumn Annals*

(4) *Book of Rites*

(5) *Book of Music*

(6) *The Analects*

He is regarded as the molder of the Chinese mind and character for he has deeply influenced the life and thought of Chinese people. His thoughts and teaching are regarded as the symbol of traditional Chinese culture.

The social chaos during the latter part of the Spring and Autumn Period caused a drastic change in the relationships between rulers and subjects. The social problem arose crying out for solution: By what principle should people's thought and actions be guided to achieve social stability?

Confucius offered the solution for the ills and evils of his time. The principle was benevolence or perfect virtue (*Ren*) . He explained it systematically, theoretically, explicitly and concisely. What is "*Ren*"? According to Confucius, it is the standards by which a "superior man" or man of virtue and high learning should live. It must involve the issue of how to conduct oneself, how to deal properly with the relationships among members of a family, between friends, and between rulers and subjects. He pointed out: " A man of perfect virtue, wishing to be established himself, seeks also to establish others; wishing to be enlarged himself, he seeks also to enlarge others. " The doctrine of loyalty and forbearance is regarded as the essence of *Ren*. *Ren* in fact is a general name for a myriad of virtues, and a standard for the value of man for Confucius.

His Five Relationships Theory, which includes ruler-minister, father-son, husband-wife, elder-and-younger, and friend-friend, is well-known in China. The responsibilities ensuing from these relationships are mutual and reciprocal. A minister owes loyalty to his ruler while a child shows filial respect to his parent. But the ruler should care for his people, and at the same time, the parent for his child too. Confucius explained his doctrine of reciprocity and neighborhood by saying that "Within the four seas all men are brothers;" "Do not do to others what you would not want others to do to you." His central doctrine is the virtue of goodness, benevolence, humanity, and human-heartedness. In short, he focuses on affection and love.

Confucius considered that good and capable people should be appointed to official posts, differing from the practice of hereditary rule. Additionally, Confucius and Confucianism emphasized the importance of benevolence, and regarded it as the highest ideal of morality. They argued that not only a ruler has an obligation to behave in a good and humane fashion, and provide decent living conditions for his subjects, but also it is profitable for the ruler himself, because the subjects will respond with loyalty and obedience in return. In other words, if the people are poor and miserable, the ruler will lose the mandate of heaven, thus, he deserves to be overthrown (Moise, 1994, p. 13). In one sense, it was an optimistic doctrine-it claimed that human beings have a natural sense of what is good.

As a famous philosopher, standing by a river, Confucius once said: "Everything flows on and on like the river, without pause, day and night". His words express the idea of change. He considered one who had perceived the meaning of change fix his attention no longer on transitory individual things but on the unchangeable, eternal law at work in all change.

The Five Constant Virtues which were stressed by Confucius were specified in the feudal ethical code. They are described in detail as the following:

(1) "Ren", the will to show benevolence to others (the root), morality

(2) "Yi", righteousness by justice (the trunk)

(3) "Li", moral ways of conduct (the branches)

(4) "Zhi", wisdom (the flower)

(5) "Xin", faithfulness (the fruit)

Confucius considers: "To be able to practice these five virtues everywhere under heaven constitutes perfect virtue". He says " If you are grave, you will not be treated with disrespect. If you are generous, you will win all. If you are sincere, people will repose trust in you. If you are earnest, you will accomplish much. If you are kind, this will enable you to employ the services of others. "

However, he failed to use the new ideas to replace the old formality and he adhered to the old formality as a means of reshaping old ideas. He advocated to govern the state with virtues but the reality has proved it was impossible. He defended the interests of the slave-owning nobles without being able to break through the shackles of the old order. Some of his idea goes against the stream of the developing history. He looked down upon women and made some disciplines—the Three Pieces of Obedience and Four Virtues. These disciplines had been the obstacle for women to play a positive role in the society for the following 2,000 years before 1949. He also said, " Only women and inferior men are hard to deal with. " The Three Cardinal Guides are: ruler guides subject; father guides son; and husband guides wife.

Confucius also organized the Three Pieces of Obedience and Four Virtues for women. According to the ethics, a woman should have obedience to her father before her marriage, to her husband after marriage, and to her son after her husband's death. He also pointed out the qualities of morality, proper speech, mod-

est manner and diligent work for a woman.

The complete system of knowledge is contained in *The Book of Great Learning*. The following are some of the verses from the book:

(1) "The way of the Great Learning lies in illustrating virtue, rejuvenating the people, and reaching perfection."

(2) "The ancients who wished to illustrate virtue throughout the world would first govern well their own state. To govern their state well, they would first regulate their families. To regulate their families, they would first cultivate their own personality. To cultivate their personality they would rectify their minds. To rectify their minds, they would first strive to be sincere in their thoughts. Wishing for sincerity in their thoughts, they would expand their knowledge. The expansion of knowledge lay in the investigation of things."

As an esteemed Chinese thinker and social philosopher, Confucius also contributed greatly to the formation and development of the science of health preservation, as one of his sayings "longevity comes from benevolence" shows. It means that one can only live a long life when he lives it in peace and harmony. Thus, according to Confucius, the level of one's cultivation and mentality is the primary factor of health, so everyone should be trained to become broad-minded. Furthermore, Confucius advised people to keep their desires within reasonable bounds because he considered human's various desires such as lust, belligerence and greed harmful to a sound heart and mind.

Confucius's followers such as Zeng Zi, Zi Si, Mencius and Xun Zi further developed important theories on health preservation. Early Confucian theory on health preservation involved nourishing the mind and the body as a whole. In other words, preserving a tranquil mind, cultivating mental faculties and avoiding sexual strain were believed to be the most important principles of Health Preservation. First of all, preserving a tranquil mind means to keep the mind at peace and in rational status, so as to keep away from wild fancy. It is believed that from the heart comes the improper thoughts and desires, which disturb the mind. Lessening the desires will ease the mind and maintain the generous and peaceful mind, while keeping physically and mentally healthy. Second, cultivating mental faculties mean maintaining a Gentle and Pleasant Temperament and Observing Rules of Nature and Following Customs. To be specific, people who maintain a high spirit and have an optimistic attitude towards life will get less disease and live longer, because when the mind is at ease, the energy in his / her body will flow smoothly, hence the blood circulation will be smooth as well so as to prevent people from getting ill easily. Facing facts and actively adapting to environment are also important elements to keep people healthy. For example, "take his food as delicious, not be particular about his clothing, and happily follow the local customs"; "live comfortably in the natural environments, observe the rules of the eight wind, conform to common customs in diet and daily life, be free from such emotions as anger, and behave in accordance with reality," (Herb China, 2007, para. 6) and the likes, are all considered as a healthy attitude towards life. Third, avoiding sexual strain is also advocated by Confucians, because the kidney stores the reproductive essence whereas overindulgence in sexual intercourse is most likely to damage the kidney-essence. Thus, the key to keep sexual activities in check lies in keeping the mind clear from greed and wild fancy (Herb China, 2007, para. 13).

Besides health preservation, Confucius also introduced physical exercise as a system making it an important part of promoting vitality of life. After he introduced a private school system, many schools began to offer physical education and various sports courses and requirements were made for students of different ages. Particularly, the Book of Rites which combined Confucianism and Chinese Medicine, talked about physicians and it contains the fundamental ideas of early Confucians on medical care. For example, it discusses particular diseases occurring at particular times of the year and therefore, different diets should apply. One should eat more sour food in spring, more bitter food in summer, more sweet food in autumn and more salty food in winter. It also reminded that foods should not be eaten if they had become rotten, if they were not well cooked, if their color had changed, or if the wine and dried meats bought from the market were not clean. He also suggested that foods should only be eaten at mealtime, and people should not over-eat (China Official Gateway, para. 5). To summarize, early Confucians made an important contribution to the development of Taoism in the pre-Qing period.

Confucian highlights a moral point. The moral imperative to effective action is one of the basic elements in his tradition. His following idea of a good family is widely accepted by Chinese till now: "educating the young, caring for the aged, and maintaining moral standards". His theories not only relate with the governing of a state, but with self-cultivation, which have influenced one after another generation of Chinese. From some of his ideas, it's easy to understand why his philosophy has influenced Chinese and some Asian countries for over 2000 years. His viewpoint "Do not do unto others what you would not like others to do unto you. " is also shared by western culture. He advises teachers to "teach students in accordance with their aptitude". The principle is also similar to the western moderate educational principles. He would like a leader to "know one's subordinates well enough to assign them jobs commensurate with their abilities".

However, some western intellectuals have negative attitude to Confucianism. For instance, a Russian educator named Borevskaya compares Confucianism and Russian Orthodox tradition. She points out "Confucian orthodox basically unfriendly to the concepts of individual, subject, personality and individuality that underlay liberal progressivism. " It seems to her Western education concerns with the liberation of individuals and the development of personality, while Chinese education is sympathetic to social and collectivist concerns. 'This education easily leads to the cementing of collectivism and totalitarianism. ' Some Chinese educators argue Borevskaya has such an opinion because she is deeply affected by Western colonialism and she has one-sided opinion or even prejudice against Chinese culture and Confuscism. In fact, people need to have basic knowledge about intercultural education for they are living in a multi-cultural world now.

Chinese traditional education theory (which is influenced by Confucian's philosophy) is not simply a conventional and harmful one. Of course, the theory is far from perfect and needs to absorb from other cultures. Meanwhile people need to be more open to different cultures for each culture has its own merits. They need to be open and international to "let a hundred flowers blossom and a hundred schools of thought content. " Chinese have to confess the present and the past can't be mentioned in the same breath at the same time for there is no changeless culture or philosophy. Therefore they should draw on collective wisdom and absorb all useful ideas from different cultures. Perhaps they may even study Russian Orthodox tradition of Christianity. Western culture may concern more elements about liberation of individuals and the development of personality, Chinese will learn to enrich their philosophy and culture. In the past 2000 years, China has been a united nation partly owning to Confucian's philosophy's influence. In order to keep the country to be stable, to have sustainable development and to play an active role in international affairs, Chinese shouldn't go from one extreme to another by valuing it without development or denying the value of Confucian's philosophy. Confucianism is closely bound to a specific society of his time. Being a civilized big county in ancient time, China slowed his pace from two hundred years ago till 1970s. Why has China been backward in the moderate society? One important factor is China didn't open its door to the outside world during the period and Chinese ignored the need to absorb new things from other nations constantly. Chinese past proud and conservative attitude made their ancient culture to be a historical burden. Therefore, it's not wise a policy to defend the old tradition without reform. Neither Chinese feudal system nor its central ideological support—Confucianism, could remain unchanged. Chinese should never reinforce the tendency to stick to the old traditions only. Of course, some parts of Confucianism can be adopted to consolidate Chinese present

society.

Two years after the death of Confucius, his former house in Qufu was consecrated as a temple by the Prince of Lu. The Confucius Temple in today's Shandong Province is one of China's three ancient building complexes. Built in 478 BC, it includes 9 courtyards, 460 halls, pavilions and rooms and it is one of the largest architectural complexes left from ancient China—comparable to Beijing's Forbidden City. In 1998, it was granted as one of the World Cultural Heritages (1998) and it also became the major cultural attraction of Qufu, his hometown.

Section 2　Mencius（372—289B. C. ）

Only two Chinese philosophers have the honor of being known to the Western world by a Latinized name: the first is Confucius and the second Mencius. Mencius, whose given name was Ke and styled Zi Yu, was from the State of Zou (part of Shandong Province) in Warring States. He was a great philosopher in the Warring States Period regarded as the second sage in the Confucian school. He inherited and developed Confucianism and carried the philosophy to a new height. His philosophy, together with Confucius', is known as the "philosophies of Kong Zi and Meng Zi" in the history of Chinese culture.

Mencius withdrew from the public service to teach disciples and write books setting up his own theory after he traveled around the States of Qi, Wei, Song and other places to disseminate his political propositions and to give play to his political ambition.

Mencius not only carries on Confucian thought of benevolence but also puts forward the thought of benevolence governance. His ideas are more articulate. He opposes ruler's unduly exploitation of the people and advocates for relieving punishment and taxes. He says "the people rank the highest, the land and grain comes next, and the monarch counts the least. " He advocates that the three conditions are integrated as a whole, indispensable with each other. However the human condition was the most important. He stresses the way of man over it of Heaven. He is aware of the values of man himself, signifying the awakening of man's consciousness of being the master of his own. He persuades the ruler to ensure people's safety and security, for it is the key to the safety and danger of the state and monarch. The positive social significance of this thought is opposing tyrant and despotic rule. He advises the rulers to support the aged and educate the young. According to his viewpoint, human beings are kind by nature and he regards this inborn kindness as a natural disposition. It can be acquired without learning or thinking. His attitude to education is "every person can be a sage. " He pointed out that "Slight is the difference between man and the beast. People have morals through continuous self-retrospection the through efforts to seek for their own natural kindness. The common man loses this difference, while the gentleman retains it. " Mencius regards it is his duty to ensure the whole world safety and happiness. He claims he is happy only when the whole world is happy, he would feel worried when the whole world is worried. He identifies his own happiness and worries with the peoples' happiness and worries. His strong sense of social responsibility has influenced the Chinese people and it has become a cultural tradition of the whole nation. Mencius's following statement had a great influence on intellectuals in ancient China: " Be good to and serve all when you are well off. Be decent and fulfill your obligations to society when you are poor. " He means a decent person should not spare his efforts in cultivating his own morality and should undertake his duty and obligations to family and society even if he cannot govern the state and bring peace to it to realize his ideal.

Following Confucians, Mencius was one of the first two scholars to define the scope of health preservation. He proposed health preservation means by attending to one's parents and taking care of their health in the remaining years of their life. Furthermore, he extended his theory to involve the whole society since everyone has parents and will be likely to become parents someday. Moreover, along with other Confucians, Mencius held that greediness would harm one's health and would even lead to one's total destruction. He pointed out that "mind nourishing means having fewer desires". In addition, Mencius highlighted good education in human society and considered it important in human civilization. As Mencius said, "…being well-fed, and warmly-clothed, but dwelling idle without education, they were close to the birds and beasts" (Behuniak Jr., 2002, p. 71). Thus, as a human, one has to make efforts all his life and above all, being a human "requires faith in an inexhaustible human potential (Behuniak Jr., 2002, p. 73).

Section 3 Mo-tse (468—376 B. C.)

Mo-tse's given name was Di. He was born in the State of Lu (part of Shandong Province). He studied Confucianism in his early years and founded Mohism. He became an opposition faction of the Confucianism finally. Mohism is a party of compact organization and strict discipline with moral principles and sacrifice spirits. Being a great philosopher in the early Warring States Period, he was a founder of the Mohist School. Mohism fell into oblivion after the Han Dynasty (206 B. C. —220A. D.).

Mo-tse's core thought is "discriminate love". He opposes the Confucian's "benevolence" because he thinks love should not be granted indiscriminately. He opposes war of any kind and puts forward the thought of non-aggressiveness. He doesn't believe people having fate. Instead, they should live on their own labor and have efforts to make a change.

He advocates the ideas of obedience to the ruling class which is the opposite of the Confucianism. The above idea reflects his tendency to value autocratic centralization of power and a desire to break down the hereditary power so as to attach importance to qualifications of the lower class.

He puts forward the proposals to eliminate rites, funerals and music as an opposition of them of Confucianism. The purpose is to save expenditure and lighten the people's burden. Most part of his opinions typically reflects the viewpoints of the lower class people.

Section 4 Xun Zi (about 313—238 B. C.)

Xun Zi, given name Kuang, styled Qing, was born in the State of Zhao. He was a great philosopher as well as one of the Confucian representatives in the Warring States Period. He traveled and studied in the capital of the State of Qi. He was appointed three times as an official in charge of the wine for sacrifice at the Studying Palace of Ji Xia. He was appointed as the head of Lan Ling County later. He resided there after retiring and lived on writing books and teaching disciples.

Xun Zi first establishes the philosophical doctrine proposing that "Man is independent of Heaven's will". He compares man with water, fire, plants, grass and animals and finds man has vapor, life, senses and morality. His conclusion is "Man is the primary and key aspect of the two opposing parts. He rejects the idea that a state's order, prosperity or decline is determined by the will of Heaven. Furthermore, he also rejects one's good or bad luck, poverty or fortune is determined by the will of Heaven. He believes Heaven has no will but takes its own course in its movement and change. According to his belief, what man should do is to know, control and make use of it. He intends to mention it is better to have a deep understanding of the nature and properties of everything under heaven to control it than conjure up the control of all.

The Book of Xun zi was the crystallization of his political thought. He chiefly inherits Confucian thought of rites and etiquette and takes them as a sort of basic social system to regulate social relations. The

first article in *The Book of Xun Zi is Encouraging Learning*. He values moralization and study after a person is born because the nature of man is evil and should be normalized and restricted by "rites and morality".

Xun Zi's epistemology is a theory of reflection of materialism for he puts forward a proposition of "achieving calmness by modesty and concentration". It has some rationality. "Modesty" to him means freedom from prejudice in the process of getting insight into the objective world. To him "Concentration" is to focus on what you are doing with full attention. "Calmness" refers to observe calmly and maintain an objective attitude. He thinks the change of the natural world is under the control of objective laws which is unprecedented and has no relations with man. Therefore he rejects the thought of correspondence between man and universe. He affirms the positive power of man before and puts forward "controlling fatality and making use of nature" as for the relation between man and nature. The opinion sets man's will above the natural world scientifically for the first time in his time.

Section 5   Han Fei Zi （280—233B. C.）

Han Fei Zi was born in the noble family of the State of Han in Warring States Period. He was a student of Xun Zi. He lost the emperor's favor and trust only because he advised the king of the Han State to change the law. He worked hard on writing books. His articles such as *Lonely Anger*, *On Difficulties and Five Bookworms* are collected in the book of *Han Fei Zi*. He was sent to the State of Qin on a diplomatic mission invited by the king of Qin. However, he was framed by Li Si and Yao Jia. He committed suicide after he was thrown in jail.

As a philosopher of the late period of the Warring States Period, he epitomized the thoughts of Legalist School of the period. Since he believes in the thought of historical development, he points out " people contest in morality; in mediaeval times, in resourcefulness in ancient times and nowadays, in effort". In order to make the country rich and the army strong, he proposes political reform, which manifests the spirits of defiance and innovation. He also advocates the idea of ruling by law. He builds a new system of the Legalist thought emphasizing the authority and justice of the law. He insists on punishing the high-rank officials if they break the law. According to the law, awarding should be granted to the common folk. His Legalist thought provides the theoretical foundation for building a new autocratic feudalistic centralization of state power. He exaggerates the opposition between people for he considers the relationship between people as a relationship of pure interests. The opinion is based on his belief of the evil nature of man. He publicizes violent repression and denies the moralization's role.

Han Fei Zi was contemptuous of the idea that the ruler should consider the opinions of his subjects. He claimed that a legalist government would benefit the people, but he was sure that the people were too stupid to recognize good government even when living under it. His contemporary Li Si went further, and argued that the ruler could ignore not only the opinions but also the welfare of his subjects. The purpose of government was to serve the interests of the ruler, not the common people. "if a ruler will not... utilize the empire for his own pleasure, but on the contrary purposelessly tortures his body and wastes his mind in devotion to the people-then he becomes the slave of the common people instead of the domesticator of the empire. And what honor is there in that?"

The legalists were future-oriented; they had no respect for tradition, and felt they could devise techniques of government superior to anything that had been known in the past.

Section 6　Sun Zi（Sun Wu）

Sun Wu, styled Changqing, was born in the State of Qi (part of Shandong Province) . He went to the State of Wu because of domestic disorder and was appointed as a general. He defeated the army of State Chu in the war between the State of Wu and Chu and occupied the capital of the State of Chu. Being a well-known strategist, he wrote 13 articles on the art of war.

The book *Sun Zi's Art of War* became the classics on the ancient Chinese military science and it influenced deeply the later development of Sino-foreign military science. The book is full of dialectic thought. The theory that the army is the first and foremost thing of a state is established by Sun Wu. Military affairs should be tackled as to achieve political purposes. He thinks the ruler should deal with military affairs from the view of politics. He points out five virtual important factors in the military affairs: the strategy to win over masses to support the war; the change of the nature; the topographic condition; quality of the military commander; the rules and regulation. He especially stresses a commander must know how to deal with military affairs from the point of view of politics and make decisions and strategies accordingly. In the book *Sun Zi's Art of War* he not only stresses a mutual relation between the five factors, but also puts forward a systematic theory that unites geographical, climatic and human factors into one. For instance, he considers one who knows his own strength and that of the enemy is invincible in the battle; there will be a complete victory when he has knowledge of the climate and geography at the same time. He is the first one to propose the use of favorable climatic, geographical and human conditions. By favorable climatic conditions he means the hot and cold weather and the four seasons. By favorable geographical conditions he means the coverage of area, the importance of position, the span of distance and favorable or adverse circumstances. By favorable human conditions he means people's support and the knowledge of both one's own strengths and those of his enemy. He believes only making good use of the three conditions could one possibly win a war.

He compares the army with water saying "… just as water has no certain form, an army has no certain battle formation. The spirit of military operation lies in accordance with the enemy's changes". According to him commanding an army is full of crafts. Some special military laws are also revealed in the book.

People have come to realize it is imperative to learn and use the knowledge of Sun Wu's changes if one wants to achieve success in his career through centuries of practice and evolution. More and more scholars and military strategists of different nations have come to this conclusion. They study the ancient Chinese learning of opposites from *Sun Zi's Art of War*. The book is the classic of the "learning of opposite" to be applied to military science and human activities. It includes expositions of subjective and objective conditions, the union of analysis and synthesis, the relationship between economy and politics, the need to develop one's strong points and attack the enemy's weak ones and to carefully examine oneself as well as his enemy. Therefore, people take it as an encyclopedia of the learning of opposites with its undying theoretical vitality.

Chapter 6

Lao Zi, Zhuang Zi and Taoism

Xuefei Yang, Xiaoxia Mao and Frits Buijs

China is a country with a diversity of religions. The four main religions are Taoism, Buddhism, Islam and Christianity. The last three were introduced to Chinese from overseas, while Taoism is the only native-born religion in China, which is characterized with rich Chinese colors. Taoism coexisted alongside the Confucian tradition and they both served as the ethical basis of the institutions and arrangements in China.

Section 1   Lao Zi and Zhuang Zi

Lao Zi

> The Dao that can be told
> Is not the eternal Dao.
> The name that can be named
> Is not the eternal Name.
>
> —Lao Zi (translated by Stephen Mitchell)

The second greatest influence on Chinese thought was no doubt Taoism, which opposed but also complemented and enlivened Confucianism (China Holiday, n. d., para. 1). As known to most Chinese, Lao Zi was a philosopher of ancient China and an important figure in Daoism. According to Chinese history, Lao Zi was born in the State of Chu in 604 B. C., with a family name of Li and given name of Er. Legend says that he was employed as a keeper of government records in Zhou. Unfortunately, he did not keep his own record very well, and virtually nothing is known of him, except that he was called the "Old Master" (N. A., 2004, para. 2). Lao Zi was an older contemporary of Confucius and it was said that Confucius intentionally or accidentally met him in Zhou where Confucius browsed the library scrolls and discussed about rituals and propriety with him, and it seemed that Confucius learned more from Lao Zi than from the library achieves (synaptic, 1995). Hence, the tradition claimed that Lao Zi was a senior contemporary of Confucius. Feeling that the search for fame and honor would only lead to perversion of human nature's simplicity, Lao Zi resigned from office and returned to his hometown. At the end of his life, he decided to go to Tibet for a peaceful and quiet life. He climbed on top of a water buffalo and got as far as the western gate of the city (N. A., 2004, para. 5). According to legend, when he passed the western frontiers he stopped for a cup of tea with the gatekeeper. The gatekeeper was very surprised at Lao Zi's wisdom that he begged him for a book of Lao Zi's teaching. In order to be permitted to leave, Lao Zi wrote the famous book Dao De Jing of 5,000 words. He was never seen again after he went westward on a water buffalo.

Lao Zi searches for a way to avoid the constant feudal warfare and other social conflicts during his time. Lao Zi expounds the interdependent relationship between the two opposites of things. He enumerates a number of things in the category of opposites such as difficulty, high and low, and something and nothing. According to his theory, if one of the two opposites does not exist, the other one will also disappear. The interaction and the interdependence of the two opposites cause change and development of things.

With keen eyes and great wisdom, Lao Zi observed the laws of heaven and earth, the changes of nature, of failure and success, of existence and extinction, and of bad and good fortunes in human society. Lao Zi saw many changes of things in society such as " no ruler of a state can be in office forever and no positions for rulers and subjects without changes". He also mentions " highland changes to be valley and valley changes to be hill" after observing the natural phenomena. He notices that nothing in the world is unchangeable. He says: "A hurricane never lasts a whole morning, nor a rainstorm all day. Who is it that makes the wind and rain? It is Heaven and Earth. If Heaven and Earth cannot blow and pour for long, how much less in his utterance should man?" His words express he believes both nature and human society are moving on and changing ceaselessly. To him, Tao is the origin of all creation and of all the force, and it lies behind all the functions and changes of the natural world. Nature and the earth are constantly in flux; the only constant in the universe is change.

What is Tao? Lao Zi says: " Something's has been mixed up to first produce Heaven and Earth. Still and solitary as it has always been, it evolves endlessly, operating as the parent of everything in the World. I know not its name. So I call it 'Tao'." Literally the word Tao means "a way" or "a road". Sometimes it denotes the "channel" of a river. In general, it means "the way to go". It includes the standard procedure of things, the correct method of their operation and behavior. Tao is the basis of a spiritual approach to living. Only when one follows Tao, can he avoid all the sufferings and warfare, and meet the order and harmony of nature. Tao is more stable and enduring than civilized institutions or power of the State. It is described as existing before the universe came into being. It is also believed to be an unchanging principle and mother of all things. It images the forefathers of the Lord. Also, it is the natural way, as well as the human way, and a model for human behavior. This way of nature's functioning has been a way of perfection. Tao is emphatically thought to be a way of harmony, integration and cooperation. Its natural tendency is towards peace, prosperity and health. If the Tao were to be followed everywhere, heaven, mankind, and the earth would form a single, harmonious unit, with each and every part cooperating towards universal well-being. Lao Zi points it out that mankind is also a natural being, and Heaven and humanity are equal. His idea of " the natural laws of Heaven" regards man as an independent part relieved from the fetters of Heaven.

The Taoist philosophy has rich content, yet it may be summed up in the following three points, namely wuwei (nonaction), ziran (naturalness), and *de* (virtue) (Chan, 2007, para. 57):

Wuwei: the concept of Wuwei, nonaction, means "non-assertive action," "non-coercive action" or "effortless action," but it does not mean total inaction. In other words, *Wuwei* is not about not doing certain things, it displays a reorientation of perception of value that would overcome the dominance of desires (Chan, 2007). The term Wuwei puts emphasis on the word Wu, which refers to "not having" which indicates a critique of a world given to the pursuit of wealth and power. One can also understand Wuwei as something like "act naturally," "effortless action," or "non-willful action" (Littlejohn, 2006). To put the above concept more simple, Taoists believe that " It is the practice of going against the stream not by struggling against it and thrashing about, but by standing still and letting the stream do all the work. Thus the sage knows that relative to the river, he still moves against the current. To the outside world the sage ap-

pears to take no action-but in fact he takes action long before others ever foresee the need for action" (synaptic, 1995).

Ziran: literally translates as "self (*zi*) so (*ran*)". As pointed out by Chan, nature" encompasses not only natural phenomena but also sociopolitical institutions (Chan, 2007). For human beings are "modeled" by heaven and earth, either in terms of their energy (*qi*) constitution or in the sense that they are governed by the same basic principles. Thus, Ziran, as an ethical concept, is extending beyond the personal into the sociopolitical level (Chan, 2007).

De: is a power of morality, or a power for good. It also refers to the power of naturalness, simplicity, and even weakness. Yet, it teaches survival skills on how to keep one's own integrity in time of disorder. This is possibly the most important point in the Taoist philosophy and has had an immense influence on the development of the Taoist religion. The following lists some of the Taoist classics:

- "An army will be shattered when it becomes strong; trees will snap when they grow strong."
- "The Tao gives birth to the unified thing (One), the One splits itself into two opposite aspects (Two), the Two gives birth to another (Three), the newborn Three produces the myriad things."
- "A huge tree which fills one's arms grows from a small heap of earth."
- "Man follows the way of Earth, Earth follows the way of Heaven..."
- "He who is content is rich; he who acts with persistence has will..."
- "Governing a great state is like frying small fish (so frequent disturbance should be avoided)."
- "Sincere words are not fine, and fine words are not sincere."
- "The net of Heaven is vast. It has large meshes, but it lets nothing escape."
- "The sage has no fixed personal will; he regards the people's will as his own."
- "The reason why the weak can overcome the strong and the soft can overcome the hard is known to all the people under Heaven."
- "If your hall is filled with gold and jade, whoever could keep them safe?"
- "It is upon bad fortune that good fortune leans."
- "There is no calamity greater than discontentment."
- "He does not merely rely on his own eyes, therefore he is wise and penetrating."

In sum, according to Taoism, Wuwei and Ziran provide a guide to the good life. Both the terms, non-action and naturalness, reflect the function of the nameless and formless Dao. On the other hand, ethical ideals are anchored in a non-empirical view of nature, which puts the concept of *De* above "virtues" in the sense of moral attainments (Chan, 2007). Deeply influenced by Taoism, ancient Chinese thinkers wish to give an explanation for the evident harmony and order in nature as a whole. The harmony and orderliness displayed in heaven and earth were the results of the cosmic presence of the Tao.

The ideologies and theories of Lao Zi were expounded in succinct and crisp sentences in *Book of Classics of the Tao and its Power*. The eighty-one-chapter book covers a wide range of subjects, including laws of the universe, laws of heaven and earth, laws about the details of social phenomena, and the principles of life and man's thinking. The works makes a significant impact upon the shaping and development of Chinese culture in conjunction with Confucius' famous Analects.

He is regarded as the founder of Taoism as well as the father of Chinese philosophy. Many of his viewpoints became principles of life, such as, the weak overcoming the strong, holding oneself aloof from worldly success, emptying the heart of desire, adopting an easygoing manner, retiring at the height of one's career, being selfless and modest. Furthermore, his works have exerted great influence on the Chinese mind and have been applied to politics, economy, military affairs, culture, business, and social intercourse. Chinese jujitsu, traditional shadow boxing, and quiescent qigong all originate in the spirit of Taoism.

Zhuang Zi

Zhuangzi is said to have lived from about 370-300 B. C. in the city of Meng in the state of Song, which is today's Henan Province. As the second greatest figure of the early Taoist school, Zhuang Zi's *Book of Zhuang Zi* is a must for those who want to study Taoism. The philosophy of Zhuang Zi and Lao Zi has a great impact on Chinese culture. Lao Zi teaches the way of the world and the virtues of survival, while Zhuang Zi is indifferent to human society. In other words, Zhuang Zi can be considered a precursor of multiculturalism and pluralism of systems of value. For example, Zhuang Zi argued that the wise man minds his own business, ignores the government, and hopes that it will ignore him (Moise, 1994, p. 14). There is a story that the King of Chu, a very powerful state, once sent two officials to offer a senior position in his government to Zhuangzi. He was sitting by a river, fishing, when they found him and made their offer.

Zhuangzhi held on to the fishing pole and, without turning his head, said, "I have heard that there is a sacred tortoise in Chu that has been dead for three thousand years. The King keeps it wrapped in cloth and boxed, and stores it in the ancestral temple. Now would this tortoise rather be dead and have its bones left behind and honored? Or would it rather be alive and dragging its tail in the mud?"

"It would rather be alive and dragging its tail in the mud," said the two officials.

Zhuangzi said, "Go away! I will drag my tail in the mud!"

From this story, it is not difficult for one to perceive that Zhuang Zi doubted the value of will-power and of too much thinking. Life is to be enjoyed, therefore, should be kept as simple as possible. Different from Confucius, who was eager to achieve high office so he could carry out reform, Zhuang Zi and his Taoist followers rejected position and power (Moise, 1994, p. 13). Zhuang Zi inherited the tendency of Lao Zi's thought. He believes that Heaven is the largest of all the perceivable things in the universe. When he mentions Heaven, he means nature or the natural environment. He believes man would lose the freedom of action by acting against the laws of nature. He maintains Man should act according to the laws of nature. He tells people that only by observing the objective and natural laws when dealing with human relations and affairs, could they achieve their goal successfully. This idea further develops the concept of "the natural laws of Heaven" conceived by Lao Zi. However, he negates the role of the man while stressing the natural law of the universe. He regards man's subjective endeavors as a destructive force against nature. The relationship between man and nature is similar to that between a piece of iron and a blacksmith. The blacksmith is able to produce whatever he likes with the iron, but the iron cannot have its choice. In his opinion, Heaven and Earth are a large melting-pot and nature is the blacksmith. Man is a piece of iron and his life is completely subject to nature. Zhuang Zi denies that man's efforts can reform nature; he attempts to bring about the return of man for he believes that man is no match for Heaven. He negates the will of Heaven on one hand and the inscrutable "fate" of man on the other hand.

Zhuang Zi's teaching makes an ardent plea for spiritual freedom, self-interested tendencies, and prejudices. His central concern may be described as the finding of absolute happiness, of transcending the distinction between one's self and the universe with the Tao. According to Zhuang Zi, by utilizing superior wisdom, a sage is no longer affected emotionally by the changes of this world. For instance, he believed that death is no more than a necessary and proper correlative of human life, and a natural and desirable step following life. It is the eternal rest after one's labor in this world, or the ultimate cure for the sick.

In addition, Zhuang Zi's Taoist philosophy later mingled with Chinese medical knowledge, popular religions, and other elements of folk culture (Moise, 1994, p. 14), including organized worship of numerous deities, and the martial arts discipline known to the West as Kungfu.

Section 2 Taoism

Taoism was founded in the mid-stage of the Eastern Han Dynasty (25—220 AD) by Zhang Ling. People suffered from successive years of wars and famines were eager for peace. *The Classic of Supreme Peace* (*Taiping Ching*), a book deeply influenced by Lao-tzu's Taoist doctrines and advocating immortals worship, began to spread far and wide. The authors of the book claimed to establish a state of peace and prosperity. The authors are three brothers Zhang Jiao, Zhang Bao and Zhang Liang and the author Zhang Daoling of the book *Five Bushels of Rice Sect* (*Wudoumi*) thus won wide support from peasants. Zhang Dao Ling gave a religious interpretation of Lao Zi's classic of *The Way and Virtue* and personified the Tao by referring to it as celestial god Supreme Master Lao Zi (born in 604 BC, or born in 1321 BC). The Classics of *the Ways and Virtues* (*Dao De Jing*) depicts the principles of Taoism. Lao-tzu wrote in his *The Way and Virtue*—Taoism's main classic: "Tao generates one. One generates two. Two generates three. Three generates all things in the universe. " Taoism holds the belief that immortals dominate all things in the world. People can ask for their blessing and protection and become an integral part of Tao through benefactions and self-discipline. They can return to nature and eventually become immortals themselves in that way.

Taoism worships all kinds of immortals, including natural gods, local gods, ancestral gods, ethnic gods and craft gods as well as previous enlightened emperors, virtuous and able officials and talented scholars. Guanyin (Avalokitesvara) of Buddhism and many deities in other religions are also worshiped. The immortals' world maintains a rigid hierarchy like the human society. Each deity of the immortals' world has his or her own responsibility.

Huang Lao Dao and Fang Xian Dao were combined into one religion and Taoism was formed. Two significant reforms occurred to Taoism in its history. More and more people from high society joined the ranks of Taoist disciples from the Jin Dynasty (265—420) to the northern and Southern Dynasties (386—589). Immortals worship gradually replaced the previous dream of establishing a state of peace and prosperity. Ge Hong, Kuo Qianzhi, Lu Jingxiu and Tao Hongjing revised the early Taoism's doctrines while absorbing Confucianism's moral principles and ethics. It won support from upper-class disciples including emperors and noblemen. Thus Taoism became a peer of the influential Confucianism and Buddhism and saw its heyday in the Tang (618—907) and Song (960—1279) dynasties. More and more classics were added to the religion's repertoire. The sixth emperor of the Tang Dynasty ordered some scholars to compile the *Kaiyuan Collected Taoist Scriptures*, in the eighth century.

Wang Chongyang founded in north China a Taoist sect named Quanzhen stressing self-discipline, while another sect of Jindan emerged in south China around the mid-12th century. Both sects absorbed philosophical ideas and health preservation theories from Confucianism and Buddhism. They later merged into a single Quanzhen Sect, coexisting ever since with the Way of Orthodox Unity (Zhengyi), which was another major sect of Taoism evolving from the Heavenly Master Sect. Priests of Quanzhen Sect lived a strict religious life, single and vegetarian, living collectively in temples all the year round. However, those from Zhengyi might get married and have children. They usually lived a secular life, having meat and holding rites for disciples to exorcise spirits and stave off disasters.

During that period, Taoist temples appeared everywhere and were filled with piles of Taoist books. Immortals live not only in the kingdom of Heaven but also in beautiful mountains and rivers on the Earth in the Taoist mythology. During the initial stage of the religion's development, Taoism was practiced in simple, crude huts or caves in remote mountains, seeking to get rid of the styles of official life and the agonies in social conflicts. Therefore, numerous Taoist temples have been built on mountains with scenic splendors. These magnificent buildings are unique in style and layout. For instance, there are famous Taoism temples in the most famous five mountains including Mount Tai (Shandong Province), Mount Heng (Henan Province), Mountain Hua (Shaanxi Province), Mount Heng (Shanxi Province) and Mount Song (Henan Province) in China. Wudang Mountain, which is located in northwest Hubei Province, is a famous Taoist mountain. Another four sacred Taoist mountains in China are Mount Qingcheng in Sichuan Province, Mount Longhu in Jiangxi Province, Mount Wedang in Hubei Province and Mount Laoshan in Shandong Province.

After the 16th century, Neo-Confucianism, a Confucian school of philosophy emerging in the Song Dynasty, began to dominate the ideological sphere. Taoism turned to the countryside and gained more popularity there, further merging with Buddhism and folk beliefs because it was discriminated against. Due to various reasons, such as lack of support, both in political terms and in financial terms, Taoism moved from the ruling class down to the ordinary people. Taoism began to decline from the mid-period of the Ming Dynasty (1368—1644), and especially during the Qing Dynasty (1644—1911). Additionally, Taoism was gradually appropriated by those who wandered off in search of the secret of eternal life. This caused the philosophy of Taoism to eventually lose credit in the eyes of the intellectuals. Taoist organizations gradually declined in the first half of the 20th century. However its doctrines still maintained a wide influence on the Chinese people across the world. The People's Republic of China has adopted a policy of freedom of religious belief. Dilapidated temples have been renovated with the aid of governments at different levels. The year 1957 saw the establishment of the Chinese Taoist Association with its local branches in all provinces and autonomous regions. A Taoist Culture Institute was founded in 1989. A Chinese Taoist College was set up in 1990. China has several ten thousand registered Taoist priests and nuns, and thousands of Taoist temples currently.

The Three Pure Ones, who are the highest Gods of Taoism, form the Trinity of Taoism. They are the Ruler of Heaven granting happiness, the Ruler of Earth granting remissions of sins, and the Ruler of Water averting all evil. The Jade Emperor, who ranks beneath the Three Pure Ones, rules other gods. However, some people believe The Three Pure Ones are purely representative of the three energies cultivated by Taoist meditations—Jing, Qi and Shen.

In Taoism, Tao produces original energy (Yuanqi). This original energy is divided into Yin and Yang which are the negative and positive principles of the universe. Yin and Yang cannot exist without each other, and they often represent opposites in relations to one another. As you travel around the black and white sections of the circular Yin-Yang symbol, white or black will increase until the opposite color is littlest, but never totally gone. The cycle repeats for the opposite color. Yin and Yang come to no end. The symbolic circle is a vivid explanation of the relationship between Yin and Yang. What seems like Yin is often supported by Yang, and the opposite. For example, one must know what an evil thing is in order to know a good thing and nothing is evil without the good thing as a comparison at the same time. Yin and Yang are changing every moment in a harmonious manner, and the whole universe depends on the changes of them. They often represent opposites. For instance, Yin represents female, while Yang represents male; Yin represents darkness, Yang represents brightness; Yin represents the moon, while Yang represents the sun. The theory represents the original thinking of materialism by indicating that the world is full of conflicts and change all the time. A good understanding of the relationship can help keep things in a balanced and harmonious state.

Man can make both his mental and physical life live forever, and become immortal through a long period of self-cultivation according to Taoism. Taoism has developed by absorbing ideas and ways from other

religious sects and schools. It is regarded as an eclectic religion. The cultivation of life means the cultivation of the spirit, breath and vitality in one's body to meet the requirements of the natural law of growth. Taoism completed its religious system by absorbing much of the Buddhist philosophy and religious theories. For instance, it makes use of some Buddhist tenets to compile its own books, and imitates the Buddhist commandments to make its own disciplines and rituals. The concepts of "hell", "paradise" and "souls" are borrowed from Buddhism. Taoism highlights self-cultivation, and the practice of it developed the idea of cultivating one's mind from Chan, which is one of the schools of Buddhism in China.

The Taoist school holds the belief that the origin of the universe and a higher being involved "Heaven and Earth". "Tao" means "a way to go" or the "channel of a river". Tao includes standard procedures for the correct methods of operation and behavior. Tao is described as existing before the universe came into being. As an unchanging principle, it is the mother of all things, the natural way, as well as the human way, serving as a model for human behavior. The "way" leads to harmony, integration and cooperation with a natural tendency toward peace, health and prosperity. If Tao were to be followed, heaven, earth and human beings would form a single, harmonious reality. It is believed that Tao generates everything and all phenomena in the world. Tao is achieved through internal self-cultivation and external self-exercise. It involves the way of meditation, tranquility, freedom from desire and worry, concentration of the mind, purification and brightness. Taoists believe gaining enlightenment is the ultimate achievement of the Tao. In order to make the ego immortal, a permanent survival of its mortal body and spirit, one should make the Tao reside in ego and integrate the Tao with ego as a whole.

The development of both Lao Zi and Confucius's theories is deeply influenced by Book of Changes. One theme of the book is the idea of change. Yin and Yang alternate in an unending sequence and an extreme situation must change to make room for opposite elements. The two branches of Chinese philosophy, Taoism and Confucianism, have their common root here. Taoism created its own religious ethics by adopting the philosophies of Confucianism. Taoism borrowed the ideas of loyalty and filial piety, and the theory of life and temperament as a central part of its ethical thought, from Confucianism. Though the doctrines of Confucianism and Taoism complement each other in many ways, running side by side like two streams through Chinese thought and literature, Taoism is different from Confucianism in many aspects. Taoism denies the value of morality, legal systems and knowledge. It advocates entering the world by renouncing the world. Taoism advocates a carefree flight from the respectability and conventional duties of society. Taoists held out a vision of a transcendental world of spirit, and they turned to nature for the secrets of life. Greatly influenced by Taoist theories, some ancient Chinese thinkers wished to offer an explanation for the evident harmony and order in nature as a whole. Furthermore, Taoist ideas exerted great influence on the thinking of the Chinese people for generations.

After the Southern and Northern Dynasties (420—534), a great number of temples were built across China and some constructions were large and broad in scale.

Taoism is the only one native religion which originated in China among the five major existing religions in China. It is more than being a religion only. It has incorporated and influenced almost all parts of culture such as literature, philosophy, painting, architecture, classical music, Chinese Medicine, Martial Arts in the past. Enchanting Taoist art came into being with Taoism's spread, which had produced a great impact on other forms of traditional Chinese art. The ideas of "going back to nature" and "yearning to become immortals" are characteristic of Taoism's aesthetic thought. Myths, designs, symbols and color peculiar to the religion have been widely employed in buildings, painting, sculptures and attire. Ancient court dance and music, sacrificial rites of ethnic minorities of southwest China have been largely kept in Taoist music and rituals.

As a religion, it embraces many cultures. It is called a "learning of absorption and assimilation". The cultural composition of Taoism includes Taoist thought, architecture, medicine, fine arts, music and literature.

Taoist literature created a unique style of poetry, with five words in a line and four, eight or 12 lines of ornate stanzas. The style later developed into the popular literary form of "Tao Qing" which is popular and easily understood. A number of renowned works with Taoist themes appeared in traditional literature. These works brought a novelty of artistic conception, a new style and a new way of wording. Take the most famous poet Li Bai as an example; many of his poems are full of thoughts of immortals and feelings of natural grace.

Taoist music included solos and choruses performed during the Taoist feasts and sacrificial ceremonies. The musical instruments included many kinds of traditional instruments such as percussive bells, chime stones, drums, stringed instruments and pipes. Taoist religious music is characterized by its special local flavor. For instance, music performed during particular religious rituals may differ due to local variations in melodies. That is to say, the Taoist cultural composition represents other kinds of compositional forms, while at the same time it is influenced by those various compositional forms.

Taoism combined the Nei Dan and Wai Dan theories with traditional Chinese medicinal theories and introduced its health preservation methods. These methods of health preservation included massage, the Daoying Qi-promoting method, the regulation of breathing, and medical skills and treatment. Qi-promoting can bring about a state of harmony in the body, and exercises can make the body flexible. The essences of the methods have made great contributions to traditional Chinese medicine.

Taoist vegetarian food and beverages have contributed much to the world's knowledge of health care and longevity. A unique Taoist food culture has evolved. It is said that the dishes of the Taoist Vegetarian Canteen combine delicacy and healing functions. The world famous Vegetarian Food in the Qingyang Taoist Temple (Sichuan Province) includes unique Taoist dishes, medicinal recipes, healthy teas and medicinal wines.

People can still find traces of Taoism in China today. For instance, the idiom "like the Eight Immortals crossing the sea" has its origin in the Taoist fairy tale, The Eight Immortals Crossing the Sea. People still put portraits of the God of the Door on their doors to keep away the demons. Some people still worship the God of Wealth in the hope of achieving big fortunes. In the countryside, people still believe the God of the Kitchen is in charge of every household's fortune and misfortune. Therefore, they burn incense on the 23rd of December to send the Kitchen God to Heaven; and they light up firecrackers and fireworks to welcome him back during the Spring Festival.

In summary, Taoism influenced Chinese culture, science and imagery for more than 2, 000 years and contributed vast quantities of classics, documents, historical relics and treasures to China.

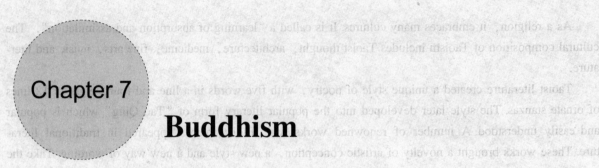

Chapter 7
Buddhism

Xuefei Yang, Xiaoxia Mao and Frits Buijs

China was a multi-ethnic country since ancient times, and there was an extensive range of objects of worship including the worship of ghosts, gods, totems, ancestors and nature in ancient China. A number of religions such as Buddhism, Islam and Zoroastrianism were introduced into China from the Qin (221-2-7 B. C.) and Han (206 B. C. —220 A. D.) dynasties. Some other religions such as Taoism, White Lotus Doctrine and Yellow Heaven Doctrine grew up in China during the dynasties in the federal society. There are no detailed statistics within the historical records of the certain number of ancient religions in China, however, the rough estimation of the number is more than 100 classifications. Buddhism and Taoism were the two dominant religions in ancient China. Because of their ideological and cultural significance, Buddhism and Taoism still influence people's lives and society.

Section 1 Origin

Buddhism is a religion and a philosophy. It means roughly the "teachings of the Awakened One" in the Indian Sanskrit language of the ancient Buddhist texts. The founder (Sakymuni) of Buddhism named Siddhartha Gautama (563—483 B. C.) was born as a prince in the ruling Kshatriya family of the Lichhavi tribe in Lumbini of Nepal. It was predicted that Gautama would become a saint and rule the world. So his father, who was the chief of the tribe, took all possible care in keeping Gautama in a palace full of luxuries and comfort, while going to great lengths to shelter him from anything that might influence his religious life. However, encountering the harsh realities of life, such as old age, sickness and death, he felt sad and declined his privileged life, glory and desire as he grew up. At the age of 29, he decided to leave his family in search of the real meaning of life and the ultimate truth to liberate human beings from sufferings (Buddhist Temples, n. d.) . To search for enlightenment, Gautama first associated himself with a group of ascetics, who were individuals pursuing spiritual disciplines to strengthen the spiritual life (AC, 2007). However, he discovered that he was not able to find enlightenment through such efforts. He chose a path of moderation-seeking to avoid all extremes afterwards. For example, he took moderate food, and swore not to stir until he had attained the supreme enlightenment. He attained enlightenment on the night of the full moon after overcoming the attacks and temptations of Mara, the evil one, sitting under a pipal tree at the age of 35. This formerly spoiled prince finally succeeded and found the path to liberate human beings from suffering and to achieve eternal happiness. He gained the title of Buddha, which means one who is awake, since Buddha Siddhartha Gautama had reached a level of understanding that had never been attained by any human in history (AC, 2007) . During the remaining 45 years of his life, Gautama traveled through much

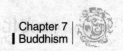

of northern India teaching numerous disciples and spreading his teaching of the way to enlightenment.

Section 2   Main Teachings

In Buddhism, any person who has awakened from the "sleep of ignorance" without instruction, and teaches it to others is called a Buddha (Wikipedia, 2007). Buddhists generally agree that Shakyamuni or Gotama Buddha was not the only Buddha (Wikipedia, 2007), and if a person achieves the wakening, he is called an arahant, meaning a spiritual practitioner who had "laid down the burden" and realized the goal of nibbana. However, Gautama, is the only Buddha among others before or after him.

There are some basic Buddhist philosophical doctrines. First of all, the world, which contains sorrow, transience and soul, is impermanent and it will be destroyed eventually. There is no substance or duration to things, because everything is unreal. Nevertheless, the only connection between one thing and the next is that one causes the next (Ross, 2007).

Second, nothing has an essence, nature, or character by itself. Buddhists all believe in the idea of "no-self," since the nature of things only exists in relation to everything else that exists, and there is no essence just as there is no substance or duration in the world. Buddhists also believe that things in isolation are "empty", which does not mean nothingness, but it means "we *cannot* know what that is" (Ross, 2007).

Third, everything has a cause. As pointed out by Ross, A momentary existence occurs as it does because of a previous momentary existence, but the cause itself is also momentary. Therefore, the goal of one's life is to escape from the cycle of cause, and to stop being born as a suffering individual who has selfish cravings and passions. The release is the highest bliss and the end of the self. To be specific, the goal of *nibbana* is to remove all causes and all the conditioned existence (Ross, 2007).

The teachings of the Buddha are classified into three major parts: the rules and regulations for the Orders of male monks and female monastics; sermons or discourses in terms of various subjects of wide-ranged significance, such as social, moral, philosophical and spiritual issues; the doctrinal commentaries which include philosophical and technical works, such as discourses, discussions on the dogma and doctrines.

The central teachings can be classified under the following three headings, namely, rebirth, karma and the Four Noble Truths. Rebirth refers to Reincarnation, Buddhist Rebirth or Renaissance (Wikipedia, 2007). It has no discernible beginning, and takes place in a variety of types of life. Karma is understood as actions of body, speech and mind. Buddhists believe that the karma of good produces "rewards" while the karma of bad produces "punishment" in either this life or in a subsequent one. To put it simple, the type of rebirth that arises at the end of ones life is conditioned by the karmas of the previous life (Wikipedia, 2007). The Four Noble Truths are among the truths Gautama Buddha realized during his experience of enlightenment. They are the Doctrine of a formulation of his understanding of the nature of "suffering": the Doctrine of Accumulation, the Doctrine of Extinction and the Doctrine of Path, respectively. They tell people that existence is full of suffering and does not bring satisfaction. The cause of suffering is craving and desire which bind beings to the cycle of existence. Suffering can be brought to an end through elimination of craving.

Except the main doctrines and teachings, there are also three essential components of Buddhism called the Buddha, the Dharma, and the Sangha, and they are regarded as the Three Treasures to Buddhists. The Buddha, which is the Awakened One, refers to Sakyamuni Buddha and those who attained Awakening similar to the Buddha and helped others to attain it. The Dharma refers to the teachings or law as expounded by the Buddha. It also refers to the universal norms or laws governing human existence. Finally, the Sangha refers to one of the two very specific kinds of groups: either the community practicing the Buddhist Way,

or the community of people who have attained the first level of Awakenings (Wikipedia, 2007). In sum, the Buddha, Dharma and Sangha are viewed essentially as One-the eternal Buddha himself.

The Eightfold Path is the means for ending suffering. It contains right views, right intentions, right speech, right conduct, right livelihood, right effort, right mindfulness and right concentration. According to Buddhism, the unsatisfied desire is the cause of all suffering including old age, disease, death... To overcome suffering and escape the cycle of life and death, to extinguish desire and destroy ignorance is necessary. Only by following the teaching can man teach enlightenment and attain perfect stillness after death, which is described as transmigration to "extinction". Buddhists are taught to show the same tolerance, forbearance and love to all people without distinction, and kindness to members of the animal kingdom.

The Ten Grave Precepts are as the following: no killing, no stealing, no being greedy, no lying, no being ignorant, no talking about others' faults, no elevating oneself by criticizing others, no being stingy, no anger, no speaking ill of the Three Treasures or the Five Commandments for layman.

To Indian Buddhism, it is said there is a hill on the slope of Mount Sumeru. The hill named Gandhara has four peaks where the Four World Heavenly Kings reside. Each of the Kings protects part of the world. In the Chinese Buddhist temple, there are Four Heavenly Kings of the Four Quarters. They guard the world and the Buddhist faith. Armed standing at the entrance to a Buddha Hall, they are guarding the eastern, southern, western and northern world. The Eastern World Heavenly King is sculptured in a white color. He plays a Pipa (four-stringed Chinese lute). He can protect the country and its people. The southern World Heavenly King, sculptured in a blue color with a sword in his hand, can protect Buddhist doctrines and develop kindliness. With a snake coiling his body, the Western World Heavenly King is sculptured in a red color to protect the people. The Northern World Heavenly King is sculptured in a green color with an umbrella in his right hand a snow weasel in his other hand. It is said he can protect the wealth of the people. The Four Heavenly Kings symbolize propitious elements, a prosperous country and the people being at peace. Each of them has a follower and 91 sons to support them. Each of the Kings also has eight famous generals who are responsible for mountains, rivers, forests and baby deities of other areas.

Section 3 Schools in China

The earliest available teachings of the Buddha are found in Pali literature and belong to the school of the Theravadins, who may be called the most orthodox school of Buddhism. Nowadays, There are ten schools of Buddhism:

1. Reality School or Kosa School or Abhidharma School

2. Satysiddhi School or Cheng-se School

3. Three Sastra School or San-lun School

4. The Lotus School or T'ien-t'ai School. (Absorb the Nirvana school)

5. The Garland School or Hua-yen School or Avatamsaka School. (Absorb the Dasab-humika School and the Samparigraha-sastra school)

6. Intuitive School or Ch'an School or Dhyana School

7. Discipline School or Lu School or Vinaya School

8. Esoteric School or Chen-yien School or Mantra School

9. Dharmalaksana School or Ch'u-en School or Fa-siang School

10. Pure-land School or Sukhavati School or Ching-t'u School

(Sources from: Buddha Dharma Education Association Inc.)

The principles of all the above schools are based on the partial doctrine of Sakyamuni Buddha (BDEA

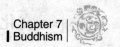

Inc. & BuddhaNet, 2007). However, the above schools may be further classified into Mahayana and Theravada; esoteric teachings and open teachings.

Section 4 Evolution and Development of Chinese Buddhism

Chinese Buddhism refers collectively to the various schools of Buddhism that have flourished in China since ancient times. The development of Buddhism in China can be roughly divided into two stages: introducing period and developing period. During the period from the Han Dynasty (206B. C. —220A. D.) to the Three Kingdoms (220—280) and the Jin Dynasty (265—420), Buddhism was introduced into different areas of China. During the Southern (420—589) and Northern Dynasties (386—534), and especially during the Sui (581—618) and Tang dynasties (618—907), Buddhism blended with Confucianism in form and essence. When a succession of Buddhism sects and schools were founded, Chinese Buddhism came into being.

Buddhism was first introduced in China from India via Central Asia at the end of the Western Han Dynasty (206 B. C. —25 A. D.). The introduction of Buddhism into China is related to a king of an ancient country in the third century according to the earliest reliable account. The king sent missionaries to teach Jing Lu. The mission achieved great success and the introduction of Chinese monk scholars and the arrival of new Buddhist scholars from the Indian subcontinent and central Asia made the region soon became the centre of Buddhist learning with distinguished monks and scholars. Later, when the merchants of Central Asia came into this region for trade, they learnt Buddhism from Chinese monks and took it as their believes (BDEA Inc. & BuddhaNet, 2007). Instead of introducing only a part of Buddhism, Chinese monk scholars introduced and developed the whole of Indian Buddhism into China. When Buddhism declined in India, the original records of many of its sects and classics could be found in China.

The exchange of Chinese and foreign Buddhist cultures was the beginning of cultural communications between China and the outside world and such exchanges lasted during the following 2, 000 years in various dynasties. Many Chinese traveled abroad to seek knowledge of and preach the Buddhist scriptures. For instance, Fa Xiang, a monk of the Eastern Jin Dynasty (317—420) traveled for a total of 15 years across 30 counties to bring Buddhist classics to China. He solved difficult questions in the scriptures and finally realized Buddhist ideals after he survived all the hardships. In his works, *Records of My Journey to India*, he gave a complete and detailed account of his experience on the pilgrimage to the West and his record contains many valuable historical and geographical materials about states in Western Regions.

The Tang Dynasty was a time of great prosperity for Buddhism in China. Although the rulers in the Tang Dynasty were Taoists, they were generally open to all religions. Many Chinese monks traveled west to bring back Buddhist works and looked for answers to their questions in their study with the rise of the Tang Dynasty. There was an individual named Xuan Zang (618—907) among them. He studied at the famous Nalanda Temple for five years and traveled around conducting research for four years after his arrival in India. He returned home in 645 and worked on translations in the Greater Wild Goose Pagoda in Chang'an. He also brought back many Buddhist classics. In his book, *Records on the Western Regions of the Great Tang Empire*, he mentioned the geography, history, culture, communication, religions, folk customs, and the ways of life in the countries and regions he had visited, including countries in mid-Asia. The book also includes a great number of myths, legends and stories of these countries, such as Afghanistan, India, Pakistan and Myanmar. In general, the book is an important document for the study of the history of these countries. Buddhism was also studied by more and more people and was accepted as their religion during the Tang Dynasty. Soon Buddhism became an important part of Chinese culture. Along with Buddhism, other

Indian culture products, such as Buddhist paintings and sculptures became very highly developed, as well. New schools of Buddhism developed and flourished, and Buddhism at that time had followers in all class groups (Walthall, 2000).

Buddhism further developed in China after the Tang Dynasty. It is said that in theory, Chinese Buddhism is characteristically different from Indian Buddhism. Chinese Buddhism changed the nature of Buddha into the "nature of mind" of Confucianism. In other words, it turns an external idol of the Buddha into an internal belief of mind. Take Guanyin (Avalokitesvara) as an example. After the Tang Dynasty, the 33 different original images (males or females), evolved into a female image holding a tiny chinaware flask in her hand. Standing or sitting on a lotus flower with a treasure vase full of dew held in her right hand, she helps the needy and relieves the distressed, cures the disabled and saves a sinking vessel whenever they call her. The basic difference between Chinese Buddhism and Indian Buddhism lies in whether one attaches importance to man or to the Buddha.

Another example of the doctrine of Chinese Buddhism is "the Buddha only works in man's own mind", and one should "realize all at once the nature of unchangeable reality in one's own mind". If one accepts the basic principles of Buddhism, he can "perceive the nature and become a Buddha at once". In the past, traditional Chinese ideology was heavily tinted with politics, and various schools and sects were closely linked with politics through different forms. Indian Buddhism was marked by the aim of deliverance "from the earthly world", while Chinese Buddhism develops to a way of living "in the earthly world". This shift marks the maturity of Chinese Buddhism. The Buddhist doctrines became integrated with traditional Chinese ethics and religious concepts. Metaphysics (Xuan Xue) was popular among the ruling classes, and had many things in common with Buddhism. Soon the two religions became one in China.

Section 5 Influence of Buddhism in Chinese Culture

After Buddhism was introduced into China, it began to communicate and merge with the traditional native culture and gradually became an important part of Chinese culture. Buddhism influences Chinese thinking and culture deeply. For instance, it has had great influence on Chinese literature, especially poetry. Chan poetry is the combination of poetry and Chan (one school of Chinese Buddhism). The type of poetry places great emphasis on a situation of nothingness, lightness, peacefulness and stillness. Wang Wei (701—761), a famous poet in the Tang Dynasty, is the most prominent figure among the Chinese Chan poets. Chinese painting is also influenced by Buddhism. Special emphasis is often laid on a state of peacefulness and freedom from care in Chinese painting. The style is exactly expressed in the water-ink landscape painting or the Chinese literati painting. The painting tends to be unworldly, intangible and light. This school is called Southern School in the classical Chinese painting, and Wang Wei is considered the greatest master. The Southern School of painting enjoys the highest fame and becomes the standard for later painters. In ancient times, the highest criterion for judging the value of a painting or a poem was to see if the art conceived was up to the level of Chan since the Tang Dynasty.

As to its artistic aspects, the sculpting and painting of the images of Buddha was part of India's Gandhara and Upagupta skills in statue modeling during the first stage. Chinese Buddhist art completed the process of changing during the Sui and Tang period. Caves were originally a form of Indian Buddhist temples, where monks could practice their self-cultivation in peace. When they were introduced in China, they quickly became blended with traditional Chinese constructions that are quite different from their original styles. Generally, only images of the Buddha and murals were presented for worship in these caves. Other constructions were built for monks to live in and to chant scriptures in front of, or beside, the caves. Chinese cave temples are depositories of treasured sculptures, murals and other relics. Among a number of famous temples are Shao Lin Temple (Henan Province), Ci'en Temple in Xi'an (Shaanxi Province), Lingyin Temple in Hangzhou (Zhejiang Province) and Yonghegong Lamasery in Beijing. The four finest temples in China are Lingyan (Magic Cliff) Temple in Jinan, Shandong Province; Qixia (Residing in Clouds) Temple in Nanjing, Jiangsu Province; Guoqing (National Purity) Temple at Tiantai County, Zhejiang Province; Yuquan (Jade Fountain) Temple at Jiangling, Hubei Province.

The Chinese Buddhist statues gradually had their own characters too. Many Buddhist statues in China were produced with the bearing of a dignified scholar after the Sui and Tang period. The Buddha Rocana in the Fengxian Temple at Longmen is a typical example. This large statue, dressed in a Chinese-style kasaya, looks kind-hearted with eyes expressing calm and insight. It fully expresses the Confucian aesthetic ideal of seeking a unity of the internal and external qualities, virtue and beauty.

Since Buddhism took root in China, there are many Chinese Buddhist schools like Chan Buddhism, Pureland Buddhism, Tiantai Buddhism, Tantra Buddhism, Sanlun Buddhism, Faxiang Buddhism and Huayan Buddhism. They all stress the importance of man's mind. All sects were in favor of the simple and easy wisdom of Buddha regarded as the gateway to enlightenment, which could be readily followed by everyone.

In conclusion, the exchanges between Chinese and Indian Buddhist cultures demonstrate how a foreign culture implanted into the soil of China must comply with the basic ethos of Chinese culture. Traditional Chinese can digest and assimilate a foreign culture. Foreign culture can serve as an impetus for the development of Chinese culture. The spirit of communication can also be found from the Chinese culture's adoption and assimilation of foreign cultures. Since it has had a profound impact on Chinese arts, architecture, literature, philosophy, religion, music, phonology and social customs, Buddhism has served as an important part of Chinese culture and became one of the Three Pillars of the traditional culture of China.

Section 6 Spreading in Asian Countries

The period of the 6th to 7th century marked the peak of Chinese Buddhism entering these countries. China served as a base relaying Buddhism to other countries at that time. For instance, 19 times envoys were sent to China from Japan being accompanied by a few hundred students and scholar monks during the Tang Dynasty (618—907). It helped the cultural exchanges between China and other countries. A large number of scholar monks sent from Korea, Vietnam, Japan and other Asian countries also studied Buddhism in China and spread it to other Asian countries. Major sects of Chinese Buddhism passed over to these countries in Eastern and Southeastern Asia during the Tang Dynasty. Buddhist cultural exchanges between China and other countries involved the import and export of culture on a large scale and during a long period. The influence was on many countries and regions of East Asia, Southeast Asia and South Asia. Buddhist cultural exchange is a "channel" and "window" for other forms of cultural exchange between China and other countries.

Part 4

Civilization and Culture

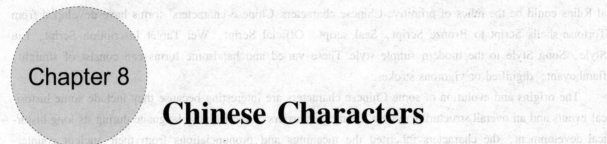

Chapter 8

Chinese Characters

Xiaoxia Mao

It is imperative to acquire a perspective through a window of the language and script when examining the cultural traits of a nation. The language and script of every nation hinge on the features and patterns of thinking as well as the rich cultural contents of that nation. A language influences the traditional way of thinking that stresses intuition and wholeness.

The "square characters" of Chinese words represent one of the oldest forms of written language in the world. It is not possible to determine each character's sound simply by looking at the strokes. It no doubt has made mastery of the Chinese language a most demanding task.

The number of Chinese characters has been growing continuously during the past 3,000 years. There were about 5,000 Jiaguwen (ancient Chinese characters) inscribed on turtle shells. The number soared to more than 47,000 in the Qing Dynasty according to the Kangxi Grand Dictionary compiled at that time. It is estimated a grand total of about 60,000 existed, and 2,000 to 3,000 characters are frequently used on a daily basis.

The Chinese characters all occupy the same spacing in printing and are figuratively referred to as "square script. " Chinese characters consist of strokes, which are classified into eight basic forms. Most Chinese characters are combinations of simpler component characters. A huge number of Chinese characters have the same sound but different meanings.

Chinese characters are isolated words which are both practical and aesthetical. The principle of coining Chinese words is: "Making pictographs based on shapes of things and finding origins from nature. " The system of the Chinese characters incorporates sounds and forms, as well as meanings. The phonetic characteristics result in its obvious musicality—pleasant in sound, clear in tempo and harmonious in rhythm. Chinese characters are syllabic while Western words are alphabetic. Compared with the Western words, simplicity of the language is a major characteristic of the Chinese language and words. Of all the United Nations documents printed in different languages, the Chinese version is the thinnest copy. Furthermore, Chinese characters are ideographs and have no direct connection with pronunciation. The Western script is abstractly rational while the Chinese characters are imaginable and perceivable. Accordingly, a group of words that have "女" (woman) as a segment such as "姐" (sister), "妈" (mother) and "姥" (grandma) may leave you a deep impression of being female roles in a family. It is easy to imagine they are all female. They give readers an intense, direct stimulus.

The coinage of the Chinese characters has undergone tremendous changes through the course of historical development. The history of the evolution of Chinese characters spans 4,000 or 5,000 years. The carved signs on the outer rims of vertical-cavity pots found in the Banpo-Yangshao Ruins and the Dawenkou Cultur-

al Ruins could be the relics of primitive Chinese characters. Chinese characters' forms have developed from Tortoise shells Script to Bronze Script, Seal script, Official Script, Wei Tablet Inscription Script, Liu Style, Song Style to the modern simple style. These varied and handsome forms can consist of straight, flamboyant, dignified or vigorous strokes.

The origins and evolution of some Chinese characters are interesting because they include some historical events and an overall structuring system. Being the carriers of the Chinese language during its long historical development, the characters inherited the meanings and pronunciations from their ancient counterparts. The Character 王 (Wang) shows a huge man and means leader in ancient script. Some scholars believed it represented an ancient weapon—axe, signifying a conqueror. 王 was termed a monarch in the pre-Qin times. Zhou Wu Wang is known as an enlightened monarch while Zhou Wang as a tyrant. Six states had their own 王 (monarchs) after the fall of the Zhou dynasty (1066 B. C. —221 B. C.). The character 王 also became one of the most popular surnames in China. Most of the characters have been readjusted and standardized since the Qin Dynasty (221B. C. —206 B. C.) and have evolved into today's characters.

Ancient Chinese characters are a large accumulation of pictographic characters to express their meanings. Pictograms are the basic Chinese characters developed from pictures to express meanings through the images of things. Pictographic characters unify form and meaning. A pictograph was an integral part of Chinese character development. The pictographic-phonetic characters are a combination of graphics and phonetics. For instance, the three dots of the character "湖" represent water and the other part, "胡", represents the sound of a lake. Though the characters such as 眼 (eye), 水 (water) and 日 (sun) do not look like their original objects, they can not only record the basic elements of the Chinese language, but also structure the sound theory of other words with their own pronunciations and meanings. Meanwhile, Chinese characters developed in other ways, including the indicative, referential, associative, synonymic and pictographic-phonetic systems.

The unit, which represents a historical concept, has been universally accepted in its long historical development.

Modern Chinese characters may seem to contradict each other. However, after tracing back their historical evolution, conformity with form and theory appears to be clear. The form and meaning of Chinese characters cannot be interpreted freely. Conformity with form means conformity with the form through its historical evolution.

All Characters are systematized and none of them stand alone. Xu Shen of the Han Dynasty summarized and classified these characters into six categories, which marked the maturation of Chinese characters.

Therefore, free interpretation is not admissible. If one character is wrongly interpreted, it will cause errors in the interpretation of interrelated characters.

Good interpretation requires the understanding of the rules for structuring characters, the knowledge of the historical evolution of the structuring characters and the mastering of an overall system of characters.

Chinese characters are difficult and complex compared to other writing systems. As a result, the task of the reform to promote and popularize common speech (Putonghua) and phonetic alphabet (Pinyin) has been carried on in China. A large scale reform of Chinese characters was continued in 1955 and 1956. During this time, more than one thousand variant characters were eliminated. The Second Scheme of Simplified Chinese Character was promulgated in 1977 and was repealed in 1986 due to general disapproval. China began to simplify the Chinese Characters to promote universal literacy. However, a return of traditional characters has recently appeared in advertising, and in restaurant and shop signs. Traditional characters are mainly used in Taiwan and Hong Kong. The simplified and traditional characters will probably continue to exist side by side in the future.

Chapter 9

Chinese Calligraphy

Xiaoxia Mao and Helen Yang

Section 1   Important Part of Traditional Chinese Culture

Travelers may notice decorative calligraphy can be found everywhere, especially in temples, pagodas, cave walls, mountain sides and monuments all over China.

Calligraphy, along with the ancient musical instrument (Zheng), chess and Chinese painting form the four skills pursued by scholars in ancient China. Calligraphy has a practical value and an aesthetic value. It can express a writer's various feelings, aesthetic ideas, thoughts, education as well as his personality through the use of a brush to write Chinese characters. Brush, ink and paper are the instruments used in calligraphy to produce varied effects. Different methods for the use of ink are used including the use of thick ink, light ink, dry ink, missing ink, wet, withered ink and swelling ink. An ink slab is indispensable for Chinese calligraphy. Generations of Chinese calligraphists have counted on it to add to the artistic effects of their works. Ink sticks include both black and colored ones. A good ink slab is not only a valuable and practical cultural instrument but also a piece of art useful in the arts of painting, calligraphy, word carving, and sculpture.

The structure of Chinese characters and their rich connotations make them an ideal calligraphic medium. A soft and elastic ink brushes is an ideal tool to express the various calligraphy styles. Brushes of different sizes and materials (sheep wool or wolf wool) are used to write characters of various types and sizes.

There are mainly five styles of calligraphy popular among calligraphers that are closely interrelated and each has its own shapes and features. The seal form is categorized by tortoise shell script, bronze script, Warring States seal script and the small seal script. The tortoise shell script was the original one. Other scripts developed later. The bronze script originated from the tortoise shell script, and was used for inscriptions on bronze objects. The Warring States seal, represented chiefly by the "inscriptions on drum stones," was more proportionate in form. It was considered poised, elegant, lively and vigorous. Developed on the basis of the Warring States seal script, the small seal script became the standardized form for seal scripts after the first Emperor of Qin unified China. Its structures are long and round with thick and thin strokes. The strokes were smooth rather than sharp at the two ends, and were considered very aesthetic.

The Official Script (Zuo Script, Shi Script) has a very decorative shape with wide, flat strokes extending on two sides. Its strokes are undulating and its horizontal strokes have the shapes of the silkworm head and the swallow tail. It achieved the highest artistic level in the Han Dynasty. The various styles may be square, dignified and refined, elegant, forceful, rigorous, plain and natural. The Official Scripts in different dynasties had their own characters. Take the Official Script in the Tang Dynasty as an example. It

stressed the outward form with thick smooth strokes and a more magnificent style but lacking vigor and appeal.

The Regular Script (Zheng Script) developed in the Wei, the Jin, the Southern and the Northern dynasties, and culminated in the Tang Dynasty. Its forms are square but varied and its strokes follow strict rules. The dots, bending and straight strokes are coordinated. Yan Zhenqin and Liu Gongquan are very famous calligraphers of the Regular Script in the Tang Dynasty.

The Cursive Script (Simple, Hasty Script) appeared in the seal script period and formed its independent style during the Han Dynasty. This script could be subdivided into official cursive script, current cursive script and wild cursive script. The structure of the official cursive script was simple and concise. There are some connections between the strokes but the words were not connected. The horizontal and the falling strokes had a vertical tendency, which typified the undulating forms of the official script. Shi You, Zhang Zhi and Du Cao in the Han Dynasty and Suo Jing and Lu Ji in the Western Jin Dynasty are among the famous official cursive script calligraphists. The current cursive script (the small cursive script) was developed based on the official cursive script. It adopted the touches and the tendencies of the regular script, but eliminated the undulation of the strokes. The words above and below are often connected and the components of the words were generally used in common forms. It was more flowing and rhythmic. It could be written swiftly for it facilitated the changing and turning of the strokes. The famous calligraphist of the current cursive script is Wang Xianzhi, the son of Wang Xizhi (the famous calligrapher of the cursive script calligraphy from the Eastern Jin Dynasty). The Wild Cursive Script (the Big Cursive Script) was even freer and wider. Some of the famous script calligraphists include Zhang Xu and Huai Su from the Tang Dynasty. The Cursive Script gradually shifted its focus from stressing utility to emphasizing aesthetic appeal in the course of its development. It became a pure form of art after losing its practical value.

The Running Script (Xing Ya Script) is a script between the Cursive script and the Regular Script. People compare it with a floating cloud or a flowing stream, for it gives calligraphy a natural and vivid impression. Its dots and strokes are connected by a gossamer line and its lively strokes follow and turn vigorously. The graceful and flowing style of the Running Script replaced the old plain style and brought the running script to a new level of perfection. Poets like Cia Xiang, Su Shi, Huang Tingjian and Mi Fu of the Song Dynasty were all well versed in running script calligraphy through which their sentiments were naturally expressed.

Maneuverability is one important element in Chinese calligraphy. It requires controlling the brush on the paper at the right speed with the right force. The speed, quick or slow, is controlled by the dexterous use of the brush. In order to create the effects of various types like brush sharpness, mid-way, side cutting, hidden or exposed point, the calligrapher has to control not only his speed but also the pressure on his brush when writing. Generally the lines should be written with force to create a feeling of substance.

There are more than ten writing techniques in calligraphy. For instance, the strokes include starting strokes, closing strokes, curved strokes and straight strokes etc. The vigor of the writing is created through the strength of the strokes. The strokes can be robust or gentle. A certain inner vigor is shown through a stroke. The momentum of writing means the tendency of the strokes. Tendencies of strokes are continuous even if the strokes are not actually continuous. Strokes and dots can be written in different forms but their tendencies are unified.

Structure is another important element in calligraphy. Structure of the script in calligraphy involves the suitable and artistic arrangement of the strokes which are based on the form and the writer's aesthetic interest. In order to make the character combinations seem full of life and animation, the layout of the points and the execution of the brush movement must stress balance, escape and supplement, facing up and reversing, capping and piercing, filling a blank, siding, covering, increasing and decreasing. Principles that contribute to the beauty of a script include density, fullness, concentration, proportion, coordination and harmony as well.

Style is the third element of calligraphy. Writers in different moods create different styles. The mood of writing refers to the spirits and sentiments of the writer expressed through the written scripts. A combination of beauty in form and in the quality of the work can give a vivid presentation of a producer's accomplishments and taste. The depth and breadth of the knowledge of a producer forms the bases of his work's form and quality. In other words, the simple lines and spots of calligraphy include the practical function of communicating feelings as well as an aesthetic function. A producer can express his mood, feelings, will, ideas and pursuit of beauty by using calligraphy as media.

Calligraphy is an expression of the outlook on culture, history and life through the various ages throughout Chinese history.

By the way, Chinese calligraphy stresses the overall layout among words and lines. A good calligraphy must have an overall harmoniousness through its changes. For example, calligraphy in the cursive script or the running script often increases the interconnection between the words and the continuity of the momentum so as to achieve a rhythm. In respect to the arrangement of words, the following aspects need to be considered: the appropriate proportions of the dense and sparse; the dark blank; the long, short, thick, or slender strokes; and the staggering of the big and small sizes. In fact, one has to practice stroke by stroke and word by word until he grasps the spirit of the practice. After a long period of practice he can become an excellent calligrapher. This practice is believed to be a good exercise to temper one's character and cultivate his personality. It is an active way of keeping writers fit and healthy. The practice is a relaxing and self-entertaining process. Many calligraphers throughout history were well known for their longevity. Chinese calligraphy has lost its practical value and has gradually become a purely artistic form. This is due to the invention of other writing instruments such as pencils, ink pens and ball-point pens. Some Chinese love this art and continue practicing it all their lives. Chinese calligraphy has spread to neighboring Asian countries for it is considered an elegant art form. It has become a unique feature of Oriental art as the Chinese culture spread to Japan, Korea, Vietnam and Singapore.

Section 2 Long History

Chinese calligraphy has undergone numerous stages such as the Stage of the Script on Shell and Bone, the Scrip on Bronze Vessels, the Big Seal Scrip, the small Seal Script, the Official Scrip, the Cursive Script, the Running Script an finally the Regular Script.

Calligraphy's development through history can be divided into three periods. The Pre-Qin Period (before 221 BC) is the period of early beginnings. According to an ancient legend story, Cang Jie was the person to make the characters. He was the historian of the Yellow Emperor and the emperor asked him to make characters. After observing the sun, the moon, the stars and phenomena in the sky as well as the traces and prints of birds and animals on the ground, he created characters using the techniques of pictography, association and indication. Of course, it is only a story. Over 100 of carved signs of more than 20 types are discovered on the potteries made 6,000 years ago in Banpo (Shaanxi Province). Some of them are the same as the characters found on the Cang Jie's Tomb carved in the Han Dynasty to memorize his achievement. The signs might be the earliest Chinese characters. Chinese calligraphy followed the appearance of the Chinese characters. An inscription on a piece of pottery, which was unearthed in the ruins of the ancient Longshan Culture (Shandong Province), has been considered the most ancient calligraphic work dated cir-

ca 4,300 years ago by many calligraphic historians. Before Chinese characters were invented, people used brushes to draw lines on pottery. It has been discovered that various thicknesses of lines (pretty and smooth) were drawn with elastic brushes on pottery in the primitive Chinese society. The characters were carved on bones and tortoise shells in the Shang Dynasty for divination practice. They are called "shell characters" by the archeologists. About one hundred years ago, a Chinese expert first recognized them on the shells and bones sold as medical herbs called "dragon bones". They are mature early Chinese characters. Among the 3,500 characters discovered, archeologists can understand the meaning of 1,500 ones. A large number of shells and bones with carved characters of the West Zhou Dynasty were unearthed in Phoenix Village (Shaanxi Province) in 1976. Each cut is clear and strong and all of them are well formed. The inscriptions on the bronze utensils came into being between the Shang (16th century—1066 B. C.) and Zhou Dynasty (1066 B. C. —771·B. C.). They are called " gold characters" since all metals were called "gold" in ancient time. They are of high value in studying the ancient society and they are specially dear to calligraphers who are interested in the ancient style. The art developed from inscriptions on tortoise shells and ox bones formed Dazhuan and Xiaozhuan. The First Emperor of the Qin Dynasty ordered the Prime Minister Li Si put the characters of the whole China standardized. Li Si made the seal characters, which were simpler and easier to write and read. Cheng Miao collected and organized the even simpler style among the folk people in the Qin Dynasty—the official script. The curving strokes of the seal style were changed into square and straight strokes, losing the characteristic of pictography. The emergence of the official style was a dividing line and land mark in the Chinese characters' development.

The second period is from the Western Han Dynasty (206B. C. —24A. D.) to the Tang period (618—907). It is the period of maturity. Chinese used to write words on books made of bamboo with brushes. When paper was invented in the Han Dynasty (206B. C. —220A. D.), Chinese started to write with brushes and paper. The Regular Script came into use at the end of the Han Dynasty. It was invented by Wang Cizhong and was developed by Zhong Yao and Wang Xizhi during the Wei and Jin Dynasty (265—420). The style reached a peak in the Sui (581—618) and Tang (618—907) dynasties. It has been used in China for more than 1,700 years and continues to be used today.

The sacred things were often carved on stones for a memory in ancient times. Some pieces of stone with carved inscriptions of the early Qin period are not steles in a real sense. The stele served 3 purposes of applications in the early time of the Qin Dynasty: measuring time, being erected in front of a house to hold farming animals and lowering the coffin down to the grave by winding a rope around it. The steles having these purpose had no inscriptions. Characters of praise began to be carved on steles in the early time of the East Han Dynasty (206—220). The steles with inscriptions carved on after this period became a treasure of culture and a corridor of calligraphy. The calligraphers of the different times carved on steles made their contributions to the process and their works of variety and beauty had been carved on steles.

Chinese calligraphy entered its golden age during the Sui and Tang period. Writing scripts with a brush gradually developed into an art form. The art involves the technique, the vigor, the momentum and the mood of writing. Philosophy has exerted a strong influence on calligraphy throughout history. Both Taoist and Confucius theories have stamped a deep brand upon calligraphic aesthetics. For instance, the Yin and Yang in the doctrine of changes, and the Way of nature, as well as the Confucian doctrine of the mean, all influenced the styles of calligraphy. Meanwhile, calligraphy has embodied the meaning of traditional philosophies in the form of art.

From the Five Dynasties (907—960) to the end of the Qing Dynasty (1644—1911), which was the modern period of calligraphic development, there has been individualistic development. Some literary works have been copied by calligraphers. Therefore, the presentation of these literary works of calligraphy also enables people to enjoy the beauty of both the art of calligraphy and literature at the same time. For instance, Su Shi, a famous poet and calligrapher of the Song Dynasty (960—1279), wrote many poems and copied them by calligraphy. People can admire the art of his calligraphy and his poems at the same time. A great number of outstanding calligraphers have emerged in ancient and moderate China. Take Wang Xizhi (321—379) and his son Wang Xianzhi (344—386) of the Eastern Jin Dynasty as examples. They created a flowing new style. Their calligraphy has the character of free and natural beauty. The beautiful style has remained very popular through later generations. Yan Zhenqing (708—784) of the Tang Dynasty created the style of regular script. His style has been followed by later generations, because his work has a strong and robust character. Mi Fu (1051—1107) of the Song Dynasty is well known for his cursive hand and running hand. The main character of his work is beautifully bold and flowing. Zheng Banqiao (1693—1765) of the Qing Dynasty created calligraphy which exhibits exotic and clumsy beauty. Yu Youren (1879—1964) blended the stone rubbing school and the model book school into one and created a new school. In modern times, due to the invention of other writing instruments, such as the pen, pencil and ball-point pen which are convenient and soon gained popularity, Chinese calligraphy lost, much of its practical and gradually became a purely artistic form. There are still quite many people, especially the older generation, who love this art and keep practicing it all their lives as a hobby.

Decorative calligraphy can be found everywhere in China, especially in temples and pagodas, on the walls of caves, on the cliffs of mountains and on the sides of monuments. Chinese calligraphy has had a far-reaching influence in countries like Japan, Korea and Indo-China.

Section 3   Master Pieces of Calligraphy

Wang Xizhi's *The Foreword to Lanting Pavilion*

Wang Xizhi created his own style using official script, regular characters, running hand and cursive script. *The Foreword to Lanting Pavilion* is a typical example of his running hand. It is said, when he and some scholars gathered at Lanting Pavilion for an old sacrificial ceremony, they drank and wrote poems to enjoy themselves on the bank of a river. The great calligrapher and poet, wrote a foreword to these poems as *the Foreword to Lanting Pavilion*. It was naturally written from the beginning to the end in running hand and regular script. The vertical columns are almost equal in length. However, since the characters are of different sizes, the vertical columns are not always straight to the bottom. The work was completed in rhymes. The thick strokes are robust but not awkward; while the narrow strokes are delicate but not weak. These strong, clear-cut lines and round mellow forms present people with a fresh, clear and exquisite work of art. Later on he failed to copy his original work several times and he felt the original effect could not be reproduced. The work is regarded as the best example of running hand school. The Emperor TaiZong of the Tang Dynasty (627—649) finally acquired the work since he treasured the work. The original artwork was buried with him after his death. His tomb was robbed and the original work disappeared. Only copies exist today. The copies written by other famous calligraphers carried their own styles.

Yan Zhenqing's *The Yan Qinli Tablet*

Yan Zhengqing was both a calligrapher and a Tang minister. He absorbed the strengths of past masters and created his own style in both regular script and running hand. His works reflect the prosperity and strength of the Tang Dynasty (618—907). The style of his 138 works, which represents his character and education, is robust, solemn and elegant. This master piece was produced when he was 71 years old. The

characters are smoothly and energetically written with an effect of forceful penmanship produced. The long slanting lines and long vertical stems of the typical brush strokes are unique. His style has vigor, elegance and an atmosphere of magnificence that can be clearly seen in *The Yan Qinli Tablet*.

Liu Gongquan's *Xuanbi Pagoda Tablet*

Liu Gongquan was a calligrapher of the Tang period. He was famous for writing regular characters. He created a style with a firm and forceful framework of strokes. His most famous work *Xuanbi Pagoda Tablet* (841) tells the story of a master monk, Dada, being favorably treated by the emperors of the Tang Dynasty. The work is an example that emphasizes a strong idea of buildup. The basic feature of the work is having "bones." He used the middle edge of the brush, square or round, and raising and pressing his strokes. The slanting lines are generally produced with a heavy force when moving to the right and with a light touch when moving to the left. The compact and stiff structure is intense inside and relaxed outside. The style of the work is sharp and vigorous with hard and bony strokes and it is a good model for beginners to copy.

Su Shi's *Book of handwritten Poems Written in April at Huangzhou*

Su Shi (1037—1101) of the Northern Song Dynasty made a strong contribution to the fields of calligraphy, painting and writing. He is well known by later generations for his running hand and regular script. He established a style with a sense of fullness and charm, which became the typical style of implied meaning during the Song (960—1279) and Yuan (1271—1368) periods.

When he was the prefectural magistrate of Huzhou, he wrote some poems about malpractice in the courts and the harm caused to ordinary people. He was sent to prison because of the poems. Later on, he was released and given a post at Huangzhou (in Hubei Province). He wrote two poems expressing his indignation and describing his hard life and sorrows in Huangzhou. His *Book of handwritten Poems Written in April at Huangzhou* consisted of these two poems written with five characters per line on paper. His poems and calligraphy complement each other to express his sorrows for his life and worries about the country. The work is considered to be his greatest achievement in running hand script. The characters were written alternately in regular form and running hand with tough, full strokes. People compare his heavy brushwork with a crouched bear and his lighter bush strokes with a flying swallow. The composition includes a good use of space. The formation of small and large script, thick and thin characters, and strong and light ink create a rhythm throughout the work. The increased quickness of the brush, like a torrent of water, expressed his gloomy mood.

Chapter 10

Chinese Painting and It's Component Parts

Xiaoxia Mao and Helen Yang

Painting and calligraphy are regarded as two treasured arts in China. Ancient Chinese learned scholars pursue four skills including Zheng (a kind of musical instrument), chess, calligraphy and painting. The four skills were as a good exercise to temper one's character and cultivate one's personality.

Section 1 Traditional Chinese Painting

Chinese painting possesses its unique national character though it has some principles in common with Western painting from an aesthetic point of view. For instance, it seldom follows the convention of central focus perspective to realistic portrayal, but gives the painters their freedom on artistic conception, structural composition and method of expression to express their subjective feelings. Chinese painting has also absorbed the best of the art forms, such as poetry, calligraphy and seal engraving. Therefore, some great painters are also great poets and calligraphers as well. Chinese painting refers to paintings painted following traditional principles formed through the ages and using the special Chinese brush and ink. It emphasizes Inspiration comes from close observation and understanding of Nature. Both the spirit and the form are reflected in the painting. It has developed its own style, techniques and a complete system of art to express the aesthetics of the nation. It involves the use of Chinese brushes, inks, ink-stones, Xuan paper, silk, etc.

Generally, Chinese painting has three categories: flower-bird painting, figure painting, and landscape painting. These three classifications can be divided into additional branches. For instance, Flower-bird painting's major objects of depiction are animals and plants divided into such branches as flowers, vegetables, fruits, grasses, insects, birds, fish, prawns, crabs, animals and etc. It can also be divided into eight parts by subject matter. The subjects are flowers, birds, fish, insects, animals, landscapes, buildings and figures. Chinese paintings are further divided into four categories according to the format of murals, scrolls, screens, fans and albums.

In the long course of historical development, traditional Chinese painting has been influenced by Buddhist art paintings and the Western arts. Figure painting mainly focuses on portraying people's life and activities to reflect the reality of society directly. Paintings based on history, reality, stories and activities of mythical characters emerged in a large number. It embodies the aesthetic consciousness of the Chinese nation, as well as presenting an overall view of social ideology in politics, religion, philosophy, ethics and art. The various aspects include morality, human relationships, feudal ethics and rites, historical stories, legends and fairy tales, social customs, Buddhist monks, Taoist priests, pretty ladies and portraits. Besides, Confucius morality and virtues, feudal ideology, the philosophy of being faithful to one's ruler are all

propagated in the highly harmonious form of figure painting art. Ancient painters used figure painting portrays social ideology, historical events and represent the spiritual and material life of the people of all classes. Chinese ancient figure painting conveyed Confucius aesthetic and artistic ideology by possessing human virtues as "humanity", "justice", "courage", "wisdom", "selflessness" and "goodness". A perfect harmony of man and nature is fostered and shaped.

Traditional Chinese figure paintings included five major categories: detailed brushwork, sketchy brushwork, outline drawing, free hand brushwork and splash-ink. Painters emphasized the distinction between the primary and the secondary, and the detailed and the sketchy. In narrative paintings, space was sectioned according to the landscape of the interior of the building. The repeated appearance of the subject figure breaks through the time and space limitation to show the course of the events. Sometimes, in order to express the figures' different characters and inner nature, they are depicted with exaggerated beauty.

Landscape painting aims to portray all natural landscape like famous mountains and rivers, fields and villages, scenic beauty and spots, city gardens, buildings, boats, bridges etc. When artists create rich and colorful natural landscapes, they embody their conception of nature, aesthetic awareness, wisdom and sentiment. The principle of Chinese landscape painting is nature is the source of artistic imagination and creation. A good landscape painting is a vivid manifestation of culture of traditional Chinese ideology. What landscape painting builds is a scene where man and nature, feelings and settings are in harmony. Painters try to preserve their understanding and perception of the whole natural world. The soul of traditional Chinese landscape painting is artistic conception.

Flower-and-bird Painting takes animals and plants as subjects. It can be subdivided into the paintings of flowers, birds, animals, fish, shells, fruits, vegetables, insects, grasses. Instead of simply focusing on the surface features of the objects, artists express their understanding, sentiment and attitude to nature, society and life to achieve the purpose of expressing ideas through certain objects. Flower-and-bird Paintings are very expressive medium and carriers of painter's emotion and ideas and knowledge. Since the flowers and birds in the painting are the medium and carriers by which the painters' emotions and ideas, sometimes a painting is not confined by the accurate description of the objects. Birds and flowers painting firmly grasps a certain relationship between natural world and the painter's experience, thinking and feeling and gives intensified expression of this affinity or association. It not only stresses the truthfulness but attaches importance to the expression of the good and the beautiful things. Sometimes artists seek after similarities and dissimilarities to exhibit the charm of the objects and their feelings.

Chinese painting has a long history over several thousand years. Traditional Chinese painting was very rudimentary in the West-East Han Dynasties and Six Dynasties (206B. C. —589A. D.). The development of Chinese painting, through the ages, constitutes an important part of the history of Chinese culture.

Figure painting is the earliest kind of traditional Chinese painting since human activities were the major objects of description. The earliest murals of human figures were found in the Zhou Dynasty (1066 B. C. — 256 B. C.). A large number of figure paintings appeared from the Warring States Period (403 B. C. —221 B. C.) to the Qin (221 B. C. —206 B. C.) and Han (206 B. C. —220A. D.) periods. Religious paintings with human figures became popular due to the introduction of Buddhism and the emergence of professional painters. The techniques used in figure painting matured between the Wei (220—265), Jin (265—420) periods.

The important period for its development should be credited to the Wei and Jin (265—420) period, the Southern (420—589) and Northern period (386—534), the Sui (581—618) and Tang (618—907) period. Gu Kaizhi of the Jin Dynasty is the representative of the first group of figure painters contributed to the foundation of the important tradition of the Chinese figure painting. Figure paintings of the Tang Dynasty were not only the imposing images of emperors but also the pretty ladies with the typical bearings of the Tang Dynasty. The character's individuality, disposition and the well-developed graceful manners were expressed. Wu Daozi, a famous painter of the Tang Dynasty, brought religious figure painting to a more lively, touching and new state.

Another important period for figure painting development was during the Five Dynasties (907—960) and the Song (960—1279) dynasties . Genre paintings and historical story paintings blossomed owing to the political and economic development of the Song Dynasty. Artists expressed complicated inner feeling, different characters, inner nature and social attributes of the characters in their figure paintings.

Paintings of gentlemen, pretty ladies and ancient people constituted the main part of the literary figure paintings of the Yuan (1271—1368), Ming (1368—1644) and Qing (1644—1911) dynasties. Artists focused on details including facial expression, gestures, and movements in sketching the hats, clothes, surroundings and other property. A painter's emotion and style was expressed.

Ancient landscape painting became an independent category during the Sui (581—618) and Tang (618—907) dynasties. Painters went beyond passively copying nature. They tried to express their understanding and perception of the whole natural world. Their thought and emotion, ideal and desire were all put into the limited picturesque scene. In order to seek the unity of the form and spirit, to realize the unity of feeling and the natural setting, artists tried to create artistic conception through an emphasis on expressing their thought and feelings.

Landscape painting from the Five Dynasties (907—960) and the Song period (960—1279) are typically characterized by harmony between nature and man, the uniformity of poetry and painting, as well as a blending of emotion with scenery. Famous painters, and many different schools, appeared thereafter. Some artists only painted a suggestion of a scene or landscape rather than realistically expressing the entire picture. The themes of the majority of landscape paintings in the Yuan Dynasty (1279—1368) were mostly about living in the mountains or about secluded fishermen. Painters in the Ming (1368—1644) and Qing (1644—1911) periods achieved the unity of poetry, calligraphy and pictures in their traditional Chinese landscape painting.

Flower-and-bird painting took rough shape until the Hans (206 B. C. —220 A. D.) and the Six Dynasties. It became fully developed after the Tang Dynasty (618—907), the Five Dynasties (907—960) and the Northern Song Dynasty (960—1279). The Imperial Flower-and-bird Painting had great development featured by fine brushwork, coloring, sketching, details, truthfulness, and elaborate style. The compendious, unrestrained Xie Yi flower-and-bird Painting appeared. Subjects such plums, orchid, bamboo, chrysanthemum became very popular among the literati painters. Xie Yi Flower-and-bird painting in ink and wash had immense influence to the development and prosperity of the Xie Yi flower-and-bird painting in the Yuan (1271—1368) and Ming (1368—1644) dynasties. An upsurge in Baimiao Flower Painting, which was featured by detailed brushwork without color, also sprang up during the Song period.

A Chinese painting is drawn on Xuan paper (a special kind of rice paper) or silk using brushes, ink, Chinese pigments and seals. Chinese painting is highly regarded for its original style and it has its own unique national characteristics and independent systems. It consists of an aesthetic system which is entirely different from that of the West. For instance, Chinese painting gives the painter freedom of artistic conception, structural composition and methods of expression in order to better express his subjective feelings instead of following the convention of a central focus perspective found in realistic portrayals. It is using the form to express the spirit. Literally, painting the feeling (Xieyi) is a fundamental approach to the Chinese pictorial art.

Another character of Chinese painting is to combine calligraphy, poetry and seal engraving in one

painting. For instance, sometimes a good painting includes a good poem written with calligraphy. This is why some well-known painting masters are also great poets and calligraphers. The indispensable elements supplement and enrich each other by contributing to the beauty of the whole picture.

Furthermore, a Chinese painting combines the object with the painter's concept of turning a natural image into an "artistic image" and filling that object with feelings. Not all the objects are drawn on the paper so as to leave some space for the viewer's imagination. People often compare a good painting as a good poem. Chinese artists learn to highlight the main part and focus on the comparison between the empty part and the filled part. They make harmonious arrangement of the empty part and the filled part. They also tend to use "moving perspective" in their works which is quite different from naturalism. Their eyes make use of the nature.

The use of lines is important in Chinese painting. There are eighteen different ways of drawing lines with the brush in figure painting. The brush techniques emphasized line drawing, stylized expressions of shade and texture, the dotting method and the application of color. The major features of Chinese painting are listed below:

- Depicting the sentiments
- Having "Qiyun" in the painting
- Using imagination to depict the marvelous
- Likeness in spirit residing in unlikeness
- Taking nature as a teacher and the heart as a source of inspiration

The experience of a painter is enshrined in the phrase "Qiyun". "Qi" is cosmic spirit, literally meaning "breath" or "vapor" that vitalizes all things and gives life and growth to them. "Yun" refers to the charm and rhyme of a painting. It is the task of an artist to attune himself to this cosmic spirit and let it infuse him with energy so that in a moment of inspiration, he may become the vehicle for its expression.

Traditional Chinese painting falls into two categories in terms of method of expression. First, it literally paints the feeling which is marked by exaggeration of form and liberal use of ink. Secondly, it meticulously uses brushwork which is characterized by strict and detailed representation of the subject. Therefore, for methods of depiction, there is fine colored brushwork, and bold, unrestrained freehand brushwork.

The Three Friends in Winter is a painting of pine, bamboo and yellow sweets under the pseudonym of Qing Teng in the style of Xu Wei (1521—1593, the Ming Dynasty). Some favorite symbolic objects are used in the painting. For example, pine is as a symbol of longevity, bamboo is as a symbol of ever flourishing, and plum blossom is as a symbol of sturdiness and chastity.

Section 2 Calligraphy's Relationship with Chinese Painting

Chinese calligraphy is of great importance among the traditional Chinese fine arts like Chinese painting. Chinese painting and calligraphy are different branches of art stemming from the same origin. The art of Chinese calligraphy arose mainly from the shape and structure of the Chinese characters and the use of a Chinese brush which is also good for painting. The lines used in painting are variations of the points and lines of calligraphy. Besides, traditional Chinese painting and calligraphy use the same kind of tools. They influence each other and create another artistic feature. Therefore, they are closely linked in terms of their expression of thoughts and feelings. The infancy of Chinese painting predated the appearance of written characters. However, a fine piece of calligraphy, known as a treasure in ink, is often more treasured by a collector of art than a good painting. Calligraphy has been regarded as a form of visual art in China.

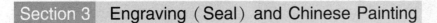

Section 3 Engraving（Seal）and Chinese Painting

The cutting of inscriptions on tortoise shells began during the late Shang Dynasty（3,000 years ago）. People started to engrave their names on utensils and documents to claim ownership or for identification in the Qin Dynasty（2,000 years ago）. The engraving on Chinese paintings with poems attached creates a harmonious impression. Throughout history, seals have also been popular among the literati who would display their seals on scrolls of calligraphy and on paintings. Painters use seals in their paintings too.

Chinese Emperors regarded a seal as a symbol of power. An emperor's seal was called Xi. It symbolized authority to all his inferiors. Today, Chinese people frequently mark their favorite books with a seal with their names on it. Government of different levels in China, issue orders that are endorsed with official seals.

Stone is the most widely used material though the materials used for engraving could be jade, gold, brass, stone or wood. China's four distinguished stones for seal-making are Shoushan Stone（pyrophyllite）found near Fuzhou of Fujian Province, Qingtian Stone（soap stone）from Zhejiang Province, Balin Stone from Inner Mongolia and Changhua stone found in Zhejiang Province.

Chapter 11

Traditional Chinese Medicine

Frits Buijs and Xiaoxia Mao

Traditional Chinese medicine (TCM), consists of traditional medical practice which originated in China and developed over several thousand years. Due to its deep roots and thousands of years' development without any outside influence from other medical systems, TCM has not only accumulated a rich experience in preventing and treating diseases, but also made remarkable contributions to the wealth of China and the treatment of diseases in the whole world. In principle, TCM employs a method of analysis and synthesis, investigating on a macro level the internal systems of the human body and their mutual relationships with the internal and external environment. It also explains the fundamental laws that govern the functioning of the human organism, health maintenance and application of the theories on the treatment and prevention of diseases. The TCM medical treatment is composed of the pillars including Acupuncture, Massage, Herbal Medicines, cupping, Moxibustion and Qi Gong. Other therapeutic methods of treatment are diet therapeutic methods, Gua Sha (pressuring and scraping the skin with a rounded object) and Taijiquan (Tai Chi Ch'uan). TCM is a treasure house in the country's fine cultural traditions.

Section 1   A Brief History of TCM and Its Development

The use of plants as medicine in China can be dated back to the origin of mankind; however, the exact origins of traditional Chinese medicine are vague. Around 2, 500 BC the word *doctor* and *medicine* already appeared in the written Chinese language. Afterwards, in the ancient time, there were many medical texts written, however, most of them did not survive the test of time (Fu, n. d.).

Between 2698 and 2596 BC, the Yellow Emperor supposedly wrote the book, *Basics Questions of Internal Medicine*, or *Huangdi Neijing*. There are now also modern scholars who think that the book was composed by an anonymous scholar over two thousand years ago. During the Shang Dynasty (early 17th century BC to 11th century BC), medical herb decoctions were being produced. Professional doctors appeared during the Western Zhou period (11th century BC to 771 BC) . *The Book of Songs* is a record of more than 50 species of plants which can be used as medicine. The *Classic of Mountains and Rivers* mentions 126 kinds of TCM and their use. People learned that the spreading of diseases could be increased by an abnormal climate and that epidemic diseases were infectious during the Western Zhou period.

The *Pharmacopoeia of Sheng Nong (Sheng Nong Ben Cao Jing)* was written, describing all the known herbal medicines of that time in the Han Dynasty. Legend tells us that the ancient "Shen Nong" tasted a hundred species of herbs in order to specify, which plants or herbs were useful for curing certain illnesses or diseases and which types were harmful to human health. The experiments were repeated and the knowledge of herbs was passed down in the *Canon of Herbs*. This accumulation of experiences leads to the birth of early Chinese medicine and health preservation. Hua Tuo (141—208A. D.) was a medical scientist in the East Han Dynasty. He applied either herbs or needles for acupuncture remarkably for simplicity and efficaciousness. He invented an effective herbal medicine called "Mafeisan" for patients during operation who suffered from gastric or intestinal obstruction. His invention and practice exhibit China's level of anesthesia and surgery at the time which is at least 1, 600 years earlier than the use of anaesthetic in the Western medicine.

Since medicine was seen as important by the emperors of the Northern Song Dynasty, the imperial governments organized a series of revisions of the old medical publications. They republished books written more than 140 years earlier. Many insightful physicians began advocating the study of these theoretical works and began to pay attention to the analyses of the pathological and pathogenic causes of diseases. As a result a thriving academic atmosphere flourished in the medical circles at that time.

Due to the TCM development during the previous centuries, eventually, in the 16th century *The General Outlines and Divisions of Herbal Medicine* (*Ben Cao Gang Mu*) was written which is the greatest contribution to Chinese herbal medicine in history (Fu, n. d.).

The Nationalist government encouraged the promotion of Westernization in China, as the government at that time did not want China to lag behind in scientific progress led by Western countries during the Revolution in 1911. Nevertheless, TCM was still used to treat illnesses and diseases in the rural communities.

Impressed by the results of the Chinese medicine which was used during the Long March (1934—1935), Mao made great efforts to revitalize medical tradition in China (AMF, 2007) . For instance, he called on doctors to improve their skills in traditional Chinese medicine and bring traditional Chinese medicine to the forefront. He said: "… only then can we shoulder the tremendous task of looking after the health of several hundred millions of people. " Doctors were encouraged to explain the theory and principles of traditional Chinese medicine from a modern scientific point of view, and to develop new ways of combining traditional Chinese medical treatments with other Chinese medicine and Western medicine. Great progress was made from the 1950s to 1965, as the government has formulated a series of guiding principles and policies to support and promote the development of TCM since the 1950s. There were at least 280, 000 doctors of Chinese medicine working in medical institutions. The Academy of Traditional Chinese Medicine and 21 colleges of Chinese medicine were organized. Additionally, some hospitals of traditional medicine were established or reinforced. Some important results were achieved by combining Chinese and Western medicine. A large number of books and textbooks about Chinese medicine and pharmacology were published.

A national working conference on Chinese and Chinese-Western medicine was held in 1980. The conference advocated the long-term co-existence and simultaneous development of the three branches of medicine: Chinese medicine, traditional Chinese medicine and Western medicine.

In China and throughout the world, TCM is gaining in importance as part of the medical sciences. In large public hospitals in Chinese cities, both traditional Chinese and Western approaches are offered as medical treatment. Very few practitioner of Western medicine in China reject traditional Chinese medicine. In the past 50 years, TCM has continued to be distinct branch of modern medical practice. Chinese doctors have made efforts to place TCM on a firmer Western scientific empirical and methodological basis. They have tried to integrate Chinese and Western medical traditions. The ongoing effort to promote and further develop TCM will surely continue to make remarkable contributions to the common health of mankind.

Section 2   Basic Fundamental Theories

The foundation principles of Chinese medicine are not necessarily uniform, and are based on several

fundamental theories. Chinese medicine is an observational medicine which gradually included theories and philosophies about the understanding of life and the universe during the centuries. These days, Chinese medicine mainly focuses on harmonizing the body on the inside and with the environment. There are many theories and principles with regard to TCM, and this section will introduce two main theories which are widely acknowledged in the field of TCM.

Yin and Yang Theory

In Chinese medicine, life is understood as the balance between Yin and Yang. Yin is the dark and negative element, which also means that it is feminine, cold, wet, soft, passive, downward seeking, consuming and corresponds to the night (YYH, 2006). It is often symbolized by water and earth. On the contrary, Yang is the bright and positive element, which also means that it is masculine, warm, dry, hard, active, upward seeking, producing and correspond to the daytime. It is symbolized by fire and air. Yin and Yang are mutually exclusive which indicates that the two elements have opposite qualities.

However, neither of the two can exist without the other. Everything contains aspects of both Yin and Yang, so that even extreme Yang contains the seed of Yin and vice versa (YYH, 2006). Moreover, the two elements are mutually transformative. To put it simply, extreme Yin (cold/wet) extinguishes Yang (fire), extreme Yang (fire) burns up Yin (water), and eventually, extreme Yin transforms into Yang and vice versa (YYH, 2006). Thus, it is obvious that there exists an interdependent relationship between Yin and Yang. Nevertheless, as mentioned above, Yin and Yang are never in an exact balance, which means that in reality Yin and Yang are always in a dynamic relationship. In normal circumstances, the balance between Yin and Yang is always constantly changing (TCM basics, 2006).

In Chinese medicine, health is represented as a balance between Yin and Yang. When the two elements are in relative balance, they constitute a state of harmony and health in the body. Out of balance it leads to illness. For example, it is generally stated that "… conditions such as insomnia and night sweats are often Yin related conditions. If the symptoms occur during the day, the condition is more likely to be related to the Yang energies of the body" (YYH, 2006). The reason why the two elements should be in relative balance is because normally, the shift of balance between them is natural. For example, when a person is angry, his/her fury signifies Yang. When he/she gradually calms down, a peaceful state overcomes the furious mood and in the end, Yin dominates. However, if the balance is constantly altered it will bring imbalance in the human body, which leads to disease and therefore, treatment must be focused on adjusting Yin and Yang back to their basic state of relative balance (TCMbasics, 2006). Traditional Chinese medicine practitioners apply the Yin and Yang theory to determine the exact nature of the imbalance in the human body and then correct it through acupuncture, herbal medicine, exercise, change of diet and change lifestyle, until the balance is restored, which indicates that the patient is healthy.

The Five Element Theory

The Five Elements, also called Wu Xing, Five Phases or Five Movements, represent the processes that are fundamental to the cycles of nature, and therefore correspond to the human body (AWOCM, 2006). The five elements are, metal, wood, water, fire and earth. According to the Five Element theory, everything in the universe, including the human body, is governed by the five elements. Each of the elements has a reason and particular organ and sense to associate with. In the Chinese medicine this can be illustrated more in detail. Fire, generates light and energy and is representing the heart (Yin) and intestine (Yang). Emotions, such as joy and overindulgence create imbalance within this element. Metal implies lung (Yin) and the large intestine (Yang) and emotions like sadness creates imbalance within this element. Wood is regarded as strong and rooted and it represents the liver (Yin) and the gall bladder (Yang). Indecisiveness and anger generate imbalance within this element. Water is related with the kidney (Yin) and urinary bladder (Yang). Fear and paranoia are the emotions which create imbalance within this element. Earth, which is seen as productive, fertile and growth, is associated with the spleen (Yin) and the Stomach (Yang). Pensiveness is the emotion which creates imbalance within this element (AWOCM, 2006).

The system of the five elements shows the characters, the interactions and the relationships among the elements. To put it simply, the five element theory describes two cycles of balance between the five elements, namely the cycle of creation and the cycle of destruction. On the one hand, wood feeds fire, fire creates earth (ashes), earth bears metal, metal collects water and water nourishes wood. On the other hand, wood parts earth, earth absorbs water, water quenches fire, fire melts metal, and metal chops wood.

In traditional Chinese medicine, this is used to interpret the relationship between the physiology and pathology of the human body and the natural environment (TCM basics, 2006) so as to guide clinical diagnosis and treatment. For instance, during treatment, a TCM practitioner may ask a patient many detailed questions which will give clues regarding the nature of his/her imbalances. As for the treatment, the TCM practitioners usually use the law of mutual generation and destruction to create more methods of treatment, such as, "cultivating the earth in order to generate metal", and "supporting the earth to restrict wood" (TCM basics, 2006).

Section 3 Health Preservation

Confucianism, Buddhism and Taoism have health-preserving theories. Confucius' idea was that, nourishing the mind would be the basis of nourishing life. He thought that treatment of the mind should precede treatment of disease, and nourishing the mind should precede nourishing life. In this health-preserving culture, Confucianism and TCM complemented each other. Only by studying and analyzing the health-preserving cultures of different schools can people have a complete knowledge and understanding of it.

Chinese physicians applied the concepts and created the traditional science of health preservation on the basis of Chinese medicinal theories. The first stage of the development of this science was from the Qin Dynasty (221—207 B. C.) to the Tang Dynasty. The main approaches were the use of elixir medicine, the Daoyin method and the sex guide. Emperor Yingzheng issued an imperial edict to seek the elixir of life during the Qin Dynasty. During the Han Dynasty, Emperor Wudi (140—87 B. C.) also issued the same imperial edict and recruited alchemists to produce such a drug. A Taoist physician named Ge Hong of the Eastern Jin Dynasty (265—420) wrote *The Works of Master Bao Pu* after many years of alchemy study. He persuaded people to learn the skills of alchemy and eat a "golden elixir." The book influenced people in the study of alchemy and the use of the golden elixir. The practice gained in popularity during the Tang Dynasty (618—907). Mineral drugs were also popular among the literati and officials during that period. Because of the harmful effects, they gradually became obsolete after the Tang Dynasty.

The well-known physician Zhang Zhongjing of the Han Dynasty explained the functions of the method in health preservation and the disease prevention. Hua Tuo, who was the master surgeon, further developed the Daoyin method with the Five-Animal Exercise. The Five-animal Exercise was patterned after the movements of the tiger, bear, deer, bird and monkey. After Ge Hong emphasized that the function of Qigong was to keep good health inside and prevent evils from the outside, Xu Xun of the Jin Dynasty proposed a way to promote the smooth movement of tendons, bones and muscles and blood circulation through Qigong

exercise. "Daoyin" materials were edited by Tao Hongjing of the Southern and Northern dynasties. He compiled these materials into a special collection that included 12 kinds of regulated breathing, a six-character formula of breathing exercises and eight patterns of movements. They are still widely practiced in China today. During the Sui and Tang dynasties, the Daoyin method was officially recognized by the imperial court as an approach to keep fit and treat diseases.

After the Song Dynasty, the second stage of the development of the Health-Preservation School was to really start emphasizing health preservation. Medical care also began to change with the use of tonics and health-promoting food. A unique health-preservation system for the elderly had essentially taken shape by the Ming and Qing dynasties. Back in the Han and Tang period, Wang Chong and Sun Simiao wrote works on the relationship of food and health preservation. Sun Simiao's *Essential Prescriptions Worthy a Thousand Pieces of Gold* was the first published book on health preservation and medical care for the elderly. Based on their achievements, a number of books about health preservation and food were produced during the Song Dynasty (960—1279). The writers stressed the scientific and practical applications of food since special importance was placed on medical care during that period. *Principles of a Proper Diet* by Hu Sihui, a Yuan Dynasty court physician, is a monograph of high academic value. It combines food nourishing and therapy by introducing nutritive functions, and therapeutic effects. It even includes the methods of cooking various kinds of food. Many scholars and literati also wrote about their personal experiences. For instance, *Longevity and Health Preservation* by Ming's imperial physician, Gong Yanxian, introduced many principles and methods of health preservation as well as a great number of secret prescriptions for maintaining longevity. Gong Juzhong, another imperial physician from the Ming Dynasty, wrote A *Guide to Five Blessings and Longevity and Snow Melted in a Hot Furnace*. These books provide advice on living environments, functional regulations, control of desires, shape-keeping, exercise and health preserving drugs for the elderly. During the Qing Dynasty, a well-known health-preservation specialist named Cao Tingdong wrote *Common Sayings Serving the Aged*. He advocated health preservation through the regulation of the spirit, the control of diet, taking care of one's daily life and Daoyin exercises.

Section 4　Cultural Features and Practical Ways of Health Preservation

TCM and the health-preserving science have evolved into special parts of the traditional Chinese culture. In *Essential Prescriptions Worthy a Thousand Pieces of Gold*, Sun Simiao summed up the morality required from physicians. They should have the desire and responsibility of healing the wounded and rescuing the dying. *The Yellow Emperor's Classic of Internal Medicine* states the idea that: "man can not become immortal or reverse the aging process, however it is possible to prevent one from becoming old before his time and to live a long life". Health care should be carried out throughout one's whole life, particularly during the crucial stage of one's life. TCM stresses the importance of natural circumstances and psychological factors and their relationship with disease. Also the principle of adapting to the change of seasons and climates is emphasized. It professes that the human body is an integral whole. There are links and relationships between the organs and the channels and collaterals. The way the body's organs function and coordinate contributes to the vitality of life. Yin and Yang are two opposite aspects constituting the human body and spirit as a whole. They maintain a state of balanced equilibrium under normal conditions. If one aspect becomes less or more than the other, physiological disorders occur, and disease begins. It is advisable to regulate and control the balance of Yin and Yang. Human life, from its start to its end, contains a series of motions causing internal contradictions in the body. The motions of life include rising and falling, entry and exit. The law of life is the process of metabolism. If the process is blocked, it will lead to disease. Every cell in the human body is always in motion, which makes physical exercise essential to the prevention of disea-ses. Furthermore meditation and Qigong have had a great influence on TCM. Taoist Qigong became medical Qigong and medical theories of nature cultivation as well as self-cultivation have been developed.

An especially important part of TCM is its ways of keeping people in good health. TCM holds that good living habits are important in preventing disease and maintaining good health. For instance, TCM believes that vital energy starts to accumulate in the morning and therefore people are advised to do massage or other physical exercises in the morning to adjust the human organism. This is the reason some Chinese go to a park or riverside in the morning to perform some mild exercises such as Qigong, Taijiquan and strolling. The negative ions of the fresh air help them to invigorate their metabolism and expel any harmful substances ac-quired during the night. TCM also advises people to go to bed early and to get up early.

Emotional traumas are a major cause of disease according to TCM. The Yellow Emperor's *Manual of Internal Medicine* (the Huangdi Neijing) pointed out that there are five kinds of vital energies coming from five internal organs, namely joy, anger, sorrow, melancholy and fear. Joy hurts the heart, anger hurts the liver, sorrow hurts the spleen, melancholy hurts the lungs and fear hurts the kidneys. This means that these emotional factors can cause diseases if there is an excess of any of them. Chinese TCM researchers at-tach great importance to the functions of the emotions in keeping physically fit and healthy. They find that a good emotional state can help improve general well-being and increase longevity. Therefore, they em-phasize a peaceful state of mind and broadmindedness. Doctors report that patients free from emotional bur-dens tend to recover from an illness sooner.

TCM has developed special ways to follow the laws of nature in the four seasons to maintain good health and strengthen the body for a longer life. *Yellow Emperor's Manual of Internal Medicine* states, "a wise way to preserve one's health is to conform to the changes in the four seasons and accordingly adjust one's living habits. " Since many meteorological factors as temperature, humidity, atmospheric pressure, rain and wind all affect body metabolism and internal secretion abilities through the function of the hypothal-amus. In the spring and summer, people should go to sleep a bit later and get up a bit earlier. TCM also maintains that the liver should not be so active in the spring, for if it is too vigorous, it weakens and re-places the role of the spleen. Thus, sweet things like dates that are rich in protein, sugar and vitamins B and C, are good for the spleen. TCM advises people to restore and build up their internal energy in the spring and summer. To protect internal energy, one should refrain from having too much cold fruit or cold drink.

TCM doctors believe invigorating the circulation of the blood is the clue to preventing cancer because it enhances the body's immunity. The best way to gain this effect is by exercise for this stimulates the blood flow and metabolism.

According to the theory of TCM, high blood pressure is closely linked with the liver and the disease is affected by irrational eating and the lack of inner energy. There is a great variety in foods to help prevent high blood pressure. For instance, the staple food of corn porridge, lotus leaf porridge and celery porridge are effective. Fruit like watermelons, bananas, haws and persimmons are also helpful. Diabetes is consid-ered a "modern disease. " TCM considers that diabetes is caused by consuming too much fat and sugar; having too much fat and sugar results in increased inner heat. It is also caused by anger, sadness and other irritants which are turned into an internal fire burning up the "Yin" liquid in the lungs, stomach and spleen. Therefore, the first step in treating diabetes is to control the diet by limiting the intake of carbohy-drates, grain and sugar. Of course, herbal medicines will also be helpful to treat the disease.

Section 5　Acupuncture and Moxibustion

Acupuncture and moxibustion are often used to prevent diseases and give emergency treatments by Chinese doctors. These techniques especially increase the rescuing rate of emergency patients. They are easy to do and can be done anywhere and at anytime. The pain-killing effect induced by acupuncture in many clinical instances led to the use of acupuncture anesthesia in surgical operations. The patient remains conscious and is able to co-operate with his doctor under acupuncture anesthesia. He not only suffers less post-operative pain but recovers faster as well.

How can a small needle perform such a magical function? Ancient Chinese discovered that blood, body fluids and energy (Qi) are the material bases for the activities of all organs. Blood and energy, which run through the main and collateral channels, link all the internal and external parts of the body together. All parts of the human body are combined by the channels as a whole. A disease is the result of a functional disturbance in one of the organs due to the disorder of energy, or an imbalance of Yin and Yang. Acupuncture and moxibustion can adjust the function of the internal organ through the channels and improve the human body's immune system. In this way, a human body's normal activities can be maintained again. The theory has been proved through laboratory and clinical research in the modern times. The magic of acupuncture and moxibustion treatment is their quick results, simple methods and little side-effects. Quite often an acupuncture treatment is accompanied with some Chinese herbs as well. The combination of herbs and acupuncture in treatments helps to achieve the desired result more quickly.

The earliest applications date back to antiquity. Pointed stone tools and stone needle were used. Iron needles replaced the stone ones after the Iron Age. A number of new acupuncture points and new methods of treatment have been discovered. Currently, more than 300 types of ailments can be treated using acupuncture.

International acupuncture and moxibustion training centers were set up in Beijing, Nanjing and Shanghai in 1975. These centers have trained several thousand practitioners from over 100 countries at the request of the World Health Organization.

Based on the same theories, the massage treatment method refers to the use of hand techniques to massage the soft tissues of muscles, joints, and the skin of the body. The ancient therapy of massage can be used to treat diseases by removing the obstructions in the meridians, stimulating the energy in the body, and relaxing the body. The techniques used in massage treatment mainly include pressing, dragging, grasping, and kneading. Massage works to promote blood circulation, reduce the displacements of joints, treat injured soft tissues and adjust the functions of internal organs.

Section 6　Qi Gong (气功)

"Qi" refers to human body's vital energy, circulating through the human body system to nourish the internal organs and to help resolve disturbances of it. "Qi Gong" literally means "breath exercise". The ancient Shang (16th B. C. —1066B. C.) and Zhou (1066B. C. —221B. C.) dynasties witnessed the records of breath practice related to Qi. A number of Lao Zi's verses suggest breath practice and the benefits of merging with the forces and elements of nature. Zhuang Zi, another Taoist philosopher, mentioned the ancients had breathed down to their heels in the form of Qi which was projected and circulated throughout the human body. A silk scroll, unearthed in a Han Dynasty tomb in Hunan Province, has a series of over 40 figures doing various Qi Gong movements.

Qi Gong is composed of Qi and Gong. Qi is defined as vitality energy or life force, Gong is practice, cultivation or refinement. Being an invaluable component of TCM, Qi Gong means to cultivate and refine through practice one's vitality or life force. Qi Gong, one pillar of the traditional TCM, suggests self-healing or enhancement or empowerment practice. It has its origin in ancient times of the Chinese history. The aim of it is to search for health, longevity with the ultimate aim of immortality. Ancient Chinese believe the primary mechanism triggered by the practice of Qi Gong is a spontaneous balancing and enhancing effect of the natural healing resources in the human system. Its exercises help to keep the balance between Yin and Yang, to keep the main and collateral channels in good shape to establish harmony between vital energy and blood. It also helps to tap the body potentialities and stimulate positive factors. In general, it became an effective measure to attain health and longevity in ancient time. Millions of Chinese people have practiced Qi Gong over thousands of years.

One form of Qi Gong practice is Tuna (exhaling and inhaling) or Tiaoxi (regulating breath). It suggests one should expel the stale and stagnated air and inhale fresh air, thus improving the functioning of the internal organs to resist senility and prolong life. Three basic categories of it are breathing through the mouth or nose, abdominal breathing and other methods of breathing and regulation in conjunction with mental activity to fill the body with Qi. The third basic category refers to directing Qi to a region two centimeters below the navel or directing Qi to the heel or breathing like a tortoise.

Another form of practice is Daoyin. "Dao" refers to the effect that the strength of the mind guides the physical movements to stimulate the internal flow of Qi in the body. "Yin" refers to the idea that the physical movements help Qi reach the bodily extremities. The modern Qi Gong exercises originated from its source. Ancient people interpreted Daoyin as physical movements executed in coordination with controlled breathing. A jade article about Daoyin of the Warring States Periods (475 B. C. —221B. C.) is preserved at the Museum of Tianjin. The inscription of the whole process of breathing in Daoyin practice is as follows: "Draw a deep breath, direct it downward and let it stay there. Then exhale and direct the breath upward like a growing sprout, in a direction just opposite to the inhaling route and up to its dead end. The heavenly essence thus goes up and the earthly essence comes down. One who follows this law will live, otherwise one will die. "

Qi Gong requires one to be relaxed, calm, natural and free from distractions during the whole process of practice. The relaxed mind can remove stress, dispel tension, improve coordination of the nervous system, and enhance one's mental self-control.

Section 7　Herb Study and Bone-Setting

Efforts to study and explain Chinese medicine's theories and therapeutic principles with a modern approach along with clinical experiences have been relatively successful.

Fruitful results have also been obtained in the studies about the effects of Chinese medicinal materials. A large number of Chinese herbal medicines have been screened for their anti-cancer properties. A few hundred types of herbs have been tested in the laboratory or through clinical means. The results have proven relatively effective in the treatment of some diseases.

Chinese herbal medicines are traditionally prepared in the forms of pills, powder, pellets, oil, tinctures, drinks, syrups, lumps and gelatin. They have also been prepared as injections, tablets, dissolvable and sprays.

Among the nationally famous Chinese pharmaceutical herb shops are Tong Ren Tang (Beijing), Da Ren Tang (Tianjin), Hu Qingyu Tang (Hangzhou) and Lei Yunshang Tang (Suzhou).

New interpretations of Chinese bone-setting methods have evolved after being studying modern medical techniques. Fairly satisfactory results have been obtained using massage treatments. Doctors also find that using a combination of Chinese and Western therapeutic methods in the treatment of fractures has a higher rate of success than by using either method alone. The new methods have proven successful in hastening the healing of injured bones by relieving pain and local swellings, helping circulation and accelerating bone growth.

Section 8 A Brief Review of the Ancient TCM Books

As mentioned earlier the first recorded TCM history can be traced back to 2,000 years ago, but it is believed that the origin of TCM can be dated back to more than 5,000 years ago (Fu, n. d.) . During the long history and the continuous development of TCM, many books were written by various authors in different periods and Dynasties.

The Yellow Emperor's Classic of Interior Medicine, China's first classic medical book, published during the Spring and Autumn as well as the Warring States periods, created a comprehensive theoretical system of TCM and health preserving sciences. The book was also the result of a joint effort by many physicians of that period, divided into two parts, Plain questions and Miraculous Pivot. It involves 168 essays in 18 volumes. The book laid the theoretical foundation for TCM health preservation. It introduced the theory of Yin and Yang and the five elements to establish an integral conception of TCM. The theory of vitality, essence and spirit is stressed as the three vital and treasured constituents of the body. It presents a study on the physiological phenomena of the human body and specifically identifies the different stages. Furthermore, it also stresses preventive therapy and put forward the health preserving principles of the correspondence between man and Heaven. Thus, the book laid the theoretical foundation for TCM health and Qigong (breathing exercise) health preservation.

Another classic medical book, named *Shen Nong's Material Medicine*, sums up experiments, using ancient herbal medicines, existing before the Qin and Han dynasties. There were more than a hundred species of medicinal herbs described according to their toxic and curative effects. They are the original classifications of medicines in ancient China. This book laid the foundation for the development of Chinese herbal science.

Treatise on Febrile and Miscellaneous Diseases was written by Zhang Zhongjing at the end of the Eastern Han Dynasty (25—220) . Based on ancient medical instructions and a broad study of many others' medical formulas, the book performed the transition from theory to clinical practice. Zhang Zhongjing proposed the four methods of diagnosis: observation, auscultation and olfaction, interrogation, plus feeling and palpation.

Wang Shuhe of the Western Jin Dynasty (265—316) wrote *Pulse Classic*. It is the earliest treatise in China on the study of the pulse. It provides a profound explanation of how various forms of pulse are related to different syndromes of disease. The work of clinical practice has taken a very important position in TCM diagnosis.

A Number of important works on surgery were published during the Song and Yuan dynasties. For instance, *Effective Formulae Handed Down for Generations* by Wei Jinglin, is the most detailed extant Chinese medical publication on osteology. It contains descriptive details about the fractures of limbs, the dislocation of fractures and joints of the spine, wounds and sprains, arrow wounds, relocation and treatment. Many of the therapeutic methods and tools, as well as the methods of anesthesia are also described. The book gives the first description of treating a broken spine by hanging the body.

Obstetrics and gynecology became an independent science during the Song Dynasty (960—1279) . A special department was created in the Bureau of Imperial Physicians. Pediatrics also reached a new high level. Qian Yi's *Key to Treatment of Children's Diseases* is the oldest surviving treatise on pediatrics in China.

Dynastic rulers had the desire to achieve immortality prior to the Qin Dynasty (221—207B. C.). It led necromancers to produce so-called panaceas. Two books, *Kinship of the Three*, and the *Book of Changes* by Wei Boyang in the Eastern Han period, were the earliest documents of alchemy in the world. Roasting and boiling medicinal herbs are key methods of TCM. Lei's *Treatise on the Preparation of Drugs* edited by Lei Xiao during the Song Dynasty (420—479) is the earliest monograph on the subject in China. The later TCM roasting and boiling methods are based on this treatise.

Theory of Pathogenic Fire by Liu Wansu and *Excessive Yang and Deficient Yin* by Zhu Zhenheng had a profound influence on physicians of the Ming Dynasty. An excessive use of drugs of a cold nature gradually surfaced. A school of tonification with "warm" medicines appeared to stop the tendency later. Scholars of this school held that most wind-syndromes and rheumatic and miscellaneous diseases were caused by deficiencies in the spleen and kidneys. They should be treated with tonics and drugs which are warm in nature. The school of tonification with "warm" medicines was an important remedy in curbing the prevalent mistakes of the time. After making keen observations about the nature of epidemic diseases based on clinical experiences, Wu Youxing wrote the book, *Treatise on Pestilence*. It dealt with epidemic diseases such as the plague, smallpox and diphtheria. The foundation for the school of epidemic febrile diseases was also laid. Li Shizhen, the great pharmacologist of the Ming Dynasty (1368—1644), developed the science of material medicine to a new height. In his book *Compendium of Materia Medica*, an account of the properties, flavor, shape, origin, method of collecting, process of preparation, pathological study and prescription of each species in herbal medicine is described in detail.

The world-famous monumental masterpiece *Compendium of Materia Medica* was written by Li Shizhen (1518—1593A. D.) in the Ming Dynasty. The immense volume of this work includes indications and prescriptions of 1892 medicinal herbs, 1,100 illustrations and 10,000 recipes. In his endeavors he traveled throughout the country to pick up specimens in the wild and to search and collect folk recipes in the course of twenty-seven years of compiling the work. His classifications of plants and animals were based on rather scientific approaches at the time.

Section 9   Differences between Chinese and Western Medicine

Based on the TCM philosophical concept, TCM believes the human body is a small universe with a set of complete and sophisticated closely-related sub-systems. The systems work harmoniously and in a balanced way to maintain the normal function of the human body most of the time. There are also systems in the human body to heal illness automatically like the defense systems. If there is any imbalance between the subsystems, the healing system may lose its power and then, illness will occur. In other words, when balance is restored, the body will heal itself from illness. TCM theory considers all organs of a body as parts of a system, and more attention is paid to assist the balance of the human body and then letting the body's healing system do its job.

Fact is that TCM is an "empirical medicine and it was developed in the old days in the absence of systemic scientific knowledge". Therefore, it is "a product of accumulated clinical observations gathered over centuries of practice." (Zhang, 2005). It is a wonder, however, that Chinese doctors could treat and cure their patients only by physical examination. The methods of diagnoses are observation, Auscultation and olfaction, interrogation and pulse reading and palpation. Two of the most important diagnostic tools in Traditional Chinese Medicine are the pulse and the tongue. Observation refers to directly observing the ap-

pearance of a patient's condition. Since "The exterior reflects the interior" the rationale behind observation is that when the inner organs are out of balance, the problems will be reflected on the skin, tongue and some other outside organs (CMS, 2004). Auscultation and olfaction are means for doctors to collect information through hearing and smelling to define the problems of a patient. Interrogation is to interview the patient and his/her relatives to find symptoms, the evolution of the disease and previous treatments. The interview is considered to be the prime importance because this is how the majority of signs and symptoms of specific complaints and underlying systemic imbalances are discovered and classified (CMS, 2004). The pulse reading and palpation refer to doctors noting down the pulse condition and then analyze the inner change of symptoms. The reason behind this is that if the organic function is normal, the pulse, frequency, and intension of pulse will be relatively stable.

From the above mentioned diagnostic tools, it is not difficult to notice that during treatment, Chinese medical practitioners usually make their diagnoses by looking at the human body's behavior as a whole during the course of an illness, and the role of medical treatment, according to TCM, is to restore balance in the human body. During diagnosis and treatment, however, decisions made by practitioners differ according to their different skills and experiences, and the same protocol might not necessarily be repeatable for other patients. Thus, the effectiveness of TCM is not well suited for a generalized class of diseases (Zhang, 2005).

Western medicine, in contrast, is based on modern biomedical science and is an evidence based medicine (Zhang, 2005). In *Philosophical Differences Between Western and Chinese Medicine*, the author points out that the method of the Western medicine is fundamentally analytical and reductive, thus, it is good at "understanding the structure and function of the human body and disease-causing agents such as bacteria, fungi, protozoa, virus, etc." (Zhang, 2005). Western medicine has just like Chinese medicine a very long history and more or less the same origin. Where the Chinese deepened their observational skills and incorporated philosophical aspects about life, in the West they started to analyze diseases and medicines in a scientific way. This led more or less to medicine which is based on the principle "seeing is believing".

Of course a Western doctor uses more or less the same analytical skills as Chinese doctors do. They also watch the patients' appearance and behavior and look for signs on the outside which reflect illness on the inside (observation). They interview the patient to asses the problem and help them to guide their thoughts (interview). They listen to the patient and search for signs and clues which may lead to the answer of the patients' problem (auscultation). Certain diseases have specific smells for which they are trained to pay attention to (olfaction). Also palpating the pulse is part of the standard patient examination (palpation). Last but not least palpation and percussion are a very important part of the patients' examination by a Western doctor (palpation).

Where the Chinese doctor can form a diagnosis and start a treatment the Western doctor will go further to confirm his thoughts and findings by testing. This analytical and scientific aspect forms a big difference with Chinese medicine. A Western doctor will not accept his diagnosis through examination only he will try to confirm it. There are many diseases which will lead to the same physical findings and complaints, but who will have a totally different origin and thus different treatment needs.

Where as the Western medicine in the beginning also started with the herbal treatment of diseases in time it started to analyze and isolate the substances in herbs which had a curing effect. From this they started to modulate substances so that the medicines would work more effective. How to modulate medicines was again derived from research on diseases and the human body and organs.

However, the disadvantage is the Western medicine is that because of the testing, it takes more time to get to the diagnosis and sometimes the test results can be confusing or can still be interpreted in different ways. Also, new medicines usually take a long time to develop and to test, and sometimes they have expected damaging side effects.

To conclude, the most obvious differences between TCM and Western medicine (WM) is TCM is experience based; WM is evidence based. As argued by Zhang, TCM is a summary of clinical observations; WM is the result of laboratory experimentations. TCM uses herbs and natural agents; WM uses more chemical compounds. TCM looks at the behavior of the system as a whole; WM looks at the structure and function of the parts, (Zhang, 2005).

Nowadays, because of the spreading and speeding up of globalization process, the Western and the Chinese medicine are more and more coming in contact with each other. Whereas Western medicine is infiltrating Chinese society, Chinese medicine and herbs are more and more researched on in the Western society.

Chapter 12

Education

Xiaoxia Mao and Catherine Gu

China has one of the oldest educational systems in the world. Schools came into existence in the Western Zhou Dynasty (11ᵗʰ century—770 B. C.) . Among the subjects taught were rites, music, archery, history, chariot riding and mathematics; these were called the "six arts." The schools were run and controlled by the government. Government officials were teachers in the schools. Private education began to make its appearance during the Spring and Autumn, and the Warring States periods (770B. C. —221B. C.). There were two kinds of schools in ancient China—the official institutions and the private schools. The official institutions were open to the children of the nobles, while private schools were run by local scholars who taught students at home. Great scholars such as Confucius, Mencious, Mo Zi and Han Fei Zi all enrolled students. This educational system remained unchanged for about 2,000 years in China. The main objective of education was to train students for the imperial examination (civil service examination) from the Han Dynasty. The continuing development of Chinese culture owed much to the imperial examination for it guaranteed that the officials at various levels of the government had a solid educational base. However, it encouraged the intellectuals to seek rich life and honour as their aims in life. They regarded education as the means to break away from the productive labor and social practices in feudal China. The Imperial Examination was abolished in 1905 and the educational system that had lasted 2,000 years in feudal China came to an end. A new kind of school called New Learning appeared. Public schools were founded in all parts of the country in which Western subject matter was offered as part of the curriculum. After 1911 China began to develop a Western educational system that encompass all levels of education from basic education to higher education.

Section 1 Imperial System in Ancient Times

In ancient China, as society developed, so did the system of recruiting officials. Officialdom and e-moluments were hereditary in the Pre-Qin period. The king selected his officials according to the closeness of blood relationship. A system of assessment and recommendation was adopted in the Han Dynasty (206 B. C. —220 A. D.) . Local governments recommended talents for the court to examine and give appointments.

One important way of selecting officials from the common people was called Ke-Ju, which could be translated as Imperial Examination, and it became the main source of officials from the time of the Sui Dynasty.

Starting from the Sui Dynasty (1,600 years till now), and developed in the Tang Dynasty, the Imperial Examination became the oldest and the most influential examination in China. Before the Sui Dynasty, Chinese emperors selected their officials according to people's family backgrounds or the references from important officers. However, most officials were selected mainly through the Imperial Examination from the Sui and the Tang dynasties by which some people's social positions were changed. After the Sui Dynasty was set up, the emperor needed many intellectuals, at various levels, in his government to govern the new country efficiently. For this reason, the emperor (Sui Yang) invented the Imperial Examination to satisfy his needs to strengthen the central power of the government over the entire country. New middle-class landlords appeared in the new dynasty and they were eager to become members of the governmental power force. Therefore, the emperor required people to take part in the provincial examination held annually from the first of November to the 21st of March each year to search for more intellectuals for his government. Many schools sent their students, who had passed the examination at the school to take the higher-level exams. Some other intellectuals, who stayed at home to learn to read and write, could also attempt the Imperial Examination. In order to improve the validity and reliability of the Imperial Examinations, the emperors sometimes would travel across the country in disguise to investigate personally. During their travels, they listened to different opinions about the Imperial Examination from both common people and the officials. Some emperors liked organizing the examination papers themselves. They even went to check the Imperial Examination sites themselves.

The Imperial Examination included the following parts: filling in the blanks from famous literary works; interviewing; answering questions about a few classical works; and presenting an argument about a method of organizing a country and writing poems. Some military officers were also selected through the Imperial Examination including shooting and weight lifting.

The Imperial Examination was developed and improved during the Song (960—1279), the Yuan (1279—1368), the Ming (1368—1644) and the Qing (1644—1911) dynasties. The Imperial Examination greatly influenced education and culture in China. It also often affected the fate of the Chinese intellectuals.

The Imperial Examination had a great impact on China in the following ways:
- It stimulated people's motivation to study;
- It contributed to the development of Chinese schools;
- It was comparatively fair to most students;
- It made it possible for the children of the common people to enter the upper class.

However, most Chinese intellectuals could not gain cultural capital by only passing the examination. They participated in the examination annually in a vain attempt to change their current position. The Imperial Examination was a rather fierce competition for most people. Some people used their network of relationships, or even bribed officers and proctors, in order to pass the exam and climb the career ladder leading to the upper class in the society.

Many intellectuals looked down upon all the other professions except that of government official. Their main aim in life was to pass that Imperial Examination in order to change their social status and fate.

Imperial Examination in the Song Dynasty

The Imperial Examination was further developed during the Song Dynasty. For instance, the examination was changed from being given once a year to once every two years, and finally, to once every three years. The palace examination was then added to the Imperial Examination. Those who passed the palace examination would receive more benefits from the government. In the test, all students' names were hidden, and all the test papers were copied by designated people before they were read and scored. Only the copied paper could be read and scored. Those experts who handled the examination papers had to live in isolation

throughout the examination. In the Song Dynasty, the most important governmental positions were occupied by those who passed the Imperial Examinations. Also, the old "handed-down" system was kept.

Imperial Examination in the Yuan Dynasty

Students were divided into different groups according to their nationalities for the Imperial Examination in the Yuan Dynasty. Those people, who were of the Han majority or from Southern China Provinces, had to take more difficult examinations. Even if they passed the examination, their official ranks were always lower than those who were of the Mongolia or SeMu nationality. This was because the emperors of the Yuan Dynasty were from Mongolia in Northern China. Due to this racial prejudice, during the one hundred years of the Yuan Dynasty, only about 1,000 people of the Han majority passed the imperial examinations and were selected to be officers.

Imperial Examinations in the Ming and the Qing Dynasties

The form of the Imperial Examinations became more and more complicated during these two dynasties. Many complex rules and regulations were added to the tests. The examination was divided into four stages: the district examination; the metropolitan examination; the joint examination and the palace examination. People were required to write an eight-part essay which was a literary composition prescribed for the imperial civil service examination. This essay was well known for its rigidity of form.

The examination emphasized the text books included in "The Four Books" (*The Great Learning*, *The Doctrine of the Mean*, *The Analects of Confucius and The Mencius*) and "The Five Classics" (*The Book of Songs*, *the Book of History*, *The Book of Changes*, *The Books of Rites*, *The Spring and Autumn Annals*). Science, history, accounting and astronomy were all ignored. Thus, the Imperial Examination became the most effective method for the common people to get rich and change their social status. As a result, the Emperors could not select the most responsible officials for his government because those who passed the examination could only write eight-part essays. They were neither creative nor capable of carrying out or pursuing their official careers. The system of imperial examinations gradually lost its vitality and hindered the development of society since the content of the examinations was narrow and stereotyped. It did not measure the candidates' practical experience, thereby degrading education and making it a mere appendage to the imperial examination system. This was especially true beginning in the Ming Dynasty when the writing of the "eight-legged essay" was taken as a criterion for passing the examination. Chinese people criticized the Imperial Examination because it was a barrier to social development and progress in the Ming and the Qing dynasties. The Imperial Examination was finally abolished in 1905.

Section 2   Testing in Modern China

Testing System in the Republic of China (1912—1949)

After the Opium Wars in the 1840s, 8325 missionaries from Western countries came to China to establish missionary schools in the coastal areas of China. They began to put into practice a colonial educational system. The enormous increase in missionary schools gradually instituted an independent educational system from primary schools to the universities. These schools were directly controlled by foreign authorities and the Chinese government could not interfere in the management of the schools. Chinese students were required to learn and use English and to adopt the foreign life styles in these schools. Meanwhile, many of China's feudal warlords and bureaucrat-compradors established some Westernized schools in which translators, compradors and interpreters would be trained. They wished to use Western technology to maintain the rule of the Qing government. Thus western arts (the military and industrial technology of the West) and foreign languages were taught. Many new schools, different from the old type of schools, were established throughout China in the late 19th century. Under such circumstances the Qing government had to conduct educational reforms and created modern schools. Natural sciences and foreign languages were added to the curricula. Thus, a semi-feudal, semi-colonial educational system came about in substitution for a feudal variety.

From 1911 to 1949, China experienced a civil war. Important changes in the late Qing educational system were made. For instance, all the required courses on Confucian classics were abolished and the requirements for applied science and professional education were strengthened. Individuals were given greater freedom to set up private schools. Girls and boys could learn side by side in some primary schools, however, girls in high schools had to learn separately from boys. None of the bourgeois reforms were thoroughly carried out while China was ruled by the Beiyang warlords (1912—1927).

The KMT (Kuomintang) Government governed most parts of China. In 1932, driven by a desire for radical changes in education, the Educational Ministry of the KMT Government began a new policy of National Graduate Jointed Exams. The degrees and careers of students would be decided and managed by the central government after graduation. However, during the warring time, the educational quality and the levels in all areas of China were rather different, causing many students to complain and oppose the policy, because it was unfair. During the 20 years under the Kuomintang's rule, the United States strengthened its influence on education in China. There were 21 institutions, 514 secondary schools and 1, 133 primary schools, funded by foreign countries, and most of them were founded by the United States.

About 80 per cent of the population was illiterate in reading and writing Chinese, and most of them were in the rural areas. Only 20 per cent of the school-age children were in school and most of them were from rich families. Specialized secondary schools and universities were mostly concentrated in large cities.

Testing System in the People's Republic of China (1949—1965)

When the mainland of China was liberated by the Chinese Communist Party in 1949, large numbers of trained personnel were urgently needed after the founding of the People's Republic of China. To fulfill the task of re-construction, the new Chinese government made fundamental changes in the old educational system. Schools of all levels and types underwent speedy development. The government also adopted National Entrance Examinations to meet the needs of the current situation. Thousands of students of different ages, who passed the National Entrance Exam, had the opportunity to enter into universities for further study. Shortly after World War II (in the 1950s), most Chinese students were from poverty-stricken families. Hence, the government paid the entire education fee for those students. Moreover, students in financial need could receive help with food or win scholarships while studying in universities. In order to alleviate the burden on students and their parents, higher education was compulsory from 1950s to 1965. The governments carried on a direct state distribution policy. All the students graduating from universities were provided positions, either in government or academic organizations. In this way, only by passing the National Entrance Exam could they receive the benefits of a decent job in government organizations after graduation. This included many students from farmers' or workers' families. Their university education, as a cultural capital, enabled them to be the educated class and gain a higher social status.

Testing System in "Cultural Revolution" Period (1966—1976)

Unfortunately, the existing educational system, the old teaching methods and teaching materials were questioned and criticized during the Cultural Revolution Period. The National Entrance Examination was a-

bolished. All Chinese high-school graduates had to move to the countryside to work and live with farmers and in order to be "re-educated". Since all the universities were actually forced to close, university students and their teachers were all sent to the countryside for "re-education". In the 1970s, universities started to open again. However, the National Entrance Examination was not resumed. Eligible students who could enter into universities had to be recommended by the leaders in the factories or in the countryside where they had worked for years.

Entrance Examination Restored (1977—present)

From 1977 to the present, the National Entrance Examination has been restored. Shortly after the "Cultural Revolution" ended, the Chinese economic situation was difficult. Many young people, who had failed to pass the entrance examination, became unemployed. During the late 1970s and early 1980s, employment opportunities were rather limited. Only the limited percentage of young people who had passed the National Entrance Examination had the chance to study and have good employment opportunities in society after graduation. The direct state distribution would offer them appealing professions. Therefore, great concern was given to the National Entrance Examination. In 1990s owing to the reform, some self-funded students were permitted to receive university education though they had failed to pass the entrance examination. This represented a major reform in higher education. From 1995, most universities only accepted self-funded students who passed the National Entrance Examination. As a result, it expanded access and opportunity for students while at the same time universities did not have to wait for funding from the central government. Students now have the freedom to seek jobs in state-run enterprises, academies, in private companies or in foreign-funded firms after graduation while some students may fail to find jobs immediately after their graduation.

The Development of Testing Systems from 1980s

Since China adopted the "open-door policy" in the 1980s, a few thousand state-funded students have been sent abroad annually to study after graduation from a Chinese university. To be eligible, these students first have to pass the EPT Test (a national standardized exam). Then, after they apply to study abroad, their working institutions must recommend them. The objective is to give Chinese young people the opportunities to learn Western advanced science and technology. Soon after this policy began (from the 1980s till the present), a tide known as "being crazy for going abroad" spread widely throughout China. In order to go abroad to study, students must pass exams such as the TOEFL, GRE, and GMAT. As a result of these standardized examinations, organized by foreign committees, the future of thousands of Chinese young people has been changed. Some young people who pass the exams may have the opportunity to study in Western countries such as America, Australiaand Canada. Those who gained degrees from Western countries and returned to China later may have easier access to higher income and more career promotion opportunities. The income gap between them and the Chinese universities' graduates is large. Some Chinese overseas students prefer to stay abroad after graduation, and they have attained remarkable achievements and acquired middle class status in those countries.

Examinations and Social Constructions in China

The Chinese are aware of the importance of passing examinations. It is believed that people can change their social positions by passing the above mentioned examinations. This belief strongly influences Chinese people's attitudes toward education, studying and examinations. In addition, the reform of the enrollment system has brought about essential changes to regular education too. More and more students attain master's degrees or doctor's degrees today. Therefore, the competitions among them are fierce to find good jobs. Since late 1990s, some excellent students look for further opportunities to gain cultural capital by passing other examinations held by the Sino-British examination organization. Passing English tests held by the foreign academy may mean gaining more cultural capital. For instance, some oral interview tests, designed by Cambridge and Qinghua universities, have been used as a compulsory channel for Chinese bank employees to gain promotions. Some Beijing middle schools require their teachers to pass oral interview tests. In view of the beliefs about the power of cultural capital to change people's positions in society, people have realized it is urgent for them to gain more cultural capital. However, these tests sometimes are excessively used and become a heavy burden to people. Standardized Examinations, like the National Entrance Examination, the English Examination Band 4 and Band 6, and the TOEFL, all play a critical role in China.

Most Chinese young people consider Chinese education to be heavily test oriented. Examinations have not only positive effects but also negative effects on them. For instance, they have to spend inordinate amounts of time preparing for the tests. They feel depressed and exhausted because of the endless tests. The reputation of the schools and the students' self-image or evaluation of themselves are increasingly linked to the test results. A student is judged mainly by his test results. Thus young people require less formal tests, it is unfair and inappropriate if their lives are radically changed and controlled mainly by examination results.

When we discuss the Chinese testing system, we should not ignore the relationships between the testing system and various aspects of China's social development. Although reform of testing system is really necessary, it is impossible to tackle the complex and controversial issue in a short period of time. Chinese education is heavily testing-oriented, which has both positive and negative effects. Teachers need to take the principle of respecting students as individuals and meet their different needs so as to achieve their potentials.

Section 3　History of Traditional Chinese Education

Schools were set up as early as the Western Zhou Dynasty (1066 B. C. —221 B. C.). Public schools in ancient times were established by the governments at different levels. Central schools were under the direct control of the central government and local schools were administered by local authorities. Emperor Wu Di of the West Han Dynasty (206 B. C. —23 A. D.) established an Imperial College as the highest institution of learning for the propagation of Confucian classics. Schools were set up in prefectures, counties, districts and townships, which constituted an educational network across the country. Succeeding dynasties, to a great extent, did the same. Great advances were made in private education during the Han Dynasty. Children from landlord families generally enrolled in private schools, since the public schools had a limited number of available spaces. There were two kinds of private schools, elementary schools and high schools. Children learned to read and write in the elementary schools, while high school students studied the Confucian classics, such as the "Four Books" and the "Five Classics. "

Ancient education reached a glorious stage during the Sui and the Tang dynasties (581 A. D. — 907 A. D.). In addition to the imperial college, there were other central-administered schools to educate the children of noblemen and high officials. The schools were specialized in calligraphy, mathematics, law and science. The schools, administered by prefectures, sub-prefectures and counties at the local level, taught Confucian classics and medical science.

Printed textbooks became very popular after block printing came into use in the 10th century. Private schools were primarily concerned with elementary education when academics emerged in the 14th century. Some landlords and merchants invited teachers to come into their homes to teach their children; some pupils were taught in their teachers' homes. Children of the common people went to public places such as tem-

ples and shrines to learn. This system was funded by the local gentry. Still, most children in private schools were from rich family backgrounds. Academic schools appeared during the Song Dynasty (960 A. D. — 1279A. D.) and most of them were run by famous scholars, who emphasized "free discussion". The method of collective discussion to study Confucian classics was used in the classroom. However, these academic schools were gradually brought under the control of the government. All schools became governmental establishments and individuals were prohibited to attend academic schools during the Qing Dynasty (1644—1911).

Military schools were established by both the central and local authorities during the Ming Dynasty (1368 A. D. —1644 A. D.). An organization known as the Department of Cultural Affairs (Guo Zi Jian) was established by the central government at the beginning of the Tang Dynasty (618 A. D—907A. D.). It functioned as the nation's highest institution of learning during the Song Dynasty (960A. D. —1279A. D.).

Confucius was the first educator to advocate moral education. He advocated the practice of the "Rites of the Zhou Dynasty" and devoted almost all his life to systematically editing and revising teaching materials known as the Six Classics. From the general analysis of the Six Classics, the motif of moral teachings in the Confucian classics can be clearly seen. The five books, except the Book of Music, became the basic courses for both government and private schools in feudal Chinese society.

Confucius selected 305 poems and songs from the original 3,000 in the Book of Songs. The central idea of the poems and songs he selected conformed to the moral standards of the "rites". The book is believed to enable one to observe society, understand life, and promote a consciousness of cooperation.

The Book of *History* of *Shang Shu*, a collection of political and historical events compiled by governments before the Spring and Autumn Period (before 256 B. C.), is another famous work of Confucius. He believed that by studying the book, one would enrich his knowledge of history and master the way previous kings ruled their kingdoms through moral teachings. Of most importance in the book was its moral teaching about filial piety and love for one's brothers.

Confucius carefully studied the rites of the Zhou period and suggested people follow The Book of Rites (Shi Li, or Yi Li). The rites he selected were those concerned with the spirit of benevolence. Confucius believed if one did not study the rites, one could not know how to conduct oneself.

Confucius studied the book *Zhou Yi* late in his life and wrote an annotation and commentaries known as *Yi Zhuan* to explain his doctrines of morality, politics and philosophy.

The Spring and Autumn Annals is a chronicle of the State of Lu. Confucius concealed the ideas of "rectification of names", "distinguishing virtue from wickedness" and "judgment on people through his use of metaphor". The book was very important in training personnel through the rules of virtue.

Confucian educators wrote different annotations to the classics along with the progress of feudal society. These different annotations to the classics promoted the development of diversified forms of Confucian educational ideology. *The Five Classics* were always maintained as the fundamental courses in the schools of the later dynasties. Moral teaching was an important part of the fine traditions of Chinese culture. The structure of moral education courses occupied a dominant position in traditional Chinese education. However, natural sciences and literary and art courses had less important positions, although they were also introduced and developed. Faced with the emerging science and industry of the modern world, traditional Chinese education was out-dated. Chinese realized this and tried to accept the challenge of the new era. This occurred after the First Opium War (1840—1842) when Western aggressors opened China's door by force. There followed a deluge of Western culture. Traditional Chinese education began to face the challenges from the West for the first time in Chinese history. Two societies and two cultures collided. A number of progressive and sober-minded scholars tried to find new methods and launched fervent discussions on how traditional education should advance. The Chinese faced either a cultural crisis or a new opportunity for development. From the 19th century, they began to import natural science and technology instead of weapons and ships. However, they neglected the translation of works in humanities. They looked only to industrial and mechanical manufacturing and other practical sciences. Some Chinese scholars did not introduce and assimilate modern mathematics and its theories and other natural sciences. Gradually people realized the importance of political and educational reform. Advocates for national salvation through science, literature and education caused repercussions in society. Until the New Cultural Movement in 1919, people realized culture was not the right approach to solve the problems of China. Modern Western natural sciences have become an important part of education for many Chinese intellectuals. It was difficult to introduce Western natural sciences and it took an even longer time to introduce Western humanities in China. Although Chinese scholars achieved some success in the introduction of various schools of Western philosophy and culture, some problems still remained in China. After the Qing Dynasty was overthrown in 1911, advanced thought exerted an increasingly profound influence on the development of China. China had experienced the biggest historical change ever in modern times after 1911. Chinese intellectuals have been troubled by the problems of how to adapt their traditional culture to the outside world, because the traditional Chinese culture and the modern Western culture are so different and independent from each other. When the two clash, the question is how to apply the principles in a way that makes use of the strengths and eliminate the weaknesses in each of the cultures. Some people are determined to pursue reform in Chinese culture, others believe their traditional culture has not lost its value in modern times and the essences should be preserved. Noted and successful scholars in modern times have closely studied traditional culture, and they took neither a nihilist attitude nor a completely assertive attitude toward the national culture. After all kinds of experiment and study during the past 150 years, Chinese scholars came to the following conclusions: the idea of total Westernization cannot and should not be considered in China and other lands. If a nation realizes modernization at the expense of giving up its own traditional national culture, then it would prove an impasse, theoretically and practically. In other words, "total Westernization and complete globalization" is not a wise choice for a nation. In fact, there will be no globalization without nationalization. The law of cultural development is to have more nationalization developed for more chances of cultural exchange.

There were several occasions when foreign culture was introduced into China on a large scale. For instance, Buddhism was introduced during the Han Dynasty and influenced Chinese culture and society in the following centuries. However, it never changed the system and structure of traditional Chinese culture based on Confucianism. After the Opium War, Western culture arrived in China. Under the influence of modern Western concepts of democracy and equality, traditional Chinese thoughts and culture underwent a transitional change, exercising a far-reaching and profound influence in the modernization of Chinese society. The relationship between a modern society and its traditional culture should be of inheritance first. It does not mean everything should be retained but there should be a process of selection and creation. Formed over several thousand years, the unique traditional Chinese culture has a strong ability to renew itself. Of course, the attempt to reform and renew the traditional culture is a difficult and gradual process. It has not been fully realized yet. After World War I and World War II, some Chinese scholars began to consider the advantages and disadvantages of both Chinese and Western cultures and attempted to search for ways to modernize Chinese traditional culture. The principle of using the essence and leaving out the dross of traditional Chinese and Western cultures are widely accepted by Chinese people. They realize that the views of "total global consciousness" and "total roots-finding consciousness" are biased. The fine aspects of Chinese traditional culture should be esteemed, while absorbing and assimilating the fine cultural products from the rest of the world. Through inheritance, reform and development, the traditional culture can be preserved and can serve

the needs of modern society.

Section 4 Approach to Education Today

Education can never be isolated from the society in which it occurs. On one hand, big changes in politics and society will produce big changes in education. On the other hand, education influences the societal process. One country's education is influenced by other cultures and this is unavoidable. The past one hundred years has produced big changes in China's history as well as its systems of education.

In the past 2000 years, before 1911, Confucian philosophies of concerning Chinese education have held a dominant position. For hundreds of years, all private schools educated students using textbooks that expounded the Confucian philosophy.

In 1902, the Qing government decreed the creation of a modern public school system in Beijing for the first time in China's history. Lots of foreign schools were organized in China by the Americans, British, Japanese and Russians after the Qing Dynasty collapsed. Most of these schools were Christian mission schools. Ten years later, most of them were handed over to the Chinese government. It was called "nationalization." Before 1949, the twin forces of nationalization and internationalization were present in China. After the People's Republic of China was established, Marxism-Leninism was given an important position in Chinese education.

In the 1950's, the government encouraged "peasant education" and made efforts to allow many farmers to learn reading and writing, because new China needed an educated populace to build the new country after World War II.

The Republic of new China destroyed the old educational system, and a new one needed to be built in the 1950's. It was a turning point in the history of Chinese education. In 1957, the Chinese government declared a new policy of education: 'Education must serve proletarian politics and must be associated with labour and production. ' (Chairman Mao, 1957) The old teaching methods and materials were questioned and criticized, Chinese education followed in the foot-prints of the Soviet Union. Some teaching materials were imported directly from the Soviet Union. In the 1950's, destroying their old family roles, many Chinese women received an education and were given work opportunities. The close political and economic relationship between the Soviet Union and China was broken in the early 1960's. This forced China to work out her own method of reconstruction. Educators were encouraged to rely on their own efforts. The trend re-emphasized the value of the Chinese culture.

The "Cultural revolution" broke out in 1966 and lasted for ten years. It was a nation-wide disaster. The old Chinese ideology was regarded as "feudalism" and was totally destroyed. The Western cultures were called "capitalism", and were thrown away too. During that period of time, education in China was in ruins.

The disastrous revolution came to an end in 1977. China re-opened its door to the outside world once again. The Chinese have realized the problems that are created by cutting off contacts with the rest of the world. In the past two decades, after China opened the doors to the outside world, Chinese people have realized that China's progress has slipped behind many other countries. The economic level in some capitalist countries is higher; their education and public health systems are more advanced. From the political leaders to the Chinese citizens, it is commonly agreed that Chinese education must accept and learn experience from foreign countries. Of course, learning foreign technology and science has been the major focus. China is attempting to learn from other nations without losing sight of its own culture and situation. The Chinese have avoided just copying others' experiences and models without thinking about how these new models affect their own conditions and environment. Since 1979, Chinese people have been allowed to go abroad to study and work again. More and more Chinese have understood the necessity of respecting different cultures and being open to multicultural differences. Foreign cultures have flourished in China since 1980's. Accompanying the dramatic increase of international trade, the intake of foreign cultures is immense. Foreign textbooks are again being used and foreigners were encouraged to teach in the universities in China. Since the late 1980's, it has again become legal to develop private educational institutions in China. These "multiple channels" of education, including both local authorities and individual institutions were created and have become enlarged since 1995.

A few years ago, some Chinese universities were permitted to have co-educational programs with universities in different countries (mainly the United States, Australia, Canada, England, Germany and England). Now, multiple educational exchange programs are in existence. Not only are Chinese students studying in other countries but foreign students are attending classes in China. Some classes taught in China have been organized by universities in other countries. Finally, some students studying in China have the opportunity to earn degrees offered from universities in other countries. During the past decades, the Chinese have made great efforts to develop and reform Chinese education. Much progress has been made. However, there is still a long way to go for further improvement. Many problems still need to be solved. For example, many girls in the remote countryside are still illiterate because of poverty and gender prejudice. In this booming period, many Chinese people in backward rural areas still have limited educational opportunities. Governments at all levels need to carry out a new policy to wipe out illiteracy in China. The government is concerned about those economically backward rural areas. Hoping Project is a program to assist Chinese children to become educated. The central government is aiming at wiping out illiteracy in the next decade. Since 2005 children in the remote areas have been able to receive a free education, including free textbooks and lunch. Of course it is a difficult task because China has a large population.

The central government continues to wield enormous influence and power over private and public education. Most Chinese families value their children's participation in general academic schooling. This schooling is needed for these children to find skilled jobs or decent career positions. The local culture and situation are ignored. Some Chinese political leaders strengthen the belief that educational revolution must accompany political revolution. Some officials in China still believe that the only purpose for school is social responsibility; the goal of education is for the social service. They ignore the idea that an important task of education is to create humanistic individualism and to foster personal development. China is in the throes of a dramatic technological revolution and changes in its society.

Educational reform is of crucial importance to meet the challenge of the new technology. One big challenge for educators is to change schools from being socially divisive places into places that promote a balance between activist study, work, enterprise with a social conscience, and creative leisure. Ideally, some Chinese educators believe that students should grow into open-minded citizens who value and respect their own lives and consider how they fit into this new global age.

Chinese young people have discovered that media material makes complex subject matter accessible and engaging. They would like teachers to adapt new computer technologies to education. Compared with plain blackboards, computer screens are more graphic, visual and interactive. They would be eager to learn to use the new technologies to enhance their lives. Since young people are concerned about their self-development, they are willing to be active participants in their education, just like young people from other countries. They also desire teachers who meet their needs and respect them as individuals. The relationship between teachers and students should be relaxed and friendly. Teachers can be friends who understand them

and respect them; teachers can be their advisers and their psychologists.

Living in a variety of social spaces, Chinese young people have their personal dreams to fulfill. In the future, they will interact in a real world full of competitions. Teachers need to help them be able to adapt to the new society.

Chapter 13

Traditional Chinese Architecture Art

Xiaoxia Mao, Catherine Gu and Min Li

Section 1 Palace

"Chinese Palace" refers to the place where the emperor lived. A palace consisted of a group of halls, constituting the most important buildings. The Chinese palace, the highest, most luxurious and valuable architecture in ancient China, represents the highest level of architectural skills of the time. The palace symbolized supreme imperial power. The layout reflected the imperial power and embodied feudal etiquettes. The front halls were usually sites to handle state affairs while the back halls were bedchambers. The left side in the front served as the ancestral temple. On the right side, the altar for offering sacrifices to the gods of the earth and the harvest was built.

According to historical records, the ruler of the Xia Dynasty built his palace during the 20th century B. C. From 667 B. C. , six kings of the Qin state built a large number of palaces scattered around the area of Xian'yang during the following 120 years. Xian'yang became the largest city in China. After Ying Zheng, the first emperor of the feudal society had conquered all of China, he constructed palaces replicating those of other states in Xian'yang. The new palaces were built with Xian'yang Palace as the centre like stars in the sky setting along the Wei River. These "stars" were considered to be the Milky Way according to the theory of astronomical phenomena. These palaces, pavilions, towers and offices were scattered over 15, 000 square km. Each one was linked by straight ways. Xian'yang was occupied by a general named Xiang Yu in 206 B. C. His army set fire to the palaces and the fire lasted for three days. The magnificent Xian'yang City was left in ruins. Soon after the war, the first Emperor of the Western Han Dynasty moved his capital to Chang'an City (near present Xi'an) because it was too difficult for him to build a new capital on the ruins of Xian'yang.

Magnificent palaces such as Changle Palace, Weiyang Palace and Jianzhang Palace were established in the Han Dynasty (206 B. C. —220 A. D.) . The Three Palaces were built on a very luxurious and large scale. Situated southeast of Xi'an, the Xingqing Palace was built during the Tang Dynasty (618—907). However, these palaces were later ruined. Emperors of later dynasties all spent a large amount of their wealth to hire the best craftsmen and to buy expensive materials to build their palaces. However, just like the ruining of the Three Places, most of the palaces that were built in later dynasties in other ancient capital cities, such as the palaces in Bianliang (Kaifeng), Jianye (Nanjing) and Luoyang, were all burned down during wars.

The Forbidden City (Beijing), Shenyang Imperial Palace (Shenyang) and the Potala Palace (Tibet) are the outstanding examples of imperial palaces as well as examples of China's well-preserved timber con-

struction.

The intricate decorations and paintings on the architectures in the Forbidden City and Shenyang Imperial Palace are mainly red and yellow. The yellow glazed tiles, the golden gates, the red pillars and walls as well as the white-marble engraved balustrades form a wealthy, noble and gracious spectacle.

Located in downtown Beijing, the Forbidden City could be divided into the southern part and the northern part in the Ming and the Qing Dynasties. The southern part is centered on the three grand halls straddling the Central Axis. It was here the emperor met with high-ranking officials to handle national affairs and grand ceremonies were also held. The northern part, centering on two palaces, was the area where the emperor lived. The Forbidden City includes the Taihe Hall, Zhonghe Hall, Baohe Hall, Qianqing Palace, Imperial Garden, Yangxin Hall and Chuxiu Palace. It reflects China's splendid ancient civilization.

Since Beijing, was built by Zhu Di as a capital city, imitated Nanjing City, the Imperial Ancestral Temple was built on the east side of the Forbidden City.

Both the emperor and his sole empress were enshrined in the Imperial Ancestral Temple of the Ming Dynasty. The emperors of the Qing Dynasty would personally come to this temple to offer sacrifices to their ancestors. These emperors followed the etiquette of "three-genuflection and nine-bow" traditions. The imperial Ancestral Temple became the Cultural Palace for Working People after the founding of the People's Republic of China.

One Ming emperor ordered that a Shejitan (Temple for Sheji) had to be installed in administrative offices at every level to show the great importance attached to agriculture. Thus, Shejitans spread over China in large numbers during the Ming Dynasty. Emperors of the Qing Dynasty would hold sacrificial events at the Shejitan on the west side of the Forbidden City whenever important events occurred. Today, the Shejitan has become Zhongshan Park.

The largest cluster of the wooden buildings in the Forbidden City used to be the symbolic heart of the capital of China. Twenty-four emperors of the Ming and the Qing dynasties lived there during the past 500 years. The Forbidden City was constructed between 1406 and 1420 during the Ming Dynasty. It covered an area of 72 hectares, with the 9999 buildings covering some 150,000 square meters. The palaces are fully surrounded on each of the four sides by a 10-meter high brick wall. The Forbidden City is renowned as the largest and most integrated, existing, ancient palace complex in China as well as in the world.

Although having been repaired and rebuilt many times during the past 500 years, The Forbidden City's basic form and layout remain true to its original pattern. It is divided into the Outer Court and the Inner Court. All the structures are arranged symmetrically in a hierarchical order along the central axis of the palace. The arrangement shows both imperial style and breathtaking magnificence. The emperor held grand ceremonies, exercised his supreme power and summoned his ministers in the Outer Court. The Three Grand Halls: The Hall of Supreme Harmony (Taihedian), The Hall of Complete Harmony (Zhonghedian) and The Hall of Preserved Harmony (Baohedian), were of significant importance. The core structures of the Inner Court are the Palace of Celestial Purity (Qianqinggong), the Hall of Celestial and Terrestrial Union (Jiaotaidian) and the Palace of Terrestrial Tranquility (Kunninggong). The Inner Court where the emperor and his family lived is again aligned along the central axis of the palace. The six Eastern and Western Palaces, The Hall of Mental Cultivation (Yangxindian), and the Imperial Garden are the other principal structures of the Inner Court.

The Meridian Gate (Wumen), the southern entrance to the Forbidden City, is surmounted by five towers. The 9-bayed main gate-tower, with a double-eave hip roof and two massive wings, forms a huge square. Grand ceremonies such as dispatching the generals into the fields of war, celebrating victories and announcing the new calendar for the following year were held here.

The Hall of Supreme Harmony (Taihedian), standing on a three-storied marble terrace, is the largest timbered structure existing in China. It was used to hold grand coronation ceremonies when a new emperor took the throne. Ceremonies for an emperor's birthday or wedding, an empress's conferment, celebrations for the Chinese New Year, and other important occasions were also held there.

Standing behind the Hall of Supreme Harmony (Taihedian), the Hall of Complete Harmony (Zhonghedian) served as a place of rest for the emperor on his way to the Hall of Supreme Harmony (Taihedian). The emperors consulted with their religious ministers in this hall. It was here that the emperor would read prayers prior to his departure for sacrificial rites at the temple of Heaven, Altar of the Earth and Ancestral Temple. During the Qing Dynasty, a special ceremony was conducted every ten years after the revision of the imperial genealogy was completed.

The Hall of Preserved Harmony (Baohedian) stands at the northern end of the terrace. The Ming emperors usually changed into their ritual garments here prior to the ceremonial installation of an empress or a crown prince. The Qing emperors used to hold imperial banquets to entertain princess's bridegroom, their fathers and other relatives who served the imperial government. Banquets would be held to fete provincial governors, Mongolian princes, civil and military officials here on the eve of the New Year. The final testing of the Palace Examination during the Qing Dynasty was also held here.

Being the core structure of the Inner Court, the Palace of Celestial Purity (Qianqinggong) used to be the place where the Ming and some Qing emperors lived and handled their daily affairs. During the reign of Emperor Yongzheng of the Qing Dynasty, the building was used as an audience chamber where he held ceremonies and received envoys presenting tributes from vassal states. Also, Foreign ambassadors were received and imperial banquets were held here at Chinese festival time. After the death of a Qing emperor, his coffin would be placed here for a few days for memorial ceremonies. After the death of Emperor Yongzheng of the Qing Dynasty, the name of an emperor's successor was placed in a box behind the plaque of "Be Open and Above-Board." The box was opened only after the emperor passed away. If the name in the box was the same as was retained by the emperor, the named person would be the designated prince and take the crown upon the death of the emperor.

The Palace of Terrestrial Tranquility (Kunninggong), the last major palace in the Inner Court, was the residential palace of the empress during the Ming and early Qing dynasties. From Emperor Shunzhi of the Qing Dynasty, it was used to pay homage to the gods of Shamanism. Three grand ceremonies would be held in the first lunar month, spring and autumn, as well as daily and monthly sacrificial rites.

The Hall of Mental Cultivation (Yangxindian) stands south of the Six Western Palaces in the Inner Court. From the time of Emperor Yongzheng of the Qing Dynasty, it was where emperors resided. The rear chamber was where the emperors lived. In the Eastern Warmth Chamber, Cixi (mother of Tongzhi) and Ci'an attended state affairs sitting behind a curtain when Emperor Tongzhi and Emperor Guangxu were young. Cixi was the real monarch ruling China for 48 years in the Qing Dynasty.

The Palace of Longevity and Prosperity (Chuxiugong) was home to the imperial concubines during the Ming and the Qing dynasties. The most noted hostess who lived there was Cixi.

Standing at the northernmost tip of the central axis is the Imperial Garden measuring 130 meters long and 90 meters wide. Arranged symmetrically in hierarchical order, 20-odd architectural structures of different appearances are interspersed with rare trees and flowers, ponds and layered rocks. The architect sought to use diverse forms of buildings and supplements to play up the imposing royal manner of the neat layout. The garden also displays a variety of different characteristics. Though similar in layout, the two groups of the buildings vary in shape, decoration and colour portraying a totally different look.

At the corners of the Forbidden City are the four corner towers consisting of nine roof beams, 18 pil-

lars and 72 ridges. These towers were used for defensive purposes.

The Gate of Divine Might (Shenwumen) is the north gate of the Forbidden City. It has three openings and an imposing tower. Housed in its tower are drums and bells used in the mornings and evenings to mark time. This gate was used by empresses, imperial concubines and royal family members. The candidates of beauties selected to be the wives of the emperors would also enter the palace through this gate.

Some furnishings displayed outside the halls also indicate the concept of hierarchy. For instance, cloud pillars (Huabiao) erected in front of the palace are a special symbol of the imperial building. A pair of bronze lions in the Forbidden City is regarded to get rid of evil spirits and show dignity and power. The bronze tortoise and crane in the yard symbolize longevity.

After the Foundation of the People's Republic of China, the new government soon opened the Forbidden City to the public as a museum. It was listed among the first group of key cultural sites to be placed under state protection by the Chinese government in 1961. In 1987, it was added to the list of UNESCO World Heritages. The Palace Museum was established in the imperial palace along with other relevant collections from the Ming and the Qing Dynasties. Being a comprehensive national museum, it mainly exhibits the history of the Ming and Qing Dynasties, the palaces and ancient works of art. Millions of cultural relics are housed in there, and most of them are art treasures from the past dynasties of China.

Section 2　Gardening

The Chinese Garden is an architectural gem of China and of the world. The four essential factors necessary for a traditional garden include hills, water, architectural structures and plants (mainly flowers and trees). The Chinese garden, as it developed, was consistently influenced by nature. Garden art, which stresses artistic and poetic effects, has achieved great success in China. It usually mixes structures with man-made landscaping, natural scenery, painting, literature and calligraphy. Horticulture is an important adjunct to the talents and achievements of Chinese architects. Imperial gardens in and around Beijing, and the private gardens in the South were two major categories in the developmental course of Chinese gardening.

Chinese ancestors used to live in natural caves during the early Paleolithic Period (500,000 years ago). During the Neolithic Age, tribal people living along the Yellow River built their simple houses in the caves or partially caved-in houses. The houses were made of mud and grass with wooden frames. Later, buildings supported by stiles high above the ground appeared. Buildings constructed with rammed earth appeared during the Xia Dynasty (21st—17th century B. C.). The classical Chinese gardens originated in the Shang (17th century—1046 B. C.) and Zhou dynasties (1046 B. C.—256 B. C.), when monarchs began to build parks for their own leisure and pleasure. In the pre-Han period, gardens were the hunting grounds for emperors and nobles without man-made landscaping. An example of this type of garden was the Gusu Stage, which was built by the State of Wu during the late Spring and Autumn Period.

Palaces were built on high and large rammed-earth terraces. Varied types of buildings were introduced and a complete construction system was gradually set up to create the simple and open style during the period of the Qin (221 B. C.—206 B. C.) and Han (206B. C.—220A. D.) Dynasties. The Emperor Wu (140—88B. C.) of the Han Dynasty built an Imperial Forest Park. It involved facilities for living, entertainment and rest. A pond was built with an isle in the center on which a pavilion was erected. This design is imbued with man's spiritual demands.

The unique private landscaped garden appeared in the Wei, Jin, Southern and Northern Dynasties periods. From this point, the Chinese garden developed toward two different orientations: imperial gardens and private gardens. Since most landlords of private gardens were officials and literati, representing the highest level of the culture of their society, private gardens are regarded as the epitome of the culture of ancient times.

During the Wei (220—280) and Jin (265—420) period, the literati class used to lead a reclusive life in natural landscapes and they endowed nature with a perfect personality. As a result, the theme of a private garden is to represent a scene of a natural landscape. Pine-trees, plum flowers, bamboo and man-made rock hills representing forests scenes were widely used in private garden design.

From the period of the Wei (220—265), Jin (265—420), and especially the Tang (618—907) Dynasties, with the widely popularized Buddhism in China, Buddhist constructions of pagodas and temples influenced Chinese construction styles. The function of construction was stressed to suit the demand of the people's cultural life. Most of the private gardens were concentrated in Chang'an (present Xi'an) and Luoyang during the Tang Dynasty (618—907). The intention was to build small gardens suitable for the functions of daily life. Private gardens usually included houses, water space, bamboo groves, pavilions, bridges, famous stones from Lake Taihu and sometimes with cranes or other birds. The elaborate scheme and the gallant style of the garden were unique.

The appearance and shape of the buildings became beautiful due to the increased urban economic development of the Song Dynasty (960—1279). Garden building was very popular among the rich literati during this period. A number of gardens were built in various cities. Private gardens were built to be suitable for people's daily lives. Additionally, public parks were rapidly developing in the suburban areas of cities. Some private gardens were also regularly open to the public.

The later stages of the constructions emphasized the blending of cultures derived from a variety of ethnic groups in China, and the growing influence of foreign cultures during the period of the Yuan (1271—1368), the Ming (1368—1644) and the Qing (1644—1911) Dynasties. Chinese architecture has reached a high level alongside the development of the material and spiritual cultures and it reflected the changes of traditional culture. It was in the Qing Dynasty that Chinese gardening made great achievement and most of the extant gardens were bequeathed in this dynasty.

China's traditional architecture attached great importance to the idea of "unity of Heaven and Man". It emphasizes the unity of nature and man, and a combination of human feelings and spirit into the natural environment. One feature highlights the great importance of the harmony between man-made scenery and natural landscaping in the garden design. The layout of man-made construction may determine a garden's style and reveal the temperament of the owner. There are a number of man-made buildings matching the natural surroundings in a garden. Take a chamber or hall for example. It is often the grandest building (a scenic attraction in its own). Since a lobby is an important place for guests to meet or entertain, the construction of a lobby calls for a large space, eye-pleasing ornamentation and an elegant architectural style. A corridor serving as a link is built between buildings so as to comprise the main part of a garden. A pavilion in any conceivable shape is a scene to attract visitors' attention. A waterside kiosk is usually a slim, graceful pavilion over a river or pond used to decorate the shore of the lake or river.

Water is an important graceful element in gardens. An expanse of clear water always occupies the center of Chinese gardens, providing brightness, openness and a sense of leisurely repose. Bridges over the water offer a range of vistas and provide a highlight for the overall design. They are to beautify the surroundings by connecting the isolated buildings, and also function as a passageway. A bridge can help to divide scenery or provide a spectacular focal point. Types of bridges can range from covered bridges to arched stone bridges to zigzagging bridges. These bridges of different styles and materials all bring harmony to the surroundings. They may pass over small ponds, streams or big lakes. The engraved balustrades of some elaborate bridges may offer a sense of dignity within the overall garden design. Therefore, they are often works of art

and add a special charm to a landscape.

A wall is a screen as well as a decoration. Some windows can be used to create shifting scenes of beauty behind the wall or join the two views separated by the wall into an integrated picture.

The theory and practice of garden building gradually matured and some professional garden builders wrote works about how to build gardens. Among the garden building principles, contrast and unity were widely accepted ones. The principles such as "more in less", "much in little", "substantiality shaded by un-substantiality", "the subordinate supplementing the chief" and "originating from nature but on a higher level than nature" are basic principles. The principles created the artistic effect of a continuation of different scenes appearing before one's eyes.

The four categories of the Chinese gardens can be classified as: the imperial garden, the private garden, the temple garden and scenic spots.

The Imperial Garden generally refers to those gardens where emperors lived and entertained themselves. Most imperial gardens are marked by particular salient features apart from the general features of classical Chinese gardens. The general layout of an imperial garden gave a magnificent, imposing impression of the absolute authority of the emperors. Expensive construction Materials were gathered from the whole country; and vast numbers of artisans could be summoned by emperors so that collective wisdom was pooled. Lakes and mountains could be maintained in their original forms of natural beauty. Lakes could be dug deeper and wider if necessary, and mountains could be built in imitation of natural scenes. The northern climate was taken into consideration as most imperial gardens were situated in Northern China. The colour palette and the planting of vegetation were all carefully considered when building an imperial garden. The gardens such as the Summer Palace (1750—1888 Beijing), the Winter Palace (Bei Hai Park, 10th century, Beijing), and the Imperial Mountain Summer Resort (1702—1792 Hebei Province) mainly retain a style which is unique to the north despite keen efforts made to imitate famous gardens in the Yangtze River area.

Beihai Park

To the west of the Forbidden City, in the center of Beijing, is a vast expense of water known as the Western Garden (also named the Supreme Liquid Pond). The pond is divided into three parts, the Beihai, the Zhonghai and the Nanhai. Beihai is considered the most famous of the three parts of the pond. The area around the Zhonghai and Nanhai is the official sites of the Chinese state government.

Beihai Park has an area of more than 68 hectares, with a water area covering half of the entire park. It is the oldest and best-preserved classical imperial garden in China.

One thousand years ago, Beihai was constructed as a pleasure palace, covering an area of seventy-one hectares. It gradually fulfilled its function as an imperial garden during the Liao Dynasty (the 10th century). The rulers of the Chin Dynasty renamed the capital Zhong Du and built an imperial palace in the capital city.

Water of Taiyechi is channeled into the capital city from Yuquan Hill (located west of Beijing). It is the largest body of water in Beijing. The main architecture of Taiyechi's Qionghua Island is Guanghan Hall built by the Yuan Emperors in the Yuan Dynasty. Several times, this hall held large scaled banquets. The man-made islet in the imperial palace was renamed Qionghua Island. It is the shape of Beihai Park. The Palace of Jade Bright and the Palace of the Moon were added on it. To some extent, the imperial activities of the royal family were confined to the Beihai area that centered on Taiyechi and Qionghua Island during the Yuan Dynasty. The emperor Kublai Khan also planned his capital around Qionghua Island. It was converted into a forbidden imperial garden at that time.

Beihai became the Western Imperial Garden of the Ming emperors after the Ming court moved its capital to Beijing in 1420. Large-scale renovations and extensions, such as the Temple of Everlasting Peace (Yong'ansi) and the Hill of White Dagoba (Baitashan) were carried out during the Qing Dynasty. In the early years of the Qing Dynasty, Yong'an Temple was built on Qionghua Island's Wansui Hill. A white dagoba was constructed at the top of the hill.

Beihai Park is an artistic masterpiece representative of China's classical gardens. On one hand, it inherited China's historical garden-building traditions; on the other hand, it widely absorbed the advantages of garden building techniques from all regions of China. It was said that three celestial mountains were in the ocean where celestial beings all lived in gorgeous pavilions. According to ancient Chinese mythology, these celestial beings possessed the pills for immortality. Beihai Park was exactly built in accordance with this mythology, turning legend into reality. Qionghua Islet, the Circular City (Tuancheng), and the Terrace of Xi Hill symbolized the three celestial hills. All the structures were laid out with Qionghua Islet as the center. Ten of the structures were built around the south-north axial line. The buildings, clustered on the eastern and northern banks, along with the woods and the lake, symbolized the harmony of man and nature. The park also displays the essence of classical Chinese gardening art. Even today, Beihai Park looks as if it were formed by nature itself.

The Hall of Receiving Light (the Chengguangdian), the main structure in the Circular City, was rebuilt after the architectural style of the corner tower in the Forbidden City. A 1.5-meter-high white jade Buddha is in the hall.

Standing high on the top of Qionghua Islet, the inverted-bowl-style white Lamaist pagoda (built in 1651) is the center of the surrounding scenery, as well as being a famous landmark in Beijing. The pagoda embodies the communication and the blending of China's traditional culture with other cultures. With the introduction of Buddhism during the Western Han period, forms of religious constructions were introduced. This white pagoda is of Nepalese style resulting from the cultural exchange between China and Nepal. The Tranquil Heart Studio (Jingxinzhai) on the northern shore of the lake is an elaborately built garden of gardens. The Qing Emperor Qianlong often read there. Later it was a place of study for the crown prince. Being an exquisite example of a classical Chinese garden, the garden is ingeniously designed and novel in style. It is surrounded by a painted wall following the shape of the hills. Chambers, pavilions, towers and water-houses in the garden are separated by water or linked with bridges. The corridor and the shore of the pond with its piled rocks, offer a three-dimensional impression of scenes and sights.

The Five Dragon Pavilions are the major scenes on the northern shore of the lake. The pavilions are connected by stone bridges at the waterfront. It was the place that Qing emperors and their royal family went fishing, watched fireworks and held parties to view the moon.

On the northern shore of the lake stands the Nine-Dragon Screen. It is 6.65 meters high, 27 meters long and 1.2 meters thick, covered with glazed, colored bricks. Nine Chinese dragons in bright colours are embedded on either side of the wall. The dragons portray fierceness and vigor, tumbling in clouds and waves. More than 600 dragons with tube-shaped heads decorate the front ridges and the fallen ridges. The Nine-Dragon Screen is considered the most precious work among the coloured glazed constructions in China.

At present, among the extant imperial gardens it represents one of the oldest, most complete imperial gardens in China or even in the world.

Imperial Mountain Summer Resort

Located 250 kilometers to the northeast of Beijing, the Imperial Mountain Summer Resort (the Mountain Hamlet to Flee the Heat) lies in a hill-encircled basin and looks out over placid lakes. The Imperial

Mountain Summer Resort is one of China's leading scenic spots as well as the world's largest extant imperial garden.

The resort encompasses more than 560 hectares. It is twice the size of the Summer Palace and is the largest extant classical imperial garden palace. It is divided into the palace area and the garden area. Rows upon rows of pavilions and halls are scattered throughout the resort. Temples and nunneries dot the deep valleys and tree-clad, undulating mountains. The entire scenery creates an effect of traditional Chinese landscape paintings.

The lake area, the key scenic spot, has a maze of islets linked by causeways and small bridges. It presents a typical south China scene. The environment is quiet, fresh and green, with lotus fragrance and willows. A vast plain covered with luxuriant grass and trees lies to the north of the lake area, where deer often roam. It appears similar to the typical Mongolian grassland. The northwestern part has wooded mountains, deep valleys and steep crags. The scenery varies from season to season. Sledgehammer Peak (Qichuifeng), a 38-meter-high solitary pinnacle, is an odd-shaped peak standing on a meandering ridge that is located five kilometers to the northeast of the imperial palace. The palace "borrows" the peak as a part of its vista like some other traditional gardens. The mountain resort consists of a palace quarter and a scenery area. The palace consists of four groups of main buildings like subsidiary buildings, barn, file house, palace… The place is high, flat and spacious and the scenery area is covered by lakes, plain and hills. The plain is like a palm, covered with trees, grass and stretches as far as visitors' eyes can see. It's as good as a typical Mongolian grass land scene with numbers of green trees dotted with the cluster of Mongolian yurts. Hill area lies west and north of the resort and is dotted with over forty groups of buildings. There are deep gorges and ridges and peaks rising and falling.

The entire palace, together with luxuriant trees, is enclosed by a wall over 10 kilometers long. There are more than 110 architectural structures such as halls, offices, studios, studies, towers and buildings for landscaping purposes built within the wall. The main palace hall is built of *nanmu*, a kind of hardwood peculiar to China. Free from brightly painted décor, the architectural style is that of an ordinary north-China gray brick house, and the woodwork is in natural, unadorned color. It is in harmony with the inscription "Simplicity and Reverence" hung on the northern wall. For instance the main hall of Frugality and Placidity is solemn and lofty, quiet and elegant, simple and unsophisticated with the green pines in the yard setting off. The outer of Hall of Refreshing Mist and Waves is simple but elegant, while the displays inside are magnificent. Ancient Chinese believed that a simple and plain lifestyle could help one realize one's true goal in life.

Wenyuan Lion Grove represents the style of southern private garden, which was constructed after the Lion Grove Garden in Suzhou designed by a famous artist of the Yuan Dynasty. It is a small island, and 16 scenic spots. Some buildings are by the lake, some perch on the hills or hidden in the woods of stone. They are decorated wonderfully, uniquely and elegantly. Another example of the learning from southern garden style is Golden Hill Pavilion. It was modeled after the Jinshan Temple in Zhenjiang (Jiangsu Province). It is opposite Chen Lake, made of stones, with three sides facing lakes and one side facing small pond and grand cliffs. The Knowledge Imparting Library seems to be a two-storey building. It has three stories in fact for the middle part is hidden to avoid the direct exposure of the books to the sun. The overall arrangement of the building is well designed and carefully planned. The library is surrounded gracefully by pine trees and piled rockery creating a quiet and elegant atmosphere. Pine Soughing Hall is a group of constructions with unique characters to the northeast of the palace. Some small-sized buildings are connected by short-walls and half-circled winding corridor, lie crisscross and form a both closed and open garden. The space gradation is plentiful. The architectural style of the Mountain Resort is unique and the construction layout is simple but nice, unsophisticated but natural. It embodies the essence of China's classic palace-garden.

The Eight Temples outside the wall have architectural features showing the best aesthetic influence of the architectural styles of various national minorities. Puning temple is an architectural combination of the Han Buddist monastery and the Tibetan Lamaism temple. It reflects communication and combination of the Han majority and Tibetan culture.

The surrounding ground embraces temples, lakes, valleys, and mountain forests. The Lake Sai here is characterized by more varied scenery compared with the open expanse of water at the Summer Palace in Beijing. The large lake has been cut up into smaller interconnected lakes of different shapes and sizes by islets, bridges, causeways, sluice gates and lake-centering pavilions. The lake area covers one tenth of the total area, which is beautiful and natural with these crossed islands, crisscross bands and bridges, covered pavilions and changeable sceneries. Buildings along the lake are laid out in the style of gardens typical of the south Yangtze River area.

The forests, vast expanses of water and mountains provided the Qing emperors a cool place in the summer time. Kangxi, Qianlong and a succession of other emperors, would spend five to six months there each year so as to escape the summer heat. This resort was more than just a summer retreat. In fact, it was a second palace away from the capital.

Private Gardens

The style of the private garden is quite different from that of the imperial gardens. Private gardens are generally small in size and they perform multiple functions of lodging, get-togethers, study, theatrical performance, and sightseeing. There are artificial mountains and tree groves in private gardens. Buildings of different types, ponds, and verdant woods express the varieties of tastes of their owners. These things are evident in the minute details that are seen. The owners have wasted no effort to achieve elegance and variations within a limited space. The scenic spots and exotic scenes are hidden in the rich foliage of trees and plants. Some private gardens have a spatial system in varying hues and contrasts; they are gardens of multiple depths facilitated by hills, water, flowers, trees, and ingenious ways in handling architectural space. In some gardens, an outstanding collection of rocks, a maze of paths, caves, and running streams create a picture of traditional Chinese landscaping.

Private gardens are mainly gathered in Jiangsu, Zhejiang, Sichun, Guangdong and Anhui provinces. In Jiangsu Province alone, there are a variety of private gardens built in Suzhou and Yangzhou. There are also a number of famous private gardens in Hangzhou of Zhejiang Province. Suzhou and Hangzhou are considered the most beautiful cities in China. One Chinese saying goes, "A paradise in Heaven, and Hangzhou and Suzhou on earth". Marco Polo praised Hangzhou as "the finest and most splendid city in the world." Classical gardens of Suzhou have been listed in the World Cultural Heritage since 1997. Suzhou is particularly well known for its Four Renowned Gardens. They were owned by bureaucrats, landlords, wealthy merchants, and scholars in Chinese history. They were built all over China during the Jin, the Song, the Ming and the Qing Dynasties with the development of the economy and the culture exchange. Traditional private gardens in northern China are usually designed in a regular and closed pattern with simple colors. They look steady and solemn. Private gardens in the southern areas are freely designed and have bright and simple colors. The construction suggests a sense of vividness. The principle of integration of variety is an important feature of these gardens. The layout planners skillfully united individual, multifunctional constructions of different styles with each other to achieve a harmonious and unified artistic effect in the gardens. The Humble Administrator's Garden (Zho Zheng Yuan, in Suzhou of Jiangsu Province) is an example. The entrance of the garden leads to a circular gate along a narrow lane between hou-

ses. In front of the gate stands a rockery as a screen to prevent one from getting a full view of the garden. When one walks along the corridor around the hills, and then arrives at the Hall of Remote Fragrance, he will suddenly see an open area with clear water in a pond, and dense trees amid which are scattered buildings and pavilions. The scheme of the scenery at the Humble Administrator's Garden provides a changing view of space. It can be found in the layout of various ancient private gardens in the south.

Some famous private gardens in Southern China are well known in the world, such as Yuyuan Garden (1577, Shanghai), Humble Administrator's Garden (拙政园) (1909, Suzhou), the Lingering Garden (Liuyuan 留园) (1595, 1876 Suzhou) Huanxiu Mountain Villa (环秀山庄) (Song Dynasty, Suzhou). Lingering Garden is the best example of using the principle of "originating from nature but higher than nature". The layout design of the garden is full of changes accomplished through the use of light and space. From a twisted, narrow stretch of courtyard to an open ground with trees and then to the pavilion, a visitor is guided with his view obscured until he suddenly comes to a bright, wide open space where the Green Shaded Room stands. The principle of "first restrain, and then relax" is used.

The Yuyuan Garden (Shanghai) is not large in size. However, there are more than 40 scenic spots which are ingeniously partitioned, offering visitors a different scene at every step. The garden is laid out in an intricate manner. It is taken as a paragon of the south Chinese landscaping styles of the Ming and Qing Dynasties.

Section 3　Temple

Buddhist Temple

Among the numerous Buddhist mountains around the country, the four famous ones are called the "Four Sacred Buddhist Mountains." They are individually named, Mount Emei (Sichuan Province), Mount Wutai (Shanxi Province), Mount Jiuhua (Anhui Province) and Mount Putuo (Zhejiang Province). The Buddhist temples built in these mountains have some typical common characters.

Religious buildings represent another achievement in the history of Chinese architecture. Temples and pagodas are the main Buddhist structures in China.

The typical Indian Buddhist design for temple construction had a tower around which monks' rooms were built, forming a single courtyard. The outstanding central tower was the characteristic architectural style. From the Sui (581—618), the Tang (618—907) and the Five Dynasties (907—979) periods to the Song Dynasty (960—1279), Buddhist temples in China exhibited their own style. The design of these temples gradually adopted the models of imperial structures. The concept of buildings being built along a central axis was introduced into the building of temples. Buddhist halls were built near the pagoda which is the center. It became the construction pattern, with the structures running along an axial line, replacing the centripetal layout. There was a supporting hall and a courtyard, with buildings on three or four sides, located on either side of the main hall. The central pagoda was moved to the back, or to one side of the hall forming a new courtyard. Sometimes two pagodas might be situated in front of the main hall or the main entrance. Some Buddhist pagodas were built in the center of a temple, because they had been the main buildings of previous temples in the Sui Dynasty (581—618). Although pagodas were not always the center of temples, they remained of central importance to Buddhist architecture. They are of various styles and exhibit strong local characteristics. The pagodas that have survived in China are mainly stone pagodas, brick pagodas, bronze pagodas, iron pagodas and all-timber ones. They become more and more decorative as time passes. Among the many ancient, multiple-storied pagodas preserved today, the earliest brick pagoda is the

Songyu Temple Pagoda erected in the 6th century in Dengfeng County of Henan Province. The earliest wooden pagoda that has survived is the Fugong Temple Pagoda built in 1056, located in Yingxian County of Shanxi Province. Two granite pagodas were erected between 1228 and 1250, located inside the Kaiyuan Temple of Quanzhou County, Fujian Province. They are the earliest stone pagodas. The pagoda next to Baiju Temple in Tibet is 32 meters high. It contains 100,000 Buddha images, thus, it is called "100,000-Buddha" Pagoda.

Located in the southwestern part of the city, Tianningsi Temple was built in late fifth century. It was rebuilt and repaired several times in the Tang Dynasty (618—907). The present name was adopted in the Ming Dynasty (1368—1644). The original pagoda was built during the Sui Dynasty (581—618) at the temple. The extant pagoda dates from the Liao Dynasty (907—1125), and is considered to be the oldest extant building in Beijing city, although some superficial decorations were added during the Ming and Qing dynasties. The temple stood in the most flourishing market district of the city and played an important role in embellishing the skyline of ancient Beijing.

Most temples of the Tibetan sect of Buddhism were built with high terraces, red and white outer walls, gilded tiled roofs and trapezoid windows contrasting strongly with conventional temples. The spacious, dim halls added a mysterious atmosphere. The artistic styles of the temples vary because of the different sects and nationalities. The Buddhist temples in Tibet and Lijiang (Yunnan Province) are very different from the Buddhist temples in other areas. The Stupas house of the Potala Palace, containing the remains of the Dalai Lamas, are elaborately constructed and decorated with gold, silver, pearls and precious stones. The pillars in the entrance hall of the Potala Palace, and the main Buddhist image in the Potala Palace, both have a strong local Tibetan style.

Faguang Temple, situated in Faguang village, 25 kilometers northeast of Mount Wutai in Shanxi province, was founded during the Northern Wei Dynasty (386—534). The temple was destroyed and rebuilt again in the Tang Dynasty. The architecture appears simple and antique. The entire temple strongly shows the special features of the wooden buildings from the Tang Dynasty (618—907).

The Suspension Temple, located in the south of Hunyuan county in Shanxi province, was founded in the Later Northern Wei Dynasty (386—534). The temple is built under precipitous rocks and overlooks a deep valley. It was reconstructed in the Chin (1115—1234), the Yuan (1279—1368) and the Ming (1368—1644) Dynasties.

Located on the northern side of Inner Funchengmen Street, the White Dagoba Temple is a renowned Buddhist Temple. Being an important religious and cultural treasure, it is one of the best-preserved temples in Beijing. Baita Temple is the popular name of the Miaoying Temple, in which stands the oldest and largest extant Lama Tower in China. The 51-meter-high Dagoba, built 400 years earlier than the white Dagoba in Beihai Yongan Temple (Temple of Everlasting Peace), was designed and constructed by the Nepalese architect, Aniko, in the eighth year of the Yuan Dynasty (1271) at the request of Kublai Khan. The Baita Temple has experienced several restorations and renovations since its original construction. The renovation, in the 18th year of Qianlong's reign (Qing Dynasty, 1753), is the most notable. The original architecture and well-preserved Buddha, coupled with newly discovered cultural relics, turn the Baita Temple into one of the most prestigious temples in Beijing.

Yonghegong is the largest, richest (in cultural relics), and best-preserved lamasery in Beijing. the Yonghe lamasery presents a vivid reflection of China's politics, architecture and arts. It seamlessly integrated the architectural elements of Buddhist architecture and the palaces of ancient China. Absorbing the Tibetan religious architectural styles and decorations into a palace's architectural structure, it is solemn, magnificent and unique.

Taoism Temple

It was said that the immortals were fond of living in buildings with multiple floors. Thus, storied buildings or pavilions of the Taoist temples ("guan" or "gong") have become features of Taoist temples (palaces). They are wooden-framed constructions, and the design follows the pattern of a central axial line with symmetrical buildings on both sides. The temples were decorated with the symbols of the eight-trigrams and higher beings (the Yin-Yang symbol), the images of the Eight Immortals, and other creatures and plants symbolizing longevity. Various art works and paintings such as frescos, sculptures, calligraphy, scrolls, poems and essays uniformly decorated the constructions. The four sections were clearly defined with easily accessible routes, suggesting a sense of solemnity, refreshment and elegance. As Taoist temples were usually built on mountains or beside rivers, they were surrounded by a natural environment and a peaceful unworldly atmosphere. There are still more than 1,500 Taoist temples in China. The Temple of Mystery (Suzhou, Jiangsu Province), the Triple Purity Hall (Suzhou, Jiangsu Province), the White Cloud Temple (Beijing), the Qingyang Palace (Chengdu, Sichuan Province), and the Taiqing Palace (Henang Province), are all examples of famous, existing temples.

The design of Taoist architecture was meant to express the ideas of Yin and Yang, the Five Elements, auspiciousness and longevity. For instance, fans, fish, deer and bats, as architectural adornments, are symbols of virtue, happiness, honor and longevity. Pines, tortoises, cranes, bamboo, dragons and phoenixes symbolize longevity, immortality, virtuousness, auspiciousness and the exorcising of evil spirits. Most Taoist constructions adopted the traditional courtyard style. Many of the novel designs, layout patterns, techniques and other unique executions of other secular buildings were designed, collected and utilized in building Taoist Temples. Those various techniques and designs served as typical references for modern Chinese architecture.

There are some paintings of Taoism topics in Taoism temples. Taoist fine arts developed in tandem with Taoist architecture, including sculptures, portraits of immortals, temple frescos and Taoist paintings. They incorporated the influence of Buddhist arts with the images of Chinese faces. They also utilized the painting styles found on Chinese bronze vessels, the Han Dynasty portrait bricks and other portrait-painting methods. Famous mythical stories, such as "The Eight Immortals Celebrate Their Birthdays" and "The Eight Immortals Sail Crossing the Sea" are often adopted as decorative themes in Taoist buildings. Chinese paintings stressed drawings with lines before the Tang period. Wu Daozi (685—758), a famous Buddhist and Taoist painter began to introduce the Indian concave and convex methods into his Chinese figure painting. He adopted Taoist concepts by having the people in his paintings wear broad, loose garments with belts and move like immortals in the sky. In his Taoist paintings, clouds and Chinese dragons are painted because the legendary Lao Zi was a Chinese dragon by birth. Since then, both clouds and the Chinese dragon have become some of the main characters in Chinese paintings.

The Qingyanggong Taoist Temple, situated in western Chengdu City (Sichuan Province) is the oldest Taoist temple in China. The temple was formerly called Qingyangsi Fair. Master Zhang Daoling founded and propagated Taoism during the East Han Dynasty (25—220) in this city. Most of the structures were built during the Qing Dynasty (1644—1911) on the ruins of the Court of Two Celestials. The main constructions include the Lingzhu Tower, the Eight Diagrams pavilion, the Hall of Three Trinity and the Qingyanggong Garden. The Hall of Three Trinity was constructed in the Tang Dynasty (618—907) and was used as the main hall in the Qing Dynasty. The construction of the hall is grand, dignified and spacious. The three figures in the hall are outstanding in China for their elegant and lofty composition. Eight wooden pillars in the hall stand for the eight Taoist deities, while the 28 stone pillars represent the 28 stars. The Eight Diagrams

Pavilion was the most remarkable structure since it strikingly demonstrated the elements of Taoist doctrine. The entire wooden and stone pavilion is harmoniously integrated without any bolts or bars. The three-storied pavilion is constructed compactly and ingeniously. The body stands on its square foundation, the embodiment of the round sky and square earth. The Taichi chart of the twelve animals is unsophisticated and graceful. The eight outside stone pillars are carved with hollowed-out churning dragons. They represent some of the country's rare stone carving treasures. This pavilion is the best wooden and stone Taoist pavilion in the world. Qingyanggong Garden (the Court of Two Celestials) has a few halls and a pavilion. The court has an exquisite layout, an integrated structure and peaceful surroundings.

Section 4 Typical Representatives

Lijiang (Dayan Town)

Located on the embankment of the Lijiang (Hu Li River) in Yunnan Province the ancient Lijiang City covered an area of 1.5 square kilometers. More than 4,000 families live in the city, which includes the ancient town and a new town. It is surrounded by the Lion Mountains in the west and the Elephant Mountains and the Golden Row Mountains in the north.

Clear spring water, named Jade Spring, flows in three streams from the west and north through the city. Different channels of the three springs reach every household. The flowing stream and drooping willows added to the nickname, "Venice of the East." The courtyards in the city have the characteristic elegance of the south. The unique decorations add more liveliness to the yards.

The old town of Lijiang was an important transfer station for businessmen on horses carrying goods to Southwest China in ancient times. The ancient town was a living museum of the centuries-old heritage of the Naxi people. The center square of the town was first built in 1126 during the late Song Dynasty. The Yuan Dynasty instituted a local administration of government in Lijiang by the 13th century. There are more than 1,000 households in this Ming Dynasty city.

The city's hereditary chief, Mu, and his family, dwelled in an elegant and magnificent mansion in the city. This world-renowned ancient city was built in a simple and artistic style and scientifically laid out. The streets are paved with local stone slabs, which are free from dust in the dry season and do not get muddy in the rainy season. Many stone bridges and arches were built during the Ming and the Qing dynasties. Different from most ancient cities with walls, Lijiang had no wall, but orderly roads and lanes extended in four directions from the central square.

It is an ancient city inhabited mostly by Naxi ethnic people. Residential houses are made of timber with screened walls in the front. Some houses have a quadruple courtyard planted with flowers. The rooftops, stones and tiles of the houses are in a definite Naxi style. The houses are linked together by a web-like network of narrow, crisscrossing stone pathways.

The old city was the home of murals painted by the Naxi, Han and Tibetan people. They were invited to paint them by the herdsman, Mu, during the Ming Dynasty. The murals cover a total area of 139.22 square meters on 55 walls of the Dabaoji Palace, Dabao Pavilion, Liuli Hall and Daque Palace in Laihe. The largest mural is 2.07 meters high and 4.48 meters wide containing 600 figures. The murals are mainly religious themes drawn meticulously and brightly colored. They are a combination of various cultures and customs of the different nationalities and religions in China. They not only reflect the open mindedness of the Naxi nationality toward other different cultures and beliefs, but also a valuable treasure of Chinese art and culture.

Being one of the four largest and best preserved ancient towns in China, the old town of Lijiang city was listed as a national historical and cultural city in 1986. It was included in the UNESCO world culture heritage list in 1997.

Pingyao Ancient City

About 70% of the ancient ground architectures and historical relics are gathered in Shanxi province. Pingyao lies in the middle drainage area of the Yellow River and on the western bank of the Fen River in Shanxi Province. It is a city with a unique style and almost perfectly preserved in China today. It is an outstanding city model of the Han Nationality style in the Ming (1368—1644) and Qing (1644—1911) Dynasties.

Pingyao has many places of interest and a large number of ancient architectures and historical relics that are rarely found in other parts of China as an important ancient city in Shanxi. There are five state-class and four province-class historical relics included in the over 300 ground and underground historical relics.

Commerce in Pingyao grew prosperous and many Chinese merchants and dealers gathered there during the Ming and the Qing Dynasties. The city gradually became the main business center of the province in ancient times. Pingyao's leading role in commerce circles not only supported the prosperity of the city but also stimulated construction in the city and many streets, stores, and dwelling houses were built. Rich merchants built shops and houses according to the geomantic quality at that time.

The ancient city wall winds its way for 6 kilometres and presents a firm barbican entrance to the city. The imposing structure, with its firm barbican entrance and the superstructure piercing the sky, create magnificent pictures at dawn or sunset.

Shuanglin Temple has over 2,000 ancient painted sculptures, which make it the most attractive and infectious art museum in China. It earned the titles of "Treasures House of the Orient Painted Sculpture Art" and "Treasure of the World."

The Ten-thousand Buddhas' Palace, one of the oldest wooden architectures existing in China, is famous for its novel structures and imposing manner. The painted sculptures in the palace were special treasures from the Five Dynasties and Ten States (907—979).

The Cixiang Temple's brick tower from the Jin Dynasty (265—420) is known for its unique sets of brackets on top of the columns supporting the beams. The roof eaves appear to have tiers of outstretched arms.

The Dacheng Palace of the Confucian Temple is magnificent and elegant. It is one of the oldest Confucian temples in China.

Ri Sheng Chang, the first Chinese draft bank, was noted for its capacity to remit money in China. Since the commercial prosperity promoted the development of finance, the bank dealt with the business of remittances, deposits and loans throughout China and Japan. Compared with other banks in Pingyao, Ri Sheng Chang was famous for its economic power. The bank grew to include 400 branches in 70 cities. They offered various commercial services to many different constituencies, from governmental agencies to owners of handicraft industries. During the most flourishing 100 years of Shanxi, the fortune center was not in the capital city of Taiyuan but in Pingyao, Taigu and Qi County.

There used to be thousands of ancient cities like Pingyao existing in Chinese history. However, many of them were reduced to relics or exist only in people's memories. The history and the culture of Pingyao are being protected as an ancient, rare treasure of human civilization unanimously recognized by the world.

Wang's Grand Courtyard

The residences in Shanxi Province represent the residential inheritance in north China. More than twenty residences, scattered throughout Shanxi, have been renovated and opened in recent years. The big court-yard of the Wangs is considered to be a typical example of a northern Chinese citizen's residence.

Situated at the southern edge of Jinzhong Basin, the big courtyard of the Wangs of Shanxi Province was built more than 200 years ago. It includes 123 yards with 1, 118 rooms, covering $45,000 m^2$. Leaning a-gainst the high northern slope, the courtyard has a southern exposure. It has a varied terrain with the build-ing superimposed over the yards which stretch out one after another.

This was an official mansion in the Qing Dynasty. There were 101 persons in the Wang family who won official titles by either passing the examinations or excelling in business. The old and well-known family pro-duced public officials for several generations. The Wangs in the village were important official mer-chants. Six hundred years of Shanxi commercial history were reflected in this yard.

In this luxurious residence, there are halls in the front and rooms at the back with three entrances and four closed sides. With a lower front and a higher back, this residence provides enough space for associa-tions with the neighbours outside. The design fully reflected the dignity of an official residence and the per-fection of the patriarchal clan system. The outside architecture presents an inspiring outline against the sur-rounding countryside. Those who were privileged to see the inside of the residence were equally im-pressed. The fort gate and wall, and the front, middle and back gates, enclosed the four circles of the yard guaranteeing the safety of their lives and wealth. The huge architectural complex may be rated as unique.

The nice combination of the northern and southern architectural styles makes it a peaceful and secluded place. It has a rich and colourful momentum, with an orderly scattered appearance that rises and falls appro-priately. Subjects for scholar paintings are applied to the decorations of woodcuts, carved bricks and carved stones. The culture of the yard merges the three religions of Confucianism, Taoism and Buddhism. Their principles and philosophies are reflected on the subject matter of the woodcuts, carved stones and carved bricks. The exquisite brick stones and woodcarvings are also unique.

The design features comfort and safety while the courtyard retains all the key elements of a residence in northern China. A large number of refined works of northern folk art have been preserved in the yard. The meaningful pillar scroll couplets and horizontally inscribed boards were also considered unique.

In 1996, the local government spent a huge sum of money to renovate the heavily damaged courtyard of the Wangs. It opened as the museum of China's residential art in 1997.

Hakkas' Earthen Buildings (Kejias' Tulou)

The Earthen Buildings are dotted around the mountain triangle where Fujian, Jiangxi and Guangdong provinces meet. There are about 30, 000 earthen buildings in South China. The huge buildings have tall, strong earthen outer walls made of earth, limestone and fine sand. They are often propped up by a frame of bamboo and wood chips. The residential architectures there embodied a distinctive culture.

About 70% of the total earthen buildings are in Fujian Province and most of the buildings remaining to-day were completed during the Ming (1368—1644) and Qing (1644—1911) Dynasties. The largest con-centration of buildings is in western Fujian Province. It was constructed by the Hakka people.

"Hakka" (Kejia) in Mandarin means "guest people" or "strangers." Hakka people were a group be-longing to the Han nationality of China. Their ancestors used to live in Central and North China more than 1, 500 years ago. War and frequent nomadic invasions in the third century caused the Hakka people severe hardships. In order to avoid these hardships and live a peaceful life, they began migrating south towards the present Jiangsu and Zhejiang provinces. Further persecutions pushed them farther south in the fifth centu-ry. They settled down in Jiangxi, Fujian and Guangdong provinces from the 10th to the 13th centuries. They built the earthen complexes to guard against invasion from local bandits. The Earthen Buildings were also

small communities built to maintain their way of life, unique dialect and cuisine.

An ancestral hall could be found in all the earthen buildings, for Hakkas worshipped their ancestors. Primary schools in many buildings show their awareness of the importance of education.

The square building, the most common type of earthen building in Fujian Province, has two main designs: one with circular galleries and one with separate units. The former emphasizes the unity of the building complex through the use of galleries, while the latter respects the privacy and convenience of individual units for different families.

The Earthen Buildings are cool in summer and warm in winter to live in. They are also fireproof and anti-earthquake, demonstrating the high artistic level of architectural science.

Part 5

Science and Technology

Chapter 14

Ancient Contribution to the World

Xiaoxia Mao

Chinese science and technology led the world for more than a millennium from the Qin Dynasty (221 B. C. —206 B. C.) to the Yuan Dynasty (1279—1368). Robert Temple, a British scholar, pointed out that over half of the inventions of the modern world originated in China.

Chinese science and technology had their own characteristics distinctive from other ancient civilizations. They were marked by pragmatism and empiricism. The Chinese made the first distance recording-chariot 1, 500 years ago. They also invented weighing apparatuses. The renowned four great inventions—paper making, compasses, printing and gunpowder, all resulted from practical needs. Pragmatic needs encouraged the monarchs of all dynasties "to organize the social resources by means of the state power" to spur the evolution of science and technology. Take research institutes for example, special scientific research institutes including the royal observatories and royal medical colleges were established very early. Pragmatism enabled China to stand in the forefront of the world for a long time. On the other hand, it also limited the development of science and technology, since the founding of many important scientific theories was not based on pragmatism.

Ancient Chinese had many experiences from their work and based their inventions on those experiences. They had a preponderance of empiricism and rarely proceeded further to explore the natural laws and form scientific theories. They stayed at the directly perceived, general phase. For example, the *Syllabus of Medical Herbs*, *Technical Wonders and Encyclopedia of Farming* were three works of the highest level in the fields of medicine and pharmacology, agriculture and technology in the Ming Dynasty. However, they were limited to recording production experiences and lacked theoretical generalization and sublimation. The stagnancy of the feudal economy produced the impetus to use these inventions for revolutionary purposes in the homeland.

Section 1   Astronomy

China is a big agricultural country. The ancient Chinese needed astronomical knowledge in making calendars to arrange farm and animal husbandry activities. The policy of "state based upon farming" was adopted by all the monarchs. Another reason for the astronomic achievements was the pragmatic ancient monarchs had to prove they were "mandated by heaven. " The emperors, who each called themselves "the son of Heaven", stressed observation of heavenly phenomena and a calendar system. They set up a special office for the observation of heavenly phenomena and for the revision of calendars, because they considered the calendar to be important to the state.

The Chinese made great contributions to calendar making, the keeping of astronomical records and the manufacturing of astronomical instruments. The tradition of stressing astronomy was not broken during the feudal dynasties, and the records on astronomy and calendars in ancient China were very prolific. There were more than 50 calendars made throughout the history of the past dynasties. A calendar was made by a famous scientist named Zu Chongzhi in the 5th century B. C. According to his calendar, there were 365. 2428 days for a year. The Chinese astronomer, Yang Zhongfu, made a further improvement with 365. 2425 days for a year. These calendars appeared more than 400 years earlier than the Gregorian calendar. Ancient scientists used continually improved observation instruments to accumulate astronomical data. As a result, they became more precise in locating the relative positions of the sun and the moon. The advanced mathematical methods and the interpolation method were used in tracing the orbits of the sun and the moon. Chinese scientists calculated astronomical constants more and more precisely with the passing of time.

China has continually made extensive records of celestial phenomena from the remote antiquity to the 18th century. The state gathered specialists to engage in astronomical research, and that data was recorded in the historical books of all the dynasties. The records all relied on the cooperation of many scientists organized by the state. The tradition continued as dynasties rose and fell. *The Shi Shen Star Catalogue* compiled in the 4th century B. C. was perhaps the world's earliest record.

Ancient Chinese made astronomical instruments such as the armillary sphere and the celestial globe. The Song scientist Su Song invented a 12-meter-high instrument that gave the correct time and served as an armillary sphere. This oldest astronomical clock was manufactured in the 11th century. The continually improved instruments were used to scan the heavens and draw star maps and charts by ancient Chinese astronomers. Guo Shoujing remolded the armillary sphere into a simplified one and raised the level of astronomical observation in China during the Yuan Dynasty (1279—1368). The principles and the external shapes were very similar to the modern equatorial telescope. Because of this technology, China was several centuries ahead of the rest of the world.

Beijing Ancient Observatory, located southwest of the flyover, dates back to the Ming Dynasty (1368—1644). Some large bronze astronomical instruments including an artillery sphere and a celestial globe are on the high platform.

Section 2　Mathematics

In the 4th century B. C., the Chinese were proficient at using the decimal system and fractions for the four arithmetical operations. China was the first country to adopt the decimal system, and the second to adopt fire for the advancement of human civilization. High governmental officials had to oversee production in the different areas of the country. *Nine Chapters on the Mathematical Art*, completed in the 1st century, is a well-known scientific work in the world. It served as a textbook in ancient China. It contained the solutions to 246 research products related to square fields, fractions, grains, equations, right triangles, averages, subtraction and addition, multiplication and division, surplus and deficiency, all closely related to production.

Zu Chongzhi (429—500) calculated the value of the ratio of the circumference of a circle to its diameter to be between 3. 1415926 and 3. 1415927, which was 1,000 years earlier than the European mathematicians solved this problem. Qin Jiushao gave detailed explanations of the root of equations of higher degree by numerical solution in his Mathematical Treatise in *Nine Sections* in 1247. This predated Horner's method by 600 years.

The abacus was first made around 190 A. D. Calculation by abacus was applied in all respects by the end of the Eastern Han Dynasty (25—220). The predecessor of the abacus was arithmetic sticks made of three and four inch long pieces of bamboo. The sticks could be used for addition, subtraction, multiplication and division. The multiplication tables were widely learned throughout the population during the Spring-Autumn Warring States period (722 B. C. —221 B. C.). However, people found the graphs to be unclear and cause errors when too many arithmetic sticks were used. The abacus was made to replace the arithmetic sticks during the Yuan and Ming Dynasties (1279—1644). The Chinese abacus was convenient and simple to perform complex multiplications, divisions, square roots and cubic roots. The simple and convenient calculating instrument is considered to be the father of the modern computer. Abacus is the simplest computer that demands operational programs.

Section 3 Shipbuilding and Invention of Compass

Chinese ground natural magnet into the shape of a spoon to indicate the north-south direction more than 2,000 years ago. The Chinese invented the scull. It is a creative propelling tool developed from the long oar, but more efficient than the oar, for it works both as a rudder and as an oar.

Large ships including the "tower ship" with ten stories were built during the 2nd century B. C. and the 2nd century A. D. The sail was improved and watertight-compartment construction was invented around the 3rd century. It ensured that other compartments were safe while sailors dispelled water and made repairs in an isolated compartment. This design helped to prevent the sinking of the ship. The earliest stern axial rudder for controlling the ship was also an invention by the Chinese. An axial rudder was found at the stern of a ceramic model ship from the Eastern Han Dynasty (206 B. C. —220 A. D.) in Guangzhou. The true axial-turning rudder was used in China between the second and fourth centuries A. D. The balance rudder and the holed rudder were invented in the 11th century.

Multiple masts had been installed on Chinese sailing ships in staggered positions as early as the third century. The main mast was tilted to the stern so that the sailing ship could sail in all wind directions and take advantage of the wind power. Wheels were also used to propel ships in China. Zhu Chongzhi built a "one thousand Li" (500 km.) ship propelled by wheels in the 5th century. Li Gao built a wheel treadling ship propelled by two wheels in the 8th century, which travels as fast as ships with set sails. A 24 wheeled ship was built in the Song Dynasty (960—1279).

Vessels constructed with the watertight compartments piled the seas between the eastern shore of the Pacific and the Indian Ocean. They also traveled the eastern coast of Africa. Zheng He, a eunuch in the Ming Dynasty, led his 40 to 60 large ships, of about 150 meters long, through seven voyages between 1405 and 1433. They traveled as far as the eastern coast of African, which was an unprecedented event in the world's navigational history.

The initial form of the compass was created around the 11th century. The compass was used for navigation and was an important instrument shortly after its invention. The use of the compass in ocean navigation accelerated the progress of human civilization. With the help of the compass, Christopher Columbus traveled around the world and made great geographical discoveries. Chinese Zheng He made seven long distance voyages in the Ming Dynasty.

Section 4 Paper-making and Printing Technology

The ancient Chinese had written Chinese characters on tortoise shells, bamboo, silk cloth and wood before paper was invented. They are either inconvenient to read and write or too costly. The Chinese began

to use worn-out fibers to make rough bast paper during the Western Han Dynasty (206 B. C.—23). Writing paper was invented in the 2nd century by Cai Lun and the raw materials extended from bast to bark fibers. He invented a new kind of plant fiber paper after many experiments. He made full use of scrap materials including bark, ramie combings, fishing nets, used cloth etc. The cost was reduced since the sources of raw materials were enlarged. Liana and bamboo fibers were also used for making paper for a few centuries. Paper was widely used across China during the Jin Dynasty (265—420). The invention of paper contributed to the flourishing of politics, education and commerce in China.

The technology spread to Korea in the 4th century, to Arab countries in the 8th century, and Japan in the 10th century. European people mastered the technology after the 12th century.

The Chinese were the first to develop printing skills. Carved plate printing was developed on the basis of stone carving and seal carving. People already printed numerous religious pictures with carved plates in the Sui Dynasty (581—618). The Chinese printed a number of books with carved plates and they were widely circulated. Confucian classics were printed on carved plates and supported by the State during the Five Dynasties (907—979). Books printed with clay types were expensive with respect to labor and materials. The movable-type printing was invented at the beginning of the 11th century by Bi Sheng, a printing carver in the Song Dynasty. Single words were carved on pieces of clay and heated in the fire until hardened. They were used as types and set into printing plates. Tin, copper and other types of metal were also used in movable type printing after the 14th century in China.

Typography spread to Asian countries and Europe. The techniques emancipated education and learning beyond Christian abbeys. Colleges appeared in various cities in Europe. The Religious Reformation and anti-feudalism campaigns were held in Europe.

Section 5　Gunpowder

The practice of making elixir pills emerged in China around the beginning of the Christian era. Ancient Chinese people, who practiced Taoism, invented gunpowder, while making their elixir pills for immortality. These pill makers discovered that a mixture of saltpeter, sulphur, and charcoal could catch fire easily and burn explosively. Gunpowder was originally used for making fireworks and fire crackers for entertainment. It began to be used for military purposes during the Five Dynasties (907—960). Gunpowder was widely used in battles during the Song Dynasty (960—1279). The *Collection of the Most Important Military Technique*, compiled in 1044, mentions poisonous gunpowder, incendiary gunpowder and explosive gunpowder along with detailed records of their composition. Gunpowder was used in fighting wars during the 10th century. The tube-shaped firearms were invented in the 12th century. Guns were used in battles in the Song Dynasty and improved in the Yuan (1279—1368) and Ming (1368—1644) Dynasties. The continuously firing weapon, invented in the Ming Dynasty, could consecutively fire twenty eight bullets.

The knowledge of making gunpowder spread to Arab countries, and from these countries it went to Europe around the 13th century. Like gunpowder, the practice of making elixir pills, an initial form of chemical research, also went to Europe via Arab countries. These inventions transformed heat energy into mechanical energy, which greatly contributed to the progress of global civilization.

Section 6　Water Conservancy Project

The Dujiangyan Irrigation System, situated in the western part of Dujiangyan City, is known as the oldest existing water conservancy project without dams in the world. It has greatly benefited local people during the past 2260 years.

The topography of the Chengdu Plain (Sichuan Province) is high in the northwest and low in the southeast. Based on the geographic conditions, Li Bing and his son Li Erlang led the local people to build the Dujiangyan Irrigation System. After eight years of work, they completed three interconnected projects to discharge the functions of water intake, flood control and sand drainage. The fractious Minjiang River has been tamed since that time, and the irrigation system has greatly contributed to the richness of the vast Chengdu Plain. The area earned a reputation as the Land of Abundance. The project marks the beginning of scientific water control in human history and is called the Living Museum of Water Conservancy.

Section 7　Bridges

The history of Chinese bridge construction may be traced back three thousand years. Some ancient bridges are still in use after thousands of years. They have both the function of practical use and also became artistic objects in the hands of skillful workers. The oldest and most famous bridge is Ba Bridge, which is a stone bridge located in the northeast of Xi'an (Shaanxi Province). Ancient bridges are classified as stone bridges or timber bridges according to their building materials. Among the ancient bridges, some representatives are scattered throughout different provinces. Baodai Bridge (Suzhou, Jiangsu Province) is the most grandiose, multi-arched stone bridge. Lugou Bridge (Beijing), with its famous stone lions engraved on the balusters was considered to be the "best and most unique in the world" by Mark Polo. Longnao Bridge (Sichuan), Fengyu Bridge (Guanxi), Jihong Bridge (Yunnan) are all among the famous ancient bridges in China.

Zhaozhou Bridge, built in 607, is located in historically famous Zhaoxian County in Hebei province. Stonemasons, Li Chun and Li Tong, designed it. It is the earliest built spandrel bridge (1400 years ago), and it is the best preserved arch stone bridge in the world. Its total length is 50.82 meters. The bridge span is long, and the rise is only 23.9 feet, providing a low profile. The arch is different from the traditional semicircle. Dragons and other mythical creatures are beautiful decorations on the balustrades of the bridge.

Wanan Bridge (Louyang bridge), located at Quangzhou in Fujian Province, is a large stone beam bridge. The construction began in 1053 and was completed in 1060. The bridge, made of granite, spans over 800 meters with 47 arches, and each beam weighs 20 to 30 tons.

Section 8　Earliest Exploration of Flying

According to historical records from the Warring States Period (403 B. C. —221 B. C.), Gongshu (Lu Ban), a master craftsman, sharpened bamboo and wood to make a wooden magpie. The magpie flew into the air and stayed in the sky for three days without falling down.

Ancient Chinese tried to make use of air buoyancy by imitating the bird. The monarch, Wang Mang, of the Western Han Dynasty (206 B. C. —23 B. C.), once ordered his subordinates to be outfitted with the wings of big birds and clad with feathers, linked with strings and buttons. They glided several hundred steps and fell.

During the Eastern Jin Dynasty (317—420), Ge Hong conceived an idea of building a "flying chariot," for he had the desire to fly like the birds. This idea was hard to conceptualize at that time.

Emperor Wen Xuan (Northern Qi Dynasty, 550—577) demanded a flying experiment in which men were lifted by kites. Sixty men fell and died during the experiment; only one man was the exception.

An ancient Chinese named Wan Fu tried attaching forty-seven large firecrackers to a big chair. He sat on the chair, holding a fan in both his hands. He asked people to ignite the firecrackers so that he could fly resorting to the force of the firecrackers and the flapping fans. Though he died in the disaster with a thunderous bang, the principles of his experiment contributed to modern day flight.

Though the ancient Chinese did not fulfill their dream to fly in the sky, they made some scientific-oriented flying apparatuses such as a bamboo dragonfly (a toy for children), a wooden vulture, and the Kongming Lantern (hot-air balloon).

Section 9　Metallurgy

People who visit the museums such as Shaanxi Museum (Shaanxi Province), Lintong Museum (Shaanxi Province) and Sanxingdui Museum (Sichuan Province) may notice that most fine bronze made in ancient China from over 3,000 years to 2,000 years ago are ceremonial vessels, musical instrument, weapons and daily-use utensils.

The Si Mu Wu Ding cauldron, which is 133cm high, 110cm long, 78cm wide and weighs 875 kg., is the largest excavated bronze relic. The sophisticated technology indicates the ancient Chinese had already mastered the principle of casting by stages to achieve complex configurations. It is fairly evident that they had also mastered welding technology and the wax-replacement methods as well.

China mastered the technology of smelting pig iron and "block iron" between the 5th and 6th century B. C. The earliest large cast iron relic found in the Hubei Province was the iron lion cast in 953 A. D. This lion weighed 50,000 kg. The Chinese also mastered the technique of making steel by repeatedly forging carburized iron blocks. They invented the process for softening pig iron. Additionally, ancient people could make puddle steel and co-fusion steel. Their method for making co-fusion steel was an advanced technique occurring before the modern crucible steel-smelting was invented. China's iron and steel metallurgy and output were the best in the world.

China was the first country to smelt zinc in or before the 16th century and the technique was later passed to Europe.

Section 10　Bell Culture—Representative of Metallurgy Technique

China has a long and brilliant history of metallurgy and casting. A small type of bell called "*Ling*" was originally baked out of pottery clay. Archaeologists discovered red pottery *Ling* from the remains of the Yangshao Culture in Henan Province in 1950s. It is hollow and there is a handle attached to its top. A mall hole on both sides of the shoulder leads to the inside of it to fix the clapper. With a height of 9. 2 centimeters and a rim diameter of 5 centimeters, it has no any decorative pattern on the surface. It was made between 3900B. C. —3000 B. C.

A bell-shaped utensil of fine grey pottery clay was unearthed from the remains of the Longshan Culture (2800B. C. —2000B. C.) in Shaanxi Province. It is rectangular in shape, hollow and fixed with a solid handle, which is similar to a bell of the Shang Dynasty (16th century B. C. —1066 B. C.). It is 11. 7 centimeters in height and 9. 4 centimeters in horizontal rim diameter and 5. 6 centimeters in vertical rim diameter. Some experts believe it might have certain connections with Chinese musical instrument *Zhong* and *Do* of the Shang and Zhou dynasties. On each side of its shoulder is a hole for fixing the clapper. A bridge and a small ball in the hollow cavities can produce the sound when the bells are rocked.

Most of the pottery *Ling* dating back to the Longshan Culture period collected by the Gansu Provincial

Museum are shaped like it. One can hold the handle and rock it to produce the sound, or it can be attached to an object to jingle. Since a ling produces a sound when it is rocked to strike the inner wall, it is not so easy to control the rhythm of sounding.

China entered the Bronze Age around the 16th century B. C. A bronze *Ling* shaped like a pair of combined tiles with a decorative ear was unearthed from the remains of the Erlitou Culture (Henan Province) in 1981. It has a decorative ear and it is 8. 5 centimeters high and 0. 5 centimeter thick. Another bronze *Ling* dating back to around 2085 B. C. was unearthed in Shanxi Province in 1983. Shaped like a pair of combined tiles. It has the height of 2. 65 centimeters in height without any decorative pattern on the surface. They are bells dating back to the early period of the Xia Dynasty or the early Shang Dynasty.

Nao (*Zhizhong*) is a kind of musical instrument bigger than *Ling*. It appeared during the Shang Dynasty in mid China (present Henan Province). It can be struck when held by the player in his hand or put on a wooden stand and it is struck from the outside to control the rhythm of sounding.

Musical bells shaped like combined pairs of tiles appeared in many areas of China from the Western Zhou Dynasty (1066 B. C. —256 B. C.) to the Spring and Autumn Period (770 B. C. —476B. C.) and the Warring States Period (475B. C. —221 B. C.). The mouth of it faces down and it is struck easily in a suspending position. Kinds of small bells named Yongzhong, Niuzhong and Bo, shaped like combined pairs of tiles, appeared in chimes or groups. They were used on events. The court promulgated the ritual and musical institutions embodied by bells and musical stones, suited to the hierarchy in the Zhou Dynasty (770 B. C. —256 B. C.). Bells displayed a symbolic function during the period. One's social position and power was demonstrated by the suspending pattern and number of bells and musical stones. The musical bell, served as a typical instrument of the ritual and musical institutions, gradually stepped down from the stage of history with the collapse of the ritual and musical institutions during the Warring States Period (475 B. C. —221 B. C.). A chime of bells and a set of musical stones were unearthed from the tomb of the Marguis of Zeng at Leigudun, Suizhou, Hubei Province in 1978. The chime of bells consisted of 65 pieces (19 pieces of Niuzhong and 45 pieces of Yongzhong). They are suspended from a stand in three tiers and nine groups. The whole chime of bells weighs more than 2, 500 kilograms and each bell bore gold-inlaid inscriptions about events, notes and temperament. All the bells can produce tow notes three intervals apart. The big and thick Yongzhong bells on the lower tier produced a deep and long sound, creating harmony and enriching the atmosphere. The Niuzhong bells on the upper part can be used as a supplement to the Yongzhong bells on the middle tier. The Yongzhong bells on the middle tier have a wide range and clear timbre, playing the major role in a performance.

The First Emperor Ying Zheng ordered to destroy all the weapons from other states and cast them into 6 big court bells and 12 statues soon after he unified the whole China. From then on, the institution and function of imperial court bells were manipulated by Emperors of the later dynasties. On the eve of the Spring Festival, the bell pealed for the ceremony in the Jin Dynasty (265—420) and officials above the rank of commander governor entered the court to greet the emperor. The Bo (Yongzhong) was used to give the correct time in the Han Dynasty.

Ancient Chinese bells were divided into Buddhist bells, Taoist bells, musical bells and bells for sounding the night watches. When a monarch held court or an official leaves his office, a bell would be struck to call together their subordinates. A bell would be struck at a feast to accompany the singing of songs.

After Buddhism was introduced in China in the East Han Dynasty (25—220), it was propagated vigorously during the Southern (420—589) and Northern (386—581) dynasties. There was a bell at every Buddhism temple. The Buddhist bells appeared on the basis of the ancient bell and served as a musical in-

strument at a Buddhist mass. The cross section of them in this period were circular in shape to propagate the Buddhist ideas of " doing no evil, doing good deeds and paying debts of gratitude" to distant places and for a long time. A bell would be struck at a Buddhist temple to draw the devotion of worshippers and the awe of ghosts and gods. People believed the stoking of the bell enabled the good and honest people to be away from suffering and to enjoy happiness. When ghosts heard the stoke of the bell in a Buddhist temple, they would stop their ferocity.

Round bells took the place of those shaped like combined pairs of tiles. The round bells were widely used in Buddhist temples because of their deep and prolonged sound. The strokes of them became sweet, spreading Buddhism to distant places. The pearls of big ones can be heard five kilometers away and the strokes of small ones can reach places half a kilometer off.

The characters in designs of the Taoist bells, the time bells and the imperial court bells also followed the shape of the Buddhist bells. The style of the Buddhist bells influenced the development of ancient bells a lot.

Ancient bells in China were at the height of development during the Ming and Qing Dynasties. They attained greater perfection and richness both in shapes and cultural connotations. There were used to celebrate grand occasions, keep a record of events, hold sacrificial rites, admonish the world or give the correct time.

The image of *Pulao*, an animal created by Chinese, was cast on many ancient bells. The legend of *Pulao* goes that the dragon has nine sons. However, none of them becomes dragons. Pulao who lives near the seashore is afraid of the big fish called the whale in the sea. Whenever the whale attacks *Pulao*, he roars. His roaring voice could shake the heaven and the earth.

The ancient bells are no longer simply for practical uses. They became a symbol of an idea, a culture and a spirit in class society. From the very beginning the bronze bells were endowed with strong emotional coloring and cultural connotations in China. The stroke of the bell at a feast conveyed feelings of joy as well as the emotion of a man with a heavy heart. Sometimes, politicians ordered to make bells for particular purpose. For instance, President Sun Yet-sen's funeral committee decided to make a bell of the mausoleum in 1925. The design implies the need to " arouse the masses of the people". It conformed to President Sun's mettle and spirit. The sponsors of China held an impressive bell-and-drum beating ceremony to enhance the spirit of striving to make the Chinese nation stronger and promoting virtue by material means, when the 11th Asian Games opened in Beijing in 1990.

Different from the loud, extrovert sound of Western bells, Chinese bells produce deep and cohesive sound. People noticed long ago how to create bells of different sound. For instance, if the upper part of a bell is bigger than its lower part, it produces a muffled sound; if a bell is vertical, it makes a slow sound; if the mouth of a bell is wide open, the sound is unbridled; if a bell is vertical, it makes a slow sound. Producers also noticed a big and short bell could produce a quick sound that could be heard within a short distance, which a small and long one could make a mild sound which can be heard far away. Ancient makers produced bells of various sizes in the light of the environmental and social factors.

Chinese splendid casting techniques ushered in the resplendent Bronze Age. Perfect workmanship brought about exquisite pieces of art. Summing up Chinese experiences gained over a long period of time, the ancient Chinese acquired a good grasp of metal smelting and casting techniques.

The process of mastering the following technique has embodied the great wisdom of the Chinese nation, scientific and the technological progress in ancient times: an accurate mixture of metals for alloy, a division of work between the extracting furnace and the smelting furnace, the replacement of the pottery base furnace by the clay furnace, the appearance of the sand furnace and the furnace of comprehensive materials, the evolution of the air blower from the air bag to the bellows, the use of the metal mould method and the lost-wax method, the ingenious application of the way of combined moulds and separate casting and the way of separate moulds and combined casting and the development from the casting of a single surface shaping furnace to the casting of pit shaping furnaces. In the book *Xun Zi*, written in the Warring State Period (475B. C. —221 B. C.), Xun Zi summarizes the essentials of bronze casting technology as Correct moulds, fine mixture of copper and tin, ingenious workmanship and consummate smelting.

Two main methods were used to cast bells in ancient China: the clay mould method and the lost-wax method.

The clay mould method has the procedures of making inner moulds, making outer moulds, drying the moulds, combining the moulds, smelting and casting. Inner moulds could be made with a scraper or a mould set while outer moulds could be made on models or with a scraper. The drying process was to make the moisture content in the mould evaporate thoroughly in order to increase the strength of the mould. Air bags and crucibles were the main smelting equipment in the early days. Bellows and large smelting furnaces were used in the Ming (1368—1644) and Qing (1644—1911) Dynasties.

The lost-wax methods includes the procedures of making inner moulds, applying wax and carving, making outer moulds, melting wax and drying the moulds, smelting and casting. After the inner bell mould was built with clay, butter mixed with wax is coated on it. Then the solidified wax is carved into the desired shape of the bell. The wax is coated with clay and an outlet is left for the wax. The melt wax flows out of the outlet when heated and a cavity is formed. Heating it continuously until the bell mold is dry thoroughly. The last step is to melt metal and do casting with the bell mold.

The Yongle Bell of the Ming Dynasty was an outstanding representative of Buddhist bells and ancient Chinese bells. The rich historical and cultural connotations of it include the largest number of inscribed characters, the first-rate acoustic properties, superb casting technology and scientific mechanical structure. The Yongle Bell was cast during the reign of Emperor Yongle of the Ming Dynasty early in the 15th century. After the Emperor Zhu Di moved the capital into Beijing, he ordered the casting of the matchless big bell (1420 A. D.) as a symbol of the greatest reverence of imperial power. It is about 46 tons in weight, 6.75 meters in height, 3.3 meters in rim diameter and 0.22 meter in the thickness of the inclined plane of the rim. It is cast entirely with Buddhist sutras and incantations in both Han and Sanskrit languages. None of the 230,000 characters casted on the bell were left out by mistake and the lines were well spaced, manifesting the effects of refinement and neatness. This unequalled Buddhist bell is the admirable and priceless treasure as well as a crystallization of superb skills of laboring people in ancient times. The bell is made from a mixture of certain kinds of metal including copper, tin, lead, zinc, iron, gold, silver, magnesium and aluminium. Ancient Chinese added gold and silver in for they realized gold was good for resisting rust and corrosion while silver enhanced the fluidity of casting fluid. The waist of the bell is thinner than the lower part to produce deep and melodious notes and enhance the harmonization of the timbre.

Researcher found a pouring head at each of the four joints between the handle and the body of the bell in 1989. This finding shows the rain-type casting technique was used to make it possible for the molten bronze to flow into the pouring heads evenly. The technique prevented forming the blow holes and air holes effectively while making the bell. The looseness of the internal structure of the bell was also avoided.

The handle of the bell was cast with the lost-wax method before the body was cast. It was placed at the joint of the inner and outer moulds for connecting casting. The root of it was threaded through the cavity between the inner mould and the outer one at the top part of the bell. It has the steel cores inside to increase the strength of the handle. The four ends of it are connected with the lower part of the cavity at the top of the bell mould. The diameter is longer than that of the upper part of the bottom of the bell handle. Any trace of

"hot crack" from the joint of the handle and the body of the bell can be found. It was possible the handle was preheated before the body of the bell was cast. Ancient already realized bronze was liable to "hot crack" but not so liable to "cold crack". The "connecting casting" technology of such a heavy bell provides much for people to learn from even in modern times.

Bronze alloy is most liable to "hot crack" in the process of cooling which is most harmful to the cast. If the cast cools too quickly, too slowly or unevenly, undesirable consequences may follow. The Yongle Bell was cast using the method of pit shaping. It cooled in the pit like a natural computerized cooling system. Some materials good for the reduction of cooling shrinkage might be inserted into the inner mould of the bell to prevent the body from being cracked by the inner mould in the cooling process. In general, the cooling technique of the Yongle Bell is not less difficult and it is more important than other aspects of the casting technology.

If the case with a weight of more than several hundred kilograms is liable to "leak-out" because of the poor quality and strength of the moulds, it would deform the surface of the cast or even make the cast a complete failure. The casting of the Yongle Bell produced great force of impact and pressure on the moulds. The method of pit shaping and pottery mould provided a good solution to the problem of "leak-out". The space between the outer mould and the wall of the pit was filled with rammed earth when the moulds were combined to increase the strength of the entire mould. The successful casting of the Yongle Bell made an outstanding contribution to the casting industry in the world.

Part 6

Literature and Art

Chapter 15

Poetry

Xiaoxia Mao and Min Li

Classical Chinese literature refers to the period from the pre-Qin Dynasty (221—207 B. C.) to the Opium War of 1840 during the Qing Dynasty (1644—1911) . Modern Chinese literature is approximately from the Opium War of 1840 to 1919. Works feature in reflecting momentous political incidents and the multifarious events of social life. They mainly revolted the foreign invasion and disclosed the darkness of the feudal system. May 4th Movement in 1919 marks the beginning of a literature revolution.

The movement aims to criticize Confucianism and promote science, democracy and writing in the vernacular Chinese. It directly impelled the development of the new literary movement. The Chinese contemporary literature begins since then.

As the earliest form of Chinese literature, poetry roots in folk songs before the written language existed and it was developed in the process of people's everyday labor, their songs and dances.

The flow of literature has been surging on for millennia. The poems in China centered on topics of human life and religion. Lyrical poems have been the orthodox genre of Chinese literature. Chinese ancestors selected the lyric poems as a medium to express their naive sentiments and unsophisticated ideals. Poems are the foundation of rhyme prose, hymns, lyrical poems and odes.

The works of lyric type have become the mainstream in the development of Chinese literature. The lyrical has also syncretized the Chinese drama, novel and prose as well as modeling art, painting and architectural decorations. Since it has become the common consciousness of literary generations, it is regarded as the foremost characteristic of Chinese literature. Poetry of China emphasizes the behaviors and supports the good conduct of Chinese people. It combines three social functions of recording history, cultivating the moral character and political teachings together, which represent the essence of the traditional Chinese poems.

Section 1   Spring-Autumn Period (the 6th and 7th century B. C.)

Chinese literature is characterized by a long tradition of realism. As the earliest anthology of ancient poems, the *Book of Poems*, compiled two thousand and five hundred years ago, was the realistic literature of China. *The Book of Poems* collected poems written in four-word verses, and is composed of 305 poems and songs from the early Zhou Dynasty (1046—256 B. C.) and the Mid-Spring-Autumn Period. The anthology was divided into three sections according to the rhythms: the Feng section (native ballads of the various states), the Ya section (music pieces from the territory of the Zhou Kings) and the *Song* section (eulogies to ghosts, deities' meritorious deeds, song along with dances).

The *Feng* section is the most important part of the anthology. It includes 160 poems collected from the

15 vassal states of the Zhou Dynasty, which are mainly folksongs expressing people's feelings, desires, and opinions, reflecting the miserable lives of the peasants, the strong desire of the young people for love, and satirizing the idle and greedy lords. Readers can take them as glimpses of ordinary people's life of that time. The most distinctive artistry lies in its realistic depiction of objects in simple but focused, elegant and lively language. In the Song section, skilled application of word rhyming, double-adjectives and alliteration enhance this part's artistic appeal. The expressive techniques of metaphor, evocation and descriptive prose interspersed with verse greatly reinforce the poetry's illustrative power.

The *Ya* section comprises the *Book of Odes and The Book of Epics*. The 105 poems in this section were intonated at courts or banquets. The works include satire on the current politics of the day and odes to former heroes.

Song comprises three parts: The Hymns of Zhou, The Hymns of Lu and The Hymns of Shang. 40 poems are included and used when the ruling class offered sacrifices to the gods and ancestors.

Confucius recollected and edited *the Songs* and made it one of his five canons. Many works in the *Book of Poems* reflected the actual social trends of that time via the aspirations and sentiments of the writers and the singers. For instance, the fatuity and cruelty of the king was mirrored in the poem, North Hill, as the words "They swill and swallow like pigs, up there... their mouth big words, oh big ones! Up there..." delivered the society's anger and grief. In the poem, *Jie Nan Shan* (bamboos on the South Hill), the King of Zhou was blamed for trusting mean people, "Not carrying out the state affairs himself causes the people to be hard pressed." "State's in a mess. Why don't you care?" All these poems contain political views to dissuade the rulers. They showed typically the characteristic of the Chinese literature of "complementing the political teachings".

Beside its political purpose, the *Book of Joy* also reflected distinctively the joy and anger, and the grief and happiness of the people. In the poem *Big Rat*, in the Wei Feng sub-section, the exploiter was compared to a big rat. It repeatedly deplored that there was no place where people were well fed and clothed. There were also a fair proportion of love poems in the book. The poem, *By the Han and the Yangtze*, describes a young man's strong desire to date his lover. In the poem *Oh, Zhongzi, Zhongzi*, a girl's standing at a nonplus for sensibilities, "Stop breaking my lovely sandal trees—I don't care about the trees, but it's my neighbors' tongues I'm afraid of. Oh, Zhongzi, I miss you, I miss you, but I'm afraid of their gossip."

The ancient songs in *The Book of Poems* were mostly plain and simple. It indicates the literature was still in the rudimentary stage. Howbeit, varied techniques of expression were shown in it.

Although the form was flexible in a sort of way, most poems in the Feng section of the *Book of Poems* contained the form of four words each line and every other line rhymed. Two literary devices "Fu", "Bi" and "Xing" were frequently employed with good artistic effects in *The Book of Poems*. "Fu" is a kind of station that represents something directly and exactly. "Bi" may be explained as metaphor. It means using some words or phrases to indicate something similar. "Xing" is a kind of rhetoric that states something at first to indicate the things you want to express. For instance, the poem, *By the Han and the Yangtze*, stated the difficulty of seeing one's lover by first describing "the tall tree gives no cover" and "the Han is too broad to be swum." These literary devices greatly enrich the forms of expression of poems and lyrics. They make it possible to create a moving mood and a moving image in a few short paragraphs. Marking a brilliant beginning in Chinese literature, *The Book of Poems* has forms and devices for expression provided with useful references for later generations. The achievement of this work lies primarily in voicing the aspirations of the time.

Section 2 Poetry of the South and "Fu" in the Han Dynasty

Poetry experienced the second prosperity in the late period of the Warring States. "*Chuci*" occurred as a poem form with free lines to make it easier to show unrestrained and flowing emotion. "*Chuci*" as a new style of poetry, established by Qu Yuan and Song Yu. Qu Yuan was the earliest known famous Chinese poet and once reformist trusted by the emperor. When the situation of the Chu Kingdom was at the crucial moment, he was exiled and unable to realize his political ideal. He wrote the immortal masterpieces : "Sorrow After Departure". "Ask Heaven", "Nine Elegize", "Deplore Ying City", "Remembering Shad City", etc … When his country was ruined by the country Qin, he drowned himself in the Miluo River. His noble personality and his excellent poems have profound and lasting influence on the later generations.

Sorrow after Departure is a long poem describing his love for his state and his disappointment at its situation. The poem marks the beginning of romanticism in Chinese poetry, as it contains descriptions of imagined scenes in heaven.

The *Nine Elegizes*, the collective of nine poems, perfectly integrated the sentiment of sorrow, realistic description and intense argumentation. Among these famous poems, *Lament on Encountering Sorrow* is his magnum opus, which laid the corner stone for Chinese romantic literature. It drew much on ancient Chinese mythology and used a large number of exaggerations in portraying characters and describing objects. Metaphors are largely used in the poem. The fairly tales in the poem further enhances the romantic flavor.

Poetry of the South referred specifically to the new style of poetry. Qu Yuan's poems were the representation of the new style, which had a rich flavor of the local color. All the works used the Chu dialect and recorded the Chu events and things.

Liu Xiang redacted an anthology of Qu Yuan and his follower Song Yu's works, and other works of his time in imitation of their style by the end of the Western Han Dynasty (206 B. C. —220 A. D.) . He entitled them, the Poetry of the Chu (Chu Ci) . It is another anthology of songs and ballads with a far-reaching influence after the *Book of Poems* in ancient China. Chu Ci is a new style of poetry absorbing the romantic attributes of myth and established the romantic style of Chinese literary creation.

"*Fu*" was a new form of rhymed prose. It emerged, or originated, from the Book of Poems and the Poetry of the South. Rhymed prose was considered suitable for reciting but not for singing. Another feature was the emphasis on elaboration and description.

Seven Discussions showed the purpose of literature to be beneficial to political teachings. It is the cornerstone of the style of the rhymed prose made by Mei Chen. It used elegant dictions to describe elaborately the six pleasures of music, gourmandism, horses and chariots, barbeques and excursions, hunting, and watching tide at beach. The exaggeration and elaboration of it impressed the mentality of the readers. Readers feel as if they were personally on the scene. Many later writers took its style as the model.

The later period of the Western Han Dynasty saw the flourish of the rhymed prose and was named the Grand Han Rhymed Prose Period. To sing the praises of the Han emperors, the writers of rhymed prose used exaggerated dictions to describe the achievements of those emperors. The greatest writer of the rhymed prose during the reign of Emperor Wu was Sima Xiangru. His representative works were "Zi Xu Fu" (Rhymed Prose of the Empty Person) and "Shang Lin Fu" (Rhymed Prose of the Royal Forest) . In the former, he used imaginary figures, Zi Xu, Wu You (nonexistent person) . His works pushed the Han rhymed prose to the pinnacle. However, his works also pushed it to an impasse because his later works overemphasized the form and the poems lacked feelings and sentiments.

An official administrative institution, Music Bureau, called *Yuefu*, was founded during the time of

Emperor Wu specially collecting and recording ceremonial chants, and the songs and ballads of ordinary people. One of the most outstanding folk ballads of them is *Peacock Flies to the Southeast*. It is about a tragic love story common in the feudal society. It tells of the tragedy of a young married couple who committed suicide as the result of the cruelty of her mother in law. Another is Mo Shang Sang. It tells about an interesting story happening in mulberry woods and created a beautiful, charming and resourceful image. The poem and its protagonist had become more and more popular in the Tang Dynasty after spread in about 600 years from Han to Sui Dynasty. The methods the people of Tang Dynasty received Mo Shang Sang were varied, such as included by types books, studied by scholars in research works, absorbed by mythology and real life and using allusions and artistry and imitation by the poets in the Tang Dynasty.

During the Northern Dynasty, the famous folk song *Ballad of Mulan* appeared. A girl named Mulan whose aged father was conscripted, unwilling to see her father fighting in a war, disguised herself as a man and joined the army in his place. She showed remarkable skill as a warrior and became a female general. Her true identity remained hidden from her members until the very end. By the end, she refused a court position and returned to her hometown to be with her family members.

> ...
> She rides with the army.
> At night the army camped by the Yellow River
> And her ear heard no father, no mother,
> But only the roar of the rushing river.
> At dawn they left the river, rode on, rode on,
> Her ears heard no father, no mother,
> But only the whinny of enemy horses, there at the border.
> Thousands and thousands of miles she marches,
> She broke through passes, she whirled past hills.
> Watchmen's gongs echoed in northern air.
> Armor and mail gleamed in wintry light.
> Their general fought hard, battle after battle,
> ...
> But Mulan asks for no post at court,
> All I beg for is a camel
> To take me home to my parents.
> ...
> She took off her warrior's coat, her warrior's cloak,
> She put on the dress she'd worn as a girl.
> She stood at the window, she let down her hair.
> She stood at the window, she made up her face.
> ...

From the lines hereinbefore, readers know Mulan had a labourious martial life, stayed for over ten years with men. She devoted her life and youth to the country. However, Mulan was not only a warrior in the battle fields, but also a young girl who had the desire to live an ordinary life. To her honor and social status could never be compared with the joy of a peaceful and simple life with her parents.

Along with the development of Musical Bureau poems, the five-word verse and the seven-word verse came into being.

Section 3　Poetry in the Wei and the Jin Dynasties

There were some important poets during this period, such as Cao Cao (155—220), Cao Zhi, Ran Ji, and Ji Kang (members of the Seven Poets of Jian'an). Cao Cao was a famous politician, strategist and an excellent poet. Here is an example from Cao Cao's *Live as Long as the Heavenly Tortoise*:

> Live as long as the heavenly tortoise
>
> And in the end you die.
>
> Cloud-breaking dragons, roaring in the sky,
>
> Drop to the earth, and are dead.
>
> But a withered old horse, lying in its stall,
>
> Dream of galloping mile after mile.
>
> And grizzled heroes, older than old,
>
> Still hope for glory.
>
> Heaven ends your life,
>
> But not Heaven alone:
>
> If you have a light heart, a happy heart,
>
> You'll live to a good old age.

Cao Cao was full of political ambition. He assimilated himself with a nag, still having his dream of galloping mile after mile. The lines of the poem manifest his political ambition and his strong will, and it is also the reflection of what is simon-pure hero of his time.

During the Western Jin Dynasty (265—316), poetry was marked by superficial and empty content, and was of euphuistic style. Lu Ji (261—305) and Pan Yue (247—300) are representative poets. Zuo Si (250—305) continued the tradition of the Jian'an School and wrote poems with realistic values which were different from the norm. Taoist philosophy influenced some poets of that time. They berhymed to express their understanding of Chinese metaphysics toward end of the Western Dynasty.

Tao Qian (Tao Yuanming, 365—427), one of the masters of the five-character poetry, was excellent in writing the joys of nature and the solitary life. He tried to escape reality and focus on nature and country life. He became the archetype of the "hermit poet" in Chinese literature. He wrote in an unadorned style that was imitated by later poets. Xie Lingyun (385—433) is another poet who wrote poems about nature, who is best remembered for his landscape poetry.

Section 4　Radiant Poetry in the Tang Dynasty: the five-character poetry

It is widely recognized that the Tang Period is a splendid era and the most prosperous period in the lyric literature development. Thousands of poems of almost all different styles were produced during this period. The book, *Complete Anthology of Tang Poems* compiled in the Qing Dynasty, includes about 50,000 poems written by more than 2,300 poets of the Tang Dynasty. Many poetic schools, boasting of divergent styles, appeared at a draught just like "all the flowers blossoming." The poetic achievements in this period surpassed all other periods both in terms of quality and quantity.

The Four Prominent Poets of the Early Tang Dynasty:

There are four outstanding pioneers of Tang poetry, they are Wang Bo, Lu Zhaoling, Yang Jiong and Luo Binwang These young and ambitious poets discarded the gorgeous style of the courtiers in the Qi and Liang dynasties, and enlarged the contents of the poems and wrote in a vigorous style.

For instance, Wang Bo's "You are my bosom friend in the world. Though in the remote corner, Yet you will be like my close neighbor" is well-known and widely recited even to this day at the farewell. Wang Bo turned his sorrow into an unconstrained sentiment, showing the writer's extraordinarily broad mind. Take a look at the following famous poem by Chen Zi'ang, *Ascending the Youzhou Terrace*, which was an another masterpiece at that time"

Ancient stages I fail to see,

Future generations I fail to meet.

Lonely in a world going on forever,

I shed tears in grief.

Although he expressed his loneliness, it involved no complaint against his predicament. He showed his broad mind and enterprising spirit through his awareness of the order of nature. The first two lines are even widely used by people today.

Pastoral poets and Frontier Poets in the High Tang Period:

The two genres of the poetical themes in this flourishing period are the landscape poets represented by Meng Haoran and Wang Wei, and the frontier poets represented by Gao Shi and Cen Shen. Wang Changling, Li Qi, and Wang Zhihuan are other famous frontier poets Some borderland poems depicted frontier scenery, military life, soldiers' homesickness, passionate patriotism and devotion to the state. Much of the poems were forceful and magnificent. In the poem, *Dirge for Liangzhou*, by Wang Zhihuan, "Futilely the Qiang flute plays in compassion for the willows. For spring breezes never go beyond the Yumen pass. ", reflected the nostalgia of soldiers staying long at the frontier garrison where was the desolate and uninhabited. Though his sentiments were intense and plaintive, the scene was open and wild, reflecting fully the valiancy of the soldiers. In Cen Shen's *Meeting a Courier Bound for the Capital*, he wrote "We meet, riding on horses, Hurrying, neither of us with paper, neither of us with ink. All you can carry home for me is words that I am still alive and well. " It stated that a courier was on his way to the capital. His future remains problematic. He was both full of ambition and a little bit pathos being away from his family. The poem reflects the aspirations of a scholar for fame, social status and the realization of his ideals in politics.

Different from these borderland poems, the pastoral poems reflected the thinking of the poets who stayed away from ado and wish for nature. Wang Wei was an all-around artist who had great success in many aspects such as poetry, painting, calligraphy and music. Most of his poems delineate the beautiful natural scenery. Su Shi, a famous poet of the Song Dynasty, appraised "in his painting there is poetry and in his poetry there is painting. " He avoided abstruse vulgarity and flowery words, broke through the ambit of poem and painting and introduced painting techniques into his poetry portraying. One example from *Weicheng Song* by Wang Wei, is as follows: Take a look at the following famous poem by Wang Bo:

Morning rain settles

The post road dust

At Weicheng.

Willows around the inn

Bud greener than green.

Drink, drink!

West of Yangguan

Who can you ever find to drink with?

The poem was a ditty hummed in the morning, about a small inn in a small city away from the capital city. It was like a delicate painting of natural scenery. His poem is delicate and pretty, graceful and vivid. It

Chapter 15
| Poetry

reflected the writer's mood just like limpidity water. Although he had been demoted to the out-of-the-way area and was separated from his close friend, he was not depressed. Instead, he was magnanimous.

"Celestial poet" and "Saint poet" in the High Tang Period:

Li Bai (701—762) is often regarded, along with Du Fu (712—770), as one of the two greatest poets in China's literary history.

Li Bai was born in Suiye (Kirgizstan) and moved to Sichuan with his father at five. He is best known for the extravagant imagination in his poetry, as well as for his great love for liquor. He spent much of his life travelling reading when he was young. After his learning was recognized by Tang Xuanzong, he was given a post at the Hanlin Academy, which served to provide a source of scholarly expertise and poetry for the Emperor. Li Bai remained less than two years as a poet in the Emperor's service before he was dismissed for his unyeildingness and an unknown indiscretion. Then he went on with his aimless wandering all over the country. Li Bai is considered as the foremost romantic poet in the Tang Dynasty. His political ambition was spoiled, so he turned to alcoholic drink to drown his sorrows and writing, which was described as "A hundred poems per gallon liquor."

A Small Hill written by Li Bai revered the chivalrous spirit and the political ambitions when young. When Li Bai realized his political ideals were in sharp contradiction to the frightfulness of social reality, he wrote Hard Goes the Way and Verses in the Old Style. During his journeys all over the country, he composed famous poems such as Departure from Baidi City at Dawn, Song of the Frontier and Watching the Mt. Lushan Waterfall. He was a genius whose works were full of passion, imagination and also elegance. His interactions with nature, friendship, his love of wine and his acute observations of life inform his best poems. His other verses, exceeding nine hundred in all, are also notable.

His poems are characterized by unusual imagination and free and direct expression of feelings:

At dawn I left Baidi towering in the midst of colorful clouds,

And reached Jiangling a thousand Li away in a day.

The screams of monkeys on either bank went on and on,

While my light boat passed by ten thousand hills.

Satisfaction and admiration will fill our hearts when we read such beautiful and dashing lines. They are so colorful, so musical, and so impressive. The image in the poem—a boat rushing forward down the gorges—is just a description of the poet himself.

From another Li Bai's poem, Song of Qiupu, comes another example: "Thirty thousand feet of snow-white hair, silvered by grief easily that long, easily that deep…" His sadness is described as being as endless as his long hair of three-thousand Zhang (1 Zhang = 3.3 meters). His powerful and unrestrained works have sentiments surging like a swift current. Cited below are parts of Li Bai's famous Tianmu Mountain, Ascended in a Dream: a Farewell Song:

Let me tend a white deer, high on a cliff,

And ride it when I visit famous mountains.

How could I bow to the ground, how could I lower my eyes,

Humbling myself to the merely noble, the merely rich?

My heart would be emptied of all happiness,

My face would forget how to smile.

The lines express Li Bai's dignity and uncontrolled character as a straightforward literator. After realizing his political ambitions could not be realized, he left the court.

Du fu (618 to 907), a renowned poet, was born in Gong County in Henan province. Readers of many different periods have considered Du Fu to be the greatest poet of the Chinese tradition.

At the age of 14 or 15 he began to write poetry and at 20 he left home and went touring. He lived in Chang'an (Xi'an) when he was thirty-five. During this period, Du Fu witnessed a typical political and social situation; the common people still lived in poverty while the emperor and his top officials enjoyed a foolishly luxurious life. His poems have been called "poetic history," just for they reflect the political and military situation of his time, and the life and miseries of the people.

Among the 1,000 poems written throughout his life, the famous ones included *Three Officers*, *Three Partings*, *My Thatched Hut Is Wrecked by the Autumn Wind and A Song of Fair Ladies*. In many of his poems, deep sympathy for the people is one of the main characteristics.

The works of Du Fu was in contrast to Li Bai's. Li Bai was called the "celestial poet". He was a Romanticist. In his poems, extraordinary imagination, bold exaggeration, beautiful dictions and sonorous rhythms blend miraculously without apparent effort, reaching a superlative level. The works of Li Bai were powerful and unrestrained, with sentiments surging like a swift current. In contrast, Du Fu's were of a quite different style. His works are depressive and marked by a modulatory melody like undulating waves, suitable for reading again and again His *Rain of Joy on a spring Night* is an example:

Oh lovely spring rain!

You come at the right time, in the right season.

Riding the night winds you creep in,

Quietly wetting the world.

Roads are dark, clouds are darker.

Only a light on boat, gleaming.

And in the morning the city is drunk with red flowers,

Cluster after cluster, moist, glistening.

Du Fu's sad life experiences made him concerned for the common people and their lives. The poem *Chariot Song* reflected people's suffering:

Chariots creaking,

Horses neighing,

Men marching, bows at their sides.

Parents and wives see them off:

Clouds of dust smother Xianyang Bridge,

They stamp their feet, they clutch the men's sleeves,

The block the road,

They weep.

…

They leave as boys wearing turbans,

They come home with gray hair.

But all of them are sent to the border,

Where battles rage and blood flows

Like flood water in a river.

…

Only weeds grow in the field?

Some strong women can hoe and plough

But the crops are planted every which way.

…

Oh, we know, how bitterly we know

The birth of a male child brings nothing to rejoice at,

And the birth of a girl child brings no sorrow.

…

But boys will be sent to war

And buried under distant grass.

Remember the white bones at Lake Qinhai,

Lying forever forgotten, rotting.

New ghosts grieve, old ghosts weep:

Listen, on rainy days you can hear them whining.

Du Fu paid much attention to state affairs and common people. The poem offers a believable panorama of real life outpouring writer's sympathy for poor people. His depressive meticulous literary style reached a high degree of professional proficiency in this poem. Since his works were regarded as the classics of realism, he was called the "saint poet."

Eminent Poets in the Mid-Tang Period:

In the Mid-Tang Dynasty, the politics suffered many rebellions and became recessionary. The poets also subsequently diverted the attention from state affairs to the trivialities of daily life, and from the glorification of landscapes to the anchorage of spirits and hopes.

Poets Bai Juyi (772—846) is one of the renowned literary figures then. His poems were written in a satirical way to describe social turbulence and people's sufferings. His *The Old Charcoal Seller* fully satirized the dark social reality. And the *Chang Hen Ge* (Song of Eternal Lament) praised the eternal love between Emperor Xuanzong in flourishing Tang and his beloved concubine Yang Guifei. The following is extract of it:

…

Such beauty? She was married to the king:

A single glowing smile so caught at his heart

That all the women at court turned boring, dull.

In the chill of spring she was ordered

To bathe with the king, in the baths at Huaqing.

The bland water warmed her wax-like skin

And she rose from the water so delicious a thing

That his favor was rightly won.

The wavy hair, the rose-like face, were lovelier still,

Crowned with a golden headdress, tinkling, bright.

…

A hundred miles west o the capital gates.

The army refuses to march on:

To pacify them, the lady must be sacrificed,

Must die obediently as the army watched.

Her beautiful jewels roll on the ground, no one cares about

Her jade comb, her golden pin,

Her lovely jacket embossed with a bird's wing.

The king covers his face with trembling hands,

Motionless, helpless.

…

His musicians, is tumblers, grow gray,

Her palace maids, her palace eunuchs, grow old.

…

He lies in bed, not sleeping, turning this way, turning that way,

…

Year after year have slid by

Since life and death were cut brutally apart.

…

He travels on a fearful quest,

Flying on clouds, blown by the wind,

Combing the universe, hunting high and low,

But her spirit is nowhere in all that endless space,

…

And then the magician hears of a solitary island,

A fairy place hidden in the sea, covered with mist and clouds.

And in those clouds were bright pavilions and shining towers

Where fairies entered and fairies left,

And she who bore one of the lost one's name

Was the loveliest of them all,

…

She entered the hall,

Her sleeves fluttering—

Almost as if, with tender grace,

She were dancing, still, to

"Rainbow Robes and Gossamer Coats."

…

Then she mastered herself, bent her eyes down,

And expressed tender gratitude for the king's concern.

…

No one else there to hear them:

"We will be together, as birds flying in pairs in heaven;

On this earth we will be two trees joined in one,

Our branches intertwined."

…

Though even heaven will end, even earth will end.

But their sorrow will last forever.

The poem adopts a romantic style and narrates the love tragedy, with rich imagination, exquisite plot, harmonious rhythm and elegant dictions. It has been appreciated by all the later generations.

In "The Song of a Pipa Player" there are these lines describing the beautiful music produced by the Pipa (a Chinese stringed instrument, resembling the guitar):

Strong and loud, the thick string sounded like a sudden shower;

Weak and soft, the thin string whispered in your ear.

When strong and weak, loud and soft sounds were mixed,

They were like big and tiny pearls falling on a jade plate.

Also in this the poem, the description of geisha's sad life reflected the miserable fate of women in the feudalist society. It also reflected Bai Ju Yi's own disaffection for the blows he suffered in his political career. The cited part is as the following:

...

We called to her, over and over, until she appeared,

But still hiding her face behind her pipa.

Turning the pegs, testing the strings,

She betrayed her feelings without playing a note,

Each string a meditation, each note a sorrow,

As if to pour the bitterness from her life.

...

I left the capital a year ago,

And now, a sick exile at Jiujiang, sorrow grows.

...

Often I sit up, alone, and sip wine.

There are folk songs, of course, there are village flutes,

But how crude they are! They grate on my ears.

Tonight I heard you play the pipa.

It brightens me like music from Heaven.

...

Tear-soaked, sorrow-laden, all sobbed out at once.

And who was weeping the bitterest tears of all?

The Deputy Chief of Jiujiang Prefecture, whose blue gown was wet.

The poem had a complicated plot with meticulous description and fluent and harmonious rhythms. It is taken as a model of the perfect combination of ideology and art by Chinese poets.

Poets of the late Tang Dynasty

In late Tang Dynasty, with the deterioration of government, the poems reflected more and more hopeless and helpless feelings of the people in a heavy way. Poets of this period fell to reminiscence and meditation on the past, and exuded a strong sentimentality. The most talented of these were Li Shang Yin and Du Mu. Some of their works are about beauty, some about disconsolation as rulers were fatuous and failed to value them. Du Mu's best poems are Spring over the South and on Deep Feelings, which recalls past glories and lament the fall of previous dynasties to express his grim pessimism about current affairs. Li Shangyin wrote a large number of poems that extracted beauty from obscure sensation and image. He produced a realm of beauty with an underlying. Meanwhile, it goes beyond hurt, melancholy depth, and felt a sense of decline. The lines from Untitled Poem have been widely recognized:

So hard for us to meet,

Harder to leave.

The spring breeze is feeble.

And the flowers are withering away,

Just as the silkworm spins silk

until it dies,

So the candle cannot dry its tears

until the last drop is shed.

Section 5   Splendid Song Poems

Although poetry was not as flourishing in the Song (960—1279) as in the Tang Dynasty, it neverthe-less carved out its own style. Poetry of the Song dynasty was less lyrical but more narrative, with more commentary. It paid great attention to description and adopted a lot of prose sentence structure. Compositions of "Ci (the Song Poem), a kind of musical poetry, contribute much to Chinese literature". "Ci" was a new type of poetry originating from the feast music at the court, and it reached floruit in the Song Dynasty. Two major styles appeared in the early period of the Northern Song Dynasty.

One type of the Song poems with a short tune and flowery diction was represented by Yan Shu and Ouyang Xiu. Su Shi (1037—1101), the greatest "Ci" poet in the later period of the Northern Song Dynasty, founded the Powerful and Free School (Heroic and Unrestrained Style). Xin Qiji was also a famous poet of this style.

Su Shi originated a new way in the Song poems, chiefly by breaking away from the decadent subject matter and adopting a bold style. With his adventurous enterprising spirit, his unrestrained, optimistic personality, his patriotism and his love of life, he diverted the course of the Song poems from singing the praises of rulers to singing the broader life and society. He was a remarkable and innovative "Ci" poet. A wide variety of issues such as society, politics, ambition and life are reflected in his works. Su Shi is not only accomplished in poem, but also in politics, gardening and cooking When Moon Is So Bright, one of his famous works, represented his innovative best:

When will the bright moon appear?

Cup in hand, I speak to the blue sky.

…

Sadness and joy,

Separation and reunion:

The world is no paradise

Waxing and waning,

Now clear, now cloudy,

The moon is never stable.

No, there's no perfection.

Not in heaven, not on earth.

If only we could live to a green old age,

Sharing her beauty, together

Though far, far apart.

From the above lines, readers notice the poem is filled with his stirring emotion and lofty spirit. He realized " there's no perfection" in the world, however, "If only we could live to a green old age, Sharing her beauty, together, though far, far apart his words" fully express his open, optimistic spirit and attitude toward life.

Another master piece of his, River Flows on to the East injected his real feelings into the picturesque scenery and the historical heroes. His conception of life, "Men go through sorrow and joy, parting and meeting" and his conception of history, "Same mountains and rivers, but different people" brought new content to the poetic themes.

Xin Qiji was a famous patriotic poet from the southern Song Dynasty, who succeeded Su Shi in developing the new style and exploring new fields of the Song poems, As a patriotic lyricist, he sang of the sorrows and joys of the time, the indignation and hope of the nation. He pushed the Song poems up to a new peak. His Song poems were unrestrained and forthright, full of patriotic ambitions. Xin's lyrics were chiefly characterized by his fervent, subjective sentiments and his obstinate ideals. His Song poems are freer with a richer language due to his apt and natural usage of allusions. Song of a Southern Country and Dance of the Cavalry are examples.

Li Qing Zhao' (1080—1155) poems are well-polished, lively and elegant. Her poems are also distinctive and vivid with a very strong artistic appeal to readers. Her works could be divided into two phases. In the first phase, her poems are sprightly and tender showing her passion for nature and love as a maiden and a young wife. The poems are sprightly and tender. However, in the second phase, her suffering and hard life greatly influenced her style. Her poems are full of sentimental feelings. Her sorrow not only resulted from the vicissitudes of her life but also from the decline of the nation. Her sorrow was very profound.

Her works were mournful and moving. Take her Sheng Sheng Man as example:

Enchanted, distracted,

Saddened, and alone,

I live a dreary life,

A weary life, and miserable,

…

Can a few cups of stale wine

Keep off the cold night wind?

…

Sitting by the window

I wait, alone, sad,

For darkness to fall.

…

Wutong leaves will drip, will drop,

And I will be so deep in misery

That even a word like "wretched" could not explain,

Could never explain.

Liu Yong (980—1053), a well-known Song Ci writer, was famous for his being good at temperament. His poems shifted the subjects to cities, towns, mountains and rivers and broadened the horizon of Song Ci.

The Dongjing folklore is richly reflected in Liu Yong's *Yue Zhang Ji*. His description of the folklore and narration of the folk culture in the song, the dance and the women taking up singing and dancing as a profession in Dongjing, the capital of the Northern Song Dynasty. His narrations not only enrich the subject matter of the Song Ci (lyrics), but also provide valuable first-hand information for our study of the folklore in Dongjing of the Northern Song Dynasty.

Section 6　Poetry in the Yuan, Ming and Qing Dynasties

Poetry began to decline from the Yuan Dynasty. Though some good poems were composed, poetry lost its dominant role in Chinese literature. The most famous poets of the Yuan Dynasty were Ma Zhiyuan (1250—1324) and Sadula (1272—1225). In Ma's Tianjinsha, the sad mood and loneliness of the author were expressed through the vivid descriptions of a particular environment. The images of "lean horse," "withered vines," "old branches" and "returning crows" all expressed the old man's depressed and senti-

mental feelings. In *Early Summer*, *Huai River Valley*, Sadula expressed his pleasant feeling and hope by the mentioning of "fish jump out of the net," "green" and "plums grow into fruit." The surrounding of Southern China's early summer was full of life in the poem.

Among the poets of the Ming Dynasty, Yu Qian (1398—1457), Wang Pan (1470—1530) and Wu Weiye (1609—1672) are the most well-known. In the *Limestone Song*, Yu Qian expressed the quality of the real man he admired and wished to be:

It was digging

Chiseling

Cutting

That led me into the world.

What can heating

Burning

Boiling

Do to hurt me, now?

Reduce me to dust, to powder,

I'm not afraid

So long as I remain stainless, and pure.

The poem reflected the author's courage, straightforwardness and strong will in confronting a hard environment.

Nalan Xingde (1651—1685), a very famous poet, wrote *Tune*: *Chanxiangsi* to show his homesickness:

Past rivers, past mountains,

On we go, to Yuguan Pass.

At night a thousand tent-lights burn.

Wing roars, snow falls,

The watchman bangs his gong

As he walks his rounds.

My heart beats sick at the noise.

I cannot dream any longer:

At home I never heard such sounds!

The feudal society experienced great changes after the Opium War in 1840. The progs such as Liang Qichao, Huang Zunxian and Tan Sitong called for the innovation of poetry. They either expressed their misgivings about China's future or their patriotism about their country in their works. Tan Sitong's lines "Ah, eight hundred million eyes are wet" "Where is China, now, on the map" and his lines in *Lines Composed in Reflection* are both good examples. Liang Qi Chao expressed his oppression through the following lines when he schemed without avail for the country:

…

But oh, such rare talents,

Such bold vision,

And nothing to do but

Cry out in his poems!

Such indignation at invaders

At aggressors:

How can we keep from crying with him?

Huang Zunxian explained his hatred to the invaders and asked the question "Land of wealth, land of beauty, sinking fast—and who can save her?" in his To Liang Qichao.

Other famous patriot poets of the Qing Dynasty include Yuan Mei (1716—1798), Gong Zizhen (1792—1840), Lin Zexu (1785—1850), Lu Song (1791—1860), Huang Zunxian (1848—1905), Tan Sitong (1865—1898), Liang Qichao (1873—1929), Qiu Jin (1877—1907) and Liu Yazi (1887—1958).

Section 7 Contemporary Poetry

Chinese poetry came into the modern times after the New Cultural Movement of 1917, and the May Fourth Movement in 1919. The New cultural movement was a truly great revolution, which opened a new chapter in the history of poetry. There are many most famous poets in that period, such as Guo Moruo, Xu Zhimo, Wen Yidou, Xu Zhimo (1896—1931) is notable for his works high level of artistry. In his famous Goodbye Again, Cambridge, his lines rhymes as "I leave softly, gently, exactly as I came... Without taking so much as a piece of cloud. But with a quick jerk of my sleeve, I wave goodbye." In the poem, "golden willow," "dancing green grass on a watery floor," and "a flood of starlight" are all vivid images of his expectations or the precious things he desires to own. Though some of his poems had some deficiencies in ideological content, they are admired for the dramatic images, ornate words and rhyme.

Mao Zedong (1893—1976), a great politician, thinker, military expert and poet, wrote many traditional poems. His Long March and Snow are famous ones. In Mao's Snow, the norland scenery in winter is described as "A thousand miles of frozen earth, ten thousand miles of whirling snow." It expressed his love of his country and the broad mind and optimism of a great man.

Li Ji's long narrative poem, Wang Gui and Li Xiangxiang, uses the ballad form and the traditional literary devices of metaphor and allusion. The poem made it a harmonious unity of ideological content and artistic quality. Another magnum opus, The Waters of the Zhang River, was written by Ruan Zhangjiang.

Chapter 16

Fiction

Xiaoxia Mao and Min Li

In the initial stages, the ancient myths, legend, and works of historians and philosophers of the Pre-Qin time provide elementary materials for short stories. The prose in this period is vivid and life-like. The essays of the masters are varied in styles. They both combine knowledge and aesthetics, representing a golden age in the history of Chinese prose, which also provide many characters found in Chinese novels. The "Spring-Autumn Annals" completed by the end of the Spring-Autumn Period is the earliest chronicle in China. It kept a record of the major events in different states during the 242 years from 722 B. C. to 480 B. C. Its wordings are precise and meticulous. Appreciation or depreciation of a person or an event is often expressed in a single word, the so-called Spring-Autumn style; its narration is dramatic and interesting, and grasp the important links of complicated events.

Some tales reflected the supernatural in the Wei (220—265) and the Jin (265—420) period as well as the Southern and the Northern (420—581) Dynasties. Supernatural stories and anecdotal stories are two categories of tales during this time. *New Accounts of Social Talk* by Liu Yiqing was a masterpiece of anecdotal stories about famous people from this period.

The emergence of Tales of the marvelous (Prose Romance) in the Tang Dynasty (618—967) marked the maturity of the Chinese short story. They went beyond merely recording anecdotes and became consciously creative literary works by scholars. "Prose romances" of the Tang Dynasty fell into three categories: supernatural stories, love stories and heroic fictions. Famous works include *The Story of the Pillow* by Shen Jiji, and *The Governor of the Southern Tributary State* by LiGongzuo. They ridiculed feudal scholars obsessed with fame and riches. *The Story of a Singsong Girl*, *The Story of Yingying*, and *The Story of Liu Yi. The Story of A Singsong Girl* express appreciation for true love between men and women. The plot of them is complex and the characters well rounded in their portrayal. Wonderful characterizations are the most successful part of the stories.

The storytelling scripts in the colloquial language came into being during the Song Period (960—1279). Lively Vernacular language appeared extensively in literary works from the Song and the Yuan period. Realistic techniques and characterization in scripts were rapidly being developed also. The character of the printed versions of prompt-book stories is the vernacular loaded with the stock expressions of professional storytellers. *Colloquial Tales from Qingping Studio* and *Five Popular stories with Complete Illustrations* are the extant books. They indicate a further development in the Chinese novel by describing more complete pictures of real society and people's lives. Love stories like *Stories of Detective and Judicial Cases and The Erroneous Execution of Cui Ning* describe the tragic love stories of young people because of the interference of the upper classes or other societal forces.

Novels flourished and formed a mighty current in literature that appealed to the newly developing urban class during the Ming (1368—1644) and Qing (1644—1911) dynasties. Chinese novels fully matured with the coming-forth of wealth of short stories and novels. , The novels' language was simple and easy to understand and received appreciation from the Chinese people as a lively and free literary form. Novels grew quickly during the Ming and Qing period, and many noted writers and works teemed at that time.

Section 1　Famous Novels in the Ming Dynasty

In the Ming Dynasty (1368—1644), the feudal economy was well developed and rudimentary capitalist production started. Urban class came into being. With the growth of printing, fiction also gained further development. Novels blossomed forth in full splendor during this period. "Zhanghui" novels, a batch of full-length chaptered novels were created during this period. "Zhanghui" means the novels are written in chapters with specific topics. Some renowned writers and works best known at that time are Luo Guanzhong and his *Romance of the Three Kingdoms*, Shi Naian and his *Outlaws of the Marsh*, Whu Chenen and his *Journey to the West*. All these full-length novels are characterized by a complicated and interesting plot, an extensive vista and scope, vivid and realistic characterization as well as elegant and evocative language. The books have enjoyed great popularity among people and exerted a tremendous influence in their minds. Many of the characters and stories in the novels are known to everyone in China.

The Romance of the Three Kingdoms:

The Romance of the Three Kingdoms, the earliest long Chinese novel written by Luo Guanzhong (1330—1400) is one of the most famous novels in the Ming period. The master narrative transforms history into epic. It has educated and entertained readers with unforgettable exemplars of martial and civic virtue, of personal fidelity and political treachery. The novel exposed the underside of society during the late Eastern Han Dynasty and the early Jin Dynasty. It also criticized the violence of the feudal rulers and emphasized the people's suffering. People's longing for a sage emperor and a stable life are expressed.

The Romance of the Three Kingdoms is part historical, part legend and myth of the fall of the Later Han Dynasty. It portrays a fateful moment at the end of the Han Dynasty (206 B. C. —220 A. D.) when the future of the Chinese empire laid in the balance. The novel includes a massive scope and a complex plot based on the historical book, folk legends, storytelling scripts and dramas. It chronicles the lives of those feudal lords and their retainers who tried to either replace the empire or restore it. The battles and complicated connections among the three Kingdoms—Wei, Shu and Wu were vividly described.

The book deals with the plots, personal and army battles, intrigues, and struggles of the families to achieve dominance for almost 100 years. It also gives readers a sense the Chinese view their history: cyclically rather than linearly. The first and last lines of the book sum this view up best: " 'The empire long united must divide…' and 'The empire long divided must unite…' " Full of complexities and variations, the structure achieves grandness and compactness rarely seen in classical Chinese novels.

The work is written in clear, concise and vivid language and a large number of Chinese idioms have originated from the novel. The dialogues play an important role in revealing the characters' personalities. Its advanced expressive technique is manifested by adopting extensive literary exaggeration and contrast in depicting the characters. Cao Cao, the lord of the most powerful state in the north, wanted to control the entire nation resorting to his powerful army and famous generals. Liu Bei controlled the southwest with the help of other famous officers and generals. The southern area was under the power of Sun Quan and his generals. Each of them was desirous to enlarge their domains. Events and wars occurred consequently among the

various feudal warlord blocs. Liu Bei is described as a wise emperor and repudiated despotism; while Cao Cao is the representative of a violent feudal ruler. The basic inclination of the novel of "affirming Liu Bei and opposing Cao Cao" revealed the feudalist orthodox conception of the writer. And the description of the personalities of the various characters was somewhat stereotyped.

The author combined realistic with romantic styles in his writing. The basic expressive technique is realistic, while the plots and the portrayal of the historical figures are often full of romantic color.

Outlaws of the Marsh (Water Margin)

Outlaws of the Marsh was written by Shi Nai'an (1296—1370), in the early Ming Dynasty. It is considered to be among the best known and best loved ancient Chinese novels. It narrated the events happened in the final years of Hui Zong, a Song Dynasty emperor reigning (1101—1125). It tells why and how one hundred men and women banded together, became leaders of an outlaw army of thousands and fought brave against addled, inept despots. It is a novel of political corruption, murder, love, martial arts; intertwining tales of bold heroes, corrupt officials and jealous lovers. Being the first novel dealing with the subject matter of a peasant uprising in China, it describes the full development of a peasant uprising from its inception to its defeat. Historians confirm that the plots are derived from fact, for some of the events actually happened, some figures actually existed. Their rebellious deeds struck a responsive chord in the oppressed masses and gradually evolved into folk legends.

The successful portraits of about 30 main characters greatly contribute to the novel's enduring popularity. Shi Nai'an learned and developed the expressive technique of revealing the inner world of the characters through their behavior and language based on folk legends, storytelling scripts and dramas. The distinctive characters are displayed mainly through their language and behaviors as well as the conflicts. The author shows great skill in treating the subtleties to distinguish the characters, though some of them have very similar personalities. The author revealed the characters' various dispositions and forms of resistance to oppression by vividly describing their different life experiences.

The plots are arranged to enhance the development of the main characters. The language has a strong colloquial style that is lively, accurate and very expressive due to the influence of storytelling scripts. Both the plot and the use of language in the novel attain a very high level. The author tells the stories of the many outlaws with an admiring attitude, and the narrations of the main characters disclose the dark side of the feudal society. Readers can easily conclude: it is the cruel and fatuous feudal rulers who drive the people to rebel.

The Pilgrim to the West (Journey to the West)

The Pilgrim to the West, is an outstanding work by Wu Cheng'en (1510—1582). The Monk Xuanzang traveled on foot to India, the birthplace of Buddhism, in search of Buddhist sutras with his three disciples, the irreverent and capable Monkey King, greedy Pig, and Friar Sand. They were subdued by the Monkey King though a lot of demons and evil spirits were encountered along their way. They finally reached the West after they endured countless difficulties imposed by various monsters and demons.

The opening chapters recount the earlier exploits of Monkey King, culminating in his rebellion against Heaven. Monkey King is the most brilliant figure who loves freedom and has a fighting spirit in the fiction. He is arrogant and unyielding in front of the gods and Buddha, he is also very obedient and loyal to his master at the same time. He defied the evil forces, overcame powerful demons and devils and upheld justice. The monk is weak, persistent and cowardly. His character embodies both the piety of a Buddhist monk and the stubbornness of a feudal scholar. His timidity and incompetence is a contrast to the Monkey

King. The Pig is a representative of the human being. He has all kinds of weaknesses, emotions and desires to seek ease and comfort. His arrogance and self-pitying behavior brings much comic relief to the work. Sandy is faithful, strong and steadfast.

It exposes the darkness and corruption of the feudal society. The world of rigid hierarchy managed by gods in the novel apparently mirrors the social reality of the actual world. The High Lord, the monks, and all the cruel monsters and demons are archetypes found in real life. Even the environment and the magical weapons were all based on reality. The novel embodies progressive and profound ideas and criticizes the social realities. The author also conveys to the readers that evil would certainly give way to justice.

The rich and fantastic imagination of the author and the reality of life are well blended in the work. The book is full of fantastic tales that are all lively, unpredictable and thrilling.

The structure centers on characters and the plot is carried out with the actions of the characters. All the difficulties which they encounter are vividly described around the complicated relationships between the main characters. Meanwhile, each story remains relatively independent.

Three Remarks, and Two Strikes

Three Remarks composed by Feng Menglong includes *Remarks to admonish the world*, *Remarks to reason with the world and Remarks to awaken the world*. Each of of Three Remarks is composed of 40 short stories with different themes classifying three categories, such as women's pursuit of true love and happiness, the faction of the ruling class, and extolling true friendship while condemning perfidious behavior.

Two Strikesviz written by Ling Mengchu contains *First Edition of Strike on the Table in Wonder and Second Edition of Strike on the Table in Wonder. Two Strikes* is composed of 78 stories and most of them are based on previously published works. The stories reflect the development of trade and the germination of capitalism during the Ming Dynasty.

The two anthologies of vernacular novelettes in the Ming Dynasty were both fairly outstanding literary masterpieces. They are regarded as the genre painting of the Chinese feudal society. They contain many descriptions of the daily lives of the townspeople, and almost all social strata and all aspects of people's lives are involved, therefore they are called the "worldly novels."

Section 2 Novels of the Qing Dynasty

The Qing Dynasty (1644—1911) was prominent for its novels in the history of Chinese literature. The Qing Dynasty witnessed a variety of literary schools. The writing of full length novels written in vernacular Chinese also made great strides. A large number of novels were created during the period. The strong development of the Reform Movement aided the reformation of literature with the gradual decline of the Feudal society in the Qing Dynasty. *Strange Events for the Last Twenty Years* by Wu Yanren is one of them. Discussions about love, marriage and codes of ethics were other major literary subjects. *The Marriage that Awakes the World* is one of those novels. The feudal society experienced great changes during the period after the Opium War. Many novels condemning the late Qing society were published. The most famous ones include *The Travels of Lao Can* by Liu E (1857—1909), *Exposure of the Official World* by Li Baojia, and *Flowers in a Mirror* by Li Ruzhen (1763—1830).

Mystery Tales Told in a Chat Room

Mystery Tales Told in a Chat Room (Strange Stories from a Liao Studio) written by Pu Songling, is comprised of nearly 500 novelettes. It was influenced by the traditions of the mystery tales from the Wei and

the Jin Dynasties and tales of the marvelous from the Tang and Song Dynasties.

Following the traditions, the author also developed further and created his own unique style. Each novelette had only four or five hundred words, but the plot is complicated and fascinating. The well-knit structure and the intricate plot provide a precious model and resource for later writers.

The romanticism in this progressive work is reflected in the characterizations of the positive figures, and the images of flower goddesses and fox fairies. Writing about ghosts and demons, the work described the world through imaginary stories to reveal the true nature of the society. He exposed the social evils and the harmful effects of the Civil Service Exam. He also satirized corrupt officials, despotic landlords and the feudal political system. Some stories expound on ethics and morals with valuable educational significance.

The novelettes are mostly about love affairs between men and ghosts, foxes or demons. The author portrayed the intense wishes of the youth to break away from the feudal code of ethics and their desire for free marriages. He depicted the peoples' revolt against feudal marriage rites and their rebellions against the evil society.

Unofficial History of Scholars

The *Unofficial History of Scholars* (*The Scholars*), composed by Wu Jinzi (1701—1754), is a masterpiece among satire novels in the history of Chinese literature. It is the first long colloquial and satirical novel in Chinese history with the intelligentsia as subject. The work depicts the lives of different scholars and famous officials in the Qing society. The subject matter is entirely about the scholars. The darkness of a feudalist history is mirrored. The author criticizes the eight-part essay of the civil service examination system by portraying the characters as a swarm of feudal scholars.

The author is good at summarizing and processing all kinds of common phenomena in daily social life. He generalized and abstracted the reality of life so vividly that the novel has achieved artistic effect which is serious but humorous, persuasive but satirical. In portraying the characters, the work is keenly insightful with its simple style.

A Dream of the Red Mansion

The Dream of the Red Mansion (*Story of the Stone*) written by Cao Xueqin is a culmination of the Chinese novel. The vast work published today contains the first 80 were written by Cao Xueqin and the last 40 chapters finished by Gao'E. The love affair of the youth is one of the themes, yet the work goes far beyond the tragic love story. It represents the feudal society's development and predicts its doomed fate. A series of complicated conflicts and struggles between the upper class and the working class, and within the ruling class, are described. The four great houses of Chia, Shih, Wang and Hsueh described in this novel were four basic political forces of feudal society. The families linked with the court and the local officials form a network of control with the feudal autocratic state power as its centre. It exhibited vividly and realistically the doom of the late feudal society, while it extolled warmly the rebels against the feudalistic way of life. It also provides a panorama of the lives of people of various levels in the degenerating empire.

Its narratives used a matured colloquial language, plain but elegant, explicit but implicit. Its dialogues fitted in with the status, cultural attainment, personality and mentality of the characters in the particular circumstances. The dialogues were so vivid that the readers would feel as if they saw and heard the characters actually. The novel also contained a number of poems, song poems, verses of dramas and parallel prose, which are compatible with the plot and the life of the aristocrats. The quality of them was fairly high, indicating the high classic cultural attainment of the author.

Life seemed to trickle spontaneously onto the pages, and unfold itself in front of the readers like a very long scroll. The plot of the novel was very ingenious. The transition from one chapter to another was like a continuous flow. Above the plot was an illusory, mystical world, hinting at the final destination of the dream of the Red Chamber and causing a sorrowful atmosphere over the dazzling events.

More than 100 characters are portrayed most splendidly. The characters in the novel were portrayed most splendidly. The characters Jia Baoyu, Lin Daiyu, Xue Baochai, Granny Liu, etc. all have become lasting artistic models. Their sentiments and thoughts were expressed very naturally. Women had a lower position in the male governed feudal society. The author had progressive ideas and created his female characters equal to men. It extols the young female characters, depicting them to be as wise and capable as men. The main character, Jia Baoyu, a rebel of the feudal noble class, had great sympathy toward the oppressed and trampled women. He represents the author's democratic thoughts and rebellious character. The author tried to tap the social origins of the tragedy of these young characters. He also wrote about the feelings of the youth as they struggled against the feudalistic way of life. The characters' sentiments and thoughts are expressed very naturally, vigorously and vividly.

The book came to the high peak of the satiric art in the field of Chinese classic novel with its broad topics, generous contents, clear and fluent language, bright and vivid style of writing. It made a great impact on other novels such as The Exposure of Official Circle, 20-Year Witness of Strange Phenomena, etc.

Section 3 Contemporary Novels

Chinese fictions developed into the modern era as a result of the New Cultural Movement of 1917. Communism began to spread in China during the first period from 1917 to 1937.

Members of the Literary Research Society (1921) created a large number of issue-oriented novels, which were guided by the dictum "literature for life's sake." Instead of analyzing solutions for the problems from political and social perspectives, the fictions discussed the problems of families and marriages and the solutions from an individual point of view. Writings reminiscing about hometown life began to spring up in the mid 1920s, which influenced the "for life" school. The novels reflected on peasants' suffering, on the awakening and the decline of small propertied classes, and landlords.

Existing side by side with the "for life" school was the "for art" school. Yu Dafu and Zhang Ziping made great strides toward creating this genre. The Creation Society and the Sun Society initiated the revolutionary literary movement in 1928. The history of the development of Chinese literature entered a new phase; meanwhile, "left" mistakes were made in the movement.

The period witnessed unprecedented achievements in creative writing. The Chinese League of Left-wing Writers was established in 1930 under the leadership of the Communist Party to wage a struggle against the KMT's cultural campaign of "encirclement and suppression." They launched a stubborn struggle against KMT and criticized fascist ideas about "nationalistic literature and art," as well as the bourgeois and petty-bourgeois ideas on art and literature. The writers put their creative activities at the services of the Chinese revolutionary struggle. They declared the literature to be part of the entire proletarian revolutionary cause. The proletarian art and literature were steadily forging ahead during the struggle. They vividly depicted China's social reality and class contradictions in a realistic attitude. During the period, the novel Midnight and the short story The Shop of the Lin Family by Mao Dun (1896—1981) shook the literary world of China. The author explained why semi-colonial, semi-feudal China could not step into a developed capitalistic society.

Chinese people suffered wars such as the Anti-Japanese War, the wars between the armies led by the Communist Party and armies of the KMT during 1930s and 1940s. The National Chinese Writers' Anti-Ag-

gression Association was established with Go Moro as its head in 1938. Discussions were conducted around 1940 about the issue of national form. The continuation of the discussions about popular-style literature and art in the first half of the 1930s advanced the development of literature. Lao She, Ba Jin, Cao Yu, Mao Dun, and Go Moro are the famous writers from this period.

Mao Zedong explained a series of fundamental principles relating to revolutionary literature in his famous speech at the Yan'an Forum on Literature and Art in 1942. He pointed out that literature and art must adhere to the orientation of serving the workers, peasants and soldiers. Writers should interact with the masses and familiarize themselves with social life, and they should reform their own world outlook. Chinese literature developed into a new phase with the speech's influence. Big changes took place in all aspects of many writers' works and a great number of fine works were produced. *The Marriage of Young Black*, *Rhymes of Li Youcai*, and *Sanliwan Village* by Zhao Shuli (1906—1970) are outstanding novels. His works reflected the profound transformation of old Chinese villages into new ones. He created images of peasants in a new light. Zhao's works were well received by the masses for they were characterized by marked Chinese flavor and style. He made important contributions to national and mass literary styles. Also, *The Hurricane* by Zhou Libo (1908—), *Lotus Lake* by Sun Li, and *Sunshine over the Sanggan River* by Ding Ling (1907—) were written in this period.

The writers who distinguished themselves not long after the Ya'an forum on literature and art were Bing Xin, Yang Shuo, Liu Baiyu, Qin Mu, Yang Mo, Qu Bo, Li Zhun, Liang Bin, Wei Wei and Ding Ling. They created many works under the impetus of the founding of the new republic and their works reflected the new life. Among the many novels published after 1949, some outstanding ones were *Violent Storm and Changes in a Mountain Village* by Zhou Libo, *Builders of a New Life* by Liu Qing, *The Morning of Shanghai* by Zhou Erfu, *Builders* by Lian Bin, *Tracks in the Snowy Forest* by Qu Bo, *The Song of Youth* by Yang Mo and *Red Crag* by Luo Libin.

After the disaster of the "Cultural Revolution" (1966—1976) was brought to an end, a new era of creativity in Chinese literature began. The 1980s were a flourishing period. The movements of realism, romanticism, modernism, and post-Modernism are all reflected in Chinese literature.

Lu Xun (Zhou Shuren 1881—1936)

Lu Xun is a great writer, thinker in modern China. He went to Japan to study medicine in 1902. Later on, he was engaged in the literary and artistic work, attempted with by to change the national spirit. Lu Xun participated in the China free motion big union successively, progress organization and was one of the "left-wing" writers in Shanghai.

He is famous for his novels, prose, poetry, literary criticism and literary history. His *The Madman's Diary* (1918) and *The True Story of Ah Q*, shaped the models for the modern Chinese novels and have established the new-vernacular literature movement cornerstone. His works are famous partly because of their deep social contents and high artistic value. His novels, like *The New-Year Sacrifice*, are collected in *Crying*, *Wandering and Old Tales Retold* have influenced Chinese people deeply.

In *the true story of Ah Q*, Lu Xun created a typical image of a backward peasant named Ah Q who was exploited by feudal forces. Ah Q habitually uses his "method of spiritual victory" in order to relieve his sufferings and satisfy his mentality of resistance and retaliation. The method includes self-respecting, self-abasing, self-consoling and self-deceiving. However, it could only bring him greater humiliation. Burning with spontaneous revolutionary zeal, he also wanted to be involved in the revolution when the revolution comes. The country-revolutionary forces sentenced him to death. The novel profoundly reflects China's social physiognomy around the 1911 Revolution and class relations in the countryside. It not only reflects the impasse of the torrential revolution and the reason for its failure, but also exposes the weak points in the Chinese national character and their negative effects on the advancement of Chinese history.

Lao She (Shu Qing Chun 1899—1966)

Being a modern novelist and playwright, Lao She published *The Philosophy of Lao Zhang* and *Two Ma and Zhao Ziyue* were published in 1920s. He finished the famous novel *Camel Xiangzi* in 1936. The outbreak of the Sino-Japanese War (1937—1945) radically altered Lao She's views. He headed the All-China Anti-Japanese Writers Federation, and wrote a number of plays, worked as a propagandist from 1937 to 1945. The representative of them is His *Four Generations Under One Roof* written in 1944. Lao She's *Teahouse* written in 1957 was frequently performed. He started to write the bibliographical novel *Beneath the Red Banner* in 1960s. However, before the book was finished, he committed suicide during the "Cultural Revolution."

Camel Xiangzi (*Rickshaw-Boy*) is a masterpiece of Lao She. It reveals author's prophetic vision of the future of China. The novel depicts the hard life of Xiangzi, an honest, upright, ordinary rickshaw-puller in Beijing. Xiangzi failed to live a decent life no matter how hard he worked. The novel's socio-historical dimensions have made it a widely used text for the cultural analysis of modern China.

Ba Jin (Li Yaotang 1904—2004)

Ba Jin is a modern novelist, prose writer, translator and editor. He is considered to be one of the most important and widely-read Chinese writers of the twentieth century. Being a well-known writer of modern Chinese literature, he wrote a number of famous novels, such as *Family*, *the Love Trilogy Fog* (1931), *Rain* (1933) *and Lightning* (1935), *the novellas Autumn in Spring and A Dream of the Sea*. His novels, short stories and poems in prose have been collected in *Works of Ba Jin*, *Collected Works of Ba Jin and Selected Works of Ba Jin*.

Ba Jin completed his best-known *Family* in 1933, one of his "Rip Trilogy" that established his reputation. The trilogy also included *Spring* and *Autumn*. In *Family*, the fledgling author exposed the darkness and decadence of feudal society by describing the collapse of a big feudal family. He praised the awakening of young intellectuals and their anti-feudal struggle. The novel had a great impact on the young people.

Chapter 17

Chinese Mythology and Legend

Xiaoxia Mao and Catherine Gu

China has its rich and colourful ancient mythology. However, a great deal of it has been lost or dispersed in other forms of literature. The mythology of the ethnic peoples of China is exceptionally rich. It reveals the lost myths of ancient times. Chinese mythology deals with all fields of the world. The major categories include myths of the cosmos, myths about man and heroes, myths about gods and myths about animals.

People could not understand some of the natural phenomena because of their limited knowledge of the world in ancient times. They personified objects in nature with their imaginations and fancies based on their experiences. Chinese myths reflect their wish to struggle against natural calamities and improve their living standards.

Mythology has an important role in the history of Chinese literature. Being one of the early types of literature, it has influenced various categories of Chinese literature, providing direct materials for later writers and artists. Many of the stories have been "rediscovered" in later literature and folklore. The rich imagination and visualization of these ancient myths were also the origin of artistic makeup and romantic creative methods of later writers.

A large number of famous ancient fables were recorded in books such as *The Classic of Mountains and Seas*, *The Book of Master Zhuang*, *Chu Ci and The Book of Master Huainan*. *The Classic of Mountains and Seas*, narrating episodes of 204 mythical figures, was a major source of Chinese mythology. It brought together a treasure trove of colorful fiction about mythical figures, medicine, natural history, rituals and ethnic peoples of the ancient world. The book is regarded as one of the most important collections of Chinese myths.

Section 1　Main Features

Chinese myths are full of human feelings. Gods, ghosts, spirits and animals are often personified. Writers describe gods the way they describe man and endow them with human nature as if they were human.

One obvious feature of Chinese mythology was that the myths were entwined with history. Chinese history, of the long period before recorded history, was partly based on legend interwoven with mythology. For example, in the mythical stories, Pangu separated heaven and earth, Nǚ Wa created humans, Suiren made fire by drilling wood, Houyi taught people to farm and Shennong discovered herbal medicine. It should also be noted that there were many versions among the minority peoples. Some were similar to the Han myths, while others had very unique ethnic traits.

Another feature was that many of the heroes described in mythology were both important characters in mythical stories and historical legendary figures.

Chinese mythology extols self-sacrifice and perseverance. In the story of Gun and Yu trying to tame the floods, the hero Gun was killed by the God of Heaven because he stole the "growth earth." Yu was born out of Gun's belly and continued Gun's cause. Yu sacrificed his entire life to fighting the flood. He did not marry until he was thirty. Then, he left his wife four days after his marriage to fight the flood again. After suffering countless hardships, he finally brought the flood under control.

Mythical stories praised rebellion against oppression. For instance, in one myth, it was mentioned after Ganjiang was killed by the king of Chu, his son Chibi determined to take revenge. He killed himself so that his friend could take his head to the king of Chu, and then kill the king for him.

Some of the Chinese mythical stories eulogize the yearning for true love. *The Cowherd and the Girl Weaver* is a well-known love story. Goddesses and men, or fox fairies and men, love each other passionately and sincerely in many stories. They indirectly reflected the yearning for true love that was stifled by feudal ethical codes.

Some writers are motivated by Confucian teachings about humanity and righteousness. They believe that good deeds would be rewarded with good results, and evil repaid with evil because they are influenced by the Buddhist tenet. It was an important theme to encourage good deeds and warn against sin (produced after the Wei and Jin, 265—420).

Section 2 Myths of Heroes

Pangu separated Heaven and Earth

The first universe was shaped like an egg in an undifferentiated and indivisible locality. An almighty giant was born into the entity. He kept growing until he could use his legs and arms with strength to separate the universe into heaven and earth. When Pangu noticed the earth and heaven still had some connection, he continued his work with a chisel and an axe until the great work was accomplished. While he was growing, the world also grew. He lived for thousands of years. Finally he died of exhaustion trying to force heaven and earth farther and farther apart. His various body parts changed into other things after his death. His left eye and right eye became the sun and the moon. His teeth and bones became rocks and metals. Pearls and jade came from his marrow. The stars were his hair and mustache. His clearer breath became clouds and winds, while the coarser part sank down to earth. The four corners of the earth were the transformation of his arms and legs. Parts of his body turned into mountains and his blood formed rivers. His flesh changed into soil, and his skin and body hair turned into trees and plants. His sweat fell as rain to nourish all living things, and the insects on his body took the shape of human beings.

The myths related the way ancient Chinese people speculated about the world in which they lived. Pangu mirrored the patriarchal society. Pangu and the world are two in one. The harmony and unity of man and nature evolved as the prototype of the Chinese worldview. This idea was later developed into theories by Chinese philosophers. For example, Dong Zhongshu, the Han Dynasty Prime Minister, pointed out: Man is a duplicate of nature. Nature and Man are functions and references of each other. There are affinities and similarities between them. The roundness of the world suggests the mellowness of Chinese thinking patterns and Chinese philosophy. The unity of the heaven, the earth and human beings suggests the holistic and integral thinking orientation. Myths influenced ancient Chinese theories about the round sky, the square earth and the egg shaped universe.

Nǚ Wa created Humans

Nǚ Wa noticed the world was lonely without human beings, she decided to add life and beauty to the world. She saw her own figure reflected in the lake water, thus she set about creating man with clay like herself. She shaped little figures by hand and breathed life into them. Soon after they left her hand and touched the ground, they cheered and danced. The figurines were the first group of men and women. Though she went about her work day and night, it was still very slow to create figures. In order to speed up her work, she dipped a rattan into the mud around her and flung it about. The mud drops fell and instantly turned into human beings. The cheerful and colorful world did not last long for many of her humans aged and died. Could she compensate for the rapid death rate? Another idea came to her mind: Why not make them mate and bear children? She summoned the young men and women and let them chase and play with each other. Every spring turned into a season of joy, courtship and marriage. Families were created in this way; and children were nursed and reared. Human beings continued to live on the earth.

This particular myth about the creation of man reflects a matriarchal society. Nǚ Wa made humans with yellow clay indicating the myth's place of origin. The making of pottery in ancient times was also out of clay near the banks of the Yellow River. Nǚ Wa was a goddess of love and matchmaking.

Nǚ Wa and Fu Xi's Marriage

The two versions of the marriage of Nǚ Wa and Fu Xi are different in form but similar in spirit. Nǚ Wa and Fu Xi were the only two people left in the world after a big flood. Since Nǚ Wa is Fu Xi's sister, they did not dare to think of marriage. However, to carry on the human race, they had no choice but to marry. They climbed up to the holy mountain called Kunlun and built two fires to pray: "If Heaven let us survive to be husband and wife, the smoke will join. " The smoke did join in a short time. Having obtained the approval of Heaven, they married and became the ancestors of man.

Another version goes like this: After the terrible flood, only Nǚ Wa and Fu Xi survived. They had to marry in order to continue the human lineage. Being too ashamed to marry since they were a sister and a brother, they decided to play a game of chase around a big tree to avoid embarrassment. Fu Xi could not catch his sister at first. So he turned around and ran the other way and Nǚ Wa fell into his arms. They assumed this to be the will of Heaven, and married.

Fu Xi, who was the son of the God of Thunder, was a dragon with a man's head. Among his many contributions to human beings were the inventions of fishing and hunting tools, such as marriage rites, artificial fire making and some musical instruments. He also invented "the Eight Diagrams. "

This brother-sister marriage reflected the marriage system in the remote antiquity. It is almost a universal motif of all human myths that man has the ability to survive and prosper after a terrible flood. As the first step toward human marriage, promiscuity was part of the proto-family in the distant past. The game playing and the marriage rites are similar in many parts of the world.

Nǚ Wa Repairing the Sky

Zhuan Xu, the God of North Heaven, had all the stars and planets arranged in the northern sky in his territory. The action offended the gods. After the god of water, Gonggong rose up with other gods in revolt, Gonggong was defeated. He was so desperate that he knocked down the Buzhou Mountain. Being the west pillar of the sky, the mountain fell apart and the sky collapsed. Horrible disasters followed then. Rains poured down and the floods shot up from the cracks and holes. Fierce animals rampaged and the sun was overshadowed by thick smoke. The earth turned into a hell!

The war of the gods resulted in the suffering of human beings. Nǚ Wa could not allow the disasters to continue. She started the arduous task of mending the sky to save the world. Rocks were collected and melted in a pot to mend the holes. She used a giant tortoise's four legs to support the four corners of the sky. Then the black dragon, ferocious animals and birds that were plaguing the people were killed by her. She burned the reeds she collected and used the ashes to block, divert and channel the big flood. The world was alive again and things returned to normal. Nǚ Wa died of exhaustion. Her body transformed into various entities in the universe like Pangu.

The flood stories were a reflection and deflection of Chinese climate and history in the distant past. Gods have the mixture of good and evil aspects in their nature in the large number of Chinese flood myths. The water gods varied in duties and performances and also were dual in their natures. A unique feature of Chinese mythology was that the gods were neither all evil nor all good. Nǚ Wa reflects the spirit of saving mankind by sacrificing oneself if necessary. China is a flood-ridden country. From the myths about flood fights, flood fighters such as Nǚ Wa, Gun and Da Yu were revered by people for their heroic deeds.

Hou Yi Shooting down Nine Suns

Ten suns used to be in the east at the beginning of the world. They were the sons of the God of East Heaven. They stayed in a boiling hot valley in the eastern seas with one giant tree. Sent by the mother who drove a cart pulled by six dragons, one of them would rise to the top of the tree. The other nine sons stayed under the tree. The sons were bored with the monotonous cycle and decided to go out to play. The ten suns burnt the world so hot that most living things could not survive. The father, Dijun, was angry and decided to teach his ten sons a lesson. He ordered a god by the name of Hou Yi to scare his sons. Hou Yi realized it was not wise to just scare them since they might be tempted to all go out again someday. So, he shot nine of the suns, one by one, to rescue the dying people. Cheers went up to the sky for his deed, and people's anger was appeased.

Hou Yi lost his patience with his servants after his wife flew to the moon. All of the servants left him except Fengmeng. He pretended to be loyal to his master. Hou Yi passed on all his archery skills to Fengmeng when he found the servant very eager to learn. He did not realize his servant was an ungrateful and treacherous man. He was murdered by Fengmeng later. What a great and simple-minded hero!

The myth of shooting down nine suns reflects the beautiful wish of man in a battle against droughts and other disasters.

Section 3 Mythological Storied Related with the Sun and the Moon

Chang'e Flying to the Moon

Hou Yi could no longer return to heaven since he had disobeyed Dijun's order to shoot nine suns. He was driven out of heaven by Dijun. His wife Chang'e kept complaining for she would not accept the fate of mortal flesh and death. She urged him to beg for the elixir from Xiwangmu to ensure her immortality.

Hou Yi felt responsible for the misery of his wife. He overcame many difficulties and arrived at Xiwangmu's palace finally. Xiwangmu was surprised to see him. She had heard of Hou Yi's bravery and his good deeds to save the world and mankind. She made an exception to help him by giving him some 6,000 year-old elixir. She told Hou Yi that if he and his wife both had the elixir, they could live an endless life. But there was only enough elixir to enable one to ascend to heaven.

Hou Yi hurried back home and explained Xiwangmu's instruction, wishing to share the elixir with his wife. However, Chang'e wanted to go back to heaven. She secretly consumed all the elixir when Hou Yi was out hunting one day. Because the God, Dijun would not permit her husband and her to go back the palace of Heaven. She had to fly to the moon which was a lonely place. The only creature to accompany her was a jade rabbit destined to pound medicine day and night. It was really hard to bear the loneliness. The sad wife wanted to rejoin her husband and beg for his forgiveness. Unfortunately, she could not descend to the earth again. It seemed she was condemned to suffer her lonely life on the moon forever.

A man called Wugang was banished by Heaven for his misconduct after many years. He was condemned to cut the cassia tree, a tree which could never be hewn because as soon as his axe was taken away, the cut on the cassia tree would heal immediately. That meant he had to keep cutting without stopping and never had any opportunity to meet Chang'e.

This story embodies man's wish to travel beyond earth. Chang'e also reflects human nature as a mixture of goodness and weakness.

Kua Fu Chasing the Sun

Kua Fu was an ancestor of a country of giants called Bofu. His hometown was a mountain called "Heaven Pillar" in the northern wilderness. Just one of his steps could cover hundreds of miles. He looked fierce for he had a yellow serpent on each of his ears and in each of his hands. He was actually a gentle and kind giant, although he was a little bit impatient.

He was determined to command respect among the gods and proye himself to be the number one giant of the world. One day, an idea came to his mind: why not challenge the sun in a race? After all, was he not the fastest runner?

He started off as soon as he saw the sun rise in the east. With a tree tall enough to reach heaven in his hand as a stick, he raised his step to chase the sun. A gust of wind and a cloud of dust were raised by his steps. All the gods fixed their eyes on him. On and on he ran in spite of great fatigue with sweat pouring from his body. Though he was very thirsty, he was excited by the shrinking distance between himself and his rival. At one point he dried the Yellow River and the Weihe River to quench his thirst. When it was sunset, he seemed to be close enough to embrace the sun. However, he was exhausted. He found himself to be too weak to stretch his arms to hold the sun. He knew he had to drink the cool and sweet water in the North Sea to kill the thirst and revitalize his body. He could no longer run but pushed his legs on to the north. His legs were too weak to support his giant body but he moved on doggedly. All of a sudden, he collapsed, shaking heaven and earth. A deafening sound reverberating across the mountains and valleys. His body became a huge mountain named Qin Mountain. His stick grew into a big peach garden. The woods kept expanding until it covered thousands of square miles called Deng Lin. The peaches of Deng Lin were revitalizing and rejuvenating.

According to the legend, some old and dying military horses were released into the woods by the first king of the Zhou, following the massive war overthrowing the Shang Dynasty. The horses were rejuvenated and grew into fierce horses. Eight horses from the woods were chosen to draw King Mu's cart to see Xiwangmu, who was the goddess of the Kunlun Mountains.

Kua Fu racing against the sun embodies the supernatural heroism of man.

Section 4 Ancestors: Yandi and Huangdi

Yandi the Holy Farmer

Yandi was the sun god, the god of farming and medicine. He invented farming and was worshipped as the Holy Farmer. He also wrote a well-known medical work called The Holy Farmer's Medicinal Herbs. He is the God of the South Heaven, where it was hot. The south is assigned the property of fire, and the sun god gives heat and sunshine to farmers. "Yan" in Chinese means fire and heat. Therefore, Chinese people called him "Yandi." It is said that he was the son of a holy dragon. When he was born, he had a human body, the head of an ox and the legs of a horse. He could talk soon after he was born. After five days he was running about. His teeth began to come out in seven days. Nine springs around him produced clear water and formed water wells to celebrate his birth.

Animal prey became scarce because of excessive hunting. When he was three, he learned to farm. He taught people to farm and to dig water wells. With the help of Heaven and a red bird, people got nine seeds of grain to plant, and the seeds yielded good crops. The good harvest and nine wells of drinkable water improved the health and lives of the farmers' away from the rivers. Farmers had surplus grain with the fast development of farming. Yandi taught them to trade and fixed the market time in order to avoid wasting farming time.

Yandi had a disharmonious relationship with his brother Huangdi. Discord was sewn between them by Yandi's assistants. After a war of unequal strength, he was defeated by Huangdi. He retreated to the south to heal his wounds and devoted himself to farming and medicine. Unfortunately, he also lost four beautiful daughters. He buried his personal grief in his heart and dedicated his life to improving farming and medicine. He produced plenty of sunshine for the growing crops as the god of farming. He also improved the methods, tools and seeds of farming. Besides, he collected medicinal herbs and tasted them himself. A large variety of plants were tasted by him several times a day though it was a risk. He even tasted poisonous plants for medical research. When he found that a plant was poisonous, he immediately took an antidote to detoxify the poison. Once, he tried a deadly poisonous plant and all his antidotes failed to eliminate the poison. Thus he died trying to develop medicine to save mankind.

China has been a farming country of a long history. The Holy Farmer Yandi is acclaimed as one of the ancestors of the Chinese nation.

Huangdi Ruling by Virtue

Huangdi's original surname was Gong Sun, and he lived in the Yellow River Valley 5,000 years ago. Huangdi's mother was stricken by thunder and lightening while travelling. After being pregnant for 25 months, she gave birth to Huangdi. He was the son of the god of thunder and was crowned as the supreme God of Central Heaven at the age of 17.

The auspicious phoenix, a bird of men, came to stay in his garden soon after he took the throne. He built his earthly palace in the Kunlun Mountains to rule both the world of gods and man. Being a very kind ruler and having all the noble virtues and merits in him, he became popular both in the celestial world and in the earthly world. Since he was a very meticulous architect and planner, he arranged and placed everything in good order. The two worlds under his rule were rigorously organized and peace prevailed.

Some gods under Yandi were taken as prisoners after the war between Huangdi and Yandi. They escaped and decided to avenge the insult. Chiyou (the god of war) started another war against Huangdi in the name of Yandi, which was unprecedented in scale, ferocity, intensity, savagery, destruction and loss of life. Chiyou was defeated and killed after many battles. After the victory over Chiyou, Huangdi reflected on the disasters that the war had caused his people. He was determined to eradicate war and ensure eternal peace and prosperity for the human world. According to the myth, he came to such a conclusion: Follow nature and follow natural laws. He should focus on the universe and Dao instead of physical objects.

From then on, he devoted himself to his subjects to ensure that their lives were filled with health,

peace, security and prosperity. Huangdi invented a large number of things for people such as musical instruments, the procedures for digging wells and medicine. Almost all possible inventions were invented by him. However, his greater concern was to rule the earth through virtue to ensure the peace and well-being of his subjects.

Huangdi was a benevolent and virtuous god and one of the ancestors of the Chinese nation. He assumed the supreme central position among the gods of the five heavens.

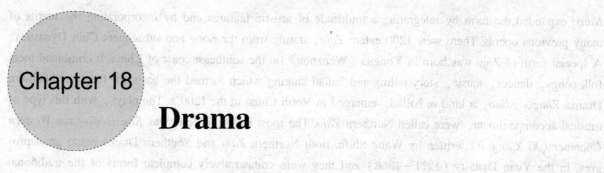

Chapter 18
Drama

Xiaoxia Mao and Catherine Gu

Section 1 the Origin and Development of the Traditional Chinese Drama

Traditional Chinese drama is a comprehensive performing art. It mirrors the culmination and distillation of Chinese civilization for the past two thousand years. It is universally considered one of the three oldest drama cultures, along with Greek tragedy and comedy, and Indian Sanskrit drama.

Traditional Chinese drama, originating from primitive folk songs and dances, creates a spectacular dramatic presentation. Singing and dancing, as elements of Chinese theater, emerged out of the production activities of early man. A beautifully colored ceramic jar excavated in northwest China's Qinghai Province in the 1970's dates back 5, 000 years. A picture of three groups of dancers is on the jar. It depicts ancient hunters celebrating a successful hunt or some other memorable occasion.

The dancers in dim, distant past, began to re-enact the struggle between Chiyou, the god of war and the Yellow Emperor, in which the latter was victorious. Dances from different periods, such as the witch-like dancing from the slavery society, pantomime from the Spring and Autumn Period (770 B. C. —476 B. C.), and ancient wrestling performances and acrobatics from the Qin (221 B. C. —206 B. C.) and Han (206 B. C. —220 A. D.) Dynasties, all influenced the development of traditional Chinese drama. Large-scale memorial ceremonies began to be held. According to historical records, a grand ceremony for driving away demons would be held annually to ring out the old year and ring in the new. Even the emperor would attend. Among the 120 young performers, one would be dressed in a bear skin to impersonate a god. It evolved into a comprehensive artistic style of singing, dialogue, music, acrobatics martial arts and pantomime. Additionally, other ceremonies to pray for a good harvest were also accompanied by dancing and singing during that period. During the Han Dynasty, the dances often described a struggle between a man and a beast. Telling folk stories and singing ballads were other sources of Chinese theater art. Figurines, unearthed from tombs of the Eastern Han Dynasty (25—220) in Sichuan Province, were of ballad singers and story tellers.

A variety of professional storytellers, balladeers and fixed performance forms, appeared in the Tang Dynasty (618—907) . Performances became to be more sophisticated then; they also became popular in the imperial palace. One song-and-dance drama known as *Lady Tayao* described the relationship between a man and his wife.

China had a fairly mature and diverse opera art which developed out of a long theatrical tradition beginning in the 11th century. The earliest form of classical Chinese drama is the *Zaju* originating in the Song Dynasty (960—1279) . Yuanben appeared in the Chin Dynasty (1115—1234) . *Yuan Zaju* and *Song Yuan*

Nanxi expanded the form by integrating a multitude of artistic features and by incorporating the merits of many previous operas. There were 1280 extant *Zaju*, dating from the Song and subsequent Chin Dynasties. A special form of Zaju was born in Yongjia (Wenzhou) on the southeast coast of China. It combined local folk songs, dances, music, story telling and ballad singing which formed the basis for the later Southern Drama. *Zhugongdiao*, a kind of ballad, emerged in North China in the 1200's. The plays, with this type of musical accompaniment, were called Northern *Zaju*. The most influential one was *Romance of the Western Chamber* (*Xi Xiang Ji*) written by Wang Shifu. Both Northern *Zaju* and Southern Drama made great progress in the Yuan Dynasty (1271—1368) and they were comparatively complete forms of the traditional Chinese opera. They influenced each other in their coexistence. The birth of *Zaju* marked the maturity of traditional Chinese opera.

Southern Drama developed regional variations, such as Haiyanqiang (Zhejiang Province), Yuyaoqing (Zhejiang Province), Yiyangqiang (Jiangxi Province) and Kun Opera or Kunshanqiang (Jiangsu Province). The last two types exerted the greatest influence and were the longest lasting in the Ming Dynasty (1368—1644).

Yiyangqiang merged with many local operas when traveling players introduced these operas to different areas of China, while the *Kunqu* opera began to decline in the Qing Dynasty (1644—1911). Local operas flourished in different areas during the Kangxi and Qianlong period of the mid-Qing period. The operatic tunes were divided into five different tunes: Kun Tune, High Tune (Yi Tune and Jing Tune), Bangzi Tune, Xuansuo Tune and Pihuang Tune. The operas from the Qing Dynasty not only inherited the Yuan Zaju and Ming Romance but also aided their development. For instance, the Ban Tune System, a tune typical of diversified tune patterns was created.

Mutual borrowing has taken place among various types of local operas and new forms have continually appeared during the course of the development of the Chinese drama. There are 368 forms of local operas throughout China and each variety acquired its name from its place of origin. Different types of drama can be distinguished by the use of local dialects and unique melodies. The same story can be told accompanied by a wide range of different tunes and musical instruments, depending on where it is being presented. Local operas can be divided into three genres. Local Operas, such as Huju, Yuju and Luju, were based on the story-telling and ballad-singing arts. Some other local operas, such as Yangge, Tea-picking Opera and Flower-lantern Opera have developed on the basis of songs and dances. Tibetan Opera, the third genre, is greatly influenced by the ballad tradition of the Tibet nationality. The five major forms of the traditional Chinese drama are Beijing Opera (Beijing), Yue Opera (Zhejiang Province), Huangmei Opera (Anhui Province), Yu Opera (Henan Province) and Ping Opera (Tangshan, Hebei Province). Interest in the Kun Opera gradually waned because it was only enjoyed by the nobles in the royal court. It was at this historic moment that Beijing Opera emerged.

Section 2 History of Beijing Opera

There are about 368 types of traditional, local, dramatic forms in China. Huangmei Opera, Yue Opera, Ping Opera, Sichuan Opera, Shaoxing Opera and Guang Dong Opera are the most popular ones. Beijing Opera has a history of more than two hundred years and a complete system of stage performance. It absorbed the various elements of the Chinese local operas during its development. It also has a complete system of stage performance compared with other types of traditional dramatic forms in China. It has achieved the highest artistic accomplishments and it is the most influential and representative of all operas in China. Beijing Opera is regarded as the national opera in China.

Beijing Opera has its origin in primitive songs and dances from ancient Chinese. The techniques and movements of Beijing Opera's dancing styles are similar to those of the Tang Dynasty (618—967).

Emperor Qianlong of the Qing Dynasty (1644—1911) loved the local dramas he experienced during his six secret inspections of the southern provinces. In order to celebrate his eightieth birthday in 1790, he summoned opera troupes from different localities to perform for him in Beijing. After the celebration, four famous troupes of Huang Mei Drama from Anhui province were asked to remain in Beijing. Beijing audiences were particularly interested in their beautiful melodies, colorful costumes and interesting facial patterns. The performances in Beijing gradually absorbed the element of Kunqu (developed in the Ming Dynasty) thus it became popular in the palace and among the upper classes in Beijing. They also absorbed the merits of other local operas and became a mature art form. When some troupes from Hubei Province came to Beijing and performed with the Anhui troupes, the two types of singing blended on the same stage and gradually gave birth to a new genre—Beijing Opera.

As time went by, Beijing Opera popularity spread all over China, becoming the most popular and influential dramatic form on the Chinese stage. Since it shows a higher artistic level in terms of repertoires and staging arts than other operas, it has exerted a prevailing influence over the others.

Section 3 Major Features of Beijing Opera

Beijing Opera is recognized for its four highly systemized categories of singing, dancing, mimicry and acrobatics. It uses the skills of Chinese martial arts and creates a unique system of stylized, fictitious movements which is strongly rhythmical. Beijing Opera mainly presented historical stories. In the past, there were 1,300 traditional plays, and about 400 of them are still being produced, most of which are based on folk tales, famous novels and fairy tales. It is a pleasure to watch if the audiences know the basic story. Among the most famous Beijing Operas are *The Monkey King*, *The Drunken Beauty*, *Crossroads*, *The White Snake*, and *Strategy of an Unguarded City*.

The costuming is based on the style of the Ming Dynasty court and civil costumes. They are a garish collection of sharply contrasting colors. Much use of deep red, deep green, white, black, yellow and blue is frequently seen because the stages were originally only lit by oil lamps when it was performed. Strong contrasting colors are freely used and the costumes are embroidered in gold, silver and colored threads. Strictly based on the rank, life style and occupation, special costumes have different colors and designs for each role.

The music is mainly composed of two styles: music which originated in Hui tune (Erhuang) and the music from Han tune in Hubei province (Xipi). In the past, Beijing Opera was usually performed on the open-air stages in streets, tea-houses, temple courtyards or markets. Therefore, the roles had to develop a piercing style of singing to be heard over the throng. The singing is highly stylized but the variations of rhythm and pitch still enable the roles to express thoughts and emotions of different characters in all situations.

The pronunciation of the language is hard to understand. Two forms (rhythmic vernacular and capital vernacular) of recitatives in dialogue and monologue are used to better characterize the personalities of the roles. Even if the pronunciation is confusing sometimes, the audience can still grasp what the actor or actress is doing. All the movements performed on the stage are created from real life and conform to the respective roles. Additionally, every movement or pose like stroking a beard, setting a hat straight, swinging a sleeve or lifting a foot has its own pattern and formula. Everything the actor does is done according to a stylized routine. Few props are used, so each move, gesture or facial expression is symbolic.

The orchestra consists of string and wind instruments as well as percussion instruments. The orchestra had to play loudly since Beijing Opera was performed on the open-air stage. The musicians sit on the stage in plain clothes and play without written scores. The most important musical instruments used for the accompaniment to Beijing Opera are two types of two-stringed fiddles, the (Jinghu) and another two-stringed fiddle with a softer tone than the Jinghu (Erhu). Examples of other traditional Chinese instruments include Yueqin, Pipa and Suona. The percussion instruments are gongs, drums of different sizes, and the castanets (the time clapper) made of wood and bamboo. The castanets play an important role in establishing the tempo. They are "time-beaters" for the actors to give them cues, and virtually direct the entire orchestra. With the castanets, stylized patterns of singing, acting, acrobatics and dialogue are all in coordination with specific musical rhythms.

A minimum of stage equipment is required. The time, relations among the roles, the characters of the people in the story, and the environment are all demonstrated through singing, body movements and speaking. With the art of illusion, Beijing Opera makes it possible to transform a small stage into the whole universe. For example, only a table with two chairs refers to a room; a whip with silk tassels indicates that the actor is riding a horse; two pennants embroidered with wheels symbolize a carriage; four generals and four soldiers represent commanders with their army; walking in a circle indicates a long journey, and lifting a foot means going through a doorway. The presence of a door is conveyed quite clearly by a performer who makes the gestures of opening it, stepping through and closing it again. This type of artistic exaggeration is brought to perfection in the superb martial arts skills of the performers when simulating battles. To sum up, expressed through techniques of exaggeration and concentration, the art of illusion is one of the most important characteristics of Beijing Opera.

One important character of Beijing Opera is that it combines many forms of art such as grand opera, acrobatic display, ballet, and the historic play. The exciting panorama of it includes the performing arts of singing, dialogue, dancing, acrobatic combat and monologue. Beijing Opera is amazing since it combines so many forms which are separated in Western drama. The above arts may all be woven into one play, or some may be emphasized rather than others. In some operas, there is mainly music and singing, while in others, pantomime, battle scenes and acrobatics are prominent.

Section 4　Different Types of Beijing Opera

Beijing Opera falls into four categories according to the time of the story. They are divided into traditional operas, costume operas, contemporary operas and modern operas. It can be classified into whole plays or just highlights of plays according to the duration of time. There was also classification related to the number of characters in a play; there could be two major characters or many characters. Beijing Opera can be categorized into "civil" pieces, characterized by singing and acting, and "martial" ones, which feature acrobatics and stunts. Some operas are a combination. Beijing Opera can also be categorized according to the four role types. Likewise, schools of Beijing Opera have their distinctly different styles and merits.

Section 5　Four Main Roles of Beijing Opera

The roles of Beijing Opera are divided into male roles, female roles, face-painted roles, roles with facial make-up and clowns.

Male roles are either young men, depicted by actors singing in a falsetto voice (Xiao Sheng) or old men, depicted by actors wearing long beards (Lao Sheng). They are the leading male actors. They are also divided into scholars or officials (Wen Sheng) or military officers and generals in battle scenes (Wu Sheng). The actors of Wu Sheng are well trained in acrobatics.

Female roles (Dan) are further categorized into the elderly, dignified ladies (Lao Dan) like mothers, aunts or widows, aristocratic ladies (Qing Yi) in elegant costumes, ladies' maids (Hua Dan) in colored costumes, horsewomen and warriors (Dao Ma Dan), and the wife of the clown role (Chou Dan or Cai Dan). Cai Dan (clowns, Choupozi) is a role in farces and comedies. She is richly attired and heavily made-up. The performance of her is amusing, funny or treacherous and ferocious. Men and women were forbidden to play on the same stage in feudal China. Therefore, male actors were required to perform the female roles.

The most famous male actors in modern times, are Mei Lanfang (1894—1961), Cheng Yanqiu (1904—1958), Xun Huisheng (1899—1968) and Shang Xiaoyun (1899—1976). They contribute greatly to Beijing Opera.

Mei Lanfang, born in an actor's family, is the great master of Chinese dramatic art and outstanding expert of Beijing Opera. He showed great skill inheriting the best traditions of the past and adapting them to a new stage. He not only created many lively and unforgettable artistic images, but turned the Beijing Opera into a colorful and comprehensive art of the highest stage effects. He formed his own original style and developed Mei School by blazing a new path for Beijing Opera. He was accepted worldwide and applauded as a great artist. He was also the first artist to introduce Beijing Opera abroad and made outstanding contributions in promoting cultural exchanges between China and other countries. He made successful tours to Japan (1919, 1924, 1956), the United States (1930) and the Soviet Union (1935, 1952). Beijing Opera has obtained the world renown and exerted much influence to the foreign stage in return through his performances. The genius of him influenced the American artist, Charles Spencer Chaplin (1889—1977) and German artist, Bertold Brecht (1898—1956).

The face-painted roles are highly exaggerated and decorated roles, depicting different characters and remarkable images. They display the nature of good, honest or evil and dishonest characters. The face-painted roles (Jing) represent warriors, heroes, statesmen, demons and adventurers. Chinese audiences also call it "oil painted face".

The elaborate and gorgeous face-painted roles and costumes are two distinguishing characteristics of Beijing Opera. Audiences know what kind of a character is being portrayed from his colors and patterns.

The make-up, with its variegated colors, the strange wonderful painted-on "masks" and the rich costumes attract most first-time viewers. Make-up is an essential element in shaping character as well as strong artistic and technical qualities. Through make-up, a performer can fully express a character's personality, thoughts and mental state by realistically creating various artistic images.

In general, red facial make-up signifies honesty, probity, courage and bravery. The black facial make-up represents the character of impartiality, fortitude, coarseness and rudeness. The white facial make-up refers to a person who is of a negative character. A blue or yellow make-up stands for negative traits such as savageness, fierceness or arrogance. The faces of devils are usually painted green since green is the color of an unstable character. Gold is for gods or emperors. People of good nature are usually painted with simple colors. The make-up of hostile generals and doubtful characters, such as bandits, robbers, rebels and bear complex marks. The military "oil painted face" has a curious, heavy appearance but dances with graceful movements and sometimes performs acrobatics stunts such as fire-spitting. A contrasting role is the Fu Jing, a ridiculous figure who is anything but heroic.

The roles, defined by their different types of make-up, are classified according to the sex, age, personality and social status of the characters. For a deeper glimpse into the "magic" of the Beijing Opera

performance, it is necessary to look into their dressing rooms. The costumes, the facial make-up, the symbolic colors and a few props (which are equally symbolic), are all aids to the comprehension of Beijing Opera. The art of face painting has been very highly developed and each painted face has a special meaning to the knowledgeable audience. Applying a "mask" requires great ability and patience. Though many characters are known instantly by their make-up, it is still difficult for some audiences to recognize and interpret each face painting.

Clowns are usually awkward, stingy, funny or foolish people. The villain is always known at the beginning of the show with a white patch on his nose. A Clown can be easily recognized by his facial pattern— a patch of white around his eyes and nose, sometimes outlined in black. He keeps the audience laughing and to improvise quips at the right moments to ease tension in some serious plays.

Section 6 　Beijing Opera Today

Beijing Opera's plot development does not conform to the general pattern of other dramas. The heroes and villains are revealed as soon as they appear on stage. The audiences are already familiar with the plots. Instead of desiring to know the outcome, they prefer to enjoy the magic of the performance and the skillful techniques of the singing, dancing and acrobatics. In addition, the sumptuous costumes, the significant embroidery, the make-up and the acrobatic battle scenes also attract audiences. The same piece may be seen over and over again.

Hundreds of fans went to tea-houses or varied theatres to watch Beijing Opera in the early days of the 20th century. However, Beijing Opera, especially those with traditional themes, was prohibited during the Cultural Revolution Period (1966—1976). Instead, The Eight Model Operatic Plays based on China's recent revolutionary experiences were offered to Chinese people during that period. Examples of newly composed plays are: *The Story of Red Lantern*, *Shajiabang* and *To Take the Wehu Mountain by Strategy*. Distorted art forms and performances on stages and in movie theatres today contribute to young people's ignorance of the knowledge to enjoy and understand the traditional themes. Great changes have taken place since 1977 and the old traditional stories began to take their place again in China. Today, Beijing Opera is popular with elderly people. The majority of Chinese young people know little about this art form. They have difficulties in understanding the movements, the pantomime, the acrobatics, the dialogue and the singing. To understand and enjoy Beijing Opera, one needs to have some background knowledge about the related Chinese historical events and stories.

More than 390 traditional Chinese Operas are still being performed throughout China. Beijing Opera is looked upon as a Chinese art form and draws a lot of attention from both Chinese and people of other nations. In recent years, some Beijing Opera troupes have been abroad to perform. What impresses the audiences of different nations the most are the sumptuous costumes and make-up, and the acrobatic battle scenes. Beijing opera holds a unique position in Chinese art as well as the world's artistic heritage. Things that are national in style appear to be appreciated and accepted internationally.

Chapter 19

Industrial Arts

Xiaoxia Mao and Helen Yang

China was the first country to manufacture true porcelain (china). Chinese arts and crafts with exquisite workmanship can be classified into special and folk type categories. Arts and crafts, using special materials and undergoing elaborate designing and processing, include ivory, jade and stone carving. Folk categories are those such as silk embroidery, paper-cuts, kites and Chinese puppet art ("Pi Ying"). China's countless tourist souvenirs remind one of the long history and the traditions of Chinese people, such as cloisonné, carved Chinese lacquer, paper-cuttings, filigree, carpets, lanterns, fans, satin or silk flowers, colored glass animals, birds and flowers, and figurines of painted clay, jewelry, calligraphy, painting, seal materials, ink-stones, ink-slabs... These unique art pieces are famous in the world.

Section 1 Pottery and Porcelain

Ancient pottery and porcelain reflect the society and the cultural development of its period. From ancient times till now, ancient pottery and porcelain have been collected as artistic objects in China as well as by the rest of the world. China is known internationally for its porcelain products.

Pottery is made from baked clay, which is shaped, dried and baked in kilns at a temperature of 950℃ to 1163℃. The surface of the clay is usually glazed producing a glassy surface. Porcelain is not only baked at a higher temperature than pottery, but is also made from a special sort of fine clay. The materials of Kaolin sand and different technological arts (the baking temperatures for instance) create porcelain articles of a very fine quality. Both pottery and porcelain products were the most common articles used in Chinese daily life.

Pottery article production has a long history, dating from 8,200—9,100 years ago. The Yellow River was the most important area of the early development of civilization in China. Most painted pottery ware was produced in various cultural regions along the upper and middle reaches of this river. In this area, there is an enormous supply of the yellow soil used to produce pottery ware. Through the materials and skills used in the making of pottery, people can observe the social customs, primitive religion and aesthetics during different ages and how they played important roles in the ancient history and culture.

The decorations of painted pottery ware are a richer and a more varied way to reflect the level of social life compared with the shape of the pottery. The important decorations, fish, frogs, birds, deer, sunflowers, trees, strings of beans and leaves, all reflect nature. Some highly developed pattern designs are extracted and derived from natural phenomena. The wonderful works combine the imitation of natural images with human feelings. In some ancient pottery works found in the Qinghai and Gansu provinces, painting is combined with sculpture. This creates a third dimension to the decorations. Being the principal ideological form,

primitive religion was also reflected in the pottery ware. Some decorations were used repeatedly on the painted pottery ware. Over time, these patterns evolved into many different variations. When one particular image was used during the entire course of development of a certain culture, the image can be regarded as totemistic art. Fish and birds are the decorated images of Yangshao (in Northern China) earthenware. Fish are considered the totem of the Yangshao (Henan province). Culture and birds were the totems of the clan society in the east of China. It is accepted that the stork and fish, painted on the pottery found in Henan, represented ancestor worship.

Pottery articles (around the Yellow River and the Yangtze River) are designed with straight and level lines. They suggest a feeling of gravity, neatness and still life. The designs of China's painted earthenware usually include arcs, curves, and round points which give a feeling of movement. The uninterrupted lines of whirl patterns on the upper part of a water pot can be viewed as pelting waves from the front, but overlooked as surging waves. The designs of clouds, double hooks and thunder also remain the styles indicating movement.

Different kinds and shapes of pottery were created for practical reasons. For example, a bottle with a sharp bottom was made in the shape of a kernel, being slim and long on both ends. This shape makes it easy to take water from a shallow stream. Many designs are imitations of animals or plants, reflecting the life of that period. For instance, pottery of the vivid and lively models of dogs, or knotted bamboo, reflect the economic life of that historical time. Some pieces of pottery are specially decorated with woven bamboo patterns or rope, which mirrors the historical relationship between the articles produced for use and the shape of the pottery.

Chinese pottery art evolved into porcelain art, and eventually incorporated the traditional shapes and designs of the bronze works. The shapes of pottery are closely related to the high aesthetic value of the pottery. The value of the pieces of pottery is related to the craftsmen's artistic ability. Using the contrast techniques, craftsmen distinguished the principle patterns in the design, and developed the image of the theme in a more harmonious and attractive way. In order to add an effect of implication and fullness, they also added some detailed variations. The design of two jointed patterns produces a dual function of the same curve and round point. The same pattern intercrossed in the design, or designing the pattern around a center, suggests a feeling of cohesion and pulsation. Craftsmen also set one pattern in another to produce a feeling of magnificence and depth.

Convincing evidence shows most Chinese characters originated directly from carvings discovered on the pottery ware from the Yangshao Culture (5,000—7,000 years ago) and the Majiayao Culture (4,050—5,300 years ago). Markings on pottery found in different regions featured a general similarity. Some markings were commonly found in different excavations proving they were used across a wide area with generally accepted meanings. The marks were predecessors of primitive Chinese characters.

Large quantities of unearthed vessels show that vitreous glazes had come into use at the time of the Shang Dynasty (16th—11th centuries B. C.). The production of pottery occurred and developed with prehistoric farming. Early pottery objects appeared at the same time as primitive farming came about. To meet the needs of the developing farming economy, the art of pottery was advanced. As the economic conditions improved, there were greater artistic achievements in the making of pottery. Pottery became the pioneer of model art works in China, even though it was primarily made for use in daily life.

Vitreous glazes came into use during the Shang Dynasty (16th—11th centuries B. C.). Pottery of this period is black glazed ceramic ware, possessing some of the characteristics of porcelain. This is the forerunner of the green and blue porcelain ware of later periods. This kind of primitive porcelain developed gradually.

Fine pottery-ware began to appear around the Han period, and the quality was extremely fine. Pottery of this period has thick, even glazes, and is very hard. It is a fusion of glazes comparable in quality to those used today.

Primitive porcelain attained a high level of artistic maturity in the Eastern Han Dynasty (25—220). A time of rapid development in porcelain manufacturing happened during the Tang and Song Dynasties (618—907). Pottery of light green Yue ware, white Xing ware, and the pleasing colors and shapes of blue and white bowls appeared during the Tang and Song dynasties. Tri-color Tang Pottery has red, green and white on one object. It dates back 1,300 years in Luoyang (Henan Province). The Tri-color Tang Pottery was valued for its integration of the national style along with a distinctive local flavor. Molding with exquisite lines is skillfully combined in the works to please the eye. Different colors dissolved together in low heat produce a fine multifarious effect. Pieces of the Tri-color Tang Pottery were used by imperial families and then were buried with the deceased. (The quantity and quality of the funeral objects were determined by the rank of the deceased.) This reveals a facet of palace life flourishing during the Tang Dynasty. The Tri-color Tang Pottery has developed into several hundred varieties and now includes the colors of yellow, purple, blue, and black.

In the Song Dynasty, porcelain-ware had more pleasing colors and shapes. The five famous kilns of Ding, Guan, Jun, Ge and Ru were the major places to produce porcelain, each with its own distinguishing styles.

Porcelain manufacturing reached its height in the Ming and the Qing dynasties. The design technique includes the developing process from Blue and White Flower (*Qing Hua*), Five Colors (*Wu Cai*), Colorful Designs (*Dou Cai*) to Designs of Various Colors (*Fen Cai*) etc.

Almost the entire porcelain industry was concentrated in Jingdezhen (Jiangxi Province) during the two dynasties. Porcelain made in Jingdezhen began to be exported to Europe during the 17th century. Porcelain painted in cobalt oxide under a glaze, in contending colors, in sacrificial red, rough ware, and misty blue eggshell are characteristic of the pottery in the Ming (1468—1644) and Qing (1644—1911) Dynasties.

Today, the three porcelain capitals in China are Jingdezhen, Liling in Hunan Province and Dehua in Fujian Province. Take Liling for example, the four salient features of Liling porcelain are white as jade, clear as a mirror, thin as a paper and resonant as a chime when struck.

Shipbuilding and navigation were highly developed in China during the Song-Yuan period. Chinese commercial ships sailed to Japan, Korea, Indo-China, Burma, Malaya, Indonesia, the Philippines, India and Pakistan. Chinese ships also sailed to Arabia, Egypt, Africa and the Mediterranean coast. Among the exported goods in the foreign trade, porcelain was one of the important export goods in China's trade with the outside world during the Ming and the Qing dynasties.

Chinese porcelain products represent China's culture and civilization as follows:

The designs of porcelain products include landscapes, plants, animals and human figures. The thought of humanity is best shown in the unity. For instance, many porcelain vases were decorated with Chinese rose designs and the Characters "si" "ji" "ping" "an" (Safe and Sound during Four Seasons). The character "ping" here is pronounced like the word "vase" in Chinese. Porcelain products in various historical stages give a strong presentation of the beauty of life, and express the strong convictions of Chinese people about their lives. Historical events are reflected artistically in porcelain products, which express people's respect for history.

Section 2　Jade

The dazzling brilliance of jade has illuminated Chinese culture. Jade was the most precious stone, a

sacred material containing the quintessence of virtue to the Chinese people. Because they think the beauty of a piece of jade is like the behavior of a loyal and honest man, they compare the shiny and crystalline jade with a good man's heart. Nowadays, Chinese people still have the habit of wearing a jade pendant at their wrists or tied around their necks to express their wishes for wealth and protection from demons.

People in many ancient books described jade's mild, smooth and lustrous quality to be like the virtue of a wise man. References to jade were gradually interwoven into literature during the long period of its development and a rich vocabulary has been developed to describe jade. For example, "pure as ice and clean as jade" is cited to express a person's lofty character, while "rather be a broken piece of jade than a whole tile" praises the integrity of those who choose to die in glory rather than live in dishonor.

China's jade art has existed for more than 12,000 years. Early objects made of jade appeared during the early Neolithic Age. Jade articles were primarily produced in northeast China and the lower reaches of the Yangtze River during the Neolithic Age. Primitive people started to use hard stone to make jade axes. The production of jade works during the prehistoric stage occurred and developed side by side with prehistoric farming. To meet the needs of the farming economy and with the conditions provided by the economy, jade production developed. Just like the making of pottery products, the materials and skills used in the making of jade can also be used as a carrier of cultural information. Archaeologist discovered a large number of jade ware used for ritual purposes at the Liangzhu Culture ruins (more than 7,000 years ago) in Zhejiang Province.

The carving of jade has been an intrinsic part of Chinese culture. Jade articles became a symbol reflecting the evolution of social life, from its use in rituals to its use as an ornament. The evolution of jade production demonstrates a change in Chinese philosophy from theism to humanism. Jade carvings take the natural lines, luster and colors of jade into consideration. During the development of jade articles over the past thousands of years, jade article experienced mainly four periods: simple decorations, sacrificial ritual articles, symbolic fittings and art works.

Jade products are clear reflections of the primitive religious ideology of their time. Jade articles were most commonly used in ritual ceremonies in ancient times. The most common jade articles for ceremonial purposes have the name of the "Bi" (round, flat pieces of jade with a small hole in the center), "Cong" (long hollow pieces of jade with rectangular sides, carved with animal faces), and "Huang" (round, flat pieces of jade with a larger hole in the center, carved with animal faces) during the Neolithic Age. They were named according to their different shapes and they played a particular function in religious ceremonies. Ancient people used the blue Bi in rituals for paying homage to Heaven, and the yellow Cong in rituals for paying homage to Earth, and the black Huang in rituals for paying homage to the North. A man-animal combination carved on the Cong may be seen as a god of war with a shield in its hand. Ancient people believed holding a piece of jade provided the man and god with magical power. A large number of artifacts were found and served as a witness to the popularity of religion at that time.

After the Neolithic Age, large jade articles were used in sacrificial ceremonies, funerals, rituals, and adornments. They reflected the ideas of the social class system and ancient religions.

People used to carve many colorful and stylistic jade ritual articles for the sacrificial ceremonies which occupied a place of great importance to the nobility of the Shang Dynasty (17th century—11th century B. C.). Jade articles became marks of different classes in the Kingdom of Heaven and the world of man from then on. Jade was a symbol of both wealth and power to the ancient Chinese, making it the most precious of stones. Jade was a privileged object of royalty, the aristocrats and the high-ranking officials for a long period of time. Jade pieces played a role in paying respect to the king, making vows, marriages and funerals.

The Chinese common people's love and wide use of jade began during the Shang Dynasty (16th century B. C. —1066 B. C.) when jade was used as a medium of exchange. The artistic style of jade ware produced in the Western Zhou Dynasty (c. 11th century—256 B. C.) tended toward simplicity. They pursued a spiritual likeness of things.

The production of jade articles evolved away from the traditional influence of the ritual system and entered a new stage of development during the Han Dynasty (206 B. C. —220 A. D.) . The pieces from this era reflected the lofty aspirations of the unified Han Empire and marked the transformation of jade production. Emperors' seals of dynastic power were also made of jade. They were called imperial jade seals. With the drastic changes in political, economic, social and ideological spheres, the functions of jade articles changed accordingly. They became more than merely ornamental works of arts. The round works of the Han Dynasty are novelties, superb in design and craftsmanship with lively looks. They absorbed the romantic style of the Chu culture, fully expressing a vigorous, firm, bold and unconstrained style.

When Taoism grew in strength during Three Kingdoms (220—280), and the Jin Dynasty (265—420), people believed jade had medicinal properties that could make them live longer. The style of the jade articles was influenced by the characteristics of gold and silver articles, sculptural art, and the painting style of the Tang Dynasty (618—967) period.

Designs of jade articles showed the common psychology of society, and the shapes mostly imitated the natural images like flowers, birds, grass, beasts in daily life during the Song Dynasty (960—1279). The jade carving craftsmanship of this period had a far-reaching influence on the later development of jade articles utilizing a wonderful hollowing-out method and vivid patterns.

Bold, robust and unconstrained styles were represented by the best jade products of the Yuan (1279—1368) period. The jade products were clear and graceful, and the curves and lines were stout, firm and clear-cut in the Ming and Qing Dynasties. The pieces also had a strong taste of traditional Chinese painting with a high level of artistry. Both the imitated antique products and the techniques reached their peaks of development.

The high aesthetic value of jade articles is closely related to their decorations. Jade articles were produced with decorations carved on them to harmoniously match their shapes. The decorations are standardized and the style is mysterious. Many of the prehistoric carved markings were also found on jade articles. Most Chinese characters originated directly from these carved markings on jade articles (many of these prehistoric carvings have also been found on bones and pottery ware) according to this convincing evidence. The advent of characters pushed society forward into the era of HuaXia civilization.

The high aesthetic value of jade articles is also closely related to their shapes. Craftsmen display their understanding of the beauty of modeling art in jade material, which has a solid, smooth quality and lustrous colors. They use techniques such as contrast, detailed variations, and continuation and repetition of a design on their decorated jade articles.

The model of many jade articles expresses the theme of man's ideas about nature, feelings, imagination and ideals. The decoration of jade articles includes a motif in the designs. This motif injects the artisans' ideas and emotions into the designs. The artisans' thoughts and feelings about natural phenomena and their evolution are communicated through many designs full of wit and fantasy. Many valuable jade works (produced during the ages of Yandi and Huangdi) based on earthenware have the budding characteristics of China's modeling art, and they represent the trend of development of Chinese art traditions. The most famous example is the Banpo human-mask motif and fish design. Two fish are painted on both sides of a man's mouth. Such an image is completely in conformity with the people's ideas. It fully accords the reality of the social life at that time and people's desire. People still marvel at such a design, which is applicable

and comprehensible even today. The achievements of jade articles became the pioneer for model art works in China.

China Art and Crafts Museum in Beijing has a complete collection of contemporary jade carving works. The four giant jade carvings among them are very special. They include: *Wonder of Shanzhidaiyue* (*The miniature Mountain Taishan*), *Table Screen symbolizing happiness*, *Sightseeing with Flower Baskets and Flowers inferring auspiciousness*. They are commonly known as the national arts and crafts treasures of China. The four giant stones are of imperial jade, which is a finer and rarer than soft jade and comes from northern Myanmar. They had been stored at the government treasury since 1949. The State Council entrusted the factory to turn these stones into art works in 1982. Some experienced, well-known old artists applied for permission to carve the four giant jade stones. Seventy eight designs were submitted by 32 well-known artists and jade connoisseurs. Forty craftsmen worked for nearly five years, starting in 1985, to finish the carving and polishing on the four pieces of jade.

Wonder of Shanzhidaiyue, made from a 363.8-kilogram jade stone, shows the majestic frame of Taishan Mountain, a sacred mountain in eastern China. The artists have crafted the peak, trees, temple houses, bridges, waterfalls, and brooks, plus 64 figures and 21 animals following the stone's natural shape, veining and bands of colors. For example, they turned the original impurity of orange color in the stone into the sun laced within a thin cloud. Another flaw has been carved into a pair of gliding cranes to evoke a famous ancient poem about Taishan Mountain.

The relief screen, carved with nine coiling dragons, is the most brilliant of the four. The stone was sawed into four 1.8 centimeter thick slabs. The slabs have been assembled into one large screen. The rolling dragons, churning clouds and the turbulent sea have been depicted, incorporating the stone's nuances of colors, dark green, apple green and opal white. On the vivid three dimensional pictures, the four brownish streaks have been turned into water jets coming from the dragons' mouths.

The chained vase, 64 centimeters high and 28 centimeters taller than the original stone is glossy and filled with a dozen species of flowers. Chain carving is the most challenging part of the work. The craftsmen must be extremely careful to avoid flaws in the jadeite, or the chain will break. The 36 interlocked rings, formed out of the same jade piece, elongate the jade by hanging the chain on a wooden stand. The stone's flaws are successfully hidden in the complexity of the flowers.

The extravagant looking perfumer, in the shape of a two-eared cup, weighing 274.4 kilograms, is the second largest of the four. The bowls, consisting of the base, cup and cover of the perfumer, are screwed together with carved spiral ridges. The perfumer is carved with dragons, a phoenix, turtles, tigers and other significant creatures in Chinese mythology as well as 10 rings dangling from the carved decorations. The perfumer is about double the height of the original stone.

Section 3　Cloisonné ("Jingtai Blue")

Cloisonné, one of the famous arts and crafts of Beijing, has brilliant colors and is splendid in design. Being a famous traditional enamel ware, the invention of cloisonné has a history of 500 years in China.

One story relates that Emperor Zhu Zhangji had a special preference for copper ware. His son, Emperor Zhu Qiyu was deeply influenced by his father and developed the handicraft, making certain advances in the color of copper ware. The new art form developed during the reign of Emperor Jing Tai, with blue being the typical color used for enameling. The color, blue, was the royal color of the Ming emperors after cloisonné was invented. Therefore, it is also called "Jingtai Blue."

Another story told of the imperial palace catching fire at the beginning of the Ming Dynasty. Most things were burnt except the precious stones and other metals which melted into a crystal-like material. The craftsmen were enlightened, and after years of study and research, they finally invented cloisonné.

Enamelware became very popular during the emperor's region. Emperor Zhu Qiyu decorated the imperial palaces with many cloisonné products. This undoubtedly influenced the development of cloisonné. It was known internationally during the last years of the Qing Dynasty and received a first prize at the Chicago World Fair. The wars during the following decade nearly caused the art to disappear in the 1940s. From 1949 to the 1980s, there has been a surge in development. Quite a number of new varieties have been created. The color range of enamels has extended to include pea green, rose, coffee, egg yellow, azure, and gold. The designs have been improved by borrowing from patterns found on old silks. The most famous products are made mainly in Beijing. The development of the skill enjoys a high reputation both at home and abroad.

The techniques of making cloisonné were very sophisticated in Qianlong period of the Qing Dynasty. As a hand-made art, the production process is rather complicated. It requires rather elaborate and complicated processes: base hammering, copper strip inlay, soldering, enamel filling, enamel firing, polishing and gilding. A variety of patterns of great subtlety and grace were also used. The technique mainly includes the following steps:

(1) Casting of bronze into different shapes

When bronze was cast into different shapes, flat bronze wires were affixed in decorative patterns. Some larger cloisonné pieces have additional parts because they need electrical welding to join the pieces together. Copper is the usual material for making the frame, since it is very flexible and can easily be hammered into various shapes. The coppersmith needs to make a frame with an even weight and thickness.

(2) Filling the hollows with different colors

Different colors were applied to fill the hollows or frame. The craftsman had a well-prepared blueprint. Any necessary adjustments were made based on his own experience or by consulting with the designer.

(3) Coloring the Frame

The craftsman adjusted the color by adding different minerals since the change of colors is a result of different chemical reactions. He applied the colors on the small compartments formed by the copper strips. Each piece of cloisonné has to be fired three times using a fresh coat of enamel each time.

(4) Firing the Copper Article

After the article is put into the oven, it turns red at a temperature of about 800℃. The piece is taken out to be cooled naturally. A re-filling will be required for the color because the little compartments sink after the firing process. The process is completed several times until the little compartments are evenly filled.

(5) Polishing the Article

After firing, the pieces of cloisonné need to be ground and polished with different materials, such as emery, sandstone, hard carbon, rubber tools, and deerskin to get a luster and smoothness on the surface.

(6) Gilding the Article

The pieces of the cloisonné are electroplated with a silver or gold liquid, charged with electric current. After gilding, a slight polish again will be the final touch for the finished product.

Section 4　Silk and Embroidery

Silk is one of China's contributions to the world. China was the first country in the world to manufacture and use silk. According to a legend, Lei Zu, wife of the mythical Huangdi, taught Chinese people the

art of sericulture. Government-sponsored silk production workshops were set up during the Shang Dynasty (16th—11th centuries B. C.). Another explanation is that some ancient women found a special kind of white "fruit" (cocoon) when they were harvesting the fruit trees. They boiled these cocoons because they were too hard to be eaten. They eventually lost their patience and began to beat them with big sticks because they still could not eat the "fruits." Silk and silkworms were discovered in this way.

People in the Zhou Dynasty (11th century—221 B. C.) produced splendid silks with subtle designs woven into the fabric as well as silk decorated with colored embroidery. The technique of weaving silk spread along the Yellow River (Northern China) and the Yangzi River (Southern China) valleys.

Silk was manufactured throughout China during the Spring and Autumn period, Warring States periods (770B. C.—221 B. C.). During this time, considerable progress was made in weaving and dying techniques.

Emperor Wu of the Han Dynasty, sent Zhang Qian as envoy to the western Asian countries (from 119B. C.). Zhang Qian's journey marked the initial contacts between China and countries of Central and West Asia. This route became the world famous "Silk Road". From then on, many Chinese goods, including silk, were carried and traded along this road. In other words, silk has been one of China's traditional exports since the Han Dynasty (206B. C.—220A. D.); and most of the silk export business transpired using camels and horses along the famous caravan route to Western Asia and Western Europe.

The silk fabrics used by aristocrats were of fine workmanship and exquisite design. Silk from the prefecture of Qi (Shandong province) was very famous. The Western Han Dynasty gauzy jacket made of silk, which was unearthed from a tomb at the Mawangdui Changsha Hunan Province, is as fine as cicada's wings and weighs only 49 grams.

Chang'an (Xi'an), the capital city of the Tang Dynasty (618—907), became the nation's leading city for silk trading as well as for other goods with growing domestic and foreign contacts.

The weft patterning technique, introduced from Persia into China during the Tang Dynasty (618—907) period, was used on silk fabrics to cater to foreign tastes. The wide range of silk fabrics included brocade, gauze, damask, pongee and satin.

Three important trading ports with the outside world were established, (Guangzhou, Quanzhou, and Hangzhou) and big Chinese commercial ships sailed to Asian and African countries to export Chinese products such as silk, porcelain, and lacquerware. During the Song-Yuan period (960—1368), the "Silk Road" was again an important overland route for the cultural and commercial exchanges between the East and the West.

Zheng He as an envoy of the Ming emperors went to Southeast Asia and to the Indian Ocean from 1405 till 1433 seven times for cultural and commercial exchange. He sailed with more than 27, 800 men on 62 big ships (with a lot of silk, gold and other valuables) in 1405. The longest voyage carried him to the eastern coast of Africa.

Chinese silk and other products were traded to Europe. Romans, especially, were crazy for Chinese silk. It was a symbol of high social stature and wealth to wear silk clothes. The Roman Empire issued an order to limit the amount of imported silk for women's clothing because of their serious financial difficulties. Later, a monk hid some cocoons in his cane and brought them to Rome. The technology of raising silkworms spread outside China.

The shipbuilding industry of the Ming and Qing Dynasties (1369—1911) enjoyed a long tradition enabling the overseas trade of silk and other goods to develop. Silk production greatly increased, and Zhejiang Province had the highest reputation in the Qing Dynasty (1644—1911). In the past decades, the silk of Jiangsu, Zhejiang, Hunan, Sichuan and Guangdong provinces enjoy an especially high reputation. Suzhou is the generally recognized home of Chinese silk in the Jiangsu province. Silk production has a history of more than 2,000 years in Suzhou. People in the Suzhou area began to grow mulberry trees, raise silkworms, reel silk and weave silk clothes during the Western Zhou Dynasty (1046—771 B. C.). One third of the silk products exported from China is from Suzhou. Suzhou became the production and trade center in the Taihu Lake valley. Silk was transported to West Asia and Europe continuously from Suzhou after the "Silk Road" was opened during the Han Dynasty.

Silk centers had moved south since the Song Dynasty (960—1279) . The Song court, and the other courts of later dynasties, set up special departments in charge of tribute silk production. Dragon robes worn by the emperor were only woven in Nanjing. Clothes for palace maids, eunuchs and common officials were made in Hangzhou, and robes for ranking officials, empresses and imperial concubines were made in Suzhou. Production and marketing of Suzhou silk thrived because of its high quality and large quantity.

Silk products from various places have evolved with their own styles. Some special characteristics of the products were influenced by the local customs, art and culture. Some products favor fine composition, others lay stress on nature or bright colors. Chinese silk has several hundred varieties and thousands of colors and designs. Beautiful silk products such as silk quilt-covers, pillow-cases, table cloths, cloth and shoes won the love of people throughout the world. One of the silk products is silk embroidery. Designs of landscapes, flowers, animals, people, and buildings are embroidered on damask silk with silk thread. The embroidery unearthed in 1958 in a tomb of the Han Dynasty (B. C.) in Changsha is a good example of an ancient Chinese high embroidery technique. This astronomical painting on silk was unearthed from a tomb at Mawangdui (Hunan Province).

Embroidery of the Su style (Suzhou of Jiangsu Province), is celebrated for its cats and goldfish. Embroidery of the Xiang style (produced in Hunan Province), specializes in tigers and lions. Embroidery of the Shu style (Sichan Province) is well known for depicting lotus carp and giant pandas. Embroidery of the Yue style (Guangdong Province) is distinguished for its mountains, water, flowers and birds. It is especially well known for its "Hundreds of Birds Worship the Phoenix," which is set against the sun, bamboo, green pines and red plum blossoms.

An important development in embroidery technique was double-sided embroidery. In double-sided embroidery, both sides of the fabric can display the same design in the same color, or the two sides have the same design but different colors (1950s), or the two sides of the double-sided embroidery have different designs and different colors (1980s, Hunang Province).

Chinese painting and calligraphy can be seen from unearthed Han Dynasty silk paintings as well as silk scrolls passed down for generations. Many contemporary painters and calligraphers have also tried their hand at painting on silk. For instance, new pigments have been developed for the purpose by some professors from the Beijing Costume University these years. It has brought the traditional arts to a new level. Some exhibitions of hand-painted silk have been held as showcasing the artistic exploration of painters and calligraphers.

Section 5　Paper-cutting

An understanding of paper-cuts is a good beginning for learning Chinese folk arts. Chinese paper-cutting is a traditional folk art and can be traced back about 1,500 years. It is especially popular in the vast countryside of China. Chinese rural women cut papers with scissors into various designs. The great charm of Chinese paper-cutting is related to the variety of characters from the local arts both ancient and modern. They often have close links with traditional Chinese festivals and customs in the rural areas. They are pasted in courtyards, rooms and on everyday goods to decorate the domestic environment and to add a cheerful atmosphere.

The content and design of the paper-cut are rich and nearly anything can be the theme of papercuts. The designs range from animal to human figures, from flowers to birds, from architectures to gardens, from historical events to heroes in the local operas. Chinese paper-cuts are diverse in styles, depicting different characteristics found in different regions. They are simple and colorful, neat and skillful, or delicate and beautiful in design. Many paper-cuts use red paper as its material, and some use white papers dyed with colors. Some paper-cuts combine cutting with painting. Paper-cuts are of many different sizes.

Chapter 20

Martial Arts

Frits Buijs and Xiaoxia Mao

Martial Arts, such as Wushu, Kungfu and Qi Gong (great exercise), are typical demonstrations of traditional Chinese culture. Being popular sports in China, they are loved and practiced by people of all ages. These practices are used for strengthening the physique, for self-defense, and, as well, for treating illnesses. Being the earliest and longest-lasting sports, they utilize both brawn and brain. Martial arts theory is based upon classical Chinese philosophy. It has developed characteristically with a unique combination of health awareness, practical self-defense, self-discipline and as an art form throughout its long history of development. A distinction is made between "external" and "internal" Wushu. The internal training of Qi Gong is essential for Chinese Wushu.

Wushu is one of the typical examples of traditional Chinese culture. "Wu" means military, and "shu" means art. "Wushu" means the art of fighting or martial arts. It is defined as making full use of one's natural physical and mental physique to build Martial Arts Techniques. Wushu is not only about punching and kicking, it is a sport which utilizes both mind and body. It is a sporting exercise and an art form, which people use to treat illnesses and to use as self-defense. These days, we reserve the term Wushu for modern Kungfu (created by the government after the Cultural Revolution) and we reserve the term Kungfu for the traditional styles of Kungfu.

Wushu is classified by one of the three methods: Internal or External styles, Southern or Northern styles (南拳、北拳) Shaolin (少林) or Ermei (峨眉) or Wudang (武当) styles.

If the strength comes from the torso and legs, it belongs to the Internal Styles. It is an External Style if the strength is derived from training more specific arm and leg muscles.

Northern and Southern styles refer to the general origin of the schools of Wushu in China. Finer distinctions are often made to distinguish the detailed differences of these two schools. Northern Styles use deep leg stances, jumping, kicking and practitioners usually move around a lot during fighting, while Southern Styles use more arm techniques, less kicking, have more high stances and are flashy in their movements.

Shaolin boxing styles refer to the form of fighting practiced at the Shaolin Temple in Henan province. Similarly, Ermei is a significant mountain with Buddhist temples in Sichuan province and Wudang is the name of a mountain used by Taoists in Hubei province.

Different forms of Wushu training include kicking, punching, jumping, throwing, blocking, grabbing, hitting and thrusting. Chinese Wushu has many strategies such as: offence and defense, retreat and attack, mobility and immobility, hard and soft, fast and slow, empty and full, with or without weapons.

Chinese Wushu has a history of several millennia. It has thrived among the common people instead of dying out. This evinces the strong attraction and vitality of Wushu in China.

During prehistoric times, the initial form of Wushu appeared as people fought against nature, were hunting for food and clothing and had to protect themselves against animals and other humans.

In slave societies, frequent wars occurred between tribes and states. People needed Wushu to fight their enemies. Techniques to build up strength and fighting skills were introduced in the Wushu training during the Zhou Dynasty. Martial dance separated from it in the Shang Dynasty and became an important part of education with particular training time and content in the Zhou Dynasty. The five elements of metal, wood, water, fire and earth, who were held by the ancients as components of the physical universe were incorporated and later the Eight Trigrams (Bagua) were formed. The development of them shows that it became an organized activity with purpose and intention in the Shang and Zhou dynasties.

Rulers of different states promoted Wushu in the Spring and Autumn and Warring States periods (770—221 B. C.). Wushu masters gathered together for competition and mutual exchange every spring and autumn during that period. The standard was two persons combat. Solo exercises were meant as training for two person fights. The latter developed into Wushu movements. With the appearance of weapons made of iron, shapes of weapons were distinctively adapted. Series of wrestling, attacking and catching were used in actual fight and physical exercises, marking a new stage of its development. Slave owners supplied a living to their fencers and made them duel until one of them was killed each time. Therefore, fencing was also an embryo of the sport often held by slave owners.

In the Qin Dynasty (221—206 B. C.), there appeared Wushu movements. In feudal societies, weapons and military techniques provided ideal conditions for the development of it. During the past thousands of years, it was meant to be used in actual combat. Wushu movements further developed in both form and content during the Han Dynasty (206 B. C. —220A. D.). The ruler advocated the people in the border areas be mobilized for military training so as to prevent the invasion of the Xiongnu nationality. It enhanced Wushu activities among the commoners to a great degree. Freehand exercise (徒手) to promote health was created as early as the 3rd century. Boxing, involving the Imitation of Animal Movement (Frolics of Five Animals 五禽戏), appeared by the 5th century through the monks at the Buddhist monastery of Shaolin. The monks performed exercises emulating the five creatures: a bear, a deer, a bird, a monkey and a tiger. A snake was added later. It started to be regarded as an art with sport characteristics and kinds of techniques and styles.

The bureaucrats and aristocrats were indulged in luxurious life and pursued sorcery for longevity during the Wei (220—265), Jin (265—420), Southern (420—589) and Northern (386—581) Dynasties.

Wushu gained remarkable development in the dynasties of the Sui, the Tang and the Five dynasties. Notable promotion was made because of the implementation of imperial examination of martial arts in the Tang Dynasty. It became a common practice since the Tang Dynasty. A series of sword performance was composed and gained popularity and vitality for its function in sports and arts in the Sui Dynasty. Officer promotion was also based in terms of their levels of martial arts. The system of military examinations encouraged people to practise it.

Standards were set for selecting warriors in the Tang Dynasty (618—907 A. D.). Many people practised it to defend their country in the Song Dynasty against foreign invaders from the Liao (907—1125) and the Chin (1115—1234) states. The government set up Wushu schools. Many non-governmental Wushu organizations also appeared. People standardized many series of its movements. As an important period in its formation, the Song Dynasty witnessed it as a kind of social entertainment. With the appearance of professional performers of Wushu, it began to have its own practical teaching diagrams, while it was performed in regulated Series. Since a variety of weapons were used in the Song Dynasty, the saber was improved and divided into eight forms. Many good saber users arose with the growth of saber skills.

The rulers of the Yuan Dynasty practically prohibited Wushu activities in the public and even group hunting in order to prevent people's rebellion against their reign. The Yuan Dynasty saw its decline. However, it was put on the stage and its series were artificially modified in the theater with the boosting of opera.

It had a rapid growth consisted of various schools and sects of different styles in terms of tactics of weapons and boxing series in the Ming Dynasty. It was regulated as eighteen skills.

Though it was banned among the common people in the early Qing Dynasty (1644—1911), organizations of it were spread in secret. Many boxing styles appeared with scores of major styles and hundreds of series of boxing movements during the Qing Dynasty. It gained unprecedented progress owing to the rise of White Lotus Society, Taiping Heavenly Kingdom Movement and Yihequan Movement in late Qing Dynasty. People practiced it in public organizations and taught it in different forms. They learned some new styles of boxing series. Wushu was divided into internal and external schools according to whether the masters of the sects were monks or not monks of Buddhism. Theorists began to view it as a whole. They looked into the internal relation and regular patterns of movement inside the human body. They emphasized the integrity of internality and externality. They also focused on the combination of mental exercises and physical exercises.

Central Association of Goshu (Wushu was renamed as Goshu) was founded in Nanjing in 1926. Provincial and municipal associations were set up. President Jian Kashi demanded Wushu be taught as a major training in the military forces and a required course offered in the institutions of higher education.

Many Wushu clubs, societies and associations have been established across China after 1949. The status of Wushu has been distinctively raised. It was officially placed as a popular sport event in 1952. It was listed among the formal courses in the institutions of physical education and sports in 1954. In 1956, it was placed as a performance event to be held regularly. The Physical Culture and Sports Commission of the People's Republic of China dispatched "Circular on Exploring and Systematizing the Heritage of Wushu" in 1979. Physical education institutions in cities like Beijing, Shanghai and Chengdu have brought up a large number of specialists of Wushu under the National Committee of Sports since 1989. Works on exploration, systematization and research on it have been done these years. Mass activities of it have flourished and spread in China as a part of popular cultural life in the spare time of the masses. A large number of graduates majoring in it have been assigned to teach in schools.

During World War II a lot of Kungfu instructors fled to non occupied parts of China where they taught their knowledge further. Here Western soldiers, who were helping with the fight against the Japanese, already came into contact with the Chinese martial arts. Later during the Cultural Revolution, a lot of Chinese instructors (with their ancient books and scripts) fled to the West where they taught their skills to Westerners who really liked these new brought skills. Because of this a lot of knowledge is preserved in the West which was lost in China. These days this knowledge is gradually coming back to China and fills holes which were created during the Cultural Revolution. In the past decades, some Wushu delegations and instructors have been sent to other countries and people from other nations come to China to learn *Wushu*. Thousand of athletes, visiting experts and scholars of Wushu have been abroad which greatly enhanced the popularity of Wushu all over the world.

Asian Wushu Tournament were held in Hong Kong, Korea, Philippines and Japan in 1980s and 1990s. European Wushu Tournament has been held in Brussels, Barcelona and Stockholm in 1980s. Athletes from over 40 countries participated in the first world Wushu tournament held in Beijing in 1991. Six international tournaments have been held in different countries since then. Wushu was placed as an official event in

the 11th Asian Games in 1990. It also became an official event in the Southeast Asian Games and East Asian Games held in 1991, 1993 and 1995. Zhejiang International Traditional Martial Arts Competition was opened in Hangzhou in 2006. More than 3,000 contestants from 18 countries and regions competed in the event.

Action Movies (martial arts movies) also open the window of Chinese Wushu and stimulate international exchange. For instance, the movie *Enter the Dragon* starring Bruce Lee was a worldwide hit, which aroused people's fascination. Cheng Long (Jackie Cheng) and Li Lian Jie (Jet Li) are very famous Chinese stars in Action Movies. The West's interests have been aroused by Action Movies such as *Hero*, *Drunken Master* and *Crouching Tiger and Hidden Dragon*.

Chinese Wushu has begun to gain popularity throughout the world. International Wushu Association submitted to the International Commission of the Olympic Games the application that Wushu be adopted in the Olympic Games in 1998. It has adopted a formal event of competition at the Olympic Games in 2008.

The ancient historian Sima Qian's work *Historical Events*, "Biographies of Roving Swordsmen" is the earliest Wushu tale of roving knights. Chivalrous swordsmen (gallant persons) as a social force were highly influential figures in society. A large number of tales about them appeared in the late Tang Dynasty. From then on, tales of roving knights have been popular as a category of Chinese literature. Creation of such tales and films continues unabated in Mainland China, Taiwan and Hong Kong. Jin Yong and Liang Yu Shen are famous writers of novels about chivalrous swordsmen. In the past decades, Wushu movies and TV dramas have become very popular in China and the world with the development of modern science and technology.

Wushu is popular in China, for it is one of the sports treasured by Chinese people. People not only gain valuable skills in self-defense, but also improve their health and well-being through physical exercise. As the most popular martial art in the world, Tai Chi Chuan (Tai Ji Quan, shadow boxing 太极拳) is widely accepted and exercised all over the world. There are several schools of Tai Chi Chuan. Wu and Yang style Tai Chi are the most practiced among them. Depending on the schools and the teachers, the number of prescribed exercise forms can vary from 24 to 108 or more. It can mainly be practiced to improve the health but it can also be practiced as a full martial art. Three principles of Tai Chi Chuan include keeping one's body soft and relaxed, mental focus and natural breathing and practicing it slowly and evenly without breaking the smooth flow of coherent movements. According to numerous studies, practicing Tai Chi Chuan is of great help to the elderly.

Wushu has been added as one of the parts in many sport competitions in the recent years. The China Martial Arts Association was founded as a national organization in China after 1949. The organization has helped to develop Wushu to become more systematic, scientific and standardized. The five major categories of Chinese martial arts competitions are Empty Hand Forms, Weapon Forms, Choreographed Routines, Sparring Competitions and Group Practice. Empty Hand Competitions fall into the subdivisions as: Long Fist (Boxing 长拳), Southern Fist (南拳), Northern Fist (北拳), Tai Chi Chuan (太极拳), Bagua (八褂), Animal-Inspired Forms (五禽戏) and so on. Long Fist features fully extended, elegant and unrestrained movements, while Southern Fist demonstrates steadiness and momentum of movements. Tai Chi Chuan reminds viewers of floating clouds and flowing streams by its beautiful and smooth stringed movements.

As to the Weapons Competitions, 18 standard weapons selected from more than 400 ancient weapons are used in them. Among all the Wushu, Shaolin Wushu is best known. It refers to Wushu performed by the Shaolin fighting monks in the Shaolin Temple.

Section 2 Moral Character Cultivation and Chinese Philosophy

Kungfu developed under the great influence of the ancient Chinese culture and borrowed widely from academic studies such as ancient medicine, ethics, religion and aesthetics. Chinese Kungfu also adapted aspects of philosophy of Confucianism and Taoism. For instance, it has been influenced by the Chinese philosophical theory that "man is an integral part of nature". An ancient Chinese philosopher named Zhuang Zi pointed out there was an intrinsic link between humanity and the universe. Kungfu masters believe one cannot achieve the aim of practicing unless he achieves harmony with the universe. During the ancient times, people chose the environment of wooded mountains, scenic places or clean and quiet places at home to practise. The theory emphasizes the enhancement of the practical effect by using the effect of environment on the human body and adapting oneself to the changes in the universe. From the names of various types of boxing such as Supreme Ultimate Boxing (Tai Chi Chuan 太极拳), Eight Trigrams Zhang (张天师八卦) and Form and will Boxing (Qi Gong 气功) people can easily notice it has absorbed ancient Chinese philosophical principles. Another typical example is that the ancient Chinese philosophical theories of the eight diagrams, the five elements and the quintessence of the universe are reflected in Kungfu. The idea that "the balance of Yin and Yang is the Way" is already stated in the oldest of Chinese philosophical works The Book of Changes. Kungfu masters believe that "the balancing of Yin (阴) and Yang (阳) is perfect practice". A series of its concepts of correspondence with Yin and Yang have been created like dynamic and static, the void and solid, the firm and soft and form and spirit.

Influenced by Daoism, Wushu practitioners seek to reach a state in which they blend harmoniously with nature. It requires practitioners to train their inner spirit and mind as well as the external bones, muscles and skin. In other words, the combination of the physical being with the mental being is stressed. A distinct aspect of it is the advocacy of morals and emphasis on benevolence, fidelity and sincerity. Benevolence, the core of Confucianism, includes love, generosity and leniency. To Wushu practitioners, their moral level is as important as their martial arts skills.

It also emphasizes a close relationship between physical exercises and the surrounding environment. Different methods of exercises are used according to the changes of natural environment and the conditions of the practitioner's body.

Since the very nature of it is based on attack and defense, the slightest neglect of moral discipline can result in injury or even death. Proverbs like "Moral education comes before Kungfu training" and "Morality is better than strength" have been upheld by the Kungfu community since the beginning. Almost all of its schools put morality first. Traditional Kungfu morality includes patriotism, faith, politeness and uprightness. Strict regulations and commandments were followed in the past. For instance, the Shaolin Temple has regulations such as "disciples should be selected with great care," and "Kungfu shall only be taught to those who have proved to be honest and upright". The rules of the Wudang School forbade adultery, theft, obscenity, viciousness and gambling. In order to respect the value of life, its community forbade attacking eight vital parts of the human body in the ancient times. The Chinese Martial Arts Association conducts competitions according to the requirements of modern sport. Competition rules and moral requirements have been drawn up according to current standards to re-emphasize Kungfu morality.

The exterior beauty found in postures, techniques and movements is well-known. People should not neglect its deep interior beauty. It emphasizes "life essence, vital energy and spirit", " form coupled with spirit" and "physical health and inner vitality". Some of the above mentioned concepts are identical to the concepts of ancient Chinese aesthetics. Therefore, understanding the interior beauty of Kungfu requires one's understanding of traditional Chinese culture in addition to one's self-cultivation.

Kungfu has also been involved in literary and artistic fields. Chinese music, dance, opera, poetry, fiction and acrobatics all include elements of it. Some ancient martial melodies like The General Command and Ambush on All Sides are still played today. The famous dances the Bow and Arrow Dance and Grand

Martial Dance combine ancient martial arts with dancing.

Section 3 Qi Gong

Qi Gong means to cultivate and refine through practice one's vitality or life force. It is composed of vitality energy (or life force) , practice and cultivation (or refinement) . Lao Zi suggested that breathing practices help to merge the life force with the elements of nature. Zhuang Zi stated that the breath, in the form of Qi, is projected and circulated throughout the human body. People practice it to search for health and longevity, with the ultimate aim of gaining immortality. They believe that the primary mechanism that is triggered by the practice of Qi Gong is a spontaneous balancing and enhancing effect of the natural healing resources in the human system.

The history of Qi Going can be dated back to the Zhou Dynasty around 3,000 years ago. Its exercises were recorded on ancient bronze sacrificial objects. *Master Lu's Spring and Autumn Annals* written in 230 B. C. is the oldest book recording Qi Gong. Its exercising methods were also recorded in China's earliest medical works like *The Yellow Emperor's Canon of Internal Medicine* written in the Warring States Period (476—221 B. C.).

Qi Gong is the overriding component of the martial arts and is central to the practice of the " internal arts. " It has become an integral part of the Chinese culture.

One form of its practice is regulating the breath to expel the stale and stagnant air and inhale fresh air to improve the functioning of the internal organs, to resist senility and to prolong life. Three basic categories, such as breathing through the mouth or nose, abdominal breathing and controlled breathing in conjunction with mental activity are included.

Daoyin is another form of practice. It was interpreted by ancient people as physical movements executed in coordination with controlled breathing. This form testifies to the effect that one's mind guides the physical movements and the physical movements help Qi reach the bodies' extremities. Daoyin was practiced in prehistoric times prior to the Shang Dynasty.

People practice Qi Gong to relieve stress and maintain peace of mind. It is used to improve the coordination of the nervous system and enhance one's mental self-control. It also helps to tap the body's potential and to stimulate positive factors.

There are nearly four hundred kinds of Qi Gong exercises, and each has its own characteristics and effects. They differ according to posture, method, form, style and purpose. Qi Gong can be divided into two forms: hard Qi Gong and soft one. Hard Qi Gong is considered a martial art (Kungfu) , while soft Qi Gong includes aspects of health-building and therapeutic Qi Gong.

Section 4 Martial Arts and the Stage Art of Drama

Spectacular Wushu techniques are an important part of Beijing Opera. It provides fighting scenes and has a big influence on the content and the audiences' taste as well. Among the large number of actors and actresses who were skilled in it, Tan Xingpei was a famous actor who combined traditional forms of Kungfu with contemporary additions such as Shaolin broadsword techniques. Mei Lanfang, the most famous Beijing Opera artist, practiced it every day. His Lady Yu Dancing with a Sword is accepted as a masterpiece of art combining Wushu and dance. Gai Jiaotian, a famous Beijing Opera artist, compared Kungfu with musical notes.

Part 7

Tradition and Customs

Chapter 21

Chinese Culinary Culture

Xiaoxia Mao and Helen Yang

Being a vast country, China's topography is varied and complicated with towering mountains, basins of different sizes, flat and fertile plains, undulating plateaus and hills. The country is mostly comprised of plains, deltas and hills in the east, and of high plateaus, deserts and mountains in the west. The climate has a marked continental monsoonal nature, characterized by great variety and extreme diversity. China is a big family of 56 nationalities with different traditions and customs. All of the above elements create a special culinary culture that is found in different areas among different peoples. Each area has a wealth of local, special features in its cooking. Variations in it are closely linked with economic development, ethnic customs and social changes. Chinese cooking styles are grouped into four (or eight) major schools. The three essentials of color, flavor and taste are emphasized in Chinese cooking. Chinese food is well known around the world for its variety and abundance.

A typical Chinese dietary style uses grains as the staple; meats (or eggs, or bean-curd), vegetables and fruits supplemented the grains. It is different from the Western dietary style. Chinese cooking places emphasis on the essentials of color, flavor and taste.

Section 1 Origin

Eating and propagation are regarded as two basic prerequisites for the existence and reproduction of human beings. Eating is the top priority of people. People dine whether they are happy or sad at weddings and funerals or on other formal occasions.

Dietary culture is an important part of traditional Chinese culture. It includes the resources of food, food production, cooling skills, customs, dietary art, and public dietary ways.

Chinese dietary culture is closely linked with its agriculture and agriculture is considered to be the foundation of China's economy. Since the introduction of agriculture, grains of cultivated crops have become the main source of the people's food instead of meat in most areas of China. A jar of carbonized millet was unearthed in the historical relics of the Ban Po Cun Culture of the Neolithic Age. It indicated that millet was grown extensively in the Yellow River area in north China five or six thousand years ago and it was the main food. Traces of paddy rice cultivation were identified in the historical relics of He Mu Du Culture. These discoveries show that rice was the main food in south China six or seven thousand years ago.

Cooking is one of the first few steps from savagery to civilization. Chinese cuisine originated during the Shang Dynasty (1600—1046 B. C.), during which time China rose to prosperity. Shang people mastered cooking techniques like steaming, frying, stir-frying and deep-frying. They considered food preparation to

be an art. Rice and wheat have been the major staple food since the Shang Dynasty. Shang people of the upper class enjoyed a wide variety of meat from cows, chickens, pigs, sheep, deer and horses. Fish of a dozen kinds was probably the best food common people could obtain. Wine played an important role in the lives of the Shang people.

The bronze wares were used for cooking as well as being indicative of social status. Delicious and nutritious food was regarded as the basis of ordinary life. People of the Shang and Western Zhou Dynasties valued highly their way of dining. More than 2,000 people—half of the staff of the imperial palace—were engaged in preparing food for the emperor and his family in the Western Zhou Dynasty (1046—771B. C.). They not only stressed clean food and culinary vessels but also decreed harmony among ingredients with respect to their size, shape, fragrance, taste and texture. Seasonal varieties were enriched with sweet, hot, spicy or sour flavors to make tasty and healthy dishes and diet changed in different seasons. Vegetables and fruits were combined with the main dishes to gain a balanced diet. They also learned to build large underground cold storage areas to keep food fresh in the winter. Effective methods used to preserve food included salting fish and meat, and pickling vegetables.

Crops and animal husbandry were equally important aspects of the agricultural structure in the Warring States Period (about 2,000 years ago). The daily meals of the Chinese people mostly consisted of non-processed crops like beans, wheat and peas prior to the Qin Dynasty (221—206 B. C.). Wild vegetables, fruits and meals with wheat were the common dietetic structure of the lower strata, while meat was common only among the nobles during that time. A variety of bronzes were popular cooking utensils and tableware among the upper class people in addition to pottery vessels.

Flour meals replaced the non-processed grains, and flour products became common in north China after the stone mill was invented to grind grains during the Warring States Period and Han Dynasty (206B. C. —220A. D.). Northern food styles, characterized by wheat flour, were complicated. People used to boil or steam cereals, or fried them into solid food. Pancake, the early cooked wheaten food, was made by making the wheat into flour, then by adding water and rolling it into cake-shaped pieces, finally by baking, roasting, steaming or cooking. The predecessor of noodle was soup pancake boiled in water, which was a special kind in the family of pancakes that originated in the Han period. Soup pancake has a shape of flat pieces that is different from the shape of today's noodle. It was the specialty of birthday banquets by then, which confirmed to the custom of having noodles on one's birthday in north China. Meanwhile, rice flour-made food is called *Ci* or *Ciba* was popular in south area. In addition to the use of stone mills, alcohol and soy sauce were also produced. More and more people in north China began to eat cooked food made of wheat. They also started to produce bean milk and bean curd (invented by Liu An) in the Han Dynasty. Bean curd is not only tasty as a dish, but also easier to digest than other vegetable protein. Since ancient times, people have advocated suitability and frugality as the most important principles in cooking. The following five were the main vegetables consumed in the Han Dynasty: Malva verticillata (*Kui*), the tender leaves of soybeans, Chinese onion, Chinese leek, garlic and turnip.

Various kinds of pancakes such as sesame seed cake and steamed dumpling made with unleavened dough were a popular food during the Wei and Jin period. The earliest leavened food, called steamed pancakes, originated at the same period. They were steamed fermented dough. They were called "Mantou" nowadays. Stuffed bun also appeared as a leavened food and has the name of " Baozi" since the Song Dynasty.

There was wonton rather than dumpling in ancient China. Later on people made Wonton into the shape of crescent moon named Jiaozi (dumpling) in the Sui Dynasty. Dumpling has become the most common food in China today.

After the Grand Canal was dug in the Sui Dynasty (581—618), ingredients and preparation variations moved. Rice grown in the southern area was brought to the north, and wheat, millet and sorghum to the south.

Almost all the products that are now grown in China were produced in the Tang Dynasty (618—907). Fishery was also developed well during the period. Breeding fish in ponds was a common practice. Chinese people have expanded their daily sources of food by developing farming, forestry, husbandry and fishing since the Ming and the Qing periods (1368—1911). Raising pigs, ducks, geese, fish, chickens, sheep, and cattle along with the cultivation of crops became very popular too.

People cut noodles into long and thin pieces and evolved them on the basis of soup pancake which appeared in the Northern Song Dynasty (960—1279). Dried noodles appeared in the Yuan Dynasty (1271—1368). Noodles were not a daily food, but a luxury in entertaining guests or patients in ancient time.

Mongolians influenced the cooking techniques in China in the Yuan Dynasty. Their Hot Pot is now considered both a northern and southern delicacy.

The first emperor of the Ming Dynasty (1368—1644) named Zhu Yuan Zhang, required thousands upon thousands of people to resettle westward unpopulated areas. It influenced the food style in the Western China.

Vegetables were scarce in the remote ages of China. Communications between China and the West became well developed, and foreign agricultural products were introduced into China during the Han (206 B. C. —220 A. D.), Tang (618—907), Song (960—1276), Ming (1368—1644) and Qing Dynasties (1644—1911). For example, Zhang Qian, who was sent to Western Regions by Emperor Wu, brought fruits and seeds of various plants back to China from the world-famous "Silk Road" in the West Han Dynasty. Seeds and fruits like garlic (from Ferghnan), linseed, walnut, coriander, pomegranate and Lucerne (from Bactria) were carried back China on the backs of camels trudging across the vast desert. In this period, a number of the food materials imported from the Western Regions also included grapes, garden peas, broad beans, carrots, onions, rose apples, peppers and watermelon. These products have since enriched the varieties of food in China.

Foreign vegetables such as eggplant (India), cucumber (India) and spinach (Nepal) were introduced to China in the Jin and the Tang Dynasties. Hyacinth beans (India) entered into China during the Southern and the Northern Dynasties. America lima beans and chili came to China in the 16th century. The sweet potato was native to the American continent. In the Ming Dynasty, sweet potatoes were brought from the Spanish ruled Philippines, to the Fujian and Guangdong Provinces by Chen Zhenlong (1593). Tomatoes were introduced into China through Europe as an ornamental plant in the early 18th century and were cultivated as vegetable in the mid-19th century in China. The introduction of foreign crops such as corn, peanuts, potatoes and hot peppers also enriched the material life and dietary culture of Chinese people. The Chinese dietary culture is the product of agricultural development and communication with other nations.

Some famous figures in China history also have had a great influence on the food culture. Confucius developed some principles of dietetic hygiene, and criteria for testing the hygiene of food. He stressed eating in moderation, and pointed out that people, although having many meat coursed, should not overeat. Some of his principles of building health through diet are wise. For example, he advocated, "Do not take away the ginger", for it is pungent, and ginger removes dampness and reduces internal heat and fever. Mencius believed that only when people were clothed and fed would it be probable to establish harmonious relations and become cultured.

Works on dietary culture have been included in various historical documents since the Han Dynasty. The two works—*Chronicles of the Han Dynasty*, and *Food Book of Prince Huainan*—of that period still influ-

ence contemporary books. Those books contain topics on cooking skills, food production, preservation of food, philosophies from various schools of thought, food quality, delicacies, dietary customs, lifestyles, distinguishing harmful herbs, wild plant resources, and food supplied to the imperial court. Some poets wrote about the food in their verses. For instance, Lu You (a Song Dynasty poet) wrote poems praising vegetarian food.

Taoism and Buddhism have influenced Chinese cooking. Taoist priests, or monks created vegetarian food. The history, culture and art of Taoism or Buddhism are extensive and profound. Vegetarian food and beverages of Taoism or Buddhism have accumulated a rich experience in longevity and health care. A unique Taoist or Buddhist food culture has formed. The highest goal of Taoism is to achieve longevity, the Taoist priests inherits esoteric Taoist prescriptions for longevity. The dishes combine delicacy and healing into one. Some Taoist dishes include medicinal recipes, healthy tea and spirit are all superior health care in China.

Cooking and eating used to be at the same place in ancient times. People sat around the bonfire and ate. A bonfire or a stove, on which meals were cooked, was set in the centre of the residence. People invented tea for dining and reading in the Warring States Period. Teapots, tables and chairs have been widely used in dining after tables and chairs appeared in the Han Dynasty (206 B. C. —220A. D.). Before chopsticks, forks, knives and spoons were used, people grasped or tore food with their bare hands. Spoon and knife became the main dining utensils in the Zhou Dynasty. Chopsticks were commonly after the Han dynasty. They were made of branches, bamboos and natural animal bones in remote ages. Ivory and jade ones also appeared in the Xia and the Shang dynasties and bronze or iron ones emerged in the Spring and Autumn Period. Those chopsticks which were made of scraped bamboo or wood were widely used.

Diet represents a part of the civilization of each ethnic group and cooking is a superb art. It is well known that Chinese cuisine is ranked among the world's best. Chinese restaurants can be found in many countries and regions of the world. Some overseas Chinese opened Chinese restaurants in England and other countries and regions in the Qing Dynasty (1644—1911). Chinese restaurants are among the most prosperous, thriving enterprises in the world. One common saying is "the three luxuries in one's life include an American house, a Japanese wife and Chinese food".

The Chinese culinary experience applies the artistic schemes and designs of painting, sculpture, music and dance, Chinese dietary culture is considered a genuine art. Many Chinese dishes look like pieces of art and they are both good-looking and delicious. The diverse flavors, the complicated and magical techniques, the artistic appearances and taste combine to make the Chinese food culture a colorful art form.

The number of well-known ancient and modern Chinese dishes reaches 8, 000 according to data on the subject. The ingredients may be roughly classified into 600 categories. The basic ways of cooking are of 48 different kinds and all of them bring out the best in the ingredients.

Chinese cooking is very delicate and has great variety. There are more than 5, 000 different local cooking styles in China. The cooking methods and cooking styles differ greatly in different areas of China. Each region of China also boasts its local delicacies. The ten most popular cooking styles in China include Beijing, Shandong, Sichuan, Huaiyang, Shanghai, Zhejiang, Fujian, Hunan, Anhui, and Guangdong. They can be divided into four main schools.

Section 2　Northern Schools

Northern school is also called Beijing Dishes, or Shangdong Cuisine. The area of the Northern school covers Beijing, Shandong, Tianjing and Henan provinces.

People say China is the "kingdom of good food" in the world, however, few people know that the Chinese cooking history virtually originated from Beijing. As early as 17,000 years ago, the Upper Cave Man at Zhoukoudian near Beijing invented the method of cooking food with artificial fire.

Beijing has been the capital city for about six dynasties in ancient times. Being the trade center, Beijing hosted many important leaders and traders from China as well as other countries in the world. These visitors influenced the cooking skills and culinary specialties in that region. Beijing is a center for different styles of cooking. Since there are many cultural and trade exchanges with other parts of the country, as well as the gathering place of officials and businessmen. A large number of skilled chefs with different cuisines styles followed these people to Beijing and they have greatly enriched the flavors of Beijing cuisine. The Shang-dong, Huaiyang, and Jiangsu-Zhejiang cuisines have all strongly influenced Beijing cuisine. For instance, the third Ming Emperor Yongle moved the capital to Beijing in 1421 and brought the Huaiyang chefs with him. Another example is the big influence of cooks from other areas. Many people from Shandong Province came to Beijing to trade and make a living, since Shandong Province was near Beijing. The Shandong cuisine has also influenced Beijing by making a point of retaining the original flavor, freshness, crispness and tenderness of the ingredients.

Beijing is famous for its delicacies of the Manchu and Han nationalities, the meat dishes for the high officials and all kinds of traditional snacks, countless famous family food.

One characteristic of the northern school is having a high caloric value to answer the demands of the cold northern climate. Northern cuisines have salty, rich flavors of the deep-fried, grilled, pan-fried or stir-fried dishes. Beijing Dishes often combine the southern and northern cuisines. Special cuisines of Beijing include Imperial Court Cuisine, Tan-style Cuisine and Red Mansions Banquet. The well-known dishes are Beijing Roast Duck（北京烤鸭）, Mongolia Hot Pot（涮羊肉）and Almond and Milk in Jelly（杏仁豆腐）.

Beijing Roast Duck

Beijing Roast Duck has the reputation of being the most delicious food of Beijing. It is a date-red color shining with oil and characterized with crisp skin and tender meat. The proper way of eating Beijing Roast Duck is to wrap two or three pieces of duck flesh, which are cut into two-inch-square slices and dipped into a sweet sauce made of fermented flour, with some green onions in a thin pancake and folded into a roll.

Roasting duck first began in Nanjing, which was the capital city of the early Ming Dynasty 300 years ago. It was brought to Beijing as one of the favored courses on the imperial menu after the capital was moved to Beijing.

There are two major schools of roast duck preparation. One school makes use of a conventional, convection oven, in which no flames come into direct contact with the duck. This method dates back to 1816. The Pianyifang Restaurant in Chongwenmen District of Beijing serves roast duck that exemplifies this technique.

When rosting Beijing Roast Duck, cooks usually select ducks weighing 2.5 kilograms, which have been raised for 65 days. They are fed a highly nutritious mush every six hours of their last 20 days to thicken the layer of fat under the duck skin. They are brushed with a glaze of honey and hung to dry for 24 hours. Air is pumped into the ducks between its skin and flesh to produce a rich and crispy texture. The ducks' stomachs are also filled with water to steam the insides and roast the outsides at the same time. They are roasted in a doorless oven, burning non-smoky hardwood fuels such as peach, pear or Chinese date, to impart a subtle fruity flavor to the skin. The ducks are roasted about 40 minutes at 270 ℃. They need to be turned over frequently throughout the roasting process to ensure even cooking. A cook needs to occasionally

中国文化导读
Guide to Chinese Culture

hook the duck and suspend it directly over the fire for approximately 30 seconds.

Beijing Roast Duck can also be roasted in electric ovens in recent years. However many customers still prefer to taste it roasted by the traditional method in famous restaurants like Quanjude Restaurant and the Hepingmen Beijing Roast Duck Restaurant. Quanjude Restaurant, founded in 1864, is considered to be the first restaurant of Beijing Roast Duck. Yang Quanren, a noted chef who used to serve in the palace, established the restaurant in Qianmen area, which was one of the most famous commercial streets in Beijing.

Hot Pot

The Mongolian version of this steaming feast is the father of all hot-pots in China. It boasts a history of more than 1,000 years for it was popular during the Tang Dynasty (618—907). Mongolia hot pot, the most popular way to enjoy lamb, was also popular in the Yuan Dynasty (1271—1368) because the Mongolian rulers were especially fond of lamb. The Qing Dynasty rulers liked pork prior to entering Beijing from northeastern China. Imperial chefs adopted the culinary style during the mid-17th century. Mutton hot pot became a winter favorite of the Qing emperors. The court kitchen in the Qing Dynasty once prepared 1,550 hot pots for a New Year's banquet.

The dietetic influence on Beijing from the northeastern part of China was gradual. Hot-pot has had three main schools, such as the Mongolian-style, Sichuan-Style and Cantonese-style during its evolution and development. The Mongolian-style utilized prime mutton cut into thin slices. Bean curd, sesame pancakes and Chinese cabbages are also important for a complete hot-pot. The sauce contains ingredients like sesame butter, soy sauce, chopped chives, glutinous rice wine, chili oil, shrimp sauce, vinegar and Chinese parsley. Mongolian Hot Pot is a Muslim specialty. Being one of the capital's most celebrated dishes, the Mutton Hot Pot used to be a brass pot with a wide outer rim around a chimney with a charcoal burner underneath. Electric pot is more popular nowadays.

Donglaishun Restaurant is the prime Mandarin hot-pot restaurant in Beijing. The New Donglaishun Restaurant has a high reputation for making Mongolia hot pot in China. The restaurant has established more than 60 restaurants throughout China. The Sichuan hot-pot is very spicy and hot since the broth is flavored with chili peppers and other pungent herbs and spices. A broad range of food, such as beef, chicken breast, pork, mushrooms, duck, sea food, and vegetables is selected to cook in the spicy broth. The Cantonese-style is sweeter and features seafood ingredients in most of the southern-style Cantonese eateries. A sweetish white sauce and all kinds of fresh sea food are included.

Since the diners cook and serve themselves, it makes for a rather active meal. People find little more desirable and pleasant than sitting down with family and friends to a hot-pot on a cold winter day. Having hot-pot has become a way of life and an entertainment that lasts for hours during winter holidays.

Imperial Diets

The imperial meals reflected the colorful, dietetic culture and multiple nationalities of the Qing Dynasty. They were also an important component of the Chinese dietetic culture. Most food that the Chinese have today is a continuation of the dietetic culture from the Qing Dynasty.

Imperial diets, prepared by the Imperial Kitchen, were fancifully named and exquisitely prepared with the best ingredients. One meal included hot and cold dishes, meat and vegetable dishes, sweet and salty pastries, soup, milk, pickles, rice, wheat food, desserts and fruits.

After the menus were prepared by the chief cook in the imperial kitchen, it was checked by the emperors. The dishes on the emperors' menus were varied because of their differing tastes. The Qing emperors' meals followed strict rules and rites and varied in content and form according to the different tastes of the emperors. Strict standards for cooking and for using raw materials were instituted. The amounts of the major ingredients, auxiliary ingredients and flavorings that were used in the imperial dishes were designated. Strict rules were used to control the size, length and height of the buns and other staple foods. Increases or decreases were forbidden.

The emperors' diets were adjusted by the imperial kitchen with the change of the seasons. Hot pot, roast duck and roast chicken were served at every meal and other dishes changed from season to season during the Qing Dynasty. According to the metabolic rule of the human body, light food could increase people's body fluids while fatty, nutritious food increased their vital energy. Lighter food was served during spring and summer, while fattier, nutritious food was offered during autumn and winter.

The meals were based on profound cultural thought. The ancient Chinese philosophy reflected in the emperor's diets shows that "harmony is precious." A vast number of dishes included food of the five cereals, and sour, sweet, bitter, salty and spicy flavors, for people believed that they needed all five flavors to obtain all the needed nutrients to maintain good health. The diverse food and reasonable blending of ingredients were intended to achieve "harmony." The Qing emperors also ate food that had medicinal properties.

During the early Qing Dynasty, most raw food stuffs came from northeast China. More cereals appeared after Qianlong's reign. Gradually, the valuable raw materials used in the imperial meals were gathered from all parts of China. Some of them were a collection of rare food in China. The custom of having the sacrificial offerings profoundly influenced the imperial meals since large quantities of sacrificial offerings were taken by the Qing court each year. Sacrificial offerings were a component of the imperial food. Some products, rarely found among the common people, such as the various kinds of grapes from Xinjiang, a kind of red rice, and prawns were in regular supply.

The dishes comprised Manchu dishes, Han dishes, and dishes cooked in both northern and southern styles, since the imperial meals were dominated by the Manchu cuisine, the Shandong and the Suzhou-Hangzhou cuisines. The three cuisines were influenced by and blended with one another. Through cooperation, the cooks of the Manchu and Han nationalities catered to the rulers' tastes and desires for the banquets and feasts. They created new imperial meals varied from the cuisines of the three localities differing from the imperial meals of the preceding dynasties.

Some former imperial chefs opened their own restaurants and served the public after the Qing Dynasty collapsed in 1911. The menus were called Fangshan (imitation imperial dishes), since the dishes were modeled after the imperial food in the palace. The Fangshan Restaurant (1925) inside Beihai Park is the most famous imperial dish restaurant in Beijing.

Section 3 Sichuan School

Sichuan cuisine has affected and even replaced more sumptuous dishes although it has only a short history. Sichuan, a rich land in China since ancient times, produces abundant domestic animals, poultry, fresh water fish and crayfish. Its cuisine is well known for cooking fish, beef and pork. Sichuan food is famous for its rich flavors and every dish has its own unique taste. The Sichuan cooking art emphasizes the aesthetic appeal of food. It offers a presentation of color and artistic appearance, as well as a wonderful aroma and flavor.

People's impression of Sichuan food is it is hot, sour, sweet pungent and salty, using fish sauce or having a strong taste. Though hot pepper plays an important role in the flavoring in Sichuan cuisine, Sichuan food also has many dishes without hot pepper. Only 20 percent of the hundreds of varieties of Sichuan dishes have a hot and numbing effect on the tongue. Specialties also include dishes without the hot

and numbing effect such as Steamed Pork Wrapped in Lotus Leaves (荷叶蒸肉), Shrimp with Green Vegetables (翡翠虾仁), Beef Stew (炖牛肉) and Stewed Scallop and Turnip Ball (锈球干贝).

Sichuan pickles have an appealing smell. Sichuan dishes are spicy and pungent, emphasizing the use of chili, frying, frying without oil, pickling or braising. The distinct features of the Sichuan style are steaming, simmering and smoking. According to a common Chinese saying, each meal of Sichuan cuisine has its own unique taste, and no two dishes have the same flavor.

The following are the well known Sichuan dishes: Diced Chicken with Peanuts (宫保鸡丁), Mapo bean-curd (麻婆豆腐), Chongqing Hot Pot (重庆火锅) and Tea Smoked Duck (樟茶鸭). Many delicious snacks like Noodles with Chili Sauce (担担面) and Chicken with Sesame Paste (怪味鸡) are also well known.

Section 4   Jiang-Zhe School

Jiang-Zhe food is called Huai Yang Dishes or Jiangsu Style dishes. The geographic area covers present Jangsu and Zhejiang Provinces. Cities along the Yangzi River like Shanghai, Nanjing, Hangzhou and Ningbo have been economic and cultural centers since Five Dynasties (907—960). Yangzhou remained an important economic and salt-trading center for more than 1,000 years after the famous man-made canal was dug. The founder of the Ming Dynasty (1368—1644), named Zhu Yuanzhang, designated Huaiyang cuisine as the official imperial court diet in Nanjing, which was the first capital city of the Ming Dynasty.

Jiang-zhe food is nutritious and preserves the food's original flavoring, while Zhejiang food is tender, mild and fresh. Huai Yang dishes stress the use of vegetables, bamboo shoots, mushrooms and water shield, as well as beef and pork. It gives the food a light, fresh taste. The fish and shrimp are often kept alive until they are cooked. The dishes served in restaurants are quite fresh.

Huai Yang dishes are characterized by the addition of a relatively high proportion of soy sauce. Compared with northern cuisine, Huai Yang dishes have a sweet and less salty taste. They utilize stewing, braising, roasting, and simmering. The flavor is light, fresh and sweet. For instance, dishes like Longjing Shrimp (龙井虾仁), Beggar's Chicken (叫花鸡), Chicken Mousse Broth with Fresh Corn (鸡茸玉米), Squid with Crispy Rice Crust (鱿鱼锅巴) have the fresh and sweet flavor. Using fermented glutinous rice is a special feature of Jiangsu-Zhejiang (similar to Huai-yang cuisine) cuisine. Some dishes such as The well known dishes include Duck Triplet (三套鸭), Squirrel Fish (松鼠桂鱼) Heart cabbage (清炖菜心) and Sweet-Sour West Lake Fish (西湖醋鱼) are served in delicious soup. The well-know dishes also include Pork Patties with Crab Meat (蟹粉狮子头), Dongpo Pork (东坡肉) and Eight-jewel Rice Pudding Wrapped with Lotus Leaves (八宝荷叶饭).

Section 5   Southern School

The Southern school refers to the dishes in Guangdong, Chaozhou and Hainan Provinces. The raw materials, cooking methods and flavorings are all different from the other cuisines. Guangdong is located in southern China, where the coast provides rich seafood. Guangdong cuisine emphasizes seafood, and unique combinations of flavorings. The cooking methods are mainly roasting, stir-frying, sautéing, deep-frying, braising, stewing, and steaming; and the character of the dishes' tastes is light, crisp and fresh.

The cooking Steamed Sea Bass (蒸海鲈鱼), Gourd cups (冬瓜盅), Salt-Cooked Chicken (盐焗鸡) highlights its freshness, tenderness and light color, relying less on heavy sauces and deep-frying. In general, freshness and cooking things quickly are the most important things in the Guandong cuisine.

Although Guangdong cuisine is unique among the Chinese cuisines, it has absorbed the cooking skills of the West and other regions of China as Western culture has been introduced. Guangdong food has also absorbed some elements of Beijing, Yangzhou cuisine while keeping its own flavor. The well known dishes like Roasted suckling Pig（烧乳猪）, Sweet-sour pork fillet with chili（糖醋咕噜肉）, Sauté chicken ball with wild pepper（Chaozhou 花椒炒鸡球）, Frittered stuffed duck with garnish（Chaozhou 八宝酥鸭）Fried shrimps in shape of date（Chaozhou 干炸虾枣）and Snow Chicken（雪花鸡, Fujian Province）all absorb the cooking skills of other regions.

Section 6　Daily Dishes

Jiaozi（Dumpling）

Chinese Jiaozi has had a very long history. Zhang Zhongjing, an official of the Eastern Han Period, created dumplings to help people keep warm in cold winters. Fillings such as lamb, Chinese medicinal herbs and hot peppers were used.

Dumplings became popular in Northern China later and different kinds of vegetables, ground meat, ginger, garlic and onion were added. A popular saying in China expresses how much Chinese love them："There is nothing more delicious than Jiaozi." It also tops the lists of delicacies and taken as the New Year's Eve food during the Spring Festival. The custom of making it as a special dish during the Spring Festival started in the Ming Dynasty（1368—1644）. People choose it as the special food during the Spring Festival to connote their wishes for good fortune in the following year, because the appearance of it looks like the gold or silver ingot used as money in ancient China. Sometimes, people add some sweets to the fillings to express their best wishes for a sweeter life. Some families in the northern countryside may prepare enough Jiaozi to last several days of the Spring Festival time. All members of a family make it together while chatting. The process of preparing for it is a lively conversation between family members too.

Ways of making Jiaozi are different in various regions. There is also no set rule of making dumpling fillings. Jiaozi is generally boiled in water and served with vinegar, soy sauce, garlic or pungent sauce. People in Henan and Shanxi provinces boil it with noodles and serve them together as " silver threads piercing through silver ingots". Sometimes people cook it by steaming or frying. It may be served with sweet jelly made from bean or potato starch.

Noodles

Different kinds of Noodles, such as rice noodles, flour noodles, and corn flour noodles are made in different ways. The Daoxiao Noodle（Daoxiaomian）may be cut with a knife over the cooking-pot as a Shanxi speciality, or they may appear in a soup with other ingredients. They may also be grilled or fried with the same ingredients as found in the soups. They may even be served cold with pimentos（Yanji Cold Noodle）as in the Dongbei area, or in a hot stew accompanied by various cereals（Zhajiangmian）in Beijing. Noodles are of different widths（flat, round, wide and thin）, varying from threads to ribbons. A kind of thin noodle is called "Dragon Beards".

Noodles can be served warm or cold, with soup or not; dressed with chili oil, and with your choice of beef, seafood, chicken, ribs, pork, egg, or vegetables. They may be mixed with fried bean sauce, pork or chicken sauce, duck chops, or soup of any concoction.

Noodles are indispensable at Chinese birthday dinner parties. They are in the form of long strings which are the symbol of longevity.

Soybean Curd

Soybean curd (Tofu) is made from curdling fresh hot soymilk with a coagulant. The white, soft, and cheese-like food, first made in China around 200 B. C. (Han Dynasty), is generally pressed into a solid block. It is not only delicious but also healthy which contains plant protein. Some dishes of soybean curd made for vegetarians and monks imitate the appearance and flavor of meat dishes.

Spring Rolls

It is a great favorite for the Chinese and much appreciated abroad. The ingredient for the filling of Spring Rolls (Chunjuan) is usually bean sprouts, mixed with shredded pork, dried mushrooms, plumped and shredded vermicelli, shredded bamboo shoots and other necessary seasonings. Spring Rolls are deep-fried in oil and served hot when the wrappers are still crisp.

Chapter 22

Tea Culture

Xiaoxia Mao and Catherine Gu

Tea is one of the three major beverages in the world. The homeland of tea is China. Tea was originally used as a medicine since Chinese discovered its pharmaceutical ingredients. Later on, Chinese regarded it as a drink, for they found that it both quenches one's thirst and helps to reduce one's internal heat. They also learned to use it to flavor their food. They mixed it into the dishes 3000 years ago.

The use of tea spread to other nations through cultural exchanges more than a thousand years ago. It became an important Chinese trade item via the ancient "Silk Road" and other trade channels. Tea is the pride of the Chinese nation for it is one of China's principal contributions to the world. Tea beverage is made from the tea leaves collected from tea trees or bushes. The tea tree plant grows well in hot, rainy tropical climates at altitudes of 3,000 to 7,000 feet. The slower growth at higher altitudes improves the flavor of the leaves. It is ready to harvest in three years at the low altitudes and in five years in the hills.

Section 1 Long History

Being the homeland of tea, China had tea-shrubs five to six thousand years ago, and human cultivation of tea plants dates back two thousand years. Tea-drinking in China can be traced back to the Zhou Dynasty (1100—221 B. C.). Shennong, a legendary hero, tasted hundreds of world plants to see which were poisonous and which were edible to prevent people from eating the poisonous plants. Though he was poisoned seventy-two times in one day, he was saved by chewing some tender leaves of an evergreen plant blossoming with white flowers; those leaves were collected from tea trees. Tea was regarded as a kind of medicine and became a drink later to refresh oneself and to calm one's mind.

Chinese started to boil and sell tea during the Western Han (206 B. C. —23 A. D.) period. Drinking tea was very popular at least in southern China during the period of the Three Kingdoms Period (220—280). Drinking tea became a fashion for those people with high social status during the Wei, the Jin (265—420), the Northern (386—534) and Southern (420—589) period. The Tang Dynasty (618—907) was the mature period of Chinese tea culture and it was customary to drink tea at that time.

Lu Yu was known as the "sage of tea" of the Tang Dynasty. His work *Tea Canon* was the first monograph about tea in China. According to his *Tea Canon*, tea was discovered by Shennong and became popular as a drink in the State of Lu because of Zhou Gong. Lu Yu described in detail the shape and properties, production place, picking and making, boiling and drinking of tea. He went to Zhejiang Province by boat in order to spread tea culture. The local people got into the habit of drinking tea and have kept it to the present day under his influence.

In ancient times, tea played an important role in China's economy. Tea was planted more widely in south China in the Tang Dynasty (618—967) and tea tax was an important financial income for royal government. The Tang Dynasty was the golden age of tea, when the beverage spread nation wide. For example, about 20 to 30 percent of the population of Jiangsu and Anhui provinces was involved in tea cultivation and trade.

Drinking tea was quite popular in the Song Dynasty (960—1279). The book *Chalu* written by Caixiang consists of two volumes. One discussed tea and the other discussed vessels. It described that there were about ten famous tea and tea brick during the period.

Drinking tea was so common in everyday life in the Yuan Dynasty (1271—1368) that even housewives in poverty would take tea as one of the seven house chores.

People in the Ming (1368—1644) and the Qing (1644—1911) Dynasties drank tea in almost the same way as we do today, except the method of drinking tea was constantly changing. Zhang Yingwen of the Ming Dynasty finished an additional volume to Lu Yu's *Tea Canon*, discussing the tea culture and its development since the Tang Dynasty. The book became the famous tea monograph of the Ming Dynasty since it further revised Lu Yu's *Tea Canon*.

Tea was one of the sacrificial offerings to gods and ancestors from ancient times in China. It was also used as a funeral offering. Tea has a close connection with religion in China as well. Since Buddhists aim at refraining from daily pleasures while sitting and enlightening themselves with Buddha's teachings, tea is the ideal drink to cultivate their moral character. In Buddhism, tea is praised as a sacred thing given by God. It is said wine can add virginity to heroes, while tea can inspire men of letters to create. Both Buddhist and Taoist monks helped to promote tea's use. Taoist monks believe drinking tea can keep them healthy and reach longevity. The belief that tea drinking benefits health is an important part of the tea culture in China. It has been supported by modern medical research in China, Japan, and America. China and Japan lead the world in research on the role of tea in preventing and fighting illness.

Section 2　Chinese Tea Culture

References to tea have been found in almost every form of literature and art, songs, dances, paintings, plays and couplets. Tea-drinking is an art in China. For instance, Li Bai, the great poet of the Tang Dynasty (618—907) wrote more than fifty poems about tea. Lu You is the great patriotic poet of the Southern Song Dynasty (1127—1279) who mentioned tea many times in his 300 poems. In the classical works, *Dreams of the Red Mansion*, which is printed in more than 100 languages in the world, there are about 300 mentions of tea. There are many traditional Chinese paintings depicting tea-drinking affairs. Lao She (1899—1966), one of the contemporary great writers, wrote a play named *The Teahouse*. In this play, many stories happened in a teahouse that reflected the Chinese society and the Chinese tea culture.

It is said tea culture and Buddhism has a close relation. In Fame Temple, built in the East Han Dynasty in Shaanxi Province, an International Tea Party was held in 1994. Exports arranged a play of Qingming Tea party of the Tang Palace. It showed again the peaceful and powerful tea culture which has the core of the quintessence of China Buddhism, Confucianism and Taoism in the Tang Dynasty.

China has 56 nationalities, and some of the minority nationalities have developed their own variations of the tea culture and their own tea style. The method of making tea is quite complicated in some places. The tender tea leaves are regarded as the first-class tea. People who drink tea also know that a cup of good tea needs good water. Different from the way of today, ancient Chinese used to boil tea as the method to boil traditional Chinese medicine. Ointment and rice flour were added to make tea cake. They boiled the tea cake together with onion, ginger, salt, tangerine peel, date and peppermint before the Tang Dynasty (618—907). The baked tea leaves were boiled directly without anything else from the Yuan Dynasty (1271—1368).

Ancient Chinese learned the appropriate time for drinking tea and the taboos of drinking tea. Feng Zhengqing of the Ming Dynasty mentioned twelve appropriations and seven taboos for drinking tea in the book *On Tea*. For instance, one of the seven taboos included not drinking tea when the vessels were not clean or the environment was not good. Ancient Chinese ate various kinds of cakes or sweetmeats when drinking tea. People may also have melon seeds, pickles, radish slip and other food when drinking.

Making and serving tea entail a lot more than merely pouring boiling water over tea leaves. In a tea house, people are able to enjoy tea and see the treasured skill carried out step by step. Serving tea is always a matter of etiquette. Usually prepared tea will be served in small porcelain cups or glasses. Take a tea cere-mony called Gongfu tea of Fujian Province for example: In any of the traditional style tea houses of Fujian and Guangdong provinces, customers can share some Kongfu tea and let time slip away. It places emphasis on making an elegant and quiet atmosphere. A dreamy environment is created where time seems to slow down and entire hours are mysteriously lost. Usually customers are asked to smell the dry leaves first. Once the tea-set is sanitary, the tea leaves will be "washed" by pouring out the first brew from the teapot. After the pouring of the boiling water, a second time, the kettle is lifted up and down as the pot fills like "a phoenix nods three times". The waitress then moves the teapot in circles and eventually pours until it over-flows. Before the customers taste the tea, they will "smell the cup" by first taking a deep breath of the con-tents. The most graceful way is to drink the tea in three delicate sips. The first sip prepares your taste buds, the second lets you focus on the tea flavor, and the third sip gives a pleasant aftertaste. It is a way to relax in this modern world full of bustles. Unfortunately, not all people have the money and spare time for this leisure.

Laoshe Teahouse, located on West Qianmen Street in Beijing, is well known for its characteristic tea products and variety shows. There are different kinds of teas ranging from flower tea, which is Beijing citizens' favorite to modern style tea. For instance, various tea including fashion-shaped tea, Dafo Longjing, West Lake Meijiawu Longjing, Fujian Jasmine Tea and Fujian Tieguanyin are provided. The teahouse was opened in 1988 and is named after Mr. Lao She, a great literary figure of China. The teahouse has a total area of more than 3300 square meters, with Traditional Chinese Tea House, Traditional Food and Tea House and Modern Tea Art House in the form of a Chinese Yard inside. Some high level perform-ances such as Beijing Opera, acrobatics, traditional Chinese shadow show are performed every day.

It is a very important business in some provinces. Take Zhejiang as an example, being one of China's leading tea provinces, they hold the Hangzhou International Tea Festival every year. This festival has brought tourist and commercial business to this area as well as promoting cultural exchange activities. Since the study and appreciation of tea culture is a new movement in China, a Tea Museum has been built in Han-gzhou.

Section 3　the Custom of Drinking Tea

Tea-drinking is a nation-wide custom in China. Some people drink tea to lose weight because it contains caffeine, pigmentation, aromatic oils, vitamins, minerals and protein. The most important constituent is caffeine, which is somewhat bitter and aromatic. It can stimulate the central nervous system, clear one's mind and increase the elasticity of the muscles. It can also reduce the harmful effects of morphine, nicotine and alcohol.

It is a necessity for some Chinese people to have tea everyday. When a guest comes, it is customary to present a cup of tea. It is a way of showing respect to visitors as well as a symbol of sharing something enjoyable. Most of the betrothal gifts of the ancient Chinese marriage include tea.

The public place for drinking tea in ancient China was the teahouse, where there were some calligraphy and paintings of eminent people. There used to be many teahouses which were ideal places for people to relax and discuss the events of the day over a cup of tea. In the teahouses, people enjoyed performances by storytellers during the daytime. Performances, including Beijing Opera, Jingyundagu, comic dialogues, and Danxian were offered in the evenings. However, teahouses gradually declined in the capital and disappeared completely in the 1960's. They appeared again in the late 1980's.

There are numerous tea houses in almost every town and city nowadays too. Drinking tea is a continuing part of Chinese culture. Tea culture includes the tea house ballad performances and storytelling. Tea houses provided stages for Beijing Opera and other performances in the past as well.

In the past, tea was drunk without flair, merely to quench one's thirst. Younger people prefer coffee and soda. Nowadays, some kinds of iced teas, sold in bottles, both tasty and good for people's health, have been accepted by young people. Bottled iced tea is widely consumed in cities because it is convenient and refreshing to drink in summer.

Section 4　Kinds of Tea

Tea is made by infusing tea leaves in boiling water. Good water, high quality tea and proper tea sets are of importance in making a good cup of tea. Appraisement of good tea is based on five principles, namely, taste, aroma, shape of the leaf, color of the liquid, and the appearance of the infused leaf.

There are hundreds of varieties of Chinese tea. They can be categorized by their color, fragrance, flavor and finely shaped leaves. Chinese tea can be divided into six categories: green tea (Southern China), black tea (Southern China), oolong tea (Fujian province, Taiwan area), white tea (Fujian province), scented tea (southern China) and tea lumps.

There are also some special kinds of tea popular in Chinese minority areas such as *Leicha* (Hunan Province), oil tea (Guangxi Province, by Miao and Dong minority) and milk tea (Inner Mongolia and Tibet). Tea is much desired to aid digestion of Mongolian and Tibetan people's meat-and-milk diet. In Tibet, the stimulating properties of teas made life in that thin-oxygen area more bearable.

Green tea is most preferred in many areas in Asia, while Indian and Sri Lanka people are big drinkers of black tea with milk and sugar, as introduced from Britain.

Green Tea

Green tea, the oldest tea with its natural fragrance, is very popular among Chinese people. Most of the vitamins in the leaves are preserved since it is baked immediately after picking. Some medical research points out that tea can not only satisfy people's requirements for vitamins and other elements, but also contain some elements to prevent people from having cancer or other diseases. The well-known green tea are Longjing Tea (Zhejiang Province, Hangzhou area), Huangshan Maofeng Tea (Anhui Province, Huangshan Mountain), Yunwu Tea (Jiangxi province, Lushan Mountain), Yinzhen Tea (Junshan Mountain) and Bilochun Tea (Jiangsu Province).

Scented Tea

Scented Tea is a mixture of green tea with flower petals such as jasmine, sweet-scented osmanthus, orchid, rose and plum. Jasmine Tea is the most common type among scented teas and Jasmine Tea made in Fujian Province is very famous. Some people drink the Scented Tea in summer and winter.

Black Tea

Black tea is a kind of fermented tea with a black color after the fermentation. The tea is drunk mostly in winter. Famous black teas are Qi Hong Tea (Anhui Province), Dian Hong Tea (Yunnan Province) and Ying Hong Tea (Guangdong Province).

Oolong Tea

Oolong tea is becoming popular with more and more people in China, for it combines the freshness of green tea and the fragrance of black tea. One batch of Oolong leaves may be reused up to six times without losing its flavor. The third cupful is considered the best and most savored.

It is also popular in Japan because of its medicinal benefits. One benefit is to assist the body building process, and another to assist in dieting according to the results of medical research. It helps to reduce high blood pressure, lower cholesterol and prevent coronary heart disease, and it aids digestion.

Since it grows on cliffs, harvesting of this tea is very difficult; thus, it is the most precious tea. Oolong tea is mainly produced in Fujian, Taiwan and Guangdong provinces. However, the most famous Oolong tea called Tieguanyin is produced in Fujian Province.

Tea Lumps

Tea lumps are in shapes of balls, bricks or tea cakes. The major producing areas of tea lumps are in southern China, such as in Hunan, Hubei, Sichuan, Yunnan and Guangxi provinces.

This kind of tea is suitable for the minority people in border regions for it is convenient to store or transport. Local residents in Inner Mongolia and Tibet prefer brick-shaped Tea Lumps and People in Yunnan Province prefer ball-shaped tea lumps.

Tocha, classified into Puer Tocha, Yunnan Tocha and Sichuan Tocha, is a bowl-shaped and compressed mass of tea leaves. The most famous tea lump is Puer Tocha (Yunnan Province). It is able to help to lower patients' cholesterol levels according to the medical test result. People regard it as a diet tea and beauty tea as well.

Section 5   Spread of Chinese Tea

More than 40 countries grow tea, and Asian countries produce 90% of the world's total output. All tea trees in these countries have their origin directly or indirectly in China.

Chinese tea was an important Chinese export along with silk and porcelain a thousand years ago and. Chinese tea-drinking customs spread in many Asian regions through the ancient "Silk Road" or other trade channels in ancient times.

Tea seed and the technique for planting tea trees were spread to Japan in the Tang Dynasty. Tea ceremony was introduced to Japan during the Song Dynasty. The Japanese tea ceremony was originally practised in the Jingshan Temple, northeast of Hangzhou. It was introduced in Japan by a monk in 1291. The tea ceremony custom was not popular in China. However, it was widely spread in Japan by Buddhist and Taoist monks. The Japanese went on to build a tea culture uniquely on their own. As a result, the tea ceremony developed into an elaborate ritual that was truly Japanese. It is still known as the famous Japanese tea ceremony.

Tea was spread to West Europe and became the favorite drink of European people in the 17th century. The name for tea comes from the same word in Xiamen (Fujian Province) dialect of China. When the Dutch carried on their earliest tea trade with China from the port of Xiamen, they learned the pronunciation and took it to Europe.

The first green tea reached Europe around 1610 on Dutch ships from Java. Tea became very popular in Dutch high society. It was first sold in medicine shops as an expensive medicine. By 1675, tea became available in food stores. Special tea rooms were built by wealthy people to have tea clubs. Between 1625 and 1657 there was a debate about tea as a medicine in both Holland and France. After M. Cressy proved his findings on tea's positive role at the college of medicine, there were few attacks on tea.

The Portuguese bride of England's King Charles II was credited with popularizing tea in her new home. Tea came into the public eye by Charles's two courtiers from Holland and tea parties. The East India Company presented some tea to Charles II in 1660 when he came to the throne. From 1684, tea made up over 90 percent of China's exports to England. Tea drinking, as a way of socializing, moved out of the coffee houses into elaborate tea gardens where men and women could meet socially. The love affair with tea inspired numerous poems in the late 19th century. By the early 19th century, tea drinking had moved into the homes of ordinary people. In the beginning, the use of green tea superseded the use of black tea in Britain. Tea became more popular in Britain and Russia than in Germany and France. Britain, as well as Russia, became the two greatest tea-drinking nations. Because green tea was easier to adulterate, people began turning toward the black tea. Black tea replaced green tea until the mid-18th century.

All European countries, except Russia and Portugal, bought their first tea from the Dutch. The first tea reached Russia in 1618 when presented by the Chinese embassy. The Russian government bought tea from China and traded furs in return. The entire journey from Chinese tea growers to the Russian market took about 18 months. When Guangzhou (Guangdong Province) was opened as a foreign port in 1880, Russian entrepreneurs set up mechanized factories in Guangzhou making brick tea for the Russian market. Two years later, the factories were moved to Hankou (Hubei Province) along the Yangtze River. From that time, the use of the samovar became widespread in Russians. Every home in Russia had one for making tea.

The development and promotion of tea has been one of China's principal contributions. Chinese tea is the pride of China, for its culture made great contributions in the history of world civilization.

Chapter 23

Wine Culture

Xiaoxia Mao and Catherine Gu

Wine has a close connection with culture in both ancient and modern times. Few countries have as long a history as China for the brewing of wine. It permeates into almost every field of life: law, philosophy, politics, ethics, morality and social customs. From various ancient wine containers and paintings of drinking customs discovered in ancient tombs of different periods, it is proved that wine occupied a high position in the Chinese culinary culture.

People loved wine partly because it alleviated drinkers' sadness and it drew sorrow away from the drinkers' mind. In ancient times, when people practiced divination, worshipped deities and ghosts or prayed for rainfall, they used wine to show their reverence. Even when a prisoner was taken off to be executed, he would drink a bowl of wine. Since wine has a special place in Chinese eyes, especially on solemn occasions, wine cannot be replaced by anything else.

Section 1 Origin and Development

Perhaps the earliest wine was fruit wine naturally fermented. Chinese learned the process of fermentation and gradually learned to produce wine toward the end of the primitive society. China is a pioneering nation of wine brewing. Chinese people began to make wine with milk about ten thousand years ago, and with grains seven thousand years ago according to the legend. The large, strange-looking wine-making paraphernalia and realistic-looking pictures of the wine-making process were found in Shandong Province in the 1970s as a part of the Dawenkou Culture. The discovery shows grain winemaking in China already reached a certain level about 7,000years ago.

From the narrations on tortoise shells and animal bones, it is clear the wine culture was already highly developed during the Shang Dynasty (17th century—1046 B. C.) and people used grains to make wine. Grain wine was very popular and drinking wine was common in the Shang Dynasty. Chinese wine culture developed to a new stage with the application of distiller's yeast during the Zhou Dynasty (1046—256 B. C.).

Men named Yi Di (in the Xia Dynasty) and Du Kang (in the Zhou Dynasty) were the initiators of brewing wine in the works like *Stratagems of Warring States*, and *Analysis of Words*. This is why ancient Chinese often use "Du Kang" as a synonym for wine. Cao Cao, the prime minister of the Three Kingdoms Period once said: "What relieves my worries? Only Du Kang does."

The technique of making wine improved greatly with the development of twice fermented liquor in the Qin (221—207 B. C.) and the Han (206 B. C. —220 A. D.) dynasties. More kinds of wine were made during the period. As early as the Han Dynasty (206 B. C. —220 A. D.), wine shop streets appeared in cities. Wine shops hung yellow triangular flags painted with the word "wine" to attract customers.

Weijin demeanor flourished in the Wei (220—265) and the Jin (265—420) Dynasties. One striking characteristic was that scholars' drinking wine became a common practice.

It was in the Tang Dynasty (618—907) that wine-making techniques reached full maturity with the application of distillation equipment. There are grape wine, *Tianmendong* liquor, medical liquor, fruit wine apart from grain wine. The scholars of this period were addicted to drinking. Bai Juyi, a famous poet of the Tang Dynasty, mentioned "spirits" in one of his poems. It can be seen in that poem that distillation was adopted during this period.

Winemaking was improved greatly in the Song Dynasty (960—1279). More than 210 kinds of wine were listed in the book *Quweijiuwen* by Zhubian.

White spirit came into being in the Yuan Dynasty (1271—1368).

There came some famous wine with the development of wine making in the Ming (1368—1644) and the Qing (1644—1911) Dynasties. Sangluo, Yanggao, Zhangqiu, Jinhua and Magu Liquor are among the kinds of famous wines.

Section 2　Influence of Wine on Politics, Literature and Art

Wine became a part of political life for most emperors and officials were fond of wine. Emperor Wu of the Han Dynasty (206 B. C. —220 A. D.) was fond of wine. The right to produce and distribute wine belonged only to the state according to his order. It brought great fortune to the government. The first emperor of the Song Dynasty (960—1279) worried whether or not his commanders would rebel like him soon after he took the power by force. Therefore, he invited his commanders, who were also his friends, to drink wine. After drinking a few cups of wine, he told them he could not sleep well. After the honest commanders realized the reason while drinking with him, they decided to hand over their military power to the emperor. The emperor succeeded in depriving the military commanders of their command by serving them wine.

Wine was consumed when commanders sent an army on expedition or when celebrating triumph. The following is another example of wine being plied by the emperor in ancient China to win over the people's support: It is said that when someone presented wine to the King of Chu, he poured it into the upper reaches of the river for all his soldiers to drink. His action enhanced his soldiers' spirit and strength. During the war between the states of Chu and Jin, the grateful soldiers of Chu rose to the challenge and defeated the Jin army in the battle during the Spring and Autumn Period (770—476 B. C.).

Wine became a permanent theme in literary and artistic creation. Much Chinese traditional literature includes references to the enjoyment of wine. *The Book of Songs* of the sixth century B. C., the first poetry anthology, consists of 305 poems. Forty of them touch on wine. It appealed to men of letters. Many anecdotes about their drinking were handed down from this literature. Poets such as Li Bai, Du Fu and Bai Juyi wrote some famous poems about wine. Li Bai, who is the most famous poet of the romanticist school of the Tang Dynasty (618—907), loved wine so much that he said: "A hundred poems flowed after cups of wine. " He often drank to drown his sorrows because his own high ambitions were hopelessly thwarted. He said he could not write good poems without wine. About one-sixth of his poems are connected to wine, and he is called "the sage of wine" . The following stanzas of his *Alone and Drinking under the Moon* are well-known in China:

Amongst the flowers I am alone with my pot of wine drinking by myself;

Then lifting my cup I asked the moon to drink with me,

Its reflection and mine in the wine cup,
Just the three of us.
...
I am glad to make the moon and my shadow into friends,
But then when I have drunk too much, we all apart;
Yet these are friends I can always count on, these who have no emotion whatsoever;
I hope that one day we three will meet again, deep in the Milky Way.

Wang Xizhi, the most famous calligrapher of the Jin Dynasty (265—420), has hand writings considered to be the best calligraphy of his time. Once, he drank wine with some poets while resting on the banks of a winding stream after a religious ceremony. They let a cup filled with wine float in the stream. The person near the cup had to compose a poem or drink three cups when the stopped or over-turned. Wang Xizhi painted a preface, called *Lanting Preface* for them on silk with a brush after 37 poems were written. It has been considered the best calligraphy ever seen.

Section 3　Wine as Social Custom

Wine represents the ideas and pursuits of the Chinese. It makes people congenial and inspires their worldly desires. Wine is always present on occasions such as weddings, anniversaries or alliance treaty signing ceremonies. Usually when people celebrate happy events such as promotions, victories and birthdays, they drink wine. Like people of many nations, Chinese have the custom of drinking wine during traditional holidays such as the Spring Festival, Dragon Boat Festival, Mid-autumn Festival and Double Ninth Festival. People may sprinkle wine on the front and on the top of the tombs when they have tomb sweeping.

People may be unrestrained and wish to make great contributions when they drink wine during a feast. They believe wine can enliven the atmosphere of a gathering and promote friendly relations. Wine-drinking has been considered a means of interpersonal and international communications. An old saying goes, "A thousand cups of wine among congenial friends are too few..." This may explain why Chinese hosts, at feasts, usually urge their guests to drink wine until they are drunk. This phenomenon contrasts with the Western custom.

Two other implications may also explain the reason: the hosts desire to show their generosity and hospitality. Cheerfully urging people to drink more wine is indicative of people's hospitality and good will. Chinese are normally quiet. After they drink wine, they tend to divulge their suppressed feelings.

Toasting is very common during a feast. When the hosts have subsequent toasts from person to person, sometimes a guest cannot consume as much liquor as expected. If the guest is able to drink a lot before he gets drunk, he may prefer "while in Rome, do as the Romans do." If he does not want to drink liquor, he may make it known at the very beginning of the meal to avoid embarrassment. Even so, if the host repeatedly tries to push him into drinking, then he may use soft drinks instead for the toast.

The current custom of drinking wine at feasts gives the impression much business is done, and many important issues are settled at the meal table when some cups of wine are drunk. To some Chinese businessmen, inviting a few people to drink wine is the most effective way to make friends with commercial partners and keep friendships close.

When people drink, they may use very intense wine drinking penalties to bring about fun. There are various drinking penalties. Some are scholarly and dependent on wit. Others are coarse and straight-forward, such as Beating Drum and Passing Flower, Floating a Cup on a Winding Pool and Finger Guessing. Finger Guessing is a popular one. Sometimes, guests get more and more vehement and noisy, as if they are quarreling when they use Finger Guessing at a feast. The drinkers may annoy other people nearby, even though they consider their actions amusing and a pleasure in restaurants.

People in the Ming and the Qing Dynasties were more fastidious about the arrangement of seats at the banquet. Even today people are also arranged in a certain order at the formal banquet. The arrangement of seats is various in different areas. For instance, the host sits facing the door at the round-table banquet. The one sitting facing the host is the vice host. The one sitting on his right is the most honorable guest and the one who sits on his left is the secondary one. The third guest sits on the left of the vice host and the one sitting on his right is the fourth guest.

There are a variety of alcoholic beverages on sale in every restaurant. Dozens of wine advertisements appear on television every day in China. It seems that wine-drinking constitutes a part of man's virility.

The feasts usually include cold dishes, hot dishes, soup and fruits. Normally, cold dishes are served before hot ones. Soup or fish is usually the last dish of a feast after the hot dishes have been served. Newly served dishes are always put near the most honorable guest. The head of the whole fish, whole chicken or whole duck is normally pointed toward the most honorable guest. It is a way to show respect to one's most honorable guest. Some Chinese hosts not only persuade their guests to drink, but help serve the dishes to show their respect and hospitality. Some Chinese drinkers believe the saying: "Those who cannot drink wine are not real men. "

Drinking customs of Chinese minorities vary from nationality to nationality. For instance, at the meal table of the ethnic Zhuang, the first cup of wine along with a chicken head will be presented to the eldest. During dinner time, the Mongolians will present three cups of wine to a guest and sing songs of wine until he finishes them. In some ethnic minority areas of southwestern China, like Guizhou Province, people offer three cups of wine to their guests. Since wine is substituted for tea when guests arrive, it seems not to be polite if the guests decline the offer.

Section 4　Kinds of Wine

Three time-honored basic ways are used to make wine: by natural fermentation, distillation, and pressing, despite the introduction of new wine-making techniques in modern China. Wines are divided into grain liquor (rice wine, wheat wine, oat wine, red sorghum wine), fruit wine (grape wine, apple wine, plum wine), Chinese herb liquor (wolfberry wine, snake wine, ginseng wine, three-genitals wine), flower wine (chrysanthemum wine and osmanthus wine), and milk wine (horse milk wine, sheep milk wine) in terms of raw materials.

Chinese alcoholic beverages are mainly classified into four groups according to the process.

Yellow Wine (Huangjiu, Old wine)

Yellow Wine has a history of 5,000thousand years predating all the other liquors. A large number of wine-storing and drinking vessels were excavated in the 1970s in an ancient tomb (Zhongshan's tomb) of the Warring States Period in Pingshan County of Hebei Province. Two of them still contain 6.7 kilograms of alcoholic wine made 2,280 ago. It may be the oldest existing wine in the world. The alcoholic content is approximately 15%, with a high nutritive value. Shaoxing Rice Wine (Shaoxingjiaofan) (Zhejiang Province) is the most famous yellow wine for its flavor and golden color. It won the prize on the 1st and the 2nd National Wine Appraisal Conference. The wine won two gold medals in international competitions in Paris and Madrid in 1985. It has a history of over 2,000years with a name of Lao Jiu (Old Wine). Some Chinese in southern areas like to use it as an excellent condiment for cooking to eliminate fishy odors and to enhance food color and flavor.

Herbal Liquors (Yaojiu)

Chinese find the liquor is good for dispersing chills and improving blood circulation. Ancient doctor Hua Tuo mixed anesthetic powder with wine to relieve patients' pain during operations. Wine is used to reduce inflammation, to relax muscles, to relieve pain and to stimulate blood circulation by physicians using traditional Chinese medicine. Some traditional Chinese medicine should be taken with wine instead of water. For example, the traditional Chinese pills to cure wounds need to be taken with wine.

Yellow Wine was also used as the base of Chinese herbal liquor (Yaojiu, Medical Liquor) in ancient times. Adding valuable medicines to wine is a Chinese specialty. Chinese herbs are added to a liquor to increase the curing effect. There are a number of Chinese herbal liquors containing herbs. For instance, sometimes snakes and soft shelled turtle are used to make Chinese herbal liquor in Guangdong and Fujian Province. Some kinds of Chinese herbal liquor can cure arthritis. Other kinds can strengthen the constitution, improve sleep quality and relieve fatigue. For instance, Bamboo-Leaf Green Liquor (*Zhuyeqing*), made by immersing bamboo leaves and dozens of medicinal herbs, has a reputation for improving health and treating diseases such as heart trouble, high blood pressure and arthritis. It won the State Council's gold medal in 1979.

White Liquor (Baijiu)

White liquor is made from sorghum, corn, wheat or barley, white liquor contains over 50% alcohol. It is divided into solid-fermented liquor, liquid-fermented liquor and semi-solid-fermented liquor defined by the terms of fermentation. It can be also divided into big yeast, small yeast and bran-yeast in terms of yeasts. In terms of fragrance, it is divided into delicate fragrance, strong fragrance, rice fragrance and soy fragrance liquor. Many Chinese in the northern area like sorghum white liquor for it symbolizes their courage and strong sentiments.

A few hundred kinds of white wine are made in different areas of China. The most famous white wines are awarded the prize in the National Wine Appraisal Conference in China. They are Maotai (Guizhou), Wuliangye (Sichuan Province), Fenjiu (Shanxi Province), Gujinggong (Guizhou) Luzhoudaqu (Sichuan Province), Dukang Wine (Henan Province) Yanghe Twice Fully Fermented Liquor (Jiangsu Province) Jiannanchun (Sichuan Province), Xifeng (Shaanxi) and Ergotou Wine (Beijing). Maotai won a gold medal in Panama Canal at a competition held in 1915 by the U. S. government. It won another gold medal in France in 1985. It was awarded a prize at the 1st, the 2nd and the 3rd National Wine Appraisal Conference in 1952, 1963 and 1979.

The brewing techniques of white wine are complicated. In the process of making Maotai for example, cultivating yeast, fermenting and distilling are done at high temperature. The grain of whole and crushed kernels, in measured proportions, is mixed, steamed and cooked. The grains are fed into fermenting pools twice during the brewing. The grains, soaked in spirits, are fermented eight times and distilled seven times during the eight months. The liquor is aged in cellars for at least three years to bring out its characteristic flavor along with its nutritious food value, because of its quality and strong fragrant smell.

Beer (Pijiu)

Chinese people drink beer in summer to relieve the summer heat, provide refreshment and facilitate fun during their spare time. Though Chinese beer has a very short history compared with yellow wine and white wine, it has become very popular in the past decades. Famous beer such as *Qingdao* Beer (Shandong Province), Yanjing Beer (Beijing) and Haerbin Beer (Hei Long Jiang Province) are very famous. Qingdao

Beer was made in Qingdao using local spring water of high quality. The beer factory was established by the Germans in the 1920s. Qingdao Beer has been exported to many countries. It won the prize on the second and the third National Wine Appraisal Conference in 1963 and 1979.

Fruit Wine

Some kinds of fruit wine such as grape wine, apple wine and pomegranate wine are made in different areas in China. Grape wine was brought to China by Zhang Qian from the Western countries in the Han Dynasty. Grape wine got very popular since the Tang Dynasty. After the development of the making technology, most kinds of Chinese grape wine taste sweeter than the grape wine made in European countries. More and more Chinese realize grape wine is a healthy wine and they have started to drink it instead of white liquor. Great Wall Grape Wine is one of the most famous among many kinds of grape wine in the Chinese market. In addition, the following kinds of fruit wine were awarded a prize on the 3rd National Wine Appraisal Conference of 1979: Chinese Red Grape Wine, Yantai Weimeisi, Qingdao White Grape Wine, Special Fine Brandy, Special-made Beijing Brandy and Yantai Red Grape Wine.

Chapter 24

Major Traditional Festivals and Their Tales

Xuefei Yang, Xiaoxia Mao and Frits Buijs

Chinese have their both traditional festivals and modern national holidays to enjoy. Six major festivals are among a number of Chinese festivals: The Spring Festival (Chinese New Year), the Lantern Festival, the Dragon Boat Festival, the Clear and Bright Festival (Qing Ming Festival), the Mid-Autumn Festival and the Double Ninth Festival. Each one has its own historical origins with legendary allusions and unique cultural connotations. They can be divided into five types: agricultural, sacrificial, commemorative, celebratory and recreational festivals. Every festival means not only a happy get-together, but also the representation of the traditional customs, religious concepts of the nation and the moral directions. The origins of some festivals can be traced to the Shang (16—11th century B. C.) and Zhou (11th century—221 B. C.) Dynasties. They are all based on the Chinese lunar calendar.

The ten public holidays are New Year's Day, International Women's Day, Tree-Planting Day, International Labor Day, Youth Day, the Children's Day, Chinese Communist Party's Birthday Celebration, Army's Day, the Teacher's Day and National Day.

Section 1　Spring Festival

The Spring Festival is the most important of all the traditional Chinese holidays since it means the beginning of the New Year (the Chinese New Year) according to the traditional Chinese Lunar Calendar. The Lunar Calendar is used in Asian countries which are, or used to be under the direct influence of the Han culture, such as Mongolia, Korea and Vietnam. The Spring Festival is not only celebrated by the Chinese Han majority and many other minorities in China, but also celebrated internationally in areas with large populations of ethnic Chinese (Poleg, 2005). Chinese New Year is celebrated with great joy and happiness from the first day of the first lunar month till its end during the colorful Lantern Festival, which is 14 days later. However, the first week is the most important, because most people celebrate it by visiting relatives, friends and going to the temple fairs.

Legends

The Chinese New Year has a history of 4,000years and there are several explanations for the origin of the Spring Festival and its celebration. One story says it originated from a Chinese term for a sacrificial ceremony held during a primitive society. People offered sacrifices of grain from farming and animals from hunting to their ancestors and to Heaven. They were tokens of their gratitude for their bounty and a manifestation of their wishes for a good grain harvest in the coming year. Varied celebrations such as dusting (New Year's

cleaning）, pasting Spring Festival couplets and pasting New Year's pictures are held before the Spring Festival. Dusting originated from a religious rite that was supposed to eliminate epidemic diseases in the time of the two legendary sage kings Yao and Shun in ancient China. All households clean their courtyard, their articles of furniture and bed-cloths from the 24th to the end of the 12th lunar month before the Spring Festival.

Another story says that in ancient China, there once lived a man-eating horned beast called Nian`(literally meaning 'year' in Chinese). Nian lived in the deep sea throughout the whole year but came out to eat cattle and people during every New Year's Eve. So on every New Year's Eve, everyone went to the deep mountain to avoid being eaten by the beast. (People's Daily, 2006). One time by coincidence, people in the area found out that Nian was afraid of the red color and bright lights and it was also sensitive to loud noises. From then on, during every New Year's Eve, people use fireworks, red colors and bright lights to scare the beast away. These customs led to the New Year celebration and it was named as "guo nian", which means to celebrate the New Year and literally "the Passover of the Nian".

The Chinese character "福" ("luck") is written on red paper and posted on door fronts. It is placed upside down indicating luck has arrived. This is because the Chinese pronunciation for character turned upside down is the same as that of the word "arrive." Needless to say, the custom expresses people's wish to be lucky and happy in the following year.

One explanation for the origin of the custom comes from a story about a man, Jiang Ziya, and his wife who lived 3,000years ago. Legend tells us that Jiang Ziya's wife married a few times before she married Jiang. Consequently, any family she married into would face trouble. She was considered to be an unlucky woman. When Jiang Ziya was granting titles of Sainthood, his wife also asked to have a title. He granted her the sainthood of being a Poverty God since she could only bring misfortune to people. Jiang also told her to stay anywhere except where there was luck. People soon started plastering the character "福" on their doors to prevent the Poverty God from visiting.

Another legend started about 700 years ago. The first emperor of the Ming Dynasty (1368—1644) was on tour during the Spring Festival celebrations. He was wearing common clothes so he would not be recognized. He saw a crowd of people staring and laughing at a caricature on a lantern. The picture was of a barefoot woman carrying a huge watermelon in her arms. Chinese women's beauty was partly judged by her bounded feet. A "watermelon" might indicate that the woman came from the western region of China since watermelons originally came from that area. The emperor sensed they were laughing at his wife who had not bound her feet and her hometown was in western China. The irritated emperor returned to the palace and sent men to look into the matter. A character "福" would be put at the gates of those who were not involved in the mischief. Soldiers would come to arrest the people whose gates did not have the character "福." The kindhearted queen asked people to spread the news. The news spread quickly and all the people posted the character on their doors. It seemed the root of the custom was meant to avoid arousing suspicion. Later on, it has evolved to mean good wishes.

Main festivities and folk customs

During the New Year celebration, you can find many festivities and habits. For example, people have their hair cut, prepare new clothes and purchase gifts and goods for the Spring Festival. Houses are festooned with paper couplets. During the New Year's Eve, Chinese wait for the New Year, paying New Year's calls, and performing the Lion Dance and the Dragon Dance.

Family reunion

One of the meanings of the celebration of the Spring Festival is the gathering of all the family members, which means that everyone in the family gets together to meet, to greet and to have feasts together. It starts from the New Year's Eve when members of families get together and stay up all through the night. In the past, good food and incenses were burnt at home to pay respect to the ancestors and gods so as to get their blessing for good health and wealth in the coming year. Red candles were lighted and the rooms were cleaned and decorated. Family members came together to enjoy the reunion atmosphere, to eat together and to chat about the past and the future. Different games were also played, such as cards and Mahjong.

Nowadays, many Chinese families follow some of the traditions, however, they also celebrate their reunions in many other ways. For example, families get together to have a reunion feast at home and watch different TV programs made especially for the New Year celebration. Given the current economic development, some families choose to travel around China or tour abroad during the Spring Festival. Some prefer to stay in well-known Buddhist temples to hear the first knocking bell sound at mid-night. In the recent years, many Chinese people prefer to have their family reunion feasts in restaurants. Fortunately, the tradition is still well kept in most rural areas.

If one likes to experience the traditional way of celebrating the Spring Festival, the best way is to stay with a Chinese family in the countryside. All members of a family, even those away on business, would have to hurry back for the family reunion feast on the Eve. Most dishes have good names expressing the wish of good luck for the following year. For example, in southern China, people will have a New Year cake made of glutinous rice flour, which has the same pronunciation as better life in the following year. In northern China, Jiaozi (dumpling) is usually on the menu. The food Jiaozi looks like a shoeshaped silver ingot, the money in ancient China. The pronunciation of Jiaozi means "fertility" in the coming year. Both the foods symbolize auspiciousness.

Gifts and Lucky Money

People usually bring some gifts to their relatives or friends when visiting them during the Spring Festival. The number of the gifts has different meanings since numbers play a special and important role in the Chinese culture. For instance, it can be found in the number of giving gifts to appeal for good fortune during the Spring Festival. "Two" is the first even number often used to indicate double, meaning " happiness comes in pairs". "Six" is the number the Chinese like a lot, for it means "everything goes smoothly". " Eight" is the number most people would like, for " eight" and "prosperity" are similar in sound. There is a saying that " if you want to succeed, don't stray from eight" in North China. This is why people like the number of " one six eight" while choosing their telephone numbers or number plates, for it means the way to success in terms of pun.

Another custom during the festival is to give red packages to children by seniors as a Lunar New Year gift. These packages contain money in certain numbers which is usually a few hundred Chinese Yuan. The amount of money in the red packages should be of even numbers, since it is believed that odd numbers are associated with money given during funerals. The act of giving red packages does not only reflect good luck and honorability, it also suggests that seniors wish to see juniors to be successful in their studies, future careers and to be healthy in the coming year.

New year markets and performances

During the following days, various traditional recreational activities take place in many parts of China. The impressive and cheerful activities usually include dragon dances, lion dances, land-boat rowing, stilt-walking, drum dances and waist drum dances, marketing and appreciating lanterns. The Chinese dragon, as opposed to the Western dragon, is a miraculous animal. The ancient Chinese Han's ancestors took it

as a totem. During the Spring Festival, people perform dragon and lion dances to make the air more jubilant. Accompanied by drum, gong, and syllables, the Northern lion climbs up and down steps, licks its feet, scratches its ears and performs acrobatic maneuvers. The dancers make elegant and natural movements in perfect union, adding much to the joyous festive air. The Northern lion more resembles a Pekinese dog. The dragon containing many dancers follows a silk ball resembling the sun and as the top animal enjoys all the privileges. In Southern China you can also find several types of lion dancing which are also performed by Chinese immigrants in Western countries. The Southern lion is more based on Kung Fu moves and is usually performed by Kung Fu schools. According to historical records, these dances were very popular during the Han Dynasty.

Couplet and Pictures

The Spring Festival couplets refer to antithetical couplets written on scrolls which convey people's wishes for peace, fortune and good-luck with concise and matching words (People's Daily, 2006). They are usually pasted on doorposts or hall pillars, as well as furniture and screen walls. Chinese couplets consist of two sentences which are interrelated in meaning and antithetic in form (Chinatownguide, n. d.). The first sentence is called the upper couplet which is put on the right side and the second sentence, namely the lower couplet is placed on the left side. The two sentences are required to contain the same number of characters and most amazingly the words standing at the same position on each side of the two lines must not only be antithetical in meaning but also harmonious in tone. All in all, the couplet conveys the idea of good luck and it constitutes a unique form in Chinese literature.

The Spring Festival couplet was born out of the peach-wood charm. As early as the Spring and Autumn Period (770B. C. —476B. C.) there was a custom among Chinese people of hanging Taofu made of peach wood and painted pictures of two gods, named Shen Tu and Yu Lei, on the door in order to ward off evil spirits. Some people also believed that peach wood would keep away disasters and diseases so that they could live a long and healthy life. By the end of the Tang Dynasty (608—907A. D.) people started to write antithetic lines on peach wood instead of the two gods (China Town Guide, n. d.). Later people started writing the couplet on red paper instead of peach boards. During the Ming Dynasty, the couplets were called Spring Couplets and were required to be put up on the door during the Chinese Spring Festival to bring good luck and joyous atmosphere.

Chinese New Year pictures are called Nianhua in Chinese. They are usually made by block printing and feature clear lines with bright colors, scenes of fortune and prosperity. Chinese people usually put those pictures up on doors and walls to mark the Spring Festival. The themes embodied in the pictures concern a range of subjects, such as, plump babies, landscape, birds and flowers, the Buddha of longevity and harvest in the fall. They all resemble good luck, festivity and other nice things wished for by the people (Chinatownguide, n. d.).

The origin of the New Year pictures can be dated back to the times of the Yao and Shun period. During the Han Dynasty (206) it started as motifs for door pictures to ward off evil spirits and usher in good luck. The art of painting was improved during the Tang Dynasty which brought further development of New Year's pictures. During the Song Dynasty (960—1279A. D.) there were more pictures produced and woodblock pictures of religious themes gradually developed during the Ming Dynasty (1368—1644A. D.). The New Year pictures reached a new height of development and were commonly used among the ordinary people during the Qing Dynasty. At that time, almost every province had their own workshops for making New Year pictures. New Year's pictures are produced in most regions of China, and each region has its own character and style.

Generally speaking, there are two schools of New Year pictures, the northern school and the southern school. Tianjin and Shandong represent the northern school and the subjects are mainly images from traditional operas, chubby babies and beautiful fairies (Chinatownguide, n. d.). The most famous southern school is represented by Suzhou and Guangdong, influenced by the traditional styles, the southern school of painting also reflects certain features of European copper-plate printing (Chinatownguide, n. d.). Today, most door pictures are produced in places such as Yangliuqing Town (west Tianjin in Hebei Province), Weixian County (Shandong Province) and Taohuawu (Suzhou in Jiangsu Province).

Fireworks

Regarded as the most exciting event, especially to children, setting of firecrackers means biding farewell to the past year and welcoming the New Year. During the whole New Years Eve and the following days, children set off all kinds of firecrackers and fireworks. At the exact moment the clock strikes twelve on New Year's Eve, countless firecrackers will burst reverberating across the night. The firecracker (bamboo tubes) is linked with a tale. A writer named Dongfang Sho in the Western Dynasty wrote a work titled Shen Yi Jing. He wrote about a group of small, odd looking people who used to live in the high mountains of west China during the ancient times. They often stole salt from villages when they had shrimps and crabs. They only feared the sounds of crackles produced by burning bamboo tubes. Villagers often burned bamboo tubes to frighten them away. Later people burned bamboo tubes on New Year Eve to exorcise evil spirits. From the Song Dynasty (960—1279), firecrackers filled with gunpowder were set off. Nowadays the purpose of setting off firecrackers is only to heighten the festive air.

Chinese say they are the off-springs of Emperor Yan and Huang. "Yan" means fire with the red color. "Huang" refers to the yellow color. Therefore the basic color in China is red and yellow. Yellow used to be the color of the emperor and the court. The color red in China means happiness and celebration. People like to decorate their houses for wedding or party in red color, buy gifts with red colored wrapping paper and wear red colored clothes in the Spring Festival.

Section 2 Lantern Festival (Yuan Xiao Festival, Shangyuan Festival)

Origin

The Lantern Festival is celebrated on the 15th of the first lunar month. The first lunar month is called "Yuan" which means "first" in Chinese. Night was called "Xiao" in the ancient times. It is said that after the death of the Han Emperor, Liu Bang, his Empress Lu usurped the throne in the Han Dynasty (206 B. C. —220A. D.). When Empress Lu was dead, two important ministers killed two members of the Lu family who were covetous of the throne. They helped a member of Liu Bang's same family onto the throne on the 15th of the first lunar month. This new emperor, Liu Heng, merged incognito with the common people of his country on that night every year to mark the event. He made the day the Lantern Festival. People carried various colorful lanterns in a public place for a big "lantern fair."

Another legend relates the Lantern Festival with Taoism. The Taoist god Tianguan, who was in charge of fortune in the human world, had his birthday on the 15th day of the first lunar month. It was said that Tianguan liked all kinds of entertainment. So people prepared all kinds of activities on his birthday in order to pray for good fortune (Chinavoc, 2007).

History

The Lantern Festival was celebrated by the people by lighting colorful lanterns and enjoying perform-

ances until the Sui Dynasty in the 6th century. During the Tang Dynasty (618—907) lanterns were usually illuminated in all the streets in Chang'an (Xi'an) and during the 7th century people were allowed to celebrate the Lantern Festival for three days (Chinavoc, 2007). During the Festival, some buildings in Chang'an were not only decorated with lanterns, but also with silk cloth, strings of pears and gold or silver pendants. When the wind blew, the whole city was filled with jingling sounds. Trees on the hills near the city were also hung with lanterns so that one could see them from kilometers away. People walked along the river bank decorated with lanterns. The lanterns and the moonlight added radiance and beauty to each other and as they were reflected on the waters, they all added to a joyous and romantic scenery.

The festival was celebrated for five days and the activities began to spread to many of the big cities in China during the Song Dynasty (960—1279). Lanterns ranged from orange lanterns, silk lanterns, colorful trotting horses and sheepskin lanterns to Kongming lanterns. Figures, landscapes and folk tales were painted on the lanterns as well. Magic, acrobatics and other performances were held in the Imperial Streets of the capital city Bianliang (Kaifeng).

Nevertheless, the largest Lantern Festival celebration took place in the early part of the 15th century during the Ming Dynasty. The festivities continued for ten days. A specific area in the downtown was set by the emperor for the lantern festivities. Even today, there is a place in Beijing called Deng Shi Kou, meaning the light market. During the day, the place was used to sell lanterns while during the evening, the local people would go there to see different lanterns on display.

There was a department of the Qing court to make and manage all kinds of lanterns during the Qing Dynasty. Lanterns in the imperial court of course were more handsome and splendid. The lantern display is still grand. In the northern provinces of China, the ice sculpture lantern display appeared to mark the Lantern Festival since more than one hundred years ago. Even today, the Ice Sculpture Lantern Fair in Haer'bin of Heilongjiang Province is still very famous. The giant ice sculptured figures may be in the shapes of pagodas, towers, bridges, animals, flowers and so on. Connected to a multitude of electric lights, the ice sculptures give this Lantern Fair a very attractive and beautiful scenery.

The Modern Lantern Festival

These days, the display of lanterns is still a big event on the 15th day of the first lunar month throughout China and the Lantern Festival has changed very little over the last two millennia, although technological advances make the celebration more colorful and attractive. Lanterns of various shapes and sizes are hung in the streets, attracting people to visit. You can also find a lot of children walking and running around on the street with their lanterns. In some northern cities the lanterns can even be made from a block of ice with different shapes and colors!

"Guessing lantern riddles" is an essential part of the Festival. The owners of the lanterns write riddles on a piece of paper and post them on the lanterns. When visitors can guess the answers, they take the paper to the lantern owner and tell the answers. If it is correct, the visitors can get a small gift from the owners. As riddle guessing is interesting and full of wisdom, it has become popular among the Chinese people.

In some cities a lantern show is also held during the festival which makes the Lantern festival more exciting. During the daytime of the festival, many performances were held, such as the dragon dance, lion dance and beating the drums. In the past times, the lantern festival used to be the only day of the year for young and single ladies to go out and meet their lovers. Matchmakers at that time were also busy arranging ' blind dates' for young people to meet each other during the lantern festival evening. Nowadays, except for the fireworks and all kinds of lanterns, many young people gather at the festival, they meet and enjoy each others company and wish for good luck, hope a bright future in the New Year.

Yuanxiao and Tangyuan

Beside entertainment and beautiful lanterns, another important part of the Lantern Festival is to eat Yuanxiao or Tangyuan. They are small dumpling balls made of glutinous rice flour with sesame, bean paste, jujube paste, walnut paste, dried fruit, sugar and edible oil as filling (China Tour Guide, n. d.). They are often cooked in red-bean or other kinds of soup, and they can be boiled, fried or steamed. They are tasty and usually a bit sweet. The round shape of Yuanxiao or Tangyuan symbolizes wholeness and unity, so people eat them to denote harmony and happiness in the family.

Section 3 Pure Brightness Festival (Tomb-sweeping Day, Spring Outing Day)

The Tomb Sweeping Day is one of the few traditional Chinese holidays that follows the solar calendar and literally means "pure brightness" which suggests its importance as a celebration of spring, clear weather and rebirth of nature (C-C-C, 2000). The custom of transplanting willow cuttings is rarely observed, yet the custom of spring outing remains. People are also encouraged to plant trees during this period of time.

Origin

The festival originally occurred on the 5th of the 24 solar terms marking the sequence of time. It developed into an important festival with the incorporation of the Cold Food Festival celebration in the Tang and Song Dynasties. During the festival, fire was banned and people only had cold food. This festival was intended to commemorate Jie Zitui, a faithful minister of Jin State in the Spring and Autumn Period (722 B. C. —481 B. C.). His master, the prince nearly became faint from hunger, Jie Zitui cut a piece of flesh from his own thigh and roasted it as food for the prince. When the prince became the King of the State of Jin, he was careless about rewarding Jie Zitui. Therefore, Jie Zitui went to live with his mother in a mountainous area. He preferred to be ignored rather than ask for a reward. Later on, the king wanted to offer Jie Zitui a position, but Jie Zitui refused the offer. He went to the mountains. The king had a fire set to force him out in vain. Jie Zitui and his mother were found dead against a burnt willow stump with his mother on his back. The regretful king ordered fire to be banned on his anniversary of death.

Honoring Ancestors and Other Activities

For the Chinese the Tomb-sweeping Day is a day to remember and honor the ancestors at their grave sites. In the past, family members gathered and traveled to their deceased ancestors tombs because they believed that the spirits of deceased ancestors looked after the family. Offering, usually chickens, eggs and some wine, and spirit money, could keep them satisfied and peaceful in the other world and the family would prosper with harvest and more children. Especially, for some rich families, the festival can be very elaborate and expensive in terms of time and money.

Nowadays, the tradition remains. Chinese visit their family graves to sweep their ancestors' tombs, pulling out the weeds and dirt around the tombs, serving sacrificed food and drinks. (Usually fruits, dishes and drinks of which the deceased ancestors were fond.) It is believed that the spirits of the deceased ancestors they visited are around the graveyard and they would come and consume the food which is placed in front of their graves. Sometimes, a family will put burning incense with the offering so as to expedite the transfer of nutritious elements to the ancestors (C-C-C, 2000). In last couple of years, more and more

people prefer to lay flowers and wreaths at the tombs instead of burning paper money to prevent fires and to protect the environment.

Besides the traditions of honoring the dead, other activities are also done during the two weeks around the Tomb Sweeping Day. For instance, it is the high time to start the spring plowing and sowing. Some people would transplant willow cuttings in front of their doors or gates to ward off evil spirits that wonder around during the Tomb Sweeping time. It is also common that people go on a spring outing and have a picnic in the nature. With the coming of spring, the days get warmer and nature wakes up and the air also becomes clean and fresh. People also often fly kites on Tomb Sweeping Day. Kites can come in all kinds of shapes, sizes, and colors. Designs could include animals, such as eagles, dragonflies, butterflies, bats, and swallows, or characters from the Chinese opera.

All in all, the Tomb Sweeping Day combines both sadness and happiness and the activity of tomb sweeping serves to pay homage to the dead and to consolidate Chinese family ties. The Chinese people consider Yan Di and Huang Di the forefathers of all Chinese. Hence many Chinese pay homage to him in provinces such as Shaanxi, Shanxi, Shandong and Henan even today.

Section 4　Dragon Boat Festival

The Dragon Boat Festival is celebrated on the 5th day of the 5th lunar month by 27 minorities in China and it is also known as the Double Fifth festival. The festival is marked mainly by holding dragon boat races and eating the food called "Zongzi" as the festival food.

The Legend

The festival dates back as far as 5,000years ago. Considering the dragon as the most powerful god, the Chinese ancestors revered the dragon as their totem and the festival is associated with dragons. The two most important activities of the festival, dragon boat racing and eating zongzi, are related to the dragon. Besides, Chinese people worshipped their tribe chiefs as the incarnation of the dragon and made the 5th of the fifth lunar month a day to hold sacrificial ceremonies for the legendary animal.

The most popular theory of the origin of the festival is that it was derived from the activities of commemorating Qu Yuan. Qu Yuan was a great patriotic poet and politician during the Warring States (475—221 B.C.). He was also an upright person who was loved by the common people. He carried a political reform to fight against corruption, however, his action antagonized other court officials. They exerted their evil influence on the Emperor, so the Emperor gradually dismissed Qu Yuan and eventually exiled him. During his exile, Qu Yuan saw the gradual decline of his motherland, however, he did not give up. On the contrary, he wrote many masterpieces and taught his ideas to other people. On the 5th day of the 5th lunar month in 278 BC when he heard that his country had lost the battle against Qin, he was despaired and committed suicide by drowning himself in the Milo River (Hubei Province). His last poem reads:

> *Many a heavy sigh I have in my despair,*
> *Grieving that I was born in such an unlucky time.*
> *I yoked a team of jade dragons to a phoenix chariot,*
> *And waited for the wind to come,*
> *to sour up on my journey*
> (source from: C-C-C, 2000)

The local people were very sad when they heard about Qu Yuan's death. Fishermen boated down the river to search for his body but no one was able to find it. To scare away the fish so that they would not eat

Qu Yuan's body, fishermen rushed out in long boats, beating drums and throwing Zongzi into the water to feed the fish. Since then, people started to commemorate Qu Yuan through dragon boat races, eating Zongzi and other activities, on the anniversary of his death, the 5th of the fifth month.

The Dragon Boat Race

The Dragon Boat races are the most exciting part of the festival but the design of the race differs from place to place. Before the race starts, the festival celebrators hold a grand opening ceremony. During the ceremony, men in new clothes walk around a boat three times, to show homage to Lu Ban (the master craftsman) with burning candles in their hands. Then they go to the Temple of Qu Yuan to pay their respect to him by carrying an image of a dragon on their shoulders. Finally, they tie red ribbons to the boats and pull them into the river for the race. During the boat race, both banks are filled with crowds and a scene of fluttering colored banners.

Dragon Boats are usually brightly painted and decorated canoes. Ranging anywhere from 40 to 100 feet in length, their heads are shaped like open-mouthed dragons, while the sterns end in a scaly tail. Depending on the length, up to 80 rowers can sit in the boat. In some regions like Luzhou of Sichuan province, the racers in a dragon boat include a commander, a flag-catcher, a drummer and some rowers. The commander and flag-catcher stand in the front of the boat. The commander synchronizes rowing movements by waving a pennant and singing a race song, while the drummer beats the drum to cheer on the rowers. Races can have any number of boats competing, with the winner being the first team to grab a flag at the end of the course.

A big wooden boat carrying ducks is arranged at the finishing line. When the race boat reaches the line, the ducks in the boat are released into the river. Amid thunderous cheers of spectators on the banks, all the racers try to catch the ducks in the river. In Guangxi, women racers were possibly also included. Racers row race boats either by hands or foot.

Zongzi and Other Traditions

Zongzi is the most popular food during the festival and it is a special kind of dumpling which is usually made of glutinous rice wrapped in fresh bamboo leaves. The fresher the bamboo leaves, the better the taste of the Zongzi since the smell of the fresh bamboo leaves is a part of the Zongzi taste. Nowadays there are Zongzi of different shapes with a variety of fillings. However, the most popular shapes are triangular and pyramidal. The most common fillings are dates, beans and meat. The custom of eating Zongzi is linked to the legend of Qu Yuan and people are reminded of the importance of loyalty and commitment to the community and society during the festival.

During the festival, some people ceremoniously drink realgar liquor for the antiseptic purposes and to resist fungus. It is said that, after the death of Qu Yuan, an old practitioner of Chinese medicine poured some realgar wine into the Milo River to make the dragon and other aquatic animals drunk, so that they could not devour Qu's corpse. Later people continued to worship him during the festival. Adults drink it as a way of protection against vermin. Children may have some wine applied to their noses and ears for the same purpose. The wine may also be sprinkled over the floors for sterilization on festival day.

The day was also a traditional Sanitation Festival, as people cleaned their houses, and hung leaves of mugwort or cattail on their doors. This custom comes from an interesting folk tale. A nation-wide peasant uprising took place at the end of the Tang Dynasty (618—907). The leader of the peasant uprising, Huang Chao, met a women holding a child of about six years in one arm and taking a child of about three in her hand. She told the puzzled commander that the elder child in her arm is an orphan and the younger one is her

own child. She would flee with only the older one, at the sacrifice of her own son, if they ran into Huang Chao's soldiers. Deeply moved, Huang Chao promised to cherish all common people. He pulled up two mugwort plants at the roadside and gave them to her. He asked her to tell all poor residents in the city to hang the mugwort plants on their doors and his soldiers would not kill them. When Huang's army captured the city, it happened to be during the Dragon Boat Festival. The custom of hanging mugwort plants on doors has been kept in some areas since then.

Section 5 Mid-Autumn Festival (Family Reunion Festival)

Also known as the 'Moon Festival', the Mid-Autumn Festival is celebrated on the 15th day of the 8th lunar month. The moon is at its lowest angle at the horizon at this time, so the moon seems the fullest, biggest and brightest during the night. The full moon symbolizes family togetherness to the Chinese people and they take the festival as an occasion of family reunion. On that day, those who are far away from home may have a sense of nostalgia in their heart when they gaze at the full and attractive moon high in the sky.

Chinese poets like to use the moon as a favorite theme in their poems. Su Shi (1037—1101) wrote a poem in the Mid-Autumn Festival, whose lines many Chinese can recall and recite: "Now clear, now cloudy, the moon is never stable. No, there's no perfection. Not in heaven, not on earth. If only we could live to a green old age, sharing her beauty, together though far, far apart. "

The custom of worshipping the moon can be traced back as far as the ancient Xia and Shang dynasties (2000 B. C. —1066 B. C.), and the word "Mid-Autumn" already existed during the Zhou Dynasty (1066 B. C. —221 B. C.). During the Tang Dynasty, the Mid-Autumn Day started to be celebrated as a festival for people to enjoy the full, bright moon, worship it and express their thoughts and feelings under it. The festival became more and more popular during the Song Dynasty. Records say that high officials and noble lords gathered at their own pavilions to admire the glorious moon, while common people admired the attraction from wine shops. During the Ming and the Qing Dynasties, the Moon Festival grew to be one of the most important festivals in China (Chinaorgcn, n. d.).

Legend

There are many beautiful legends about the moon in China. However, when gazing at the moon, one is often reminded of Chang E, as the story *Chang E's Flying Towards the Moon* is known to all Chinese. According to the Chinese folktale, Chang E was Hou Yi's wife. Hou Yi was a hero who took pity on the common people during a disaster. After he shot down nine drought-causing suns, the common people's lives were saved. A Taoist priest offered him the elixir of life for his good deed. Hou Yi told Chang E if one had all the pills, he would fly to the moon and live forever. If two people shared the pills, they would live an endless life on earth. He planned to have this life together with his wife someday. However, one day while he was out, the curious wife, Chang E, swallowed them all. Immediately she found herself flying up to the moon. She and a jade rabbit lived a lonely life in the Moon Palace. The shadows on the moon make the story all the more credible and fascinating to the imaginative mind.

Another legend tells of an old man in the moon who is the Divine Match-maker. It is said the moon is endowed with the power to decide a person's matrimonial destiny. The old man in the moon used to tie the feet of young men and women with red cords for marriage. Thus, in ancient times, some unmarried young people lighted candles and burned joss sticks under the Mid-Autumn moon to pray for a happy marriage.

All in all, there are many stories with regard to the Moon Festival, but all show their love and longing for a better life.

Moon Cakes

Almost every Chinese festival is accompanied with some special food and round moon cakes do not only mark the food specialty during the Moon Festival, it is also the symbol of both the fullness of the moon and family togetherness.

Cakes of different sizes, usually about 10 cm in diameter and 4 ~ 5 cm thick, are stuffed with a variety of fillings such as bean paste, fruit, egg yolk, dates, lotus seeds, walnuts, pineapple, pork, sesames and so on. The traditional ones consist of a thin tender skin with a sweet and slightly oily filling and they have an imprint on top consisting of the Chinese characters for "longevity" or "harmony" as well as the name of the bakery and the filling in the moon cake. They used to be sacrifices offered to the moon. A popular legend for the origin of the moon cakes goes like this: In 1280 A. D. , the Mongolians defeated the Song Dynasty and controlled China during the Yuan Dynasty (1280 A. D. —1368 A. D.). Under the Mongolian rule, the people in the late Yuan Dynasty were oppressed and treated like slaves (Wong, 2002). Common people were forbidden to use ironware out of fear that they would rebel and use ironware as their weapons. Nevertheless, a well planned revolution was still on its way in 1368. During the August Moon Festival in that year, a leader of the peasants established contact with people by distributing moon-cakes with a note inside with words written "kill the Yuan soldiers on August 15". Since the Mongolians did not eat moon-cakes, the secret messages could not be discovered by them. After the overthrow of the Yuan rulers, people eat moon-cakes on that day every year to celebrate the victory brought about by this successful method of contact.

The festival was gradually modified to exemplify a happy family reunion. Even today, family members continue to share elaborately-made cakes (symbolic offering to the moon spirits). During the festival, family members gather together beneath the clear moonlight and snack on tasty moon cakes and various kinds of fresh and dry fruits.

Section 6 Double Ninth Day (Chong Yang Festival)

The Double Ninth Day is on the 9th day of the 9th lunar month. "Chong" suggests double, and "Yang" means nine according to *The Book of Changes* by Confucius. The festival is based on the theory of Yin and Yang, which are the two opposite principles in nature. The ninth day of the ninth lunar month is a day when the two Yang (odd) numbers meet. Since the Chinese word to express the number nine and the word "longevity" have the same pronunciation, the ninth day of the ninth month has become a special day for the elderly people to enjoy themselves or the young people to show their respects to the elderly.

The festival can be traced back to the Warring States period (475BC—221BC) where it was originally a day for farmers to celebrate bumper harvests of crops. The festival became more popular during the Han Dynasty (206 BC—220 AD).

Legend said that around the 6th century there once lived a person called Huangjing. He was a student of Fei Changfang who became an immortal after many years of practicing Taoism. One day when the two were climbing a mountain, Fei Changfang told Huangjing that on the ninth day of the ninth lunar month, disaster will come to Huangjing's hometown. To avoid the disaster, Huangjing had to make a red bag for each one of his family members and put a spray of dogwood in every one before they left home and climb to the top of the highest nearby mountain. Most importantly, all had to drink some chrysanthemum wine (China Daily, 2005). Huangjing went home and did exactly what he was asked to do and saved his family. From then on, climbing a mountain, carrying a spray of dogwood and drinking chrysanthemum wine became the traditional activities of the Chongyang Festival. In the Tang Dynasty (618—907), Chongyang festival was made the official festival and it was marked by activities such as climbing heights, drinking chrysanthemum wine and enjoying chrysanthemum flowers and so on.

Nowadays, although the tradition of carrying dogwood died out, climbing mountains and appreciating chrysanthemum still remains as a custom. Indeed, the 9th lunar month is a good time for going out and sight-seeing, since the sky appears to be clear and the weather is mostly fine. Standing on a height looking afar, a panoramic view of a blue sky with pale clouds and green mountains makes people feel carefree and joyful. It is also the ideal time for chrysanthemums. In the ancient time, people used to pick the lower leaves on the Chongyang festival and brewed the mixture of the leaves and grains into wine. People considered that the wine had medicinal effects on curing illness such as eye diseases, headaches and stomach problem, since it was believed that the flower had medical usage.

Chapter 25

Different Dragon Cultures

Xiaoxia Mao Miao, Zhang Miao, Jonathan Hoddinott and Adam A. Marx

The modern concept of the European dragon goes far back to the Roman Republic. In that period someone combined the Serpent of Greek myths with the Persian idea of a winged beast to create the Roman Dragon. The common characteristic is that they have wings and either have two legs in the front two arms are similar to humans in ability or all four will be legs. There are no set colors for the dragons in European myths so they can range from black to red and anything in between but almost all colors breathe fire. The most common of all is the fact that every dragon in Western culture has the dragon being an evil presence. Many stories have the Dragon guarding hordes of gold that they took over time or they constantly burn the farmers' crops with their ability to breathe fire.

In Greek Mythology, stories of Hercules battling many dragons are scattered throughout texts. One of the most notable stories includes Hercules battling a Nine-Headed Hydra. When he cut off one of its heads, two more heads immediately grew back in its place. Hercules was finally able to defeat the dragon by cauterizing the wound where he removed a head.

Medieval Europe holds many accounts of dragons and dragon slayers. Saint George was a famous dragon slayer and traveled around Europe slaying dragons to protect princesses and villages. In fact, stories of King Arthur and many other knights of the day often include details of intentionally traveling to far off places to win the heart of a princess by slaying the dragon that has taken her captive. Dragons of these times were very much viewed as the antithesis of good and were often wreaking havoc on kingdoms and villages. Dragons were certainly given a status of intelligence for their ability to formulate these plans of kidnapping. On a lighter note, dragons have continued to be portrayed in the light of evil even in animated movies. The movie *Shrek*, which was released several years ago, has a dragon in it that kidnaps a princess and an Ogre named Shrek saves her from her doom.

Some popular dragons in today's myths would be from Beowulf's red dragon in which he died fighting because of his old age. A lot of recent movies have featured dragons that often attack anything they see. There is also a game called Dungeons & Dragons which is a role-playing game. That means they create characters and act as if they were really the characters they just created. Often battles would end in a fight with an evil Dragon deep in a Dungeon where the dragon would keep its treasure.

Even newer than the movies is popular culture references of dragons such as Trogdor from the website www. homestarrunner. com which is a web comic based site. Though it is a comic website, it is a very popular site visited by thousands of people. Many dragons will appear on T-shirts and other common apparel thanks to the popularity of the dragon as such an evil character.

Chinese dragons and European dragons are very different. It is hard for some westerns to ever think of

dragons as anything but a mean spirited, ill tempered, greedy beast. Different from the dragon monster in the Westerner's legend, the Chinese dragon is a mythical creature according to Chinese imagination. It can walk or fly, and it has such divine powers as to summon wind and rain. Chinese call themselves "descendants of the Chinese dragon" and their country is called the "land of the Chinese dragon." In traditional Chinese culture, the dragon symbolizes power, auspiciousness and prosperity. It has become a symbol of the striving ethos of Chinese culture, and it is one of many reflections of the great aspirations of the ancients.

Section 1　The Origin of the Chinese Dragon

Opinions are divided on the origin of the Chinese dragon despite much study. Archeologists have widely different views based on different materials and various viewpoints. Some believe a pig is one of the origins of the dragon. Some jade dragons have a studded nose, a long snout and a long mane on the neck and back. Besides, pigs were the earliest and most commonly domesticated animals during the prehistoric period in China. Hence, the creation of a dragon image was based on people's own lives and productive activity.

Some other scholars believe the clam-shell dragon patterns can be explained from an astronomical viewpoint. Chinese forefathers divided up the skies into four palaces due to their four directions. In each palace, the major constellations were conjured up in the shape of an animal and named as such. For instance, The North Palace is a combination of the turtle and snake. In the Xishuipo tomb, on the east side of the excavation is a dragon pattern. The design of this pattern conforms entirely to the natural astronomical phenomena in the skies.

Since the dates from these periods, most literature and records about prehistoric times are frequently confused and contradictory. It is hard to trace the dragon to its origin through literature and records of the past. Still, from the materials, one can demonstrate the birth of the dragon was closely related to the development of primitive farming production. The dragon's image was derived from more than one animal.

The most common theory is related to the ancient people's totem. Six or seven thousand years ago, people lived under extremely hard conditions. They did not have the power to control nature, but believed that certain species of animals or plants possessed such power. Totems emerged then. The members of the tribe call their totem "dragon." Whenever they conquered another totemic tribe, they added part of that totem to the snake to show they had annexed the other tribe. Through constant enrichment and exaggeration, the image of the "dragon" was finally a creature with a deer's antlers, a camel's head, a hare's eyes, a snake's neck, a clam's belly, a carp's scales, a hawk's talons, a tiger's paws and a bull's ears. The figure of the dragon was first found on painted pottery made six or seven thousand years ago, unearthed in Gansu Province. The evolution of the shape, from the snake to the dragon, starting with the head can be seen on a jade dragon of 5,500 years ago excavated in the Inner Mongolian Autonomous Region. A group of prehistoric excavations and relics has been found decorated with dragon images. These relics included jade and pottery with designs and patterns made from clam shells found in Shanxi, Henan, Gansu and Inner Mongolia.

Fuxi and Nǚwa, the two earliest mythical figures, are the two ancestors of mankind. Both of them have the face of a human and the body of a snake or a dragon. Huangdi (26th century BC) is said to be the common ancestor of the tribes in Central China. In some legends, he eventually went up to heaven riding a divine dragon. The later leaders of the tribe, such as Yao, Shun and Yu, are all said to have blood relation with the dragon. From the tribal society in Central China to the Fuxi and Nǚwa, all are said to be either a dragon incarnate or to be related by blood to the dragon. The tribes in China all worshiped the dragon totem. From this, the significance of the dragon in Chinese traditional culture is clear.

Section 2 Dragon Image and the Royal Class

After the establishment of the Xia Dynasty in the 21st century BC, the dragon was gradually considered as the ancestor of the royal families only. It further strengthened the dragon's dominant position in Chinese culture. The initial stage in the development of the dragon design occured during the Xia, the Shang and the Zhou dynasties (2,000to 4,000years ago).

Liu Bang overthrew the Qin Dynasty and established the Han Dynasty (206BC—220AD). In order to prove he was legitimate to ascend the throne, some men fabricated stories saying Liu Bang's mother gave birth to him after she became pregnant through an affair with a red dragon in her dream. Since then, emperors and dragons were connected.

An emperor was believed to be the "son of Heaven" and was referred to as a real dragon who ruled the land by divine right. The furniture and articles used by the emperors were usually called "dragon seat," "dragon bed" and so on. During the Tang Dynasty (618—907), Wu Zetian made the dragon design the principal pattern on the imperial robe. In the Yuan Dynasty (1206—1368), the court adopted the five-clawed dragon as the design on the imperial robe and forbade the common people from using such a design. Images of dragons often decorate royal palaces. In the Qing Dynasty (1644—1911), the imperial robe was more exquisitely and sumptuously made with an embroidered dragon decorated with colorful silk thread, gold and silver wires and peacock feather yarn. Tiny pearls and rosy coral bits were also used as decorations on the dragon imperial robe. The image of the dragon can be seen everywhere in the Imperial Palace (Forbidden City). For instance, The Hall of Supreme Harmony is a world of dragons. On the Nine-dragon Screen Wall, nine dragons are prancing on an expanse of waves. Their mighty and signified images symbolize the sacredness and solemnity of the monarchical power. Images of dragons often decorate walls, pillars, tables and desks in royal palaces too. Even small things like mirrors, hairpins, and combs are decorated with the images of dragon in royal palaces.

Section 3 Dragon and Folk Customs

The Year of the Dragon is the most important of the 12-year calendar cycle. The Dragon King folk tales are very popular in China. People depended much on water for their existence in the early agricultural society. They believed their patron saint, the dragon, was living in the water. It was said the Dragon King lived in a magnificent palace built with crystal and jewels in the depths of the sea. He was able to stir up trouble on the sea or summon clouds and give rain. The golden cudgel, used by the famous Monkey King, is said to originally be a talisman in the Dragon Palace to pacify the sea.

People used to pray to the Dragon King for rain to relieve them from disaster whenever there was a severe drought. Many temples for the Dragon King were built and used for ceremonies. The Dragon King in the folktales is sometimes a benevolent savior and at other times an evildoer; if there was no rain after all their prayers, people would have a grievance against the dragon.

The dragon dance is a folk dance popular in China. There are a variety of stories about the origin of the dragon dance. One story tells that the Dragon King fell ill and recovered with the help of a doctor. To express his gratitude, the Dragon King told the doctor to make a model dragon after his image and wave it each year so that the weather would be fine. Hence the dragon dance was widely spread throughout China and the world during the Spring Festival.

China's traditional Dragon Boat Festival falls on the 5th day of the 5th lunar month when people in South

China offer sacrifices to the dragon. The dragon-boat race is held in regions with rivers and lakes in South China. The dragon boat is made in the shape of a dragon, and it is long and narrow. The crew comprises over a dozen oarsmen and a drummer. The rowers would bend to the oars to the accompaniment of the drumbeats. The spectators would also beat drums and gongs during the race. They also set off firecrackers to enhance the festive atmosphere.

In the spring days of gentle breezes, the kite resembling a dragon can be seen flying in the sky. The long dragon kite is the most spectacular among various kinds of kites.

Section 4　Dragon and the Confucian Temple

Many mountains contain "dragon" in their names; the same is true of the names of rivers. The names of numerous towns, villages, gardens and temples are also blended with the word "dragon." The most famous of the dragon columns are in Qufu, Shandong Province, the birthplace of Confucius. Though the dragon was used as the symbol of monarchical power, Confucius, the founder of Chinese traditional ethics, was considered a saint and was thought to have some relationship to the dragon. His 28 columns are carved with dignified, coiled dragons in the Dacheng Hall of the Confucian Temple. It symbolizes he was a dragon in the mortal world.

Part 8

China—a Big Family of 56 Nationalities

Chapter 26

Minority

Xiaoxia Mao, Miao Zhang and Xuefei Yang

China serves as the home to 56 ethnic groups (each of the 10 largest ethnic groups has a population of more than one million). The Han (Huaxia) majority makes up 91.96% of the total population of China. The Central People's Government has given materials and financial aid to the minority population since 1949. It has led to marked improvements in their living standards and the quality of their medical care. As a result, the minority people have experienced an increase in birth rate and population growth.

The combined population of China's minority nationalities reached over 67 million (double the 1949 figure) in the 1990s. The average annual growth rate stands at about 2.9%. Han people have only one child per couple according to the family planning policy of 1979. However, the national autonomous areas have been permitted to pursue their own family planning policies in light of their local conditions. For instance, Hezhe is the smallest ethnic group in China with a population of 1Y400 people in the 1990s. Poverty, plus an utter lack of medical services affected them so much that they were on the verge of extinction with only 300 people left by 1949. The Hezhes live in the northernmost Herlongjiang province. The Hezhes set up a nationality township in Fuyuan County in 1956 under the new government's regional autonomous policy.

In most Chinese cities and county towns, two or more ethnic groups living together are common. Although they live together, their individual compact communities are kept. The communities of the different ethnic groups have provided political, economic and cultural exchanges among themselves throughout China's long history. For instance, in Xinjiang, Yunnan, Guizhou and Guangxi, certain minority people live in compact communities but contain members of a number of other nationalities. The Tibetan nationality has a population of 4.5 million, mainly living in Tibet, Qinghai, Gansu and Sichuan provinces. The minority nationalities have developed their own various customs and social norms with regard to diet, dress, housing, marriage, funerals, festivals, entertainment, rituals, taboo down through the ages. The 55 minorities speak more than 60 languages, and 20 minorities have their own written languages.

The four major religions in the world (Buddhism, Islam, Catholicism and Christianity) have their adherents among the minority nationalities. Many minorities used to adopt one religion or another in the past. Chinese minority people have their freedom of religious belief since 1949 (their beliefs were rejected by the Han during the "Cultural Revolution" from 1966—1976).

Section 1 History of Their Development

The minority nationalities have taken form after going through a long period of historical development of more than 2,000years in China. China was inhabited not only by Hans, but by numerous other nationali-

ties including the Dongyus, the Yues and Mans, the Rongs, the Qiangs, the Jis, the Xiongnus, the Wusuns and the Donghus far back in the Qin (221—206 B. C.) and Han (206 B. C. —220A. D.) periods. Wars frequently broke out among these nationalities during the Wei (220—265 A. D.), the Jin (265—420), the Southern (420—589) and the Northern Dynasties (386—581), and a few independent kingdoms sprung up across the land. Major migrations were frequent under such circumstances. It, in turn, sped the process of assimilation among the nationalities. For instance, most of the national groups like the Xianbei and Xiongnu were assimilated by the Hans over the course of the years of migrating into the Central Plains during the period.

There was remarkable progress in the political, economic and cultural fields from the late sixth century to the early tenth century. The Han members of the imperial ruling class forged close ties with the minority national groups in different parts of the country during the Sui (589—618) and the Tang (618—906) periods. The groups of Tujue, the Huihe, the Qiang in the northwest, the Mohe, the Qidan and the Meng-wushiwei in the northeast, the Wuman and the Baiman in the southwest, the Tufan in the west were the ancestors of many of the minority nationalities in China today. Mutual contacts, cultural exchanges and fusion among the various peoples of the country have continued unabated from the tenth century onward, down through the Song (907—1279), the Yuan (1279—1368), the Ming (1368—1644) and the Qing (1644—1911) Dynasties up till the present day.

During the ancient feudalist society, the Han people and the minorities were never considered equal. Either the Han ruling classes were in command, riding roughshod over the minorities, or some minority group sat on the throne, ruthlessly encroaching upon the rights of the Hans. The Northern Dynasties (Xianbei minority, 386—581 AD), the Yuan Dynasty (Mongolia minority, 1279—1368) and the Qing Dynasty (Man minority, 1644—1911) ruled by the minorities for only three periods in Chinese history.

However, the relations between the Hans and the minorities were not simply exploitation. Over the centuries, they have gradually developed cooperative relationships in political, economic and cultural spheres.

It is difficult to quickly put an end to the discriminatory attitudes of the Han majority which prevailed over the past centuries. These attitudes were aggravated by some political ("left") errors with respect to ethnic problems from 1958 to 1977. Those nationality policies that proved effective in the past were revived and carried forward again from 1978. Since 1978, the government has taken numerous steps to deal with the problems, aiming at pushing forward economic and cultural development in the minority areas and building a legal and harmonious relation. Of course, completely resolving all of the historical misunderstandings still existing between the Hans and the minority groups is not a simple matter. It will take a considerable period of time to thoroughly resolve the issues.

Section 2   Policy of the Central Government

The Law on Regional Autonomy for Minority Nationalities constituted in 1984 reserves the rights for each minority group to administer its own internal affairs and ensure the unification and independence of the country. The law empowers self-government organizations four major aspects: 1) Economically, they may resolve out their own policies in accordance with the local condition and needs under the guidance of the state plans. 2) Income expense can be freely allocated to financial affairs within autonomous areas. 3) They may independently develop their own educational system (based on state educational policy); in terms of making local plans for education, determining the organization of schools, forming of schools, educational system, curricular language of instruction and enrolment procedures in education. 4) Absolute rights in developing their minority culture in literature, art, publishing, journalism, broadcasting, film and television. For example, film studios in Inner Mongolia, Guangxi, Xinjiang and Ningxia have been organized to primarily produce films reflecting the lives of the minority peoples; moreover, state-funded art schools have been set up in Inner Mongolia, Xinjiang, Guangxi, Tibet, Ningxia and Yanbian.

Minorities' medicine and pharmacology have been set up for health services, the development and contribution is very unique and effective. For instance, the famous Tibetan medicine with 1,000 years of history, Dai medicine from Yunnan province, all the medicine material are sourced from local herb and foodstuff, they adopt modes of treatment suited to their own local conditions. Many of them developed their own effective, time-tested prescription and acquired special healing arts. The Chinese government has been very supportive so as to develop these ethnic medicines and pharmacologies. A number of new medical institution are set up as well as improving the existing institutions in Tibet, Inner Mongolia and Yunnan province.

Owing to the discriminatory and oppressive policies carried out by the Kuomintang regime (1911—1949) in the mainland, most minority people lived in poverty and insufficient medical care. Due to the historical inequality, many minority regions are still rather backward in their economies. New government not only provide continuous fund and material aids to minorities regions on annual basis, but also transfer skilled technicians, doctors and teachers to help those areas economically, culturally and educationally since 1949.

In addition, the government has built minority teacher training schools, minority professional secondary schools, minority technical secondary schools and minority colleges. In Tibet, for instance, the students of minorities in senior middle schools receive substantial stipends including allocations of money and grants for food and clothing.

The Central Government set up China's ethnic work organizations (10 organizations) to promote the socialist relations of equality, unity and mutual assistance among all nationalities and to strengthen their solidarity. Some minority deputies (381 deputies, 10.9% of the total deputies) are selected to serve in the National People's Congress. The government has adopted the following measures to assist the minorities in developing their economies:

● All current policies, regulations or measures that fetter productive forces will be revised.

● Raising the state purchasing prices for agricultural produce, livestock and animal products to increase the people's income and ease their economic burdens.

● The government will conduct detailed surveys of the natural resources within each area and help them to formulate guidelines for economic development. In Inner Mongolia, work has begun on building four major open-pit coal mines for energy exploitation.

● The government will make efforts to popularize the contract responsibility system. Each individual's income is determined by his output.

● The government will allocate special subsidies to the minority areas primarily for economic construction.

● The central government will call upon the Han areas to offer the technical and financial aid to the minority areas in exploiting the natural resources. For instance, the sight-seeing industry of Yunnan is being supported and developed. The travel industry has experienced a rapid development in the past decades. Some major tourist cities such as Kunming (the site of the "99" International Horticultural Exposition), Lijiang (included on the UNESCO world culture heritage list in 1997), and Dali are well known in the world.

● The government encourages the border trade of minority areas with other countries (which are their neighbors). Examples would be: the border trade between Guangxi and Vietnam, the border trade between Tibet and Nepal, and the border trade between Xinjiang and Russia.

Section 3 Some Minorities

Mongolians and Inner Mongolia

The ethnic Mongolian mainly live in Inner Mongolia, while the rest are distributed throughout Xinjiang, Liaoning, Jilin, Heilongjiang, Qinghai, Gansu, Ningxia, Hebei, Henan, Sichuan, Yunnan provinces and Beijing. In the early times, the Mongolians were nomadic people engaged mainly in livestock, hunting and growing cereal crops. Grain, beef, mutton, dairy products and rice are their main foods. Since they engage in livestock, they generally dwell in yurts (circular domed portable tents) and live on a diet rich in milk products, cheese and mutton. Those living in the agricultural districts have houses built of clay and wood or bricks and wood. Although Mongolian people have begun to live in permanent settlements since the 1950s, most traditions remain until today. Horses to the Mongolians are important and children learn to ride on horses even when they are barely able to walk. Sheep are Mongolia's most important livestock and most herds move four times a year, once during each season. Meat is the most common food, while vegetables are rare in Mongolia since the herders usually do not have gardens (Gruys, 2007). In an internet site called Blue Peak, Gruys (2007) reveals how the real Mongolian barbecue is cooked:

'A popular way of cooking meat is putting hot rocks in a large container, adding mutton and some water, and closing it tightly for several hours. The meat, served in large chunks, gets very tender. The fat, which is drunk hot while it is still liquid is for the real mutton fan only… This is the real Mongolian barbeque, a far cry from the so-called Mongolian grill restaurants that sprang up in the west.'

The dress of Mongolian people shows the minorities' peculiarities since it is very much suited to the nomadic way of life. They dress is made of cotton and has long, wide gowns with silk bands at the waist. Males also wear hats or turbans and little ornamental knives attached to their waistbands. The women wear long braids, intertwined with red and blue fabric. Both men and women wear leather coats, felt boots and fur caps to withstand the cold winters.

Originally, the Mongols based their religion on the forces of nature. The moon, sun, stars and even rivers were worshipped. There were countless numbers of gods which all had a universal supernatural presence. Before the reign of Genghis Khan, a succession of Mongol empires created a rich legacy of art and culture on the grassy plains of northern China and a number of their folk tales and ballads have been handed down orally over many generations. Lamaism was introduced into Mongolia in 1260 by the priest ruler of Tibet and gradually it became the major religion. Mongolians had their own language (belonging to the Altaic family) by the beginning of the 13th century.

The Mongolians have a fine cultural tradition. Their earliest written work on history is titled, Inside History of Mongolia. Since then, a number of important historical and literary works have been written in the language. The National Origins of the Mongolians is another example. There are also important works covering the natural sciences and medicine. Many classical literary works from the Han and the Tibetans have also been translated into the Mongolian language. Mongolians are also good singers and dancers and Inner Mongolia is also called "the sea of songs". Among the most characteristic Mongolian dances are the Horse Sabre Dance and the Wine-cup and Chopsticks Dance, both performed with brisk steps. The Mongolian horse-head guitars produce low, wide, melodious and pleasant sounds. Mongolians are also well known for their proficiency in horsemanship, wrestling and archery.

The summer festival known as Nadamu Fair features traditional Mongolian sports and events such as wrestling, horse racing, archery, singing, and dancing. For foreigners, the capital city, Hohhot, is the best place to see the festival. Contests in track and field, ball and chess games, art performances and business transactions have been added to the program since 1950s. Prizes vary from a goat to a fully equipped horse. Being one of the major highlights of Mongolian life, Nadam attracts people living dozens of miles away. To get there, they travel on horseback, by cart or by motor-car. Many Mongolian herdsmen bring their family members dressed in their national costumes along with them. When they arrive at the fairgrounds, they spread out their wine, butter tea and other foods in picnic fashion and exchange toasts. Young people deck out their horses with bells, new saddles and new stirrups. They travel in groups, chatting and laughing merrily all their way to the Nadam. The fairgrounds of Nadam become alive with the sounds of singing, clapping and cheering. The performances include Mongolian songs and graceful Andai Dances. All competitions draw large crowds of people. Herdsmen sell their products such as wool, medicinal herbs, and furs, and, in turn buy products like silk, cloth, boots, compressed tea, cotton and some special articles for Mongolian use.

Mongolians were originally herdsmen roaming the Ergun River banks and later moved to the grasslands of western Mongolia. They were living on the upper reaches of the Onon, Kerulen and Tula rivers and in the Hentey Mountains by the 12th century. Genghis Khan organized a powerful Mongolian army early in the 13th century and conquered various Mongolian tribes to found the Mongol Khanate. Genghis Khan unified the Mongol tribes in 1206 and his descendants, Kublai Khan, completed his conquest and established the Yuan Dynasty (1271—1368). In 1368 the Yuan Dynasty was evicted from China by the Han Chinese who created the Ming Dynasty. Under the Qing Dynasty the Manchus gained control of the Inner Mongolian tribes and the Mongolians were severely ruled. As Manchuria came under the control of the Japanese in 1930s, Inner Mongolia was turned into a puppet of the Japanese Empire. Both ancient and modern history witnessed the hardship, rise and fall, struggles and rebellions of the Mongolians against the feudal rulers and invaders.

Inner Mongolia is an Autonomous Region in the north of China. Bordering the Republic of Mongolia and Russia, Inner Mongolia is the widest and third biggest province in China. With an area of 1, 18 million square kilometers, which occupies 12% of China's land territory, Inner Mongolia has 24 million inhabitants (Travel China Guide, 2004). There are 49 ethnical groups living in Inner Mongolia such as Mongolian, Daur, Oroqen, Ewenki, Hui, Korea and Manchu. However the majority of its population is Han Chinese, which takes up 79% of the whole population (中国内蒙古, 2008).

Due to the high longitude, Inner Mongolia's climate usually tends to be quite extreme. It has a cold, long winter with frequent blizzards and a warm, short summer (China Culture, 2008). Thus the best time to visit Inner Mongolia is from May till September. Inner Mongolia boasts vast areas of natural grassland. For example Hulunbuir and Xilin Gol are major tourist areas. However, you will find exotic primitive forests in the far north and the Greater Hinggan range contains about one sixth of the country's forests.

Inner Mongolia plays an important role in the program of China's western development. It is not only known for its natural resources of timber, skins, and medical herbs, it is also rich in minerals. The mineral deposits, such as coal, iron, manganese and chromium are an essential part of the economy of the western region and greatly promote frontier trade and foreign economic and technological cooperation with other areas. Manzhouli and Erenhot are examples of the 18 frontier land ports which were opened to the outside world. Furthermore, the extensive grasslands provide conditions for animal husbandry and its fertile plains produce good crops of wheat, oat and glutinous millet. Throughout 50 years of economic construction, especially during the efforts of the past two decades, Inner Mongolia has developed into an important base for commodity grains, livestock products, raw materials and energy in Northern China.

Except for the rich natural resources, Inner Mongolia is also one of the most important ecological pres-

ervation areas in northern China. Providing an ecological environment is the primary task in the implementation of the western development. The ecological construction demands sustainable development, which includes creating forest and grassland out of the farm land by planting grass and forbidding husbandry in pastoral areas, constructing key ecological counties at state-level, constructing protective shelters for man-made forests, controlling and preventing sand erosion, protecting natural forest in the Greater Hinggan Mountains, and ecological immigration (People's Daily, 2000).

Take the water supply issue in Inner Mongolia as an example. Since most areas of Inner Mongolia have a water shortage, improving the water supply, encouraging effective use of water and solving the potable drinking problems are urgent tasks. Solving these problems would not only guaranty both social and sustainable economic development in the area, it would also, on the one hand, serve as a defense to prevent sandstorms from destroying the northwest and the capital city, Beijing. On the other hand, it would also mitigate the drought conditions along the Yellow River and the flooding of the Songhua and Liaohe river valleys in Northern China.

Hui (Huihui)

Hui is one of the large minority nationalities in China and Huis reside in many places in China. The largest Hui communities are in Ningxia, Qinghai, Gansu, Henan, Hebei, Shandong, Xinjiang and Yunnan provinces. In 7th century, Arabians, Persians came to southeasten China for trade and they finally settled in Hangzhou, Yangzhou and Quanhou, more and more Arabics came to China and formed the new nationality Huihui in 13th century. They intermarried with Hans, Mongolians and Uygures.

The Hui suffered massively from exploitation and oppression at the hands of reactionary rulers. For example, in the wake of the defeat of an uprising staged by the Huis, about 70% of the Huis in Gansu were slaughtered and their ranks in Shaanxi were decimated. The Kuomingtang government (1912—1949) did not officially recognize the Hui nationality as an independent nationality, and carried out the same repressive policy as the Qing court. Since 1949, the new government issued a policy of regional national autonomy in areas where the Huis live in compact communities to ensure their equal ethnic rights. The Ningxia Hui autonomous Region and two autonomous prefectures in Gansu Province and six autonomous countries in some parts of the country have been established so as to protect the Huis right. After 50 years, infrastructure, raw material and daily necessary supply have all been implemented in Ningxia Province. Some large water conservancy projects along the Yellow River have also been built in Ningxia.

Previously, Huis were farmers, only few engaged in commerce or handicraft industry. They have close relation with the Han in terms of economy and culture. They speak and write the same language as Hans, they dress no difference from the Hans. However, they use Persian and Arabian languages in their religion. Islamism is their common religious faith. Islam first entered China in the mid-seventh century from Central Asia. The Silk Road helped to spread Islamic religion in China. In Yuan Dynasty, the history witnessed an Islamic zenith of prosperity. Their customs and culture are greatly influenced by Islamic religion. Like all the Muslims in other lands, the Huis pray and hold religion activities in mosque. China has more than 30,000mosques now. The four famous old Mosques in China are the Fairy Crane Mosque (1275) in Yangzhou, the Huaisheng Mosque (built in the Tang Dynasty) in Guanzhou, the Qingjing Mosque (1309) in Quangzhou, and the Fenghuang Mosque (Phoenix Mosque, built in the Tang Dynasty) in Hangzhou.

Three of their major festivals are the birthday of Mohammed, Fast Breaking and Corban which were introduced in China in 651 during the Tang Dynasty. They abstain from eating pork. The deceased are interred without being encased in a coffin according to Hui's funerary customs.

250

Generally, the Huis form their own villages in the countryside and their own neighborhoods in cities. For instance Nujie (Cow Street) in Xuanwu district of Beijing is the area where Huis gather.

In Chinese history, many contributions made by Huis are the highlights for Chinese culture and civilization. They introduced the knowledge of astronomy, calendar calculation, gun manufacturing and medicines from West Asia. This nationality has produced quite a few famous statesmen and intellectuals during the past 400 years. Some of them are well known, such as the statesman, Saidianchi Zhansiding (the Yuan Dynasty, 1211—1279), the navigator, Zheng He (the Ming Dynasty, 1371—1435) and the progressive thinker, Li Zhi (the Ming Dynasty, 1527—1602). A sizable number of accomplished poets, scholars, painters and dramatists are also from the Hui nationality.

Uygur Nationality and Xingjiang

The Uygur have lived at the foot of Tianshan mountain areas for several centuries. the Uygur nationality is largely concentrated in the Xinjiang Uygur Autonomous Region. Some have spread into the Hunan Province. Their language belongs to the Turkic group of the Altaic language family. The two systems of their writing include Arabic phonetic letters and a recently developed romanized script. Islamism is their religion, it influences family life, marriages, food, finery and customs. The most important festivals are the Corban Festival, the Almsgiving Festival, the Kaizhai Festival and Noulu Festival.

Xinjiang was known as the Western Region about 2,000 years ago. The earliest ancestors of the Uygurs were a tribe known by various names such as Huige, Gaoche, Tiele, and Huigu in ancient times. They used to colonize in the north and northwest region of China, suffered from wars between tribes before migrating to the Western Regions. They allianced with other tribes to fight against the Turks in the 7th century. After a long period of intermixing with Tubos, Mongolians and Qidans, the nationality of Uygur was gradually formed. From the 19th century, the Uygur peoplerepeatly struggled against the foreign colonialists' rule and the repressiveness of the Qing Dynasty. They also displayed just as much heroism in fighting the Kuomintang government before 1949. The Xinjiang Uygur Autonomous Region was established in 1955, Uygur is the major nationality.

Both males and females are fond of wearing small, gorgeously colored floral caps which look like an attractive handicraft article. Men like to wear a type of robe and women wear long braids, long skirts and a loose-sleeved, bright-colored garments covered by a black vest.

Due to the unstable historical situation, it took a long time for the Uygurs to transact from stock breeding to agriculture. They are specialized in growing wheat, maize, paddy and cotton. Livestock breeding and fruit farming are their important agricultural sidelines. They are the expert in planting melons and grapes. Those two types of fruits are famous throughout the world by their unique way of farming.

The Uygurs love eating all kinds of meat: beef, mutton, chicken, duck and fish. "Nang" which is a type of wheaten cake is their staple food. When they have festival dinner, one speciality dish is served, it is know as "Zhuafan".

From Han Dynasty (206BC—220AD), Uygur nationality has made great contribution in the Chinese literature field. The long narrative poems, Knowledge Gives Happiness and A Turkic Dictionary, handed down from the 11th century, are important works. Avanti's Stories derides those repressive imams in humorous terms.

The Uygurs are well known for singing and dancing. Their dances are fast and involve many changes in movement. The traditional dances such as the Balancing Bowls, Big Drum Dance, Iron Ring Dance, Puta Dance and Sainaimu are popular folk dances that are generally enjoyed. Their lively dances demonstrate bravery, diligence, openness and optimism. Their instruments encompass more than a dozen types. Because

their music and dance are so renown nationwide, the government actually sent organizations to investigate, record and collate a number of the ancient types of Uygurian music during the past decades.

Xinjiang is surrounded by a number of snow-capped mountains, such as Pamirs, the Karakorum and the Altai. The Tianshan Mountains traverse the middle region. Xinjiang contains some large basins like the Turpan, the Junggar and the Tarim. The vast grasslands enable this region to be one of China's major stock-breeding centers. Xinjiang's fine-fleeced sheep and horses are well known in China. Mining, oil, and coal in this area are important resources in China.

Some new cities emerged in Xinjiang in the 1950s. The most outstanding example is Shihezi City, which used to be an expanse of wilderness. The city develops farms, factories, roads and housing as well as being a pioneer project of 20 modern factories.

Miaos

The Miao ethnic group's population is about 7,400,000. About half of the Miaos live in Guizhou. Some of them scattered into other provinces such as Yunnan, Guangxi, Guangdong and Sichuan. Their ancestry can be traced back to the "Chiyou" tribe, a primitive society in the Central Plains. Their ancestors began to construct their own kingdom in the lower reaches of the Yangtze River during the Shang (17th century—1046) and Zhou (1046—256 B. C.) Dynasties. They started to migrate to the southern part of China later on. During the Qin (221—207B. C.) and Han Dynasties (206B. C. —220A. D.), their predecessors lived in close communities in western Hunan and eastern Guizhou. They gradually moved westward to settle down where they are now living. Much of the Miao area is hilly or mountainous. Major crops like wheat, rice, paddy, maize, potatoes, peanuts, tobacco, sugar cane and cotton were all planted by them due to a mild climate and sufficient rainfall.

Their language which consiscts of three dialects, was one stream of Miao-Yao group of the Han-Tibetan language family、unfortunately it had lost. The Miaos also utilize mandarine.

They believe in many gods and spirits, and worship their ancestors and dragons. Some of them believe in the Catholic or Christian religion.

The Miaos are musical and dance talents; they have produced many fine music pieces and their famous folk dance is Lusheng Dance, because the dance is accompanied by this reed pipe instrument called Lusheng. Miao's New Year's festival is celebrated in late autumn or early winter, between the 9th and 11th month of the lunar calendar, the date varies from region to region. The theme of the celebration is about good harvest and praying for good weather and prosperity for the next year. The celebration starts from spring cleaning throughout the village and then 3 days festival activities. On the eve of the festival, every family served rich food and wine. Early in the morning of the festival day, families offer the food as sacrifices to their ancestors. After breakfast, it's all about visiting family and friends. Their music and dance highlight the occasion from place to place, there are big parties where women line up in an arc formation to dance meanwhile accompanied by the Lusheng instrument played by men. There are crowd gather in a square, with their traditional costumes and dancing festive dances. As the night comes, the village resounds with rolls from the big bronze drum monted in the towers. These drum rolls ammounce the commencement of another festival activity. Young men are the most active. They tour the villages with lanterns and playing reed-pipes, also they look for girl friends to be their partners in "cross-singing".

The highly artistic works by the Miao people include drawn-work, embroidery, batik printing, paper-cuts and hand-woven patterned work. Their batik printing has a history of more than 1,000years. They developed the technique of using multiple colors in the 1950s.

Men of the Miaos grow their hair long and wear turbans, collarless shirts and loose-fitting trousers. They also like to tie sashes around their waists. The Miao women wear their hair in buns. They wear turbans on their heads and have floral sashes at their waists. They wear decorative accessories of bracelets, earrings and necklaces.

Zhuangs

Having 18 million population, Zhuang is the largest minority group among the 55 ethic group. Half of the Zhuang live in Guangxi Zhuang Autonomous Region, which established in 1958. The rest scattered in Yunnan, Hunan and Guangdong province.

The Zhuangs originally were part of the ancient Yue ethnic group. They used to live throughout a wide area south of the middle and lower reaches of the Yangtze River before the Qin Dynasty (221—207 B. C.).

The language belongs to the Zhuang-Dai branch of the Zhuang-Dong group of the Han-Tibetan language family and includes two major dialects that are similar in grammar and vocabulary. The written language of the Han serves as their script, though a Zhuang script based on the Latin alphabet was worked out in 1955 with the help of the Chinese government. Having an ancient and time-honored culture, the ancestors of the Zhuang began to engage in metal-casting. Characteristic of their splendid culture are their bronze drums and fine brocades. Five hundred ancient drums unearthed in Guangxi are evidence that the Zhuangs had the technique 2,000 years ago. These drums were covered with exquisite pictures and produced resonant sounds. They were used for military, recreational and worship activities. The biggest drum is more than one meter in diameter, and some weigh 500 kilograms. The Zhuang brocades are exquisite and are famous for their unique designs. For instance, their ancient ancestors produced the Flower Hill cliff fresco, located in Guangxi. The ancient drawing was made with hematite powder on the face of a limestone cliff. It depicts more than 1,300 lifelike images of people and animals across the 135 meters long picture.

The arts of embroidery and brocading were done by the Zhuang women as early as the Northern Song Dynasty (960—1127). The Zhuang women were well known in China for their brocading skill at the beginning of the Ming Dynasty.

The songs of the Zhuangs are quite fine and improvised on the spot. The verses of their songs often contain riddles, questions and metaphors. The sacrificial festival and the New Year's festival are happy occasions and are celebrated on a grand scale with singing and dancing. Antiphonal mass singing parties are held with the coming of spring and during the fall each year. Zhuang dances have distinct themes, and forceful and nimble steps. The dances are also characterized by jocular and humorous gestures, and realistic emotion. Their common musical instruments include the Chinese cornet, bronze drum, Chinese wind pipe, vertical bamboo flute, Chinese flute, a stringed instrument made of horse bones, and the cymbal.

Rice and corn constitute their main food. When guests and friends visit the Zhuangs, pork, beef, mutton, salted fish, and pickled meats will be served at meals.

The main colour of their clothes is black. Men wear black turbans and short jackets with buttons down the front. Women wear unique style of decoration, such as earrings, silver hair pins and necklace. They trim their blouses and trousers with lace and tie small aprons around their waists.

Manchu

The Manchu has 9,821,000population. The majority of Manchus reside in Liaoning Province in Northeneast part of china. The rest distributed throughout the country, even in big cities such as Beijing, Chengdu, Guangzhou.

The ancestry of the Manchus can be traced back more than 2,000 years to the Sushen tribe, and later to the Yilou, Huji, Mohe and Nuzhen tribes native to the Changbai Mountains and Heilong River in north-

east China. Middle of the 16th century, a political and military chief called Nurhachi of the Nuzhen tribe unified the whole Nuzhen tribe that scattered all over China for decades of years. Nurhachi initiated the "Eight banner" system of military organization and founded the country of "Kin". In 1635, Huang Taiji (1592—1643) the eighth son of Nurhachi chose the name of "Manchu" to replace Nuzhen for his people. In the following year, when he ascended the throne, he adopted Great Qing the name of his dynasty.

The Manchus originally lived in the forests and mountains in northeast of China, they were good at archery and horsemanship. Children were taught to ride horse and hunting gear at six or seven. Even women were skilled equestrians just as men. Manchus have their own script and language, which belongs to the Manchu-Tungusic group of the Altaic language family. Later in 17 century, as more and more economic and cultural contact between Han and Manchus, many local Manchus picked up Mandarin Chinese too.

Most of the Manchus believe in Shamanism. They also worshiped the Big Dipper, their ancestors and nature. Killing and eating dog meat is forbidden by the Manchus.

The traditional costumes of male Manchus are a narrow-cuffed short jacket over a long gown with a belt at the waist to facilitate horse-riding and hunting. They let the back part of their hair grow long and wore it in a plait or queue. Women coiled their hair on top of their heads and wore earrings, long gowns and embroidered shoes.

There are some famous Manchu novelists. For instance, one of the most important long novels in Chinese history, Dreams of Red Mansions, is written by the great Manchu novelist, Cao Xueqin. It is a great realistic piece of literature reflecting Chinese society during the Qing Dynasty. The novel has been translated into different languages and published in more than 100 countries. It won its place in the history of world literature.

The Manchus are also quite musical. They often sing and dance to the accompaniment of flutes and drums.

Manchu's jade and walnut carvings are also noted for their fine workmanship.

Children were required to regularly pay formal respects to their elders, usually once every three to five days.

Yi

The Yi ethnic group, with a population of 6,672,000 is mainly distributed over the provinces of Sichuan, Yunnan and Guizhou, and the Guangxi Zhuang Autonomous Region. There are more than one million Yis in Sichuan Province.

Historical records written in the Han and the old Yi languages show that the ancestors of the Yi ethical group were closely related with ancient Qiang people in west China. They migrated to south and joined the local southwest inhabitants, in the Wei (220—265) and Jin (265—420) dynasties, they came to be known as "Yi," the character for which meant "barbarian." They lived in the area of Lake Dianchi in Yunnan Province and in Chengdu of Sichuan Province. Around the 8th century, a slave state named "Nanzhao" was established, until 1950, they maintained a feudal and imperialist society in the areas of the Sichuan and Yunna Provinces.

Their language belongs to the Yi branch of the Tibeto-Burman group of the Han-Tibetan language family which includes six different dialects. The Yis used an ancient type of pictographic written script. Today they have a new written script, devised and standardized since the 1950s. A number of works of history, medicine, literature and the genealogies of the ruling families, written in the old Yi script are still seen in most Yi areas. More and more Yi people learned to use the Han language and characters in their daily life due to cultural and economic exchanges with the Han. One achievement of the Yis' literature is Ashima, a long and colorful narrative poem handed down for generations.

An anthropologist discovered that Yi's early stage calendar was a great contribution in analyzing ancient Chinese culture. Yi's ancestors introduced a ten-month calendar ten thousands years ago, the calendar divided each month into 36 days, each season into two months, which is 72 days. The remaining 5 or 6 days are kept for the New Year celebration. This 26 cycle and 72 cycle have influenced the Han Chinese since ancient times and the two numbers are used extensively even today. There are a lot of proverbs and idioms featuring these two figures. For instance, there are 36 Stratagems from the famous ancient works Sunzi Military Stratagems, and there are 72 mythical transformations found in the Monkey King from the famous ancient literature Journey to the West (by Wu Chengen, 1500—1582).

The Yis pray in many gods as well as their ancestors. Some of them living among Han people and believe in Buddhism. People live in the plains, take rice, wheat, maize and yam as their staple food, those reside in mountainous areas, maize, buckwheat and yams are their principal food, they also consume vegetable, fruits, legumes, pork, mutton and beef.

Their costumes show great variety and differ from place to place. Their annual Torch Festival is a celebration of bumper harvests by all the Yis. The festival begins after nightfall when villagers turn out in mass with flaming torches in their hands. They set up pine torches around their fields in order to frighten away the pests and then they sing, dance and drink toasts to each other throughout the night accompanied by a four-stringed plucked instrument with a full-moon-shaped sound box (Yueqin). A very popular dance among them is the Axi Jumps over the Moon. Another important traditional festival is the October New Year. The Yis' New Year falls on the most auspicious day of the last month of Yis'calendar. It is held to celebrate the gathering of the harvest, to offer sacrifices to their ancestors and to pray for favorable weather, and good harvests during the coming year. People slaughter pigs as sacrifices to their ancestors and warm themselves around the fire. Three days later, they begin to exchange visits with relatives and friends, giving presents of meat and wine to each other.

Naxi

The majority population of Naxi nationality in the Yunnan province is of the Naxi nationality. It traces its origins to the Maoniu tribe who lived in the time of the Han Dynasty (206B. C. —220 A. D.). They moved southward and settled in the present Lijiang, Weixi and Zhongdian areas of Yunnan Province in the 7th century.

Some local people in the town play Dongjing Music. Dongjing Music was used in ancient China as part of elaborate musical ritual activities. It was used to promote inner peace and the Taoists adopted it for physical and spiritual exercises. The music used to be popular among the educated elite in China during the Ming and Qing dynasties. The Naxi headman brought the music back from Nanjing city, Fujian and Sichuan provinces during the Jiajing period (1522—1566) of the Ming Dynasty. However, Dongjing music almost did not survive in central China with the spread of western knowledge in the late Qing Dynasty (1644—1911) and the warring years. Fortunately, the Naxi people absorbed and preserved the ancient Han music. In fact, the remaining Dongjing music survived due to the remote and isolated geographical location, the peaceful environment and the intelligence of the Naxi people. Local people set up an Ancient Music Association in 1988 to play Naxi ancient music (Dongjing Music). Some pieces of the Dongjing Music are from the Tang Dynasty (618—907) and the Song Dynasty (960—1279).

The Naxi people today engage in agriculture, handicrafts, husbandry and the tourist industry. The Naxi men dress more or less as their Han compatriots do. The women wear big-sleeved, long and wide jackets and vests, pleated aprons and sheepskin capes embroidered with symbolic constellations representing

their life "under the canopy of the moon and stars. " The Naxi people celebrate their ethnic festivals with vitality in early spring. The ancient traditional culture of the Naxi ethnic group was the Dongba culture, based on the Dongba religion. Some Naxi people believed in Taoism or Buddhism. Their culture was passed on through literature and arts. Called the living fossil of Chinese pictographic characters, the Dongba language belongs to the Yi branch of the Tibeto-Burman group of the Han-Tibetan language family, comprising two dialects and two written scripts known as "Dongba" and "Geba. " The language has more than 1, 300 separate words taking up 20, 000volumes. More than 1, 400 types of scriptures cover the wide fields of religion, philosophy, history, literature, art, astronomy, medicine, calendar, geography, painting, music and local customs.

Chapter 27

Mysterious Tibet

Xuefei Yang, Xiaoxia Mao and Frits Buijs

Section 1 World Eaves

Known as "the Rooftop of the World", "Shangri-La", "the Land of Snows", Tibet has long been seen as a unique place in the eyes and imagination of the World. Tibet (Xizang) in Chinese meaning the "Western Treasure House", lies in the southwest part of the Qinghai-Tibetan Plateau, which is on average over 4,000 meters above sea level and with a geographical area of more than twice that of France, Tibet only has a total population of 2. 7 million (Harper, 2002).

Geography

Tibet is known for the world's highest mountain and has many rivers and beautiful lakes. The northern part is a high plateau, which reaches 5,000 meters above sea level, and contains a wildlife reserve, which takes up 300,000 square kilometers. In the flight from Chengdu (Sichuan Province) to Lhasa, people are awed by the seemingly endless rows of snowcapped, jagged mountain peaks which distinguish Tibet from Sichuan Province. The northern part of Tibet is also famous for its lakes. Nam Co, for example, the largest "holy lake" in the region, is known for its crystal clear blue water and covers almost 2,000 square kilometers and (China. org. cn, 2008). On this colorful high land, people can also find a wealth of rich wildlife, dazzling sunlight and clear blue skies. For instance, one can find large flocks of sheep and herds of cows in the luscious grass meadows and groups of ducks and swans swimming in their natural habitant (China. org. cn, 2008). Due to the breath-taking natural scenery, the "holy lake" attracts endless tourists both from home and abroad.

In the southern, eastern and western parts you find a valley, which is approximately 1200 kilometers long and 300 kilometers wide and the mountains on either side of the valley are usually around 5000 meters high. No wonder it is said that it is common to "travel 3,000 meters vertically to the bottom of the valley to continue the road" (UP, 2007). Beside valleys, the region is also famous for its rivers. For example, the Yarlung Zangbo River which originates in the South Tibet Valley and Yarlung Tsangpo Canyon, and runs downstream to Arunachal Pradesh. Lake Paiku which is 6 kilometers wide at its narrowest point is surrounded by mountains on three sides that reach circa 6,000 meters high. Lake Puma Yumco which literally means "the blue jewel which is floating in the sky" is 13 kilometers wide.

Mount Everest, also called Qomolangma, meaning "Mother Goddess" in the Tibetan language, is the world's highest peak (8,848. 13 meters high) and has the shape of a giant pyramid (China. org. cn, 2008). Mount Everest is part of the Himalaya range and is located at the border between Nepal, Tibet and

China. Every year thousands of climbers visit and climb the Qomolangma. There are mainly two climbing routes namely the northeast and the southeast ridge. Comparatively, the southeast ridge is easier and it is most used by climbers. However, conquering Qomolangma is not an easy thing to do. The death zone of the mountain is a very difficult part for the climber to survive since the temperature there can drop fast and everything will be deeply frozen. Plus with the strong winds, slipping and falling can occur easily. Moreover, the atmospheric pressure on the top of the mountain is very low, so the climbers may encounter the vital problem of lacking oxygen, in one word, exhaustion, extreme cold, lack of oxygen and the dangers of the climb, all make the conquering of the Qomolangma almost impossible. Nevertheless, the unique scenery of Qomolangma has attracted worldwide attention. "Clouds, which often envelope Qomolangma like a shroud, sometimes appear to surge by like a tidal wave, at other times they drift gently away like smoke from a chimney, or other occasions appear not to be moving looking as mysterious as a veiled beauty. Visitors often sit patiently at the foot of Qomolangma for hours simply to catch a glimpse of the spectacular scenes" and "Glaciers, natural treasures in varied shapes, constitute yet another aspect of the majestic scenery of Qomolangma …" (China. org. cn, 2008).

Climate

Tibet used to be a mysterious and isolated area because of its mountains and the climate as well. The climate is severely dry most months of the year. Dust storms frequently appear and sometimes visitors feel that the wind and the sand grinding at the steep, jagged mountains seem to deny human travel. It is only on witnessing the sophistication of the big cities that one discovers what a land of contrasts Tibet is. The western part of Tibet, however, receives a small amount of fresh snow each year. While the northern part of Tibet has the high temperature in summer and the low temperature in winter, the temperature in Tibet can vary as much as 60 degrees from morning to afternoon. Nevertheless, the special and tough geographical and climate conditions coupled with strong solar radiation and frequent high winds, can also offer many prospects for the future development of solar and wind energy inside Tibet.

Economy

The economy is dominated by subsistence agriculture. In the high plateau region, livestock, including sheep, cattle, goats, camels, yaks and horses, is the primary source of income and occupation. Due to limited arable land, it is only in recent years that Tibet has cultivated vegetables in greenhouses to provide sufficient vegetables for its own population. Other main crops grown in Tibet are barley, wheat, buckwheat, rye, potatoes and assorted fruits. Tibetans' main economic support comes from stockbreeding and husbandry. They also produce the highland barley grain called "Qingko." The staple foods of Tibetans are Zanba (parched qingko barley or pea flour mixed with tea and butter), wheat, mutton and beef. In some areas, rice and noodles are also a regular part of the diet. Local residents' favorite hot drink is tea with butter or milk, sour milk and cheese, Zanba and milk tea with butter. Yak is the most common food. The Tibetan diet is simple and dominated by the food which is for hands. For example, the diet of local people mainly consists of yak. During their festivals, local residents drink a wine made from highland barley. The industry that brings the most income is handicrafts which includes Tibetan hats, jewelry (silver and gold), wooden items, clothing, quilts, fabrics and carpets. Recent years have seen a rapidly expanding tourist industry. Especially after the construction of the Qingzang Railway in July 2006, Tibet received 2. 5 million tourists in 2006, including 150,000 foreigners. According to the Chinese Central Government, between 2000 and 2006 the Tibetan economy "grew at an average rate of 12 percent" (CCTV, 2007), which indicates that there exists a good potential for Tibet to develop its economy in the coming years. Lastly, we have to mention that Tibet has a big variety in flora and more than 5, 760 varieties of plants (of which about 50% have economic value).

Transportation

Records show there were no highways in Lhasa, except for a one-km-long clay road before the founding of the People's Republic of China in 1949. In the 1950s, the Chinese army cleared away rock slides and repaired the roads, which were mere trails for yak herders. The Sichuan-Tibet Highway (between Chengdu and Lhasa) and Qinghai-Tibet Highway (between Xining and Lhasa) were opened. The region had more than 43, 000km of highways of highway by the end of 2005 with half of the road at an elevation of 4, 000meters above sea level. It is expected to reach 50, 000km by 2010. In the past, a one-way drive to Tibet took 15 days on the dangerous highway. Nowadays, it only takes 24 hours and the road to Tibet is much better. Lhasa began the first airline flight to Beijing in 1965. Tibet has opened four airports and a dozen air routes to major cities in China. Still Tibet relies heavily on road traffic and the aviation industry cannot satisfy Tibet's increasing development. Because of the special geological and climatic conditions, only one of the highways of the current five national highways connecting to Tibet is open all year round. Transportation had been a bottleneck for the social and economic development. Chinese built Qinghai-Tibet Highway in 2006 which is the "lifeline of Tibet". With the development of its highways, airport and railway, Tibet will soon become a popular tourist destination, which will bring far more change to it. It provides Tibet with a good development opportunity. For instance, a considerable number of Tibetan people still live self-contained lives and over 85 percent of them live in farming areas. The railway will connect Tibet to the vast rail transportation area. Rapid transmission of information will bring great change and improve local people's living condition. It may be the biggest opportunity in recent decades. Tourism, one of the pillar industries of Tibet, will be rapidly developed for the train ticket prices are lower comparing with the high airplane ticket. Tibet relies heavily on external aid from other areas and the transportation cost of goods from other areas will be reduced too. Qinghai-Tibet Railway will be extended from Lhasa to border areas and there are plans to integrate it into the railway networks of neighboring countries. China has become India's second largest trading partner. Indian official announced in June 18, 2006 to reopen the Natu La Pass border trade market closed for more than 40 years. The railway may make Tibet change from a closed frontier region into a potentially huge market in South Asia. It is expected Tibet will appear to be a place of great vigor and vitality.

Despite numerous hardships and difficulties, the Qinghai-Tibet Railway has finally been completed. It will take only 48 hours from Beijing to Lhasa with the test run of the railway on July 1, 2006. Passengers from those cities can now go to Tibet by train after two technical bottlenecks of laying tracks on the frozen earth and carrying out engineering projects. The conditions of insufficient oxygen and severe coldness at high altitude have been overcome when building the railway. When trains travel on the Qinghai-Tibet plateau at an average altitude of over 4, 000meters, some special difficulties to passengers such as low air pressure, insufficient oxygen and strong ultraviolet radiation have been lightened or solved in the train.

During the past 50 years, the Chinese central government has made an effectual attempt at building a substantial infrastructure in Tibet. Tibet is not an isolated part of the earth any more. Televisions are everywhere and the Internet is widely available in the large towns and cities in Tibet. With the rapid development of the travel industry in recent years, Tibet has become more open to the outside world. It received about 390, 000tourists within one month after the Qinghai-Tibet Railway was put into service after July 1, 2006. The region's tourism bureau said Tibet received 16, 700 overseas visitors in July, 2006 and Tibet is at the beginning of a new era.

Lhasa-an ancient city, with a history of over 1,300 years, is the heart and soul of Tibet, an object of devout pilgrimage and a mysterious place to visit for tourists all over the world.

Geography and Climate

Lhasa is home to about 255,000 inhabitants, including Tibetan, Han, Hui people as well as other ethnic groups. Tibetan people take up 87 percent of the total population in Lhasa. Lhasa, which lies on an altitude of 4,000 meters above the sea level, and in the center of the Tibetan Plateau, is the highest city of the world. Due to its high altitude, tourists who visit Lhasa usually have to spend their first day getting used to the low atmospheric pressure and the feeling of being light headed due to the lack of oxygen. With its flat land and mild weather, the city is neither too cold in winter nor too hot in summer. Lhasa is famous as the 'city of the sunlight' (China. org. cn, 2008) as it receives 3,000 hours sunlight annually. The sun is so intense that visitors may feel it burn the skin even on cool days and time seem to lose its relevance and be marked less by the clock than by the sun in the blue sky. The rainy season comes in July and lasts for three months and it is regarded as the best reason of the year since it rains mostly at night and is sunny again during the day. The city lies near the Lhasa River known as the 'merry blue waves,' which runs through the snow covered mountains and finally ends in the Yarlung Zangbo River. The vortex of color, refreshing air and the beautiful environment of Lhasa allow visitors' imagination to soar as high as the snowcapped peaks.

As Lhasa is a rich museum featuring ancient ruins, ancient architecture, ancient monasteries, ancient stone tablets and ancient gardens (CTIC, n. d.). The city has more than 100 scenic spots altogether, which make Lhasa an attractive and mysterious place to visit. No wonder that after arriving, visitors are usually interested in walking in the parks and visiting Buddhist monasteries.

Potala Palace

Potala Palace is a well known palace and fortress. Built by Songtsan Gambo for his bride Princess Wen Cheng in the 7th century, Potala Palace covers an area of 102. 5 acres. Legend says that Potala was supposed to be the residence of Avalokitesvara or Guan Yin who is supposed to be the father of the Tibetans and reincarnated as King Srongtsan Gambo (UP, 2007). Built at an altitude of 3, 700 meters, stretching 400 meters from east to west and 350 meters from north to south on the side of Marpo Ri ('Red Mountain') in the center of Lhasa Valley, the main building is made of stone and wood and has 13 stories measuring 110 meters high and the inside the building contains a 1,000 rooms and 10,000 shrines. The roof of the magnificent palace is covered with gilded bronze tiles.

Potala Palace is composed of the White Palace and the Red Palace. The White Palace was painted white to resemble peace and quiet and is used for political affairs and daily life (Travel China Guide, 2007). It has seven floors and was first built during the lifetime of the Fifth Dalai Lama in 1649. It was expanded in size by the Thirteen's Dalai Lama during the early 20th century. The entire Palace is for Dalai Lamas of various generations to live and handle government and Buddhist affairs (CTIC, n. d.). The fourth Floor is the largest hall (The Grand East Hall) is the site for holding momentous religious and political events. The fifth and sixth floors are offices and the top floor consists of the East Chamber of Sunshine and the West Chamber of Sunshine. They were the places where the Dalai Lama studied, lived and worked (Travel China Guide, 2007).

The Red Palace is completely used for religious affairs, such as religious studies and Buddhist prayer. Major buildings in the Red Palace include the Hall for the Holy Stupas, four chapels, and three galleries on each floor of the Red Palace. The Hall for the Holy Stupas, also called The Saint's Chapel, is the holiest shrine of the Potala Palace. Granted as "a grand building in the world", the stupas is 14.85 meters high, and it is totally wrapped with 110,000 taels of gold and inlaid with 1,500 gems (CTIC, n.d.). The inner walls which are nicely painted to describe the glory and power of the Fifth Dalai Lama and the corridors which also contain religious murals, such as the figure of Buddha, Bodhisattvas and Dalai Lamas. They tell stories of Buddhism and historical events, such as the marriage between Songtsan Gambo and Princess Wen Cheng, and the Fifth Dalai Lama's visit to Emperor Shunzhi in Beijing in 1652 (Travel China Guide, 2007). There are four chapels around the Hall for the Holy Stupas. The North Chapel centers on a crowned Sakyamuni Buddha on the left and the Fifth Dalai Lama on the right. The stupa tombs of the Eighth, Ninth and Eleventh Dalai Lama are also situated there. The South Chapel is dedicated to Padmasambhava, the 8th century Indian monk and saint who introduced Esoteric Buddhism to Tibet. The East Chapel centers on Tsong Khapa, founder of the Gelug tradition. His two meter high figure is surrounded by lamas who briefly ruled Tibet in the past. The Western Chapel contains five golden stupas. The biggest stupa, which is 14.85 meters high, contains the mummified body of the Fifth Dalai Lama, and is covered by more than 3,000 kilograms gold foil and decorated with thousands of pearls, gems, corals, ambers and agates, which is also the most luxurious tomb (Travel China Guide, 2007). The first and third galleries on different floors show murals and collections of bronze statues and figures respectively, while the second gallery is used for visitors to rest and buy souvenirs.

Since 1959 the central committee of the Chinese Communist Party and China's State Council repaired and protected the Potala palace and in 1988 special funds were granted to Tibet for a large scale repair of the Palace (CTIC, n.d.). Between 1989 and 1994 the central government spent 53 million Yuan and tons of gold to repair the Potala Palace as the first stage of the renovation project. In 1994 the Potala Palace was inscribed to the UNECSO World Cultural Heritage List. In 2002 the second phase of the renovation project started and it was finished in 2006.

Jokhang Monastery

Jokhang Monastery (Da Zhao Temple) is a famous Buddhist temple located in the center of Lhasa. During its construction in 647, to commemorate the marriage of the Tang Princess Wen Cheng to King Songtsan Gambo, it was called the Tsulag Khang or "House of Wisdom". After several renovations, the monastery now is a combination of large buildings covering more than 25,000 square meters and nowadays it is also known as the Jokhang which means the "House of the Lord". In 2000 it was listed by UNESCO as a world culture heritage site and the monastery is also regarded as the spiritual center of Lhasa. Together with the Potala Palace, Jokhang Monastery is another popular tourist attraction in Lhasa.

Adopting the architectural style of the Tang Dynasty as well as the style of Nepal and India, the monastery has four stories with gilded tiles of bronze on the roofs. The Jokhang temple complex has several decorated shrines and rooms, and standing in the square of the Monastery, one can view the entire complex. There is a path leading all the way to the main hall on the eastern side of the yard. The most important room however, is the Hall of Sakyamuni, which is 1,300 years old. Above the main entrance there is a "Dharma Wheel" confined between two deer's, which represents the unity of all things and symbolizes Sakyamuni himself (TravelChinaGuide, 2007). The statue of Sakyamuni at the age of 12 sits in the middle of the hall. On the second floor you will find several famous statues, such as Chenresig, King Songtsan Gambo and his two foreign wives, Princess Wen Cheng and Princess Bhrikuti of Nepal. There are four giant golden tops crafted in the Tang style during the mid 14th century and the 17th century on the top

floor. Located in the center of the Lhasa city, the tower with golden tops is like a holy bird spreading its wings in the sunshine

The Jokhang Monastery is a crowded place for worship in contrast to the Potala Palace. It is surrounded by a colorful entourage of monks, pilgrims and venders. One can see pilgrims with their prayer wheels walking around the Jokhang Monastery chanting scriptures. Some pilgrims even bow and then prostrate themselves on the ground every few steps as they circle the temple. To the curious visitors, the worship itself and the variety of costumes is a cultural vortex in Jokhang Monastery. People may feel as if the history of Tibet passed before their eyes after visiting Potala Palace and Jokhang Monastery.

Norbuilingka Park

Norbulingka, meaning treasure garden in the Tibetan language, is situated in the western suburb of Lhasa city. Built by the Seventh Dalai Lama in the 1740s, the park occupies an area of 360,000 square meters with 374 rooms and it is the biggest manmade garden in Tibet. As it is also a garden where the Eighth Dalai Lama used to live, exercise politics and hold festivals during summer, it is also called the 'Dalai Summer Palace' (CTIC, n. d.).

The park is divided into three parts: the palace area, the area in front of the palace and the forest area. Forests make up about 50% of the park. The main buildings such as the Golden Palace, the New Palace and Sutra Hall were constructed in 1954, and the palaces are heavily painted with murals which show strong Han characteristics. The theme of the murals includes Tibetan officials, Sakyamuni, preaching under a Bodhi tree, Tibetan history from its founding by the Holy Monkey, the vicissitudes of Tubo Kingdom (633—844), Tibetan Buddhism to Panchen Lama and Dalai Lama's interviews with Chairman Mao Zedong in Beijing (Greatwalltours, 2007). Norbulingka Park does not only reflect the ethnical and religious features of Tibet, but also embodies the architectural style of inland China. In 2001 it was listed by UNESCO as a World Cultural Heritage site.

Barkhor Street

Situated in the center of Lhasa, the Barkhor Street has a history of more than 1,300 years. The street was built in the 7th century when the Tibetan King, Sontsen Gampo, decided to construct the monastery. He brought his family and servants to settle there in order to supervise the project. Due to the magnificence of his project, thousands of Buddhist pilgrim were attracted, and as a result a trodden path appeared. Even today, there are still many pilgrims holding the prayer wheels and walking clockwise from dusk to dark (Travel China Guide, 2007). People built houses in the area, and over time, it became a religious and commercial center of Lhasa. Today the streets around here are the hub of Lhasa's commercial zone and around the circuit are shops, teahouses and hawkers. Numerous interesting goods can be bought in the market such as, souvenirs, ornaments, Tibetan knives, Tibetan robes and hats, tapestries, religious musical instruments, gold and silver ware and prayer wheels (Greatwalltours, 2007). Life styles of the old city are still preserved there. It is said that the Barkhor is 'essentially a pilgrim circuit that proceeds clockwise around the periphery of the Jokhang Temple' (Harper, 2002). The Barkhor Street is not only the largest market place in Lhasa, it is also a place full of religious atmosphere.

There are so many other lamaseries to see in Lhasa and so little time to show them to most visitors. Three famous lamaseries among them are Gandan Lamasery, Drepung Lamasery and Sera Lamasery. In those temples, visitors can enjoy the yak butter sculpture (Suyouhua), appliquéd embroidery, and murals; all of which are famous treasures in Tibet. In temples, visitors will find ribbons in the hands of some Buddhas. They are called "hada," which are the most precious gifts to the Honourable.

Most Tibetans live in the Tibetan Autonomous Region. The rest are scattered throughout the Qinghai, Gansu, Yunnan and Sichuan provinces. The minorities in Tibet are the Lhoba, Naxi, Moinba, Hui, and Nu. Originally the Tibetans lived in close communities in the area along the Yarlung Zangbo River. Tibetans are an old nationality in China. According to historical records, their ancestors gathered along the banks of the middle reach of the Brahmaputra before the Qin and Han Dynasties (about 2,000 years ago). Tibet first entered the period of the slave society during the 6th century. The Yarlung tribe assumed leadership of the local tribes and selected a leader called "Btsan-po" (king). Tibetans came into contact with Hans and other ethnic groups during that period.

The Yalung tribe became more powerful and its leader, King Srong-btsan Sgam-po, welded its disparate tribes into a monarchy. He unified all of Tibet under his rule by founding the Tufan Dynasty. It was at approximately this time that the Tang Dynasty was at its height of power. The Tufan had frequent contacts with the Tang Dynasty. These contacts ultimately resulted in royal marriages. The marriage between Princess Wencheng from the Tang imperial court to a Tibetan king has been legend in Chinese history. In 634 AD, Songzan Ganbu, king of Tufan, sent an envoy to Chang'an (Xi'an), the capital of the Tang regime, and asked for his marriage to the imperial princess of the Tang Dynasty to be arranged. After quite some years and much hesitation by the Tang court, Songzan Ganbu finally saw the arrival of Princess Wencheng. They married in 641 AD when the king was 25. When Princess Wencheng first arrived in Tibet, she found the capital was largely swampland where grass and weeds abounded. Only a few buildings can be found there. Princess Wencheng set up her tent on a piece of sandy ground as a palace. She had in her retinue a large number of Chinese craftsmen and she assisted the king with the construction of the capital. Soon after, the city quickly developed into a prosperous place. Princess Wencheng was given credit for Lhasa's emergence as an ancient city. Under the influence of Princess Wencheng, her husband became more and more deeply involved in Buddhism. The result was that many temples, run by professional monks, began to appear in many parts of Tibet. Indian monks and inland Chinese monks arrived in increasing number too. With the help of the princess, the Great Brightness Temple and the Little Brightness Temple were built in Lhasa. Some hospices were put up near the Jolhang Temple for pilgrims from afar, and houses for many local residents were built nearby. It formed the beginning of the old quarter of Lhasa, centering round what is known as Octogon Street. Songzan Ganbu then started building extensions on his old palace on Red Mountain-the magnificent Potala Palace's earliest form. Both the geographical position and the climatic conditions make Lhasa the best choice for the site of the capital. Lhasa, also known as "Sunlight City," has the famous Potala Palace (built 1,300 years ago) and some Buddhist temples. The Potala Palace, the Buddhist temples of Jokhang Monastery (built in the middle of the 7th century), Zhaxi Lhumbo (1447, the largest temple of the Yellow Sect), Drepung Monastery and Sagya display Tibet's brilliant culture and architectural forms. For instance, Potala Palace, 13-stories of majestic construction with towers as high as 170 meters, is composed of unique edifices built layer upon layer. The New Palace in Norbu Lingka (Treasure Garden) was once the Summer Palace of the Dalai Lama.

King Khri Idegtsug btsan of Tibet married Princess Jin Cheng of the Tang court in 710. Such events served to build closer ties between the Tufan and Tang dynasties. These two princesses introduced Han culture and production techniques to Tibet. The Tufan also sent young people to study at Chang'an (Xi'an) and invited Han artisans to offer instructions in their techniques.

A slave uprising broke out in Tibet and the Tufan Dynasty was overthrown during the later half of the

9th century. Local warlords set up their own independent regimes and were constantly in conflict with each other for more than 300 years. In the meanwhile frequent contacts with all the Tibetan factions were maintained and economic and trade relations were established during the Song Dynasty (960—1279).

Tibet was formally incorporated into China's domain as an administrative area during the Yuan Dynasty (1279—1369). In 1253, the first Yuan emperor granted the titles of "Imperial Tutor" and "Prince of Dharma," on separate occasions to the religious leader of Tibet and left him in control of the Tibetan area. The Yuan emperor also established a unified local Tibetan regime marking the beginning of the merging of clerical and secular ruling in Tibet.

The Ming court (1368—1644) preserved the Yuan system of administration in Tibet by taking over its government organs and institutions. The first Qing emperor conferred on the Tibetan religious leader (the Fifth Dalai Lama) an honorific title and set up a council to take charge of the administration of Tibet in 1653. After this in 1791 the Qing court promptly sent a large expedition to Tibet to drive out all the invaders from Chinese territory.

The government of the Republic of China set up a Commission for Mongolian and Tibetan Affairs in 1912. The central government granted the title to the late Dalai (after the death of the 13th Dalai) and dispatched an official to pay homage to his memory in 1933. The Tibetan local government signed a 17 article agreement with the Central People's Government to bring about the peaceful liberation of Tibet.

Tibet was a serf society under the rule of feudal manorial lords and the production and economy were stagnating before 1950. Most people lived in dire poverty. The population steadily declined and existed of about one million in 1950. The democratic reform of 1959 led to the abolition of the feudal system. The reforms ended the long standing feudal system and emancipated all the serfs and slaves. Great changes have taken place in Tibet after Chinese intervention. Take Lhasa as example, it has now developed into a medium sized city covering an area of 52 square kilometers and is home to 2,574,000 people.

Tibetan medicine and pharmacology occupy an important place among China's minority nationalities. A number of Tibetan medical books have been edited and published. Progress has been made in the research and production of Tibetan medicines. Some of them are effective in curing gastric ulcers, hypertension, tracheitis and arthritis. The famous works such as Tibetan Astronomy and Calendrical Calculations and The Four Volume Medical Canon have been collated and published too. A hospital of Tibetan medicine with an affiliated research institute has been established in Lhasa with the support of the government. The research institute has produced more than 300 different kinds of local drugs for the local people.

Tibetans have their own language and writing. Their language belongs to the Tibeto Burman group of the Han Tibetan language family. The language is composed of three dialects that represent three administrative areas. The earliest written script of Tibetans is dated back to the 7th century.

The Tibetan culture has a long history and is rich in content. The vast amount of literary heritage in existence today includes about 25,000 volumes of complete works, including biographies, historical and religious writing, folk rhymes, poems, maxims, fables, folk stories, dramas, as well as works on medicine, astronomy, and treatises on grammar and orthography. Folk literary works such as The Biography of King Gesar and Sakye Motto written in Tibetan are treasured in the world of literature. The Chinese government has supported to preserve and sort out Tibetan culture. A dozen classical Tibetan works, including The Story of Gesser Khan, The Story of Nor-bzang, Sakya's Maxims with Notes, The Story of Six Youths, The Story of a Monkey and a Bird, The Story of Milarepa, The Story of Young Zla-med have been published. Their colorful customs and folk arts are fascinating to the world too. The Tibetan publishing house, established in 1971, also collected and re-edited a large number of folk rhymes, maxims and folk tales. A number of classical Tibetan plays have been refined and re-staged to win mass appeal in China and abroad.

In the 1950s, and especially after 1976, the Chinese government did much to preserve and interpret Tibetan culture. A special fund was also used to finance the renovation of the historic monuments in Tibet. A large number of their works have been collected and re-edited. Some Tibetan plays have been refined and re-staged to win mass appeal. The well-known ancient monasteries like Potala Palace, Drepung, Sera and Trashilumpo have been repaired a number of times in the past decades. Currently, every village has its own primary school and every county has its own middle school. Most primary schools offer at least four cour-ses—Tibetan, Chinese, math and English. Tibetan students are exempted from tuition fees.

Section 4 Religion

Religious rituals are numerous in Tibet. Visitors may observe pilgrims prostrating themselves before the gates of a temple or circling around a religious monument on their knees for several hours each day. Wandering down the corridors and through the numerous temples, people can hear the melodic chant of sacred scriptures and the rhythmical beat of ceremonial drums. They can hardly forget the light from the tem-ple windows filtered through the smoke of burning incense, illuminating the faces of devoted monks.

Most Tibetans believe in Lamaism (a branch of Buddhism). "Dalai" means vast sea in Mongolian. "Lama" means "teacher" or "superior being." Lamaism is divided into five sects: Red, Flowery, Black, White and Yellow. Each sect has a head lama known as the Living Buddha to control its own sect. For the Yellow sect, the two Living Buddhas are Dalai and Bainqen Erdeni. Tsong Kha-pa (1357—1419) was the founder of the Yellow Sect of Lamaism. When he was alive, he had two famous disciples named Dalai and Panchen. They were deemed the reincarnations of him and succeeded to the throne of the Living Buddha af-ter his death. They were titled, the First Dalai Lama and the First Panchen Erdeni. Afterwards, the titles were inherited by the succeeding Living Buddhas. The Fourteenth Dalai Lama and the Eleventh Panchen Er-deni exist today. On each side of the statue of Tsong Kha-pa is a throne; the one on the left was for the Dalai Lama when he came to preach; the one on the right was for the Panchen Erdeni.

The Fifth Dalai Lama (1617—1682) declared, when a Dalai Lama dies, his spirit passes into an in-fant boy, born at the moment of the Dalai Lama's death. In order to find the right child, the dying Dalai Lama would predict information about looking for the child. The investigation lasted for years since there were many babies born at the same moment. Two notable features of an acceptable or ideal baby were a large head and generous ears to indicate wisdom. Objects belonging to the Dalai Lama were identified to es-tablish whether the child was the living incarnation of the Dalai Lama. When the baby was two to six years of age, he would be brought to Lhasa from his home for training. The parents were also brought to Lhasa and given a noble status. The Regents exercised full power until the Lama reached the age of eighteen.

To avoid the many disadvantages of this method of choosing the Dalai Lama, Emperor Qianlong intro-duced a new method of "drawing lots from the gold urn" in 1792. Many children were selected from various places after the death of the Living Buddha. Each child had a lot with his name inscribed on it. The lots were to be put into a gold urn and lamas were to recite Buddhist scriptures. It was a process to reincarnate the death according to Buddhists' beliefs. While people were watching, the high commissioners sent by the em-peror would pick up the lot that was dropped out of the shaking urn and show it to the people. The child with his name on the dropped lot would be the reincarnation of the Living Buddha.

Buddhist influence has penetrated every sphere of social life including their manner of behavior and cus-toms, since almost all the Tibetans believe in Buddhism. It may be difficult for some visitors to fathom the degree of devotion of these people's religious beliefs. It is equally difficult to imagine the will that impels pilgrims to travel for months on foot to worship at one of Tibet's many religious centers.

In the 1950s, the government formulated a policy for political unification, and for the separation of religion from civil administration. According to the law, Chinese have freedom of religious belief. However, during the "Cultural Revolution" (1966—1976), people's freedom of religious belief was not protected. The government changed its "leftist" policy and protects Tibetans' normal religious activities again from 1978.

Most Tibetan festivals are religious (their New Year is November 1st according to their own calendar). Tibetans celebrate these festivals with religious singing and dancing. Their many folksongs are varied and with a wide range of subjects. People accompany the songs with their own unique musical instruments. For instance, the Raba dance is a vigorous local dance popular in Tibet. Women beat a flat drum while dancing and men do stunts. Their unique traditions, lifestyle and culture are even preserved until today. During the annual August Fruit Awaiting Festivals, Tibetans hold grand celebrations for their harvest. National songs and dances are widely performed.

Section 5　The Local Residents and Their Lives

The Local Residents

Tibet has a population of 2.81 million (CTIC, 2006) with 400,000 living in Lhasa city and suburbs. Visitors have their first encounter with Tibetan life the moment they step off the airplane. They may notice an old Tibetan farmer chasing some yaks off the runway, or a woman with her children passing by. Suddenly, a Tibetan man riding a donkey appears. To visitors, the most striking part of Tibet is its people. They may be captivated by a group of yak herders wearing traditional Tibetan clothes with embroidered hats and boots. Even the yaks seem to be in costume with their intricately stitched harnesses and red tassels hanging from both horns.

Although they endured centuries of hardship, the people of Tibet are friendly to visitors coming from all over the world. Their warmth and openness is accentuated by the contrast with the rugged and intimidating landscape. The smile of a toothless herdsman, and especially the warmth and devotion in his eyes, must be experienced firsthand to fully connect with the local people and their culture. Whenever foreign visitors stop in villages, curious local children will appear with their inquisitive eyes staring at the visitors. The juxtaposition of the traditional with the very new can be perceived as well. It is normal to see an older woman traditionally dressed walking along with her daughter talking into a cell phone since the Tibetan young people are dressed in the latest fashions.

Tibetan Food

Due to the high altitude of Tibet, the water boils at 90°C, which makes cooking with water impossible, so the diet and food of Tibet are also unique (UP, 2007). The Tibetans mainly eat meat, milk and other high-protein foods.

The basic Tibetan meal is tsampa, a kind of dough made with roasted barley flour and yak butter with water and teror beer. There are two main ways of preparing and eating the tsampa. One is to make a tsampa dough with the Tibetan buttered tea. Sometimes, curds or sugar is used to add flavor. The other is to make porridge together with beef or mutton and vegetables such as turnip (CTIC, 2008). Tsampa is eaten with fingers. For visitors, the food is worth trying, however only a Tibetan can eat it everyday and still look forward to the next meal (CTIC, 2008).

In winter, the Tibetan people live on meat which contains heat energy, such as dried beef and mutton, in order to withstand the coldness. Due to the dry deep winter, bacteria in the meat are killed so usually the dried meat is eaten raw. Figure meat is also a common food in Tibet. Fresh meat is boiled in a pot together with ginger, salt and other spices. People take the meat by hands and cut it with knives. Honorable guests will be served the tails of white sheep. Other meat, such as sausages are also served by the Tibetans and there are four types of sausages, namely, blood, meat, flour and lever (UP, 2007).

Tibetan families also consume a good amount of milk products. Normally speaking, milk is drunk fresh or made into other products, such as Yoghurt, butter and curds (CTIC, 2008). Butter and curds can be used for food or drink with tsampa or tea. As mentioned in the famous poem, the story of Gesar, Yogurt has been a Tibetan food for more than a thousand years old (UP, 2008).

Clothes

Having lived in the Qinghai Tibetan Plateau for centuries, the Tibetan people made their own unique costume which reflects their history, culture and the characters of the local people.

A Robe is a typical Tibetan cloth which is made of sheep skin or wool and it is common for people living in the northern part of Tibet to wear it. A sheepskin is usually sun baked and then cleaned and soaked before it is tailored to wear (UP, 2007). As there is a huge temperature difference between day and night, the robe is used as a quilt during the night since it is very long and warm. Interesting enough, the robe has two big pockets with one in the front and the other at the back for people to carry things, including a five or six year old child (UP, 2007). When it is getting hot during the daytime people wear their left sleeve only and expose the right shoulder.

Tibetan farmers who live in the warm climate of the south wear woolen clothes with the buttons sewn to the right. Men's clothes are hemmed in colorful cloth or with silk at the collar, cuffs, front, and lower edges. While women wear sleeveless outwear except for cold winter (Zhang, 2007).

Tibetan people like to wear jewelries, considering a beautiful dress with colorful ornaments as the symbol of beauty and wealth (Zhang, 2007). Nowadays, under the influence of Buddhism, the Tibetan people like to make use of red, yellow, orange, blue, and dark green for articles of personal ornament. For instance, gu'a, (amulet) is worn by young people, they wear them at the chest because it is believed that gu'a can guard its wearer and bring him/her fortune (Zhang, 2007).

Chapter 28

Traditional Chinese Minority Festivals

Xuefei Yang, Xiaoxia Mao and Frits Buijs

China is a country with a territory of 56 nationalities. Some festivals are national, some are regional and some are only observed by certain ethnic groups. The 56 nationalities have their common festivals and their own specific festivals. Their traditional festivals fall roughly into three categories: agricultural, religious and social festivals.

Section 1 Nadamu Festival

The Nadamu Festival is a traditional and the biggest festival in Mongolia. It is usually celebrated in July when the pastures have plenty of water, lush grass and thriving herds. Nadamu is not only a Mongolian term for entertainment, but also used to be a test of courage and strength for nomadic people and warriors for centuries (Zunduisuren, 2006). The Xiongnu frequently invaded the mainland of northern China during the Han Dynasty (206 B. C. —202 A. D.). In order to establish peaceful relations between the Hans and the Xiongnus, the Han emperor was willing to accept the application of the Xiongnus by arranging Wang Zhaojun, one of the emperors wives, to marry the chief of the Xiongnu people (Mongolian people). Wang Zhaojun was said to be one of the four beauties in ancient China. Nadamu entertainments were offered by the Xiongnu to honor the marriage and archery, hose racing and wrestling were introduced in the Nadamu entertainments.

The first emperor of the Yuan Dynasty (1206—1368) would hold archery, horse racing or wrestling matches whenever he called a conference with the Mongol Khans to make appointments, enact laws, remove officials, reward the meritorious or punish the guilty. The Nadamu Festival celebration was held on a larger scale with richer content and shaped in a new form during the Qing Dynasty (1616—1911). It began to be organized regularly and officially. The governments of the township, county and prefecture might hold their own Nadamu Festival celebrations once a year or once every three years. Winners were given various types of prizes ranging from a sheep or pieces of brick tea to a silvery-white camel with a silver ring on its nose and pearls, silks, jewels and satins on its back. The winner was to be granted such honorary titles as "a wrestler fierce as a tiger" or "a wrestler fierce as a lion. "

As the festival means "three manly games", the Nadamu Festival is marked by three traditional events, namely, wrestling, horse racing and archery. They are the only ones that are held throughout the country. Other games such as horse lassoing, track and field sports, tug of war, volleyball, basketball, motorcycling, are also played in many different cities.

Wrestling

At the beginning of a wrestling match, some knight-like men strode once around the area shouting "The best wrestlers come and wrestle!" Immediately, two wrestlers jump into the arena waving their arms. They pitch into a tough competition to deafening cheers from the audience after shaking hands with each other. The beautiful traditional clothes wrestlers wear include leather or canvas jackets dotted with bronze nail heads, short three-color skirts, loose embroidered silk trousers and high boots. Genghis Khan was a good wrestler when he was young. When he selected and checked military commanders, wrestling was an important component. Common Mongolians viewed it as one of the three skills a man should master. The game spread through many mid-Asian countries in the middle of the 13th century.

Horse racing

Horse racing is another fascinating part of the Nadamu Festival and the game itself is one of the most rejoiced and honored traditions in Mongolia. The playing field for the game is spacious with colorful flags around the starting and the finishing line. There are 6 six races for horses of different ages, and each race has about 400 horses in average participating and the race distance varies depending on the age of the horses. (Steppes travel, 2007). All the competitors are teenagers who present a youthful and martial bearing with turbans on their heads and colorful ribbons around their waists. They stand abreast along the starting line with their horses beside them. At the sound of the starter's horn, they mount their own horses at lightning speed and whip the animals as they gallop towards the finishing line. The competitors' horses run as fast as a discharged arrow flies. The first competitor to reach the finish line is granted the title "a valiant rider on the prairie."

Archery

Most Mongolians are good archers since they have been living by hunting in the vast grasslands from generation to generation and the sport of archery originated around the 11th century, during the time of the Khanate warfare (CSEN, 2007). With the advanced production and technology, archery is more used as a game than a means of living by the Mongolians in the past decades. Archery competitors dress in traditional costumes and use a bent bow constructed of horn, bark, and wood during the game. Women are also allowed to participate and the distance from the stand to the target is different between men and women. Usually men shot from 75 meters and women from 60 meters and an archer who shoots in the target more than others becomes Champion or Mergen. (CSEN, 2007).

| Section 2 | Aobao-Worshipping Festival (Ebo-Worshipping Festival, the Takele'en Festival) |

"Aobao" in the Mongolian language means a stone pile or bulging pile. It is a sort of solid, conical pagoda piled up with stones or adobes, wicker baskets of sand, or trees. A wooden pole at the top of the pagoda reaches over three meters high. On the top of the wooden pole hang colored strips of cloth with sentences of scripture on them. They were used as road signs or boundary markers as they were usually erected near wide thoroughfares or on hills. Later on, they were vested with religious implications and became places for people to offer sacrifices to the mountain god or the road god.

The early Mongolian people believed Aobao was the residence of gods. Therefore they were extremely pious in offering sacrifices. People would pay homage to the gods by adding some stones or lumps of earth

when passing by. They may take a little stone from the Aobao with them before going on a long journey hoping it would keep them safe.

Aobao Festival, which takes place from April to June of each lunar year, is the traditional worshipping festival of the Evenki ethnic minority, who mostly reside in Heilongjiang Province and the Inner Mongolia Autonomous Region in Northeast China (Zhu & Sun, 2005).

People of all ages will offer sacrifices to Aobao when there is an abundance of grass and water in spring and autumn. They insert twigs in the Aobao, hang flags with lections on them, display Buddha portraits and make offerings of all kinds. Lamas burn incense and chant Buddhist scripts. People walk around the Aobao three times, praying for happiness. They offer valuable goods, such as livestock, jade, coins or crops, to the gods of heaven and earth, hoping the deities will bring them happiness and health. At the end of the sacrificial offerings, traditional festivities are performed. The herdsmen dance and sing to their hearts' content and young people take the opportunity to look for the partner of their hearts. Nowadays, the Aobao Meeting is considered more as mass entertainment rather than religious worship, featuring sport activities and commercial events that are similar to the Mongolian Nadam Fair (Zhu & Sun, 2005).

Section 3　Lesser Bairam (Ruz Festival, the Festival of Feast-breaking)

Lesser Bairam is one of the three major Islamic festivals. It falls on the 1st day of the 10th month of the Islamic calendar and lasts three days. The festival is celebrated by the Muslims of Hui, Uygur and some other minorities in China.

The holy month of fast for Muslims is the 9th month of the Muslim year called Ramadan. That month is believed to be when the Koran was revealed as guidance for Muslims. The Muslim canons require every Muslim adult to fast during Ramadan. People don't take any food or water from sunrise to sunset throughout the fasting days. Some people such as children, pregnant women, the sick and the aged are not required to fast. Smoking, drinking and conjugal relations are also banned during the fasting hours. Muslims are required to resist selfish desires and rid themselves of evil thoughts during this holy month to demonstrate their filial piety to Allah. Muslims spend the night repeating the prayers, reading the Koran and giving praise to God.

The new moon appearing on the 29th or the 30th of Ramadan marks the beginning of the Lesser Bairam and the consummation of the fast. If the moon happens to be shadowed by clouds, the fast is to be prolonged one to three additional days. Muslims clean the mosques, streets, and courtyards in the Lesser Bairam. They also bathe themselves and put on new and beautiful clothes to go for the festival prayers. Male Muslims in their holiday best go to the fields or assemble in the mosques for special prayers on the very first day of the festival. They visit their friends and call on each other to exchange holiday greetings. They also visit the tombs of their kin. During the following few days, female Muslims visit their friends and relatives. Muslims of Hui, Salar and Dongxiang nationalities entertain their guests with foods such as chicken, mutton, fried cakes, deep-fried dough sticks, almonds, fruit and tea, while the Uygurs usually treat their guests by preparing raisins, almonds, honey and milk tea. Young people give various festival performances during the holidays. Some of them favor the Lesser Bairam as their wedding day.

Section 4　Corban Festival (Zai Sheng Jie, Xian Sheng Jie)

The Corban Festival is an important Islamic festival. It lasts three days, from the 10th of the 12th month according to the Islam calendar. The festival is observed by the Islamic peoples in Xingjiang, Qinghai,

Ningxia and Gansu in northwestern China.

The Corban Festival is known as Erde Corban. "Erde" means festival, and "corban" means the slaughtering of sacrificial animals. The festival derives from an Arab legend. A Prophet of the Arab people called Ibrahim dreamed that Allah ordered him to kill his son as a sacrifice to test his loyalty on the 10th of the 12th month of the Islamic calendar. Ibrahim decided to do as he had been ordered on the day. Allah was moved by his devoutness and had a black lamb sent to him. Allah told him to kill it instead. Later, Arabs celebrate the Corban Festival every year to express their gratitude to Allah for his kindness.

Muslim families sweep their houses, slaughter sheep or cattle, fry dough rings, and toast pancakes to mark the occasion. People dress in their finest clothes after a Muslims bathe and go to a mosque for services early on each morning of the festival days. Amid clarion and melodious music, they shake hands, embrace and exchange words when they gather at the gate of a mosque. Then they follow an imam into the mosque hall to hold the festive rite, watch the slaughter of the sacrificial animal and listen to the imam chanting from the Koran. The rich slaughter a sheep, a cow or a camel after the rite as an offering to the imams and other Muslim leaders, relatives or friends. The bones and blood are to be buried to keep them sacred.

Muslims usually visit their relatives or friends with gifts. The hosts treat their guests to mutton, deep-fried cakes and fruit. While taking the foods, they cordially exchange blessings. Young Muslims sing and dance in the courtyards or on the grounds late into the night.

Xinjiang's Uygurs hold their grand entertainments in a particular way. They set up colored canopies, cloth tents and wooden board sheds around the entertainment area. Various refreshments like roasted stuffed buns, Shashliks, deep fried dough rings, cold noodles and all kinds of fresh and dried fruits are displayed on the wooden desks or carpets in the tents or under the canopies. All the foods are for the holidaymakers. Sala is an old group dance for men among the three ethnic dances. Wearing colorful costumes, red and green striped triangular aprons, the dancers make rhythmical movements to the left and to the right. The dancers shout "Hey! Hey!" to rhythmic drumbeats and other local musical strains. Another dance called Sailem is mainly performed by female dancers. Wearing colorful embroidered hats, silk jackets, silk skirts and glistening head ornaments, the dancers dance to varied musical strains. The doulangsailem is a group dance performed by people of all ages. It consists of varied whirling or leaping movements.

People in Xinjiang also participate in sports such as goat wrestling and horse racing during the festival. Before the goat wrestling begins, a venerable elder prays for the success of the competitors, while the competitors on horseback give their blessing to him. Then he places a small goat at a designated spot. The competitors race their horses toward the goat on the crack of a starting gun. Competitors try to wrestle away the goat from the one who has seized it. The winner is the one who reaches the appointed spot with the goat in his hand. He would treat all the other competitors a share of the boiled mutton, which is called the "mutton of happiness."

Xinjiang's Kazak people offer another entertainment that lends much joy to the festival. Pairs of boys and girls on horseback slowly ride abreast towards an appointed spot in the first half of the entertainment. The boy makes witty remarks or offer courting words to the girl riding with him. However, the girl must not display any opposition no matter what he says. When they reach the appointed spot, the boy quickly gallops back, while the girl chases after him at full speed. After she catches him. If she won't give her heart to him, she may whip him and he must not whip back. She just pretends to whip him or gently whips him if she likes him. The boy would stop galloping to have more talks about love with her in the later case.

Section 5 Hua'er Festival (Flower Festival)

Hua'er Festival has been celebrated for generations among the minorities of Tus, Huis, Salars, Bo-

nans and DongXiang in Qinghai, Gansu and Ningxia provinces of northern China. The celebration is usually held in spring and summer and lasts for three to six days, although it varies from place to place. The festival is joined by the local temple fair and pilgrimage. It attracts thousands of people coming from all directions to sing their will.

"Hua'er" (flower) is a typical folk tune expressing the emotions of young people. The folk tune has the name of "Hua'er" and "Shaonian" (youth), for girls and boys are addressed as "Hua'er" and "Shaonian." The Hua'er is made up of rhymed lines, a tune and tone. It consists of three to six lines as a metaphor and the rest revealing the subject matter.

There are 200 odd named tunes existing today. Some named tunes are named in accordance with subject matters and some are named after nationalities. Tone means the melodious notation of the Hua'er. It falls on the second and the forth scale among the five scales of ancient Chinese music. The performance style and form vary by nationality and region. For instance, the Tu people sing Hua'er with their accented rhythms and peculiar melodies, while the Salar Hua'er is presented with a sweet trill tone influenced by Tibetan folk songs.

There are different versions about the origin of the festival. One originates in the famous Mount Lotus Hua'er Festival of Gansu. When the celestial Guang Chengzi took the fairy Lotus past Kangle County, the fairy Lotus fell in love with a local young man. Guang Chengzi was angry and changed the fairy Lotus into a mountain. Deeply moved by their love, people built a temple in memory of her infatuation. People saw a young couple rising from the mountain on the day of the completion of the temple. The couple was singing the Hua'er with a lotus in the woman's hand and a colored fan in the man's. A gust of breeze blew down a lotus leaf; the couple ended their Hua'er with "Oh flower, the lotus leaf."

Later, people of the Lotus Mountain area also sang as the couple did to end the song. They carried lotus flowers and colored fans in their hand while singing. A barrier rope is placed across the path to invite a passerby to answer the Hua'er on the way to Mount Lotus. One is not permitted to continue walking unless he sings a reply.

When a contest is carried out between groups, the groups echo each other, raising and answering questions by singing. It is a taboo for the young singers and their elders to sing in the same group. A conductor is designated to be in charge of raising and answering questions in each group. He must strictly relate the answering Hua'er to the subject matter, or the group of five to eight people will sneer at him. Winners at the festival are entitled Master Hua'er singers. The competition of singing Hua'er in a dialogue style is the highlight of the festival. After the top candidates stand out, then the singing contest is carried on outside among these outstanding singers. The final winner will be entitled the "Anshou."

Section 6 Tibetan New Year

Losar is the Tibetan word for 'new year', lo means year and sar means new in the Tibetan language, and doubtlessly, Losar is the most important festival in Tibet. The festival is celebrated for 15 days during the month of December and January according to the Tibetan calendar (India Guide, 2008).

All Tibetan families start to prepare holiday food such as butter, milk tea, Qingke wine, fried barley and dromar refreshments before the festival in mid December. It is done in order to pray for a good harvest in the coming year. Each household does a thorough cleaning and throws away all the waste at crossroads which are harmful to the health and happiness of the family in the last few days before the New Year.

Besides the thorough cleaning and the house decorating, special dishes are also cooked before the New Year. For example, there is one noodle dish served called guthuk which is made from meat, wheat, rice, sweet potatoes, cheese, peas, green peppers, vermicelli and radishes. There is also another kind of festival dish called Guto which are dough balls similar to dumplings and contain various fillings. However, there are surprise objects hidden inside Guto, such as stones, charcoal, chili and wool. Family members who happen to have stones in their dough will be seen as stonehearted in the following year; if a person finds chilies in their dough, it means he is sharp tongued. If charcoal is found, it means the person is cruel hearted and the person who finds coal in the dough has a black heart. However, white colored ingredients like salt, wool or rice are inside the dough is considered as a good sign. Each family member should have nine bowls of food; each bowl must contain some leftovers to be put into a basin. After the dinner, with the basin and a torch in hand, family members inspect every room. This activity is called "driving-away-ghosts."

People also draw auspicious patterns on walls to bring good luck. Moreover, homes are decorated with flour paintings of the sun and the moon, and small lamps illuminate the house at night (India Guide, 2008). Meanwhile, a sheep head, Qingke wine and a wooden container called a Qiema are displayed on a table. The container, which is engraved with the designs of flowers, jewels, tusks and so on, is fully loaded with buttered Zanba, roasted broad beans and roasted wheat. Ears of Qingke are stuck into the container.

Before the daybreak on the Tibetan New Year, people burn pine rosin and place dyed Qingke barley and ears of wheat on their roof. Early in the morning, women carry buckets of auspicious water home from the river while other family members stay in bed, waiting for the auspicious water to wash their faces. When men and women are all dressed up with colorful new clothes, the mother of the family places the Qiema before them. Everyone takes a little Zanba while saying prayers like "all the best" and "Happy New Year." People also honor the gods in their household shrines and place offerings before them.

The first few days of the New Year are exclusively family affairs when greetings, gifts are exchanged and food is shared (India Guide, 2008). Relatives and friends visit each other as well, and during the visits. A visitor usually takes a fistful of Zanba powder out of a Qiema carried by the host and scatters it in the air. He repeats this three times and eats the fourth fistful. The visitor first dips his ring finger into the wine three times and flicks it in the air, and then he drinks three mouthfuls when a cup of Qingke wine is offered. Hada (a kind of silk cloth) is presented among close friends. The most common color is pure white. Some can be six or seven meters long and three or four meters wide. The longer the Hada offered, the more respected the receiver.

The hosts and the guests are free to have food and wine. They chat or sing and dance at the same time. People love to dance a cheerful tap dance known as "Duixie" in the Tibetan language. There are also many other types of dances, for instance, a dance called the Guozhuang dance which originates from people dancing around a cooking stove in the past. In the dance, dancers tap their feet on the floor to the music rhythms. Another popular dance called Xuanzi earned its name from a unique Tibetan musical instrument (a three stringed plucked instrument).

Besides dancing, people also celebrate the festival by many other ways of entertainment, such as holding sports games like horse racing, archery, wrestling and yak racing. In some locations, there are folk song competitions. They make bonfires in the evening and revel late into the night.

Section 7   Water-Splashing Festival

The Water-splashing Festival is the most important traditional festival observed by the Dai minority in Yunnan Province. It is also the New Year of the Dai Calendar. The festival originated in India as Brahmanism believers held the idea that bathing in the rivers on the 20th or the 21st of April can help them wash off all

evils. The festival is usually celebrated in the middle of April and it lasts for three to four days. Aged people who could not bathe themselves in the rivers were to be bathed by their children, relatives or friends. These rites greatly influenced the Dai inhabited regions of Yunnan and grew into the present festival.

There are some legends about the origin of the festival. The most popular one tells about a demon occupying and inflicting untold misery upon a village of Yunnan where the Dai people lived. He did all kinds of evil deeds, for instance, his puff of strong wind would bring an evil raging fire and his spitting would bring about a turbulent river. He also forcibly took 12 beautiful Dai girls as his wives. All the people hated him and many brave Dai men devoted their lives to killing him in vain, because his magic was too powerful to conquer. One day, when he was drunk, he told one wife that his head could be cut off only by using his hair. Discovering his weakness, the girls planned to kill him when he was fast asleep. After they succeeded in cutting off his head, it dropped on the floor and kept rolling around. It set fire to whatever it touched. The fire would only be out when the head was held tightly by one of the wives. So the girls took turn to hold the head for a period of one year, and each year when they changed turns people had to splash water on the woman who had been holding the head for the past year to wash away the blood (Li, 2005). Dai people began to hold the Water-Splashing Festival every year to celebrate the victory. Water is the symbol of holiness, goodness and purity to the Dai people. They splash water over their friends and relatives to express their wishes for peace and prosperity.

Water splashing is not only featured as a festival but also as an entertainment. Before the festival, pigs and chickens are slaughtered and other food and drinks, such as rice cakes and wines are prepared for the coming celebration. Girls soak sweet smelling flowers in water to create fragrant water which is splashed during the festival. Children make bamboo water throwers. People decorate their doors with colored paper cuts.

On the first day of the festival, people get up early and take baths in the morning. Young people, attractively dressed, go to the mountains for wild flowers to decorate their rooms. Buddhist believers go to temples to listen to sutra recitations and lectures on historic tales. Also activities such as launching rockets and dragon boat rowing are held (China Daily, 2003).

All the people come to broad streets that are lined on both sides with containers of clear water to splash water on the second day. Gentle splashing is done to venerable elders by pulling away an elder's collar and gently tipping the water into the opening. The water then gently flows down the elder's back. The target should accept the splashing and reciprocate with good wishes and blessings. They splash the water over their relatives and friends wishing them good luck and freedom from diseases or adversities when the festivities begin. They splash water from a basin or a gourd ladle over each other. The more water one bears, the happier he feels. Energetic splashing is done to young people. Some young men splash water over girls in bamboo dwellings to express their symbol of love.

Young people toss bags on the third day. Young unmarried girls stand in a line facing boys in another line before the game of tossing bags begins. Players blindly toss their bags to the opposite players at first. After some time, those who take a fancy to each other only toss the bags to each other. A girl may snatch away the head cover of the sword of the young man she loves and run home. When he comes to her home to fetch the head cover he looses, the girl has food and wine waiting for him. During dinner, they express their feelings to each other.

Some hollow logs over two meters long are filled with gunpowder and fixed on a stand. It is a magnificent spectacle with sparks ejecting dozens of meters up into the sky when they are lit at night. People also set off a kind of fireworks called Gaosheng. It consists of a long erect bamboo pole with a number of short gunpowder-filled bamboo pipes fixed on its top. People fill the biggest pipes of Gaosheng with five objects. When the pipes are lit, they soar up into the sky and produce brilliant fireworks.

Kongming lanterns are also seen at this festival. It is a symbol of auspiciousness and brightness in the world. A Kongming lantern was invented during the Three Kingdoms (220—280) for sending messages by the army. It is made of thin bamboo strips and tough paper which can be seven meters tall and two meters in diameter. Hot air sends the lanterns up into the sky and they slowly drift about while they are lit in the evening.

The Water Splashing Festival is also marked by singing and dancing. Young people dance to the accompaniment of the traditional musical instruments such as the Dai gong, the Lusheng, and the elephant-leg-like drum. All festival celebrators stand in rings singing and dancing. Among the various dances, Peacock dance, Yilahou Dance and the Bamboo Hat Dance are the most popular ones.

Reference

1. Ai Shan. Practical Ways to Good Health Through Traditional Chinese Medicine. Beijing: China Today Press, 1997.

2. Bai Shouyi. An Outline History of China, Beijing: Foreign Languages Press, 2005.

3. Behuniak Jr. J. Disposition and Aspiration in the Mencius And Zhuangzi. In Journal of Chinese Philosophy, 2002, 29 (1).

4. China Handbook Editorial Committee. Geography. Beijing: Foreign Languages Press, 1983.

5. Chen Jinwan. Famous Dishes and Great Cooks. Beijing: Foreign Languages Press, 2004.

6. Chen Zhucai. Life And Lifestyles. Beijing: Foreign Languages Press, 1985.

7. Ding Zuxin. Gems of Chinese Poetry. Liaoning: Liaoning University Press, 1986. 4.

8. Feng Weinian. Say China in English. Xian: Xian Electricity University Press, 2004.

9. Gu C., Chan R. C. K., Liu J., and Kesteloot C.. Beijing's socio-spatial restructuring: immigration and social transformation in the epoch of national economic reformation. In Progress in Planning 66. Elsevier. 2006.

10. Harper D., Cambon M., Mayhew B., Gaskell K., Miller K., Huhti T. and Org M.. China 8th Edition. Lonely Planet, 2002.

11. He Daokuan. A Descriptive And Explanatory Approach. Beijing: Foreign Language Teaching And Research Press, 2004.

12. Ji Jianghong. Guiding Tour Around Whole China. Beijing: Beijing Publishing House, 2004. 1.

13. Jing Weihua. A Survey of Chinese Society and Culture, Beijing: Chinese Electricity Press, 2005. 8.

14. Jin Hailin. The Traditional Chinese Festivals and Tales. Chongqing: Chongqing Publishing House, 2005. 11.

15. Li Zhihua. Chinese National Geography. Beijing: Chinese National Geography Press, 2006.

16. Lu Yu (Tang Dynasty). Tea Classical Works. Beijing: Chinese Working Press, 2003. 10.

17. Moise E. E., The Present & The Past, Modern China. A History. Longman Group UK Limited, 1994.

18. Ma Yin. China's Minority Nationalities. Beijing: New World Press.

19. Meng Shude. West China. Beijing: China Intercontinental Press, 2001. 6.

20. Ning Aihua. A Passage to China. Qingdao: China Ocean University Press, 2004.

21. Shen Chen. The Teaching of Cultures in Foreign Language Eduation. Beijing: Beijing Language and Culture University Publishing House, 1999.

22. Song Li. Highlights of Chinese Culture. Harbin: Harbin Industry University Publishing House, 2005. 10.

23. Sun Peiqing. History of Chinese Education. Shanghai: HuaDong Teachers' University Publishing House, 2000.

24. Sun Weixin. Highlights Of China. Shanghai Century Publishing Group, Interpretation Publishing House, 2004. 8.

25. Tang Xilin. The Story of Pingyao. Shanxi: Shanxi Scientific Technology Press, 2004. 10.

26. Wang Jianjun. Chinese Education History. GuangDong: GuangDong High Education Publishing House, 2003.

27. Wang Pijun. The 11th Panchen Erdeni Qoigyi Gyaibo. Beijing: China Pictorial Publishing House, 2005. 8.

28. Wang Yi'e. Taoism in China. Beijing: China Intercontinental Press, 2005. 10.

29. Wen Yucheng. Reporters See Wang Family Courtyard. Shanxi: Shanxi Economy Press, 2004. 1.

30. Xiang Jianguo. China Focus. Beijing: China Intercontinental Press, 2005. 5.

31. Xiao Xiaoming. Panoramic China. Beijing: Foreign Languages Press, 2006. 1.

32. Yang'en Hua. Aspect of Chinese Culture. Beijing: Qinghua University Publishing Press, 2006. 4.

33. Yang Min. Chinese Culture: An Introduction. Beijing: High Education Press, 2006. 7.

34. Zhang Guanglin. Islam in China. Beijing: China Intercontinental Press, 2005. 10.

35. Zhang Qizhi. Traditional Chinese Culture. Beijing: Foreign Languages Press, 2004.

36. Zhang Lianming. Chinese Family Feast Dishes. Shandong: Shandong Science and Technology Press, 1993.

37. Zhao Puchu. Answers To Common Questions About Buddhism. Beijing: Foreign Language Teaching And Research

Press，2001.9.

38. Zhi E'xiang. The Basics of Traditional Chinese Culture. Beijing：Foreign Languages Press Beijing，2005.

39. Zhong Linyuan. China Today. Beijing：China Today Press，2006.

40. Zhou Tailiang. Catholic Church in China. Beijing：China Intercontinental Press，2005.10.

41. Zhou Yi. An Introduction to Chinese Culture. Chongqing：Chongqing University Press，2003.9.

42. Zhu Qixin. A Primer for English-Speaking Guides. Beijing：China Travel & Tourism Press，1999.

43. Zhu Qixin. The Sights of China. Beijing：China Travel & Tourism Press，2004.9

44. Zhu Yifei. Places of Historical and Cultural Interests in China. Shanghai：Shanghai Foreign Language Education Press，1996.

45. 北京大学中国传统文化研究中心. 中华文化讲座丛书. 北京：北京大学出版社，1994

46. 黄春和. 白塔寺. 北京：华文出版社，2002.5

47. 纪江红. 游遍中国. 北京：北京出版社，2004.1

48. 啸天. 承德故事. 北京：人民日报出版社，2006.6

49. 徐文涛. 拙政园. 苏州：苏州大学出版社，1998.12

50. 杨振铎. 世界人类文化遗产天坛. 北京：中国书店，1999.3

51. 颐和园管理处. 颐和园. 徐州：中国矿业大学出版社，2000.1

52. 章采烈. 中国生态特色旅游. 北京：对外经济贸易大学出版社，1996.5

53. 查建英. 八十年代访谈录. 北京：三联书店，2006.7

54. 翟博. 法门寺传奇. 西安：陕西旅游出版社，1994.9

55. About. com，

（2007）. Hutong and Siheyuan in Beijing, traditional Beijing architecture. In About. com：China Online. Retrieved on 24-07-2007 from the World Wide Web：

http：//chineseculture. about. com/library/weekly/aa020501a. htm

56. About. com，

（2007）. The Terra-Cotta Warriors. In About. com：China Online. Retrieved on 29-07-2007 from the World Wide Web：
http：//chineseculture. about. com/library/weekly/aa061501a. htm

57. AC，

（2007）. Buddhism's Origin and Development India and Beyond. In AC. Retrieved on 12-08-2007 from the World Wide Web：

http：//www. associatedcontent. com/article/13229/buddhisms_ origin_ and_ development. html

58. AMF（Alternative Medicine Foundation），

（2007）. Traditional Chinese Medicine. An Alternative and Complementary Medicine Resource Guide. In The Alternative Medicine Foundation. To be retrieved on 22-01-2008 from the World Wide Web：http：//www. amfoundation. org/tcm. htm

59. AWOCM（A World of Chinese Medicine），

（2006）. The Five Elements in Chinese Medicine. In A World of Chinese Medicine. To be retrieved on 23-01-2008 from the World Wide Web：

http：//www. aworldofchinesemedicine. com/chinese-medicine-five-elements. htm

60. BDEA Inc. & BuddhaNet，

（2007）. Buddhist Studies：The Chinese Buddhist Schools. In Buddha Dharma Education Association Inc. Retrieved on 12-08-2007 from the World Wide Web：

http：//www. buddhanet. net/e-learning/history/b3schchn. htm and

http：//www. buddhanet. net/e-learning/buddhistworld/china-txt. htm

61. Behuniak Jr. J，

（2002）. Disposition and Aspiration in the Mencius And Zhuangzi. In Journal of Chinese Philosophy, Volume 29, Number 1，Blackwell Publishing.

62. Beijing Guide，

（n. d.）. Chinese Culture-Dragon and Phoenix. In Beijing China Travel Guide. Retrieved on 23-07-2007 from the World Wide Web：http：//www. kinabaloo. com/chinese_ culture_ 5. html

63. Beijing International,

(2007) . Summer Palace. In Beijing Official Website International. Retrieved on 23-07-2007 from the World Wide Web:
http: //www. ebeijing. gov. cn/Tour/ScenicSpots/Parks/t20040123_ 101281. htm

64. Bilin China,

(2004) . Beijing City Space Layout, City and Countryside Coordinated Development. In Success Fortune China with Bilin International. Retrieved on 17-07-2007 from the World Wide Web: http: //www. bilinchina. com/beijing-business-city-countryside-coordinate. html

65. BTA (Beijing Tourism Administration),

(2007) . Siheyuan (quadrangle) . In Beijing Tourism Administration. Retrieved on 24-07-2007 from the World Wide Web: http: //english. visitbeijing. com. cn/impression/Culture/

66. BTM Beijing,

(2004) . Satellite Towns to East Population Pressure. In Beijing This Month. 2004/03/01. Retrieved on 18-07-2007 from the World Wide Web:
http: //www. btmbeijing. com/contents/en/btm/2004-03/whatshot/population

67. Buddhist Temples,

(n. d.) . Gautam Buddha-The Originator of Buddhism. In Buddhist Temples. Retrieved on 12-08-2007 from the World Wide Web:
http: //www. buddhist-temples. com/gautam-buddha. html

68. C-C-C,

(2000) . Celebration of Tomb Sweeping Day (Qing Ming Jie) . In The Chinese Culture Center of San Francisco. Retrieved on 13-12-2007 from the World Wide Web:
http: //www. c-c-c. org/chineseculture/festival/qingming/qingming. html

69. (2000) . Celebration of the Dragon Boat Festival. In The Chinese Culture Center of San Francisco. Retrieved on 17-12-2007 from the World Wide Web:
http: //www. c-c-c. org/chineseculture/festival/dragonboat/dragon. html

70. CCTS,

(2007) . Introduction of Beijing City. In China Circulation Tours. Retrieved on 18-07-2007 from the World Wide Web:
http: //www. cctsbeijing. com/china_ guide/attraction/city_ beijing/city_ beijing_ history. html

71. CCTV,

(2007) . Tibet's economy grows at an average rate of 12 percent last 6 years. In CCTV International. Retrieved on 15-01-2008 from the World Wide Web:
http: //www. cctv. com/program/bizchina/20070621/104983. shtml

72. Chan, A.

(2007) . Lao Zi. In Stanford Encyclopedia of Philosophy. Retrieved on 07-08-2007 from the World Wide Web: http: //plato. stanford. edu/entries/laozi/#LaoSto

73. China Culture,

(2008) . Inner Mongolia. In *China Culture org*. Retrieved on 11-03-2008 from the World Wide Web: http: //www. chinaculture. org/gb/en_ map/2003-09/24/content_ 21549. htm

74. China Daily,

(2003) . Water Splashing Festival. In China Culture. Retrieved on 11-01-2008 from the World Wide Web:
http: //www. chinaculture. org/gb/en_ curiosity/2003-09/24/content_ 29269. htm

75. China Daily,

(2005) . Chongyang Festival. In China Daily. Retrieved on 21-12-2007 from the World Wide Web: http: //www. chinadaily. com. cn/english/doc/2004-01/09/content_ 297522. htm

76. China Official Gateway,

(n. d.) . Confucian Philosophy on Health Building. In China Official Gateway to News & Information. Retrieved on 03-08-2007 from the World Wide Web:
http: //www. china. org. cn/english/imperial/26119. htm

77. China. org. cn,

(2008). The Landscapes of Tibet. In China. org. cn-China's Official Gateway to News & Information. Retrieved on 14-01-2008 from the World Wide Web:

http://www. china. org. cn/ch-xizang/tibet/picture_ album/english/landscapes/landscapes. html

78. China Summer Palace,

(n.d.). The Summer Palace. In China Summer Palace. Retrieved on 20-07-2007 from the World Wide Web: http://www. chinasummerpalace. com/

79. Chinatown Guide,

(n. d.). Traditional Chinese Culture. In China Private Tour Guide Service. Retrieved on 10-12-2007 from the World Wide Web: http://www. chinatourguide. net/12_ 10. htm

80. China Travel Agent,

(2007). Huaqing Hot Springs. In China Travel Agent. Retrieved on 27-07-2007 from the World Wide Web:

http://www. china-travel-agent. com/city_ guides/view. php? city = xi'an&id = 1000719401

81. China Travel Guide,

(2007). History of the Great Wall. In China travel guide. Retrieved on 19-07-2007 from the World Wide Web: http://www. travelchinaguide. com/china_ great_ wall/history/

82. Chinavoc,

(2007). Lantern Festival. In China voc com. Retrieved on 12-12-2007 from the World Wide Web: http://www. chinavoc. com/festivals/lantern. htm

83. CMS, (2004). Diagnostic Methods. In the Chinese Medicine Sampler. To be retrieved on 24-01-2008 from the World Wide Web: http://www. chinesemedicinesampler. com/diaginterview. html

84. CSEN, (2007). Naadam Festival. In The Center for the Study of Eurasian Nomads. Retrieved on 08-01-2008 from the World Wide Web:

http://www. csen. org/Mongol. Nadaam/Mongol. text. html

85. CTIC (China Tibet Information Center),

(n. d.), Scenic Spots in Lhasa. In China Tibet Information Center. Retrieved on 16-01-2008 from the World Wide Web: http://www. tibetinfor. com/tibetzt/lasa/scenic/menu. htm

86. CTIC (China Tibet Information Center),

(2008). Tibetan Food. In Tibet. cn. Retrieved on 18-01-2008 from the World Wide Web: http://www. tibet. cn/tibetzt-en/tibetanfood/everyday/1. htm

87. CSEN,

(2007). Naadam Festival. In *The Center for the Study of Eurasian Nomads*. Retrieved on 08-01-2008 from the World Wide Web:

http://www. csen. org/Mongol. Nadaam/Mongol. text. html

88. Fu H.,

(n. d.). The Origins of Traditional Chinese Medicine. In Purify Our Mind. To be retrieved on 22-01-2008 from the World Wide Web:

http://www. purifymind. com/OriginsMedicine. htm

89. Great Wall Tours,

(2007). Norbulingka (the Summer Palace). In Great Wall Tours. Retrieved on 17-01-2008 from the World Wide Web: http://www. greatwalltour. com/greatwall_ pages/provinces/tibet/nobulinka. htm

90. Gruys R.,

(2007). Mongolia-Life in the Countryside. In *Blue Peak Travel Photography*. Retrieved on 12-03-2008 from the World Wide Web: http://www. bluepeak. net/mongolia/countryside. html

91. Gu C., Chan R. C. K., Liu J., and Kesteloot C.,

(2006). Beijing's socio-spatial restructuring: immigration and social transformation in the epoch of national economic reformation. *In Progress in Planning 66*. Elsevier.

92. Herb China,

（2007）. Health Preservation. In Herb China. Retrieved on 02-08-2007 from the World Wide Web：

http：//www. herbchina2000. com/h6_ preservation. shtml

93. Harper D. , Cambon M. , Mayhew B. , Gaskell K. , Miller K. , Huhti T. and Org M. ,

（2002）. China. 8th Edition. Lonely Planet.

94. India Guide,

（2008）. Losar-Tibetan New Year. In India Guide. Retrieved on 11-01-2008 from the World Wide Web：http：//festivals. iloveindia. com/losar/index. html

95. Lhasa Today. In China. org. cn-China's Official Gateway to News & Information. Retrieved on 16-01-2008 from the World Wide Web：

http：//www. china. org. cn/ch-xizang/tibet/picture_ album/english/lhasatoday/lhasatoday. html

96. Littlejohn R. ,

（2006）. Laozi（Lao-tzu）. In The Internet Encyclopedia of Philosophy. Retrieved on 08-08-2007 from the World Wide Web：http：//www. iep. utm. edu/l/laozi. htm

97. Li X. ,

（2005）. Water-Splashing Festival in Xishuangbanna. In China Internet Information Center. Retrieved on 08-01-2008 from the World Wide Web：

http：//www. china. org. cn/english/null/127243. htm

98. Liu Z. ,

（2007）. Beijing-From an Ancient City to an International Metropolis. Speech on Capital Alliance Meeting. Retrieved on 18-07-2007 from the World Wide Web：

http：//ca2007. nationalcapital. gov. au/downloads/papers/Zhi_ Beijing. pdf

99. Moise E. E. ,

（1994）. *The Present & The Past*, *Modern China. A History*. Longman Group UK Limited.

100. N. A. ,

（2004）. Lao Zi. In Chinese Mythology. Retrieved on 07-08-2007 from the World Wide Web：http：//www. godchecker. com/pantheon/chinese-mythology. php? deity = LAO-ZI

101. Li X. ,

（2005）. Water-Splashing Festival in Xishuangbanna. In *China Internet Information Center*. Retrieved on 08-01-2008 from the World Wide Web：

http：//www. china. org. cn/english/null/127243. htm

102. Naumann S. ,

（2007）. A History of Xi'an. In About. com；China for Visitors. Retrieved on 26-07-2007 from the World Wide Web：http：//gochina. about. com/od/xian/p/Xian_ History. htm

103. Oriental Travel,

（2007）. Beijing, China（Capital City of China）. In Oriental Travel. Retrieved on 17-07-2007 from the World Wide Web：http：//www. orientaltravel. com/China/Beijing. htm

104. People's Daily Online,

（2005）. Beijing city planning unveiling a new blueprint. In People's Daily Online. January 16, 2005. Retrieved on 18-07-2007 from the World Wide Web：

http：//english. peopledaily. com. cn/200501/16/eng20050116_ 170800. html

105. People's Daily,

（2006）. Chinese Spring Festival, origin and customs. In People's Daily Online. Retrieved on 29-11-2007 from the World Wide Web：

http：//english. peopledaily. com. cn/200601/25/eng20060125_ 238211. html

106. Poleg D. ,

（2005）. Chinese New Year and Chinese Spring Festival. In DanWei, Chinese media, advertising and urban life. Retrieved on 29-11-2007 from the World Wide Web：

http：//www. danwei. org/china_ information/chinese_ new_ year_ and_ chinese_ s. php

107. Ross K. L. ,

(2007) . The Basic Teachings of Buddhism. In The Proceedings of the Friesian School, Fourth Series. Retrieved on 12-08-2007 from the World Wide Web:

http: //www. friesian. com/buddhism. htm

108. Sima Q. ,

(2000) . Records of the Grand Historian. In Guoxue. Vol. 47. Retrieved on 01-08-2007 from the World Wide Web: http: //www. guoxue. com/shibu/24shi/shiji/sj_ 047. htm

109. Steppes Travel,

(2007) . Naadam Festival. In Steppes Travel. Retrieved on 08-01-2008 from the World Wide Web: http: //www. steppestravel. co. uk/naadam-festival-page1411. aspx

110. Synaptic,

(1995) . Lao Tse & Daoism Resources. In The Ejournal Website, Critical Thinkers Resources. Retrieved on 07-08-2007 from the World Wide Web: http: //www. synaptic. bc. ca/ejournal/laotse. htm

111. Tales of Old China,

(n. d.) . Tales of Old Peking, The Great Wall. In Tales of Old China. Retrieved on 19-07-2007 from the World Wide Web: http: //www. talesofoldchina. com/peking/btwall. htm

112. TCM Basis,

(2006) . The Basic Content of Yin-Yang Theory. In TCM Basis. To be retrieved on 22-01-2008 from the World Wide Web:

http: //www. tcmbasics. com/basics_ yinyang_ theory. htm

113. The Application of Yin-Yang Theory to the Field of Traditional Chinese Medicine. In TCM Basis. To be retrieved on 23-01-2008 from the World Wide Web:

http: //www. tcmbasics. com/basics_ yinyang_ application. htm

114. The Potala. In China Tibet Information Center. Retrieved on 17-01-2008 from the World Wide Web: http: //www. tibetinfor. com/tibetzt/bdlg/index. htm

115. Traditional Chinese Festivals. Retrieved on 30-11-2007 from the World Wide Web:

http: //www. china. org. cn/english/features/Festivals/78322. htm and retrieved on 20-12-2007 from the World Wide Web: http: //www. china. org. cn/english/features/Festivals/78311. htm

116. Travel China Guide,

(2007) . Mausoleum of Western Han Emperor Liu Qi (Hanyangling) . In Travel China Guide. Retrieved on 27-07-2007 from the World Wide Web:

http: //www. travelchinaguide. com/attraction/shaanxi/xian/hanyang. htm

117. Travel China Guide,

(2007) . Potala Palace. In Travel China Guide. Retrieved on 16-01-2008 from the World Wide Web:

http: //www. travelchinaguide. com/attraction/tibet/lhasa/potala. htm

118. Travel China Guide,

(2007) . Big Wild Goose Pagoda (Dayan Ta) . In Travel China Guide. Retrieved on 27-07-2007 from the World Wide Web:

http: //www. travelchinaguide. com/attraction/shaanxi/xian/bigwildgoose. htm

119. Travel-in-China,

(2007) . Mausoleum of the First Qin Emperor. In Travel-in-China. Retrieved on 27-07-2007 from the World Wide Web: http: //www. travel-in-china. com/attraction/Xian-Mausoleum-of-the-First-Qin-Emperor. php

120. U. P.

(2007) . A Quick Tour of Tibet. In Purdue University. Retrieved on 14-01-2008 from the World Wide Web: http: //omni. cc. purdue. edu/ ~ wtv/tibet/tour. html

121. Walthall M. K. ,

(2000) . Buddhism: The Journey from India to China. Retrieved on 14-08-2007 from the World Wide Web: http: //www. ccds. charlotte. nc. us/History/China/04/walthall/walthall. htm

122. Wikipedia,

（2007）. Beijing. In Wikipedia. Retrieved on 17-07-2007 from the World Wide Web：http：//en. wikipedia. org/wiki/Beijing#History

123. Wikipedia,

（2007）. Buddhism. Retrieved on 12-08-2007 from the World Wide Web：

http：//en. wikipedia. org/wiki/Buddhism#Doctrine

124. Wikipedia.

（2007）. Chang'an. In Wikipedia. Retrieved on 26-07-2007 from the World Wide Web：

http：//en. wikipedia. org/wiki/Chang%27an

125. Wikipedia,

（2007）. Summer Palace. In Wikipedia. Retrieved on 20-07-2007 from the World Wide Web：http：//en. wikipedia. org/wiki/Summer_ Palace

126. Wong B. K. ,

（2002）. Mooncakes. In The Family Culture. Retrieved on 21-12-2007 from the World Wide Web：

http：//www. familyculture. com/holidays/mooncake. htm

127. World Heritage Convention,

（2003）. Periodic Reporting on the Application of the World Heritage Convention. In World Heritage, UNESCO. Retrieved on 22-07-2007 from the World Wide Web：

http：//whc. unesco. org/archive/periodicreporting/APA/cycle01/section2/438. pdf

128. YYH,

（2006）. TCM Acupuncture Theory, Treatments, Protocols and Resources. In Yin Yang House. To be retrieved on 22-01-2008 from the World Wide Web：

http：//www. yinyanghouse. com/theory/chinese/acupuncture_ information

129. Zhang C. ,

（2005）. Philosophical Differences Between Western and Chinese Medicine. In Sinomed Research Institute. To be retrieved on 24-01-2008 from the World Wide Web：

http：//www. sinomedresearch. org/c19_ PhiloWest. htm

130. Zhang H. ,

（2007）. Colorful Tibetan Clothes. In Sino way travel. Retrieved on 18-01-2008 from the World Wide Web：

http：//www. chinadiscover. net/china-tour/tibetguide/tibet-culture-clothing. htm

131. Zhu H. , Sun S. ,

（2005）. Aobao Meeting. In China Corner. Retrieved on 08-01-2008 from the World Wide Web：http：//china-corner. com/article_ list. asp? id = 740

132. Zunduisuren B. ,

（2006）. Naadam Festival. In Visit Mongolia. Retrieved on 04-01-2008 from the World Wide Web：http：//www. visitmongolia. com/naadam_ festival_ tour. htm